D1519852

THE POLITICS OF IRONY
IN AMERICAN MODERNISM

THE POLITICS OF IRONY
IN AMERICAN MODERNISM

MATTHEW STRATTON

Fordham University Press

NEW YORK   2014

Fordham University Press has no responsibility for the persistence or accuracy of URLs for external or third-party Internet websites referred to in this publication and does not guarantee that any content on such websites is, or will remain, accurate or appropriate.

Fordham University Press also publishes its books in a variety of electronic formats. Some content that appears in print may not be available in electronic books.

Library of Congress Cataloging-in-Publication Data

Stratton, Matthew.
    The politics of irony in American modernism / Matthew Stratton.—
First edition.
        pages cm
    Includes bibliographical references and index.
    ISBN 978-0-8232-5545-0 (hardback)
    1. American literature—20th century—History and criticism. 2. Irony in literature. 3. Satire—History and criticism. 4. Politics in literature. 5. Politics and literature—United States—History—20th century. 6. Politics and culture—United States—History—20th century. 7. Literature and society—United States—History—20th century. 8. Modernism (Literature)—United States. I. Title.
    PS228.I74S87 2014
    810.9'18—dc23

                                                                    2013026383

Printed in the United States of America

16 15 14   5 4 3 2 1

First edition

THE
AMERICAN
LITERATURES
INITIATIVE

A book in the American Literatures Initiative (ALI), a collaborative publishing project of NYU Press, Fordham University Press, Rutgers University Press, Temple University Press, and the University of Virginia Press. The Initiative is supported by The Andrew W. Mellon Foundation. For more information, please visit www.americanliteratures.org.

For Ambrose Albert and Giacomo Francis

Contents

Acknowledgments

The shortcomings of this book are exclusively mine, but whatever is of value can be traced to a large group of people to whom I am most sincerely grateful. This has been true since the night when Jacques Lezra suggested I "historicize what Americans mean when they say that irony has a politics." By the time I realized that his advice represented equal parts morbid curiosity and sadistic humor, it was too late to turn back; I therefore thank him first and foremost for seeing the joke through to the end.

Thomas H. Schaub never failed as interlocutor and comrade, casting a friendly but ruthless critical eye over too many abstract propositions and forcing me to rethink basic assumptions by sharing his encyclopedic knowledge of U.S. literary, cultural, and political histories. Russ Castronovo, Gerhard Richter, and Rob Nixon gave powerful feedback when it was sorely needed. My understanding of irony and of my own argument was immeasurably improved by prolonged engagement with interlocutors from many disciplines, areas of expertise, institutions, and states: Todd Shepard, Jack Opel, Thomas H. Crofts, and Matthew Hussey never once asked me to shut up and were instrumental in helping me work through generals and particulars. Helen Tartar, Tom Lay, and my readers at Fordham University Press were thorough, smart, sensitive, generous, and invariably correct. Thanks to Yale University Art Gallery for the Mabel Dwight lithograph on the cover and to Pete Mueller for permission to reproduce his cartoon. I am also grateful to the Office of Research and the Division of Humanities, Arts, and Cultural Studies at UC Davis: a Faculty Development Award and a Publication Assistance Grant gave me valuable time, money, and ultimately an index.

When the topic of irony seemed impossibly, even foolishly, large—as it frequently does—I would not have persisted without advice, encouragement, and friendship from those who were under no obligation to provide it: Rebecca Walkowitz, Susanne Wofford, Henry Turner, John Tiedemann, Stephen Bernstein, Tom Foster, Eric Rauchway, Jonathan Freedman, Cristanne Miller, Elizabeth Rivlin, Dave Junker, Rich Hamerla, Catherine E. Kelly, Michael Alexander, Paul Jones, Beth Quitslund, Kevin Haworth, and Joyce Wexler helped more than they probably realize. Jonathan Greenberg went out of his way to share his invaluable *Modernism, Satire, and the Novel* when I really needed it. Librarians at the Manuscript Division of the Library of Congress, the Labadie Collection at the University of Michigan, Pennsylvania State University Libraries, and the Manuscripts, Archives, and Rare Books Division of the New York Public Library did much more than fetch cartons and make copies. Special thanks are owed to two scholars whose intellectual companionship improved every page, who generously read and commented on portions of the manuscript, and who never hesitated to cry foul and argue the finer points late into the night: Andrew Escobedo and Michael LeMahieu.

I am surrounded by an astonishing group of people in the English Department at the University of California, Davis. They represent the very best combination of brilliance and kind decency that one could hope to find in any community; as the campus confronted discouraging, shocking events over the past few years, I learned that they are also admirably brave, and I am deeply proud to count them as friends and colleagues. John Marx not only asked all the right questions and dissuaded me from some wrong answers but read chapters and shared insights and advice galore. Within a few days of our first meeting, Margaret Ferguson subjected my argument to thirty minutes of the most pitiless interrogation it had seen, making me all the more grateful for the years of friendship and sage advice since then. Nathan Brown took special pains with one chapter in particular while introducing me to entirely new levels of agonistic friendship. The book as a whole is far better for my exchanges with Nathan, Kathleen Frederickson, and especially David Simpson, who offered game-changing feedback at several critical junctures. Colin Milburn steered me over one particularly jarring bump in the process, while Seeta Chaganti, Gregory Dobbins, Alessa Johns, Claire Waters, Joshua Clover, and Christopher Loar helped me negotiate many other hurdles along the way. I am particularly lucky to be surrounded by a peerless group of Americanists, who continue to share their precious time, expertise, and friendship: Hsuan Hsu, Mark Jerng,

Evan Watkins, Desirée Martín, Danielle Heard, and especially Elizabeth Freeman and Michael Ziser. My project and my life would look very different if it weren't for Gina Bloom, Frances Dolan, Flagg Miller, Scott Shershow, and Scott Simmon, each of whom fed the beast in vital ways at truly critical moments. I shall probably never be able to repay them, as I won't be able to repay the family with whom I do and don't share blood: Vickie Simpson, Albert and Bette Stratton, Craig and Rebecca Stratton, Stephanie Beltz, Ed Cooper, Cam and Deb Shapansky, and the whole wide world of Millers, Ghiardis, Van Driesches, McDermotts, and Mahoneys. Ian Afflerbach was inestimably helpful in the preparation of the manuscript and set a new standard for graduate student assistants. An early version of Chapter 1 appeared in *Arizona Quarterly*, and an early version of Chapter 3 appeared in *Twentieth Century Literature*.

Over the years, I have given Elizabeth Carolyn Miller ample justification to hope that my own ironies would actually just die already. Instead she continues to refute the old notion that irony and love are necessarily opposed; these pages are as much hers as they are mine.

Irony and How It Got That Way:
An Introduction

For of course Irony has a history . . . if we cannot tell what Irony is, we can tell by what gradations it has become what it is.

— J.A.K. THOMSON, 1927[1]

Here's a familiar story: in the weeks after September 11, 2001, the editor of *Vanity Fair* proclaimed "the end of the age of irony." A week later, a *Time* columnist suggested, "One good thing could come from this horror: it could spell the end of the age of irony." The editor of the *New York Observer* said that survivors wanted to comprehend the incomprehensible events, and that this desire itself "makes irony obsolete"; a publisher told *Entertainment Weekly* that "somebody should do a marker that says irony died on 9-11-01." Subsequent weeks, months, and years saw these quips multiply into the latest iteration of what turns out to be quite an old contest, wherein cultural critics either implored this half-baked prophecy to fulfill itself or adopted the opposing position, arguing that "As jingoists call for a New Sincerity, we need irony—the serious kind—more than ever."[2]

Of course, by now the ostensibly empirical question of whether or not irony "died" on 9/11 is long settled; even if you haven't read *The Onion* or you somehow missed the ascendancy of Jon Stewart and Stephen Colbert from comedians to respected and influential political analysts, a slew of critical studies and popular pundits have reassured us that irony is indeed still alive and kicking, performing its ancient function of critique and entertainment. This is true, even if writers like Joan Didion would complain in 2003 that "in New York . . . 'the death of irony' had already been declared, repeatedly, and curiously," only to mutter again in 2008 that the election of Barack Obama transformed the United States into an "irony-free zone."[3] Thus scholars working in philosophy, cultural

FIGURE 1. "The Last Shred of Irony." P.S. Mueller, © 2001.

studies, and political theory have produced intellectually robust defenses of irony—ranging from R. Jay Magill Jr.'s *Chic Ironic Bitterness* (2007) to Cynthia Willett's *Irony in the Age of Empire* (2008), Elizabeth Markovits's *The Politics of Sincerity* (2008), Amber Day's *Satire and Dissent* (2011), and Jonathan Lear's *A Case for Irony* (2011)—that demonstrate how irony continues to be a salient feature of manifold cultural discourses and articulate myriad reasons why democratic societies don't just seem to like irony but *need* irony. Not only does the consensus seem to be that irony "has thankfully proven itself to be far from dead, as many predicted and some even hoped for," but such defenses plainly outnumber continuing complaints about the "anti-democratic implications" of the supposed fact that "we have in recent decades been building a towering Fortress of Irony."[4] Moreover, such defenses of irony have proved more convincing than novelists or critics pining for "a post 9/11, postironic novel" that would "move beyond irony and youthful nihilism."[5]

That irony—along with satire, one of its frequent compatriots with an equally long and contentious history—is still "alive" is perhaps too obviously true, even if what precisely irony means in a given situation is less obvious. The question at hand is not whether irony exists but what possibilities competing discourses about irony disclose and foreclose for literary studies and cultural politics: not because examples of ironic discourse are apparent everywhere from television shows to novels but because the dispute has never been one of empirical fact, let alone of literary-historical analysis. Rather, the dispute provides just the most recent evidence of the fact that irony has long served as a capacious and malleable term to describe subjectivities and texts, as well as relationships among individuals, collectives, thought, language, representation, and history. When Paul Krugman recently described Newt Gingrich's crocodilian "defense" of Medicare as a moment when "irony died," for example, the economist joined a rhetorical tradition stretching back much further than the previous decade.[6] In 1955, after U.S. troops left the Korean peninsula and Senator McCarthy was ejected from his bullying pulpit, literary critic R.W.B. Lewis remarked that a culture of conformity had produced a situation wherein "irony has withered into mere mordant skepticism. Irony is fertile and alive; the chilling skepticism of the mid-twentieth century represents one of the modes of death."[7] In 1951, Theodor Adorno announced that "The medium of irony, the difference between ideology and reality, has disappeared [*Ihr Medium . . . ist geschwunden*]"; before the military action of World War II was close to settled, a popular film critic would claim, "Irony is out for the duration."[8] And thirty-five years before that, when a president who "kept us out of war!" sent troops to France with the public blessing of thinkers who were expected to know better, a young radical named Randolph Bourne declared that "Only in a world where irony was dead could an intellectual class enter war at the head of such illiberal cohorts in the avowed cause of world-liberalism and world democracy."[9] If cultural diagnosticians have greatly exaggerated the reports of irony's demise, they have consistently done so by insisting upon the exceptional, acute nature of what a longer view reveals to be recurrent symptoms of a chronic disease within the body politic.[10]

Irony has evolved as a concept over the millennia, expanding beyond and yet never fully shedding its previous characteristics and associations; one of my central assertions is that irony continues to be invoked as a kind of proxy for other kinds of debates not in spite of the fact that it is such a malleable and capacious term but because it is. If irony notoriously seems to require multiple definitions to be useful, all of those definitions themselves require histories, qualifiers, and disclaimers of their own; in the context of its periodic demises, complaints about irony's definitional difficulties serve as a complementary obverse to the resources those multiple significations provide as a conceptual constellation. In 1917—well before listeners consulted M. H. Abrams's glossary to complain about Alanis Morissette's imprecise song "Ironic"—American music critic James Huneker saw that "Irony is a much abused word," and a Cambridge lecturer in 1926 claimed that "if ever a word has suffered, and suffers, abuse in common speech, it is 'irony.'"[11] And indeed, writers about irony invoke the difficulty of definition almost as epic poets invoke the Muse and have usually viewed this as a difficulty to be overcome as a precondition for literary analysis. This has been a modern convention at least since an 1899 essayist flatly stated that "To frame a definition of irony is almost impossible, since the figure has been so variously employed," and runs through Claire Colebrook's estimable primer on the subject, which commences with the admission that "by the very simplicity of its definition [irony] becomes curiously indefinable," via Paul de Man's more expansive observation that "Definitional language seems to be in trouble when irony is concerned."[12]

There may be situations wherein "irony is in essence a very simple quantitative device, like exaggeration,"[13] and there may be a form of irony best analyzed under the category Max Eastman called "The Humor of Quantity" (1921). After all, one might not otherwise speak of a person as "too ironic" or possessing "not enough irony," and a *New Yorker* cartoon couldn't plausibly depict a stunned pedestrian beside a book being advertised as "Now with 50% less irony!" Attempts to understand irony systematically, however, are relatively recent and resist mere quantification. In 1920, literary critic Frances Theresa Russell remarked that "The science of Esthetics is a tribute to our zeal in attempting to define the indefinable word beauty. Nearly as elusive of categoric bondage is *irony*; but for its capture no formal scientific crusade has as yet been organized," and twenty years later an article in the logical-positivist journal *Erkenntnis* reflected that "The glitter of triumph in a man's eye has hardly been studied by optics, nor has the tone of irony or sincerity in his voice been investigated by acoustics."[14] Nonetheless, excellent studies have persevered to delineate and analyze its discursive history running from Aristotle, through Roman rhetoricians and German Romantics, all the way through New Criticism, or Gilles Deleuze, or Paul de Man, or Richard Rorty, or Linda Hutcheon. Book-length taxonomies of the term began appearing in English in 1927 with J.A.K. Thompson's *Irony: An Historical Introduction*, and that task has been more than capably addressed about once per decade since that time. I doubt that there is a literary-philosophical history of irony that would improve upon the magisterial triad of Joseph Dane's *The Critical Mythology of Irony*, Linda Hutcheon's *Irony's Edge: The Theory and Politics of Irony*, and Colebrook's *Irony*, all of which take a long and wide view of an old concept to guide those who want to know how Aristotle and Quintilian meant something quite different from Adorno and Deleuze. Krugman is clearly not a New Critic, but there are ways in which de Man's irony can be subsumed under a broad intellectual history including Friedrich von Schlegel and what Edward Said called "a new New Criticism"; the theorists who have composed these critical histories are all worth visiting and revisiting. I have not attempted to compose such a history.[15]

FIGURE 2. Roz Chast, *The New Yorker* October 15, 2001. © Roz Chast/The New Yorker Collection/cartoonbank.com.

While drawing upon the philosophical and literary inheritance of preceding centuries, I have traced a genealogical account of irony's history running roughly from 1900 to the mid-1950s. I have done so in order to illuminate the emergence of a particularly influential period where "irony" exploded as a term to describe features not only of life and art but of the possibilities for aesthetics to orient the lives of social individuals toward political goals. For if irony has always been attached to questions of appropriateness and desirability—Aristotle's remarks are contained in the *Nicomachean Ethics*, after all—the best of the bibliographic, literary historical, and philosophical works about irony also attest that irony has a "politics." And it is precisely in either theorizing (or simply invoking) a politics of irony that the critical consensus reaches an impasse that appears as the literal dilemma at the heart of the "irony died" conversation: whether (and what kind of) irony is good for democracy, and what kind of democracy is good for people. One side of the divide finds critics quoting or tacitly inheriting an Hegelian, anti-Romantic "irony" as the linguistic and conceptual point of convergence in the otherwise rather different work of Richard Rorty and Hayden White, where irony is "invaluable in our attempt to form a private self-image, but pretty much useless when it comes to politics."[16] This is due to the supposed fact that "As the basis of a world view, irony tends to dissolve all belief in the possibility of positive political actions. In its apprehension of the essential folly or absurdity of the human condition, it tends to engender belief in the 'madness' of civilization itself and to inspire a Mandarin-like disdain for those seeking to grasp the nature of social reality."[17] In the specific terms of literary politics, this position frequently emerges as a preference for realism and naturalism, since highly ironic or satirical modernist and postmodernist novels may entertain readers but can never "move them to formulate a legislative program, to join a political movement, or to share in a national hope."[18] Such readers retreat into theory instead of forming broad consensus among diverse interest groups pursuing pragmatic justice, we are told, and what remains is only a "spectatorial, disgusted, mocking Left" who prefer "cultural politics over real politics, and to mock the very idea that democratic institutions might once again be made to serve social justice."[19] Rorty and White express no real interest in irony as a term of critique that precedes them. Nonetheless, it is only irony that could work as the central term in their attempts to yoke particular dispositions toward unruly language, while simultaneously dismissing definitions of politics that are too unruly for their own neat formulations and visions of democratic life.

On the other side of the divide, one finds precisely opposite counterclaims from Rorty's immediate targets of non–Old Lefts: Herbert Marcuse, for example, who asserted that "In the face of the gruesomely serious totality of institutionalized politics, satire, irony, and laughing provocation become a necessary dimension of the new politics."[20] More recent theorists such as Denise Riley make similar calls, for "A public irony must flourish, for the sake of the political and ethical vigour of language"; political theorist Cynthia Willett continues in this vein, emphasizing that "this is especially true in an age of empire, for what could more effectively unmask the ignorance and hubris of imperialism than comic irony?" since "comedy illustrates that irony is not only an effective tool in the private realm, as Richard Rorty has argued; irony can also play a democratic role in public and political realms." The most influential work of Donna Haraway goes even further, to call for a form of irony "No longer structured by the polarity of public and private."[21]

Whether following Wayne Booth in warning against the "political limitations of unstable irony" or whether public irony is understood as "a critical distance that undermines all politics," otherwise divergent thinkers present the highly contested as the seemingly commonsense: "Today, the mere spectacle of democracy . . . lives on in the work of Richard Rorty," a translator of Alain Badiou states, "whose preference for 'irony' over real politics is well documented."[22] Here, it is precisely the opposition of "irony" and "real politics" that best represents the political liability and opportunity presented and exploited by the word "irony." Like the "liberal irony" with which his name has too frequently become coterminous, "Rorty" can mark any number of positions in the debates surrounding both irony and politics, and a striking commonality emerges in these different articulations of the "politics of irony": if both "Rorty" and "irony" function as a shorthand for any number of competing political positions, such assertions about the politics of irony tend to rely on delimited definitions of irony in order to reinforce conventional wisdom about and assumed definitions of *politics*.

No other distinctively literary and philosophical figure has been invoked so regularly as a topic of public discussion, and no other figure could have possibly met so many sticky ends during moments of acute cultural crisis. Indeed, it's difficult to think of another term that might be used in equivalently portable ways to characterize personal, political, and national identities—and intersections among these identities—so that one frequently finds the formulations revealing more about the writer than about the object of analysis. Thus in the opposition of different claims about irony, seemingly insuperable impasses continue to arise. In 1912, for example, Agnes Repplier thought that "A deep vein of irony runs through every grade of society"; how then should one proceed in evaluating the truth of counterclaims that rely upon old associations of irony with an elite, such as Dale Bauer's recent conclusion that in the same period as Repplier was writing, "irony did not circulate generally in the middle and working classes"?[23] What one should not do is hope to find information that would settle the truth of the question once and for all but rather proceed to trace the ways that the disagreement in such pronouncements reveal more fundamental assumptions about texts, writers, readers, and the world in which they act.

The use of "irony" to make broader claims about textual and collective identities certainly isn't limited to class but includes many other categories of identity. It should raise multiple eyebrows to proclaim that the working class is particularly adept with syllepsis, that Zimbabweans are averse to symbols, that Swedes are natively skeptical, or that finally, at long last, Americans can rest easy now that metaphor has gone to the grave. And yet these kinds of claims have long been made about irony in a wide variety of specifically political contexts: "The Mexicans," an *Atlantic Monthly* writer claimed in 1920, "whatever else they may be, appreciate satire and irony"; seven years later George Saintsbury thought that both the English and "the Jews 'have it by kind.'"[24] Adorno seemed to know natively that "Irony, intellectual flexibility, and skepticism about the existing order have never been highly regarded in Germany," while a patriotic American writer agreed during World War II, since "We Americans in particular are such addicts of satire . . . but I feel doubtful if German soldiers openly sing any such ironical paeans to an efficient Nazi commissary."[25] For Anglophone writers, the most familiar contest is that between American and British sensibilities: historian J. R. Pole remarks that "English intellectuals appear to derive more satisfaction than sorrow from the conviction that Americans have no sense of irony," while novelist Jonathan Franzen claims that the difference is of kind rather than quantity, for "American irony is sincere irony, as opposed to the truly ironic English irony."[26] Where H. L. Mencken—himself no stranger to irony—derided the anti-intellectualism in "an essential character of the American . . . his tendency to combat the disagreeable with irony," critic Gilbert Seldes was sure that "irony . . . is not what America lives on," whereas "The Frenchman . . . turns to irony as his natural mode."[27] Terry Eagleton traduces only a regional portion of the population, suspecting that if "we encountered a creature looking much like us but incapable of irony, then we might well suspect that it was some cunningly devised machine, unless once more we were living in certain areas of California."[28] In its various uses as a conceptual tool to categorize groups of people, "irony" invariably casts as much light upon the values of the user of the term as it does upon the object of the characterization, and it is the goal of this project to illuminate how these values promote or obscure differing politics.

Ascribing characteristics to particular categories of people, events, and texts under the rubric of irony has been particularly common and contentious when it comes to another familiar dyad: modernism and postmodernism. It is not surprising that critics have arrived at conclusions that are just as divided as they are when it comes to individuals, nations, classes, races, and genders. For twenty-five years, many critics have followed Alan Wilde's opposition between a "disjunctive irony (the characteristic form of modernism), [which] strives toward a condition of paradox . . . before inevitably achiev[ing] an aesthetic closure" and the postmodern "suspensive irony," with "its yet more radical vision of multiplicity, randomness, contingency, and even absurdity."[29] This divide—where a "brand of irony distinctive of the postmodern is essentially skeptical, hence the psychological disengagement . . . contrasts with the irony of modernism which is essentially the irony of the avant-garde—that of tireless self-conscious self-creation"—is then used as a stable structure for, say, a political analysis of feminist epistemology or a more totalizing "politics of modernism."[30]

I have no particular quarrel with competing assertions: that postmodernism "abandoned the grand themes of modernism and instead turned to popular culture, making irony and pastiche the key aesthetic elements," or that irony was instead already the "supreme moral and aesthetic achievement and the dominant value" of modernism.[31] In fact it is precisely competing assertions that I wish to keep in play against one another. This is because of the difficulty in seeing any real utility in choosing sides in what is finally a question of nonfalsifiable categorization: whether it is true that what "we postmoderns find most unacceptable and intolerable in high modernism itself, [is] namely Irony" or whether instead we are all "steeped in high modernist irony," whether one form is "political" or another is "antipolitical" is finally a question of persuasion and definition as well as decision.[32] There are assuredly ways in which postmodernism should be understood not as a break from but an "intensification of modernist irony"; it is no doubt true that irony is "A complex term which is closely associated with postmodernism, although it has a relevance as an aspect of modernist art," and there are specific ways in which it can be true that "modernism brought about the rise of irony" to establish "irony as art's dominant aesthetic value."[33]

Finally, though, the benefits of deciding among these positions are unclear, except insofar as the decisions themselves reveal larger networks of interconnected assumptions, discourses, and practices. To choose one of these positions would require the introduction of an exterior criterion of value that would merely refine or expand the category under consideration rather than settle a question; the questions "Is it modernist?" or "Is it postmodernist?" and "Is it ironic?" or "Is it unironic?" or "Is modernist irony political or antipolitical?" are finally much less interesting and productive than the question "What definition of irony and what definition of modernism and what definition of politics are necessary in order to make X a true statement?" If it is true that "the concern with political commitment tends to make the writers of the generation after the high modernists skeptical of modernist ambiguity and irony," it is only true insofar as one works within particularly delimited understandings of categories that are—and should be—constantly under renegotiation.[34] In narrating and theorizing a cultural history of modernist ironies, I hope merely to respond to the fact that "under the aegis of modernism, irony is often invoked as a kind of 'text sanitizer' with regard to recurring ideological blindness and complicities with colonial and other all too familiar ideologies."[35] Michael North has rightly dispatched the notion that "irony is [necessarily] a minority strategy deployed against modern society" because that formerly popular argument not only relied on an unsustainable opposition between high modernisms and mass culture but "depends on the assumption that irony is not already a common feature of that society."[36] These chapters trace some particular ways in which writers in both canonical modernism and mass culture (with no particular divide adduced between them) used the term "irony" to describe themselves, their texts, and their world, and did so with a conscious sense of the interrelation among "modernism," "politics," and a rich, historically located multiplicity of "ironies."

Attempts to distinguish ontologies of "modernism" and "postmodernism"—and the forms of irony that are indexed to them—are subject to the same dynamics as attempts to distinguish between "political" and "antipolitical" irony because the results of one's investigations are inevitably functions of what definition of "modernism" or "postmodernism" one adduces at the outset. The "New Modernist" studies has done much to expand the definitions of modernism and to explode the previously limited associations of high modernism with fascism, or intensely alienated individualism, or reactionary Southern regionalism, and the aim of this project is not to load another definition onto the growing stack of additional modernisms. Rather, I locate a constellation of writers who are conventionally understood as modernist, who consciously and explicitly mobilize the concept of irony to compose and describe their own work and the work of others, and whose politics remain contested at least partially because they fall outside a relatively narrow continuum running from Left to Right. Far from using "irony" to describe a withdrawal from praxis, these writers locate the root of collective change within the embodied minds of individuals leading inextricably public and private lives, simultaneously assisted and threatened by the tendency of putatively democratic states to become authoritarian, and especially of the demonstrable tendency of liberal institutions to become violently illiberal.

In the end, all of the different forms of irony can be subsumed under a category of difference: the difference between what is said and what is meant (verbal irony), between what an audience knows and what a character knows (dramatic irony), between the effects one intends in an action and how that action brings about precisely the opposite effect (cosmic irony or *Weltironie*), between the coherent, knowing subject and the capability of that subject to transcend and examine the conditions of its own subjectivity and thus partake of an infinite, negative freedom (some Romantic, some modernist ironies). This seems particularly germane in the United States, which has frequently paid comfortable homage to difference rather than allowing or encouraging various differences to flourish. If post-9/11 commentators were precisely *prescribing* an end to irony in favor of more tractable credulity toward authority and information (sadly, they got their wish), Bourne and Adorno and Lewis were *describing* the erasure of difference: the difference between ideology and reality had disappeared, and with it the possibility of contentious democratic dissensus minimally presupposing such differences. From this dialectic of prescription and description, I hope to show, emerges a nonprescriptive brand of activist literary politics legible under the aegis of "irony."

None of this is to imply that one can't productively adduce a particular version of irony as a central term for particular uses, as generations of criticism and theory plainly attest. A Lacanian critic can, for example, coherently state that irony "reveals the limitations of a given Symbolic formation and hence its necessary relation to the real" while stipulating that "The Real is but the internal limitation of a given discursive formation, its own systemic negation. It is not irony per se," and we know what he means.[37] After considering Jonathan Lear's sustained assertion that irony "in contemporary use is a diminished version of what Kierkegaard meant," readers can gauge for themselves whether the "idea that one still needs to grasp what irony *really is* can look like mystifying hokum."[38] Ultimately, however, such assertions about "real irony" and "irony per se" and "irony itself" do seem mystifying and occasionally mystical, as they instantiate an impulse to control and stabilize not only the meaning of irony but disagreement about the work of language itself.[39] To compose a genealogy of irony as it emerges within the first part of the twentieth century therefore requires resisting the temptation to say what irony "really is," other than the fact that "irony" is and has been a particular way of speaking about a wide variety of cultural phenomena and discourses.

This book attempts to discover inductively what it has meant for irony to have a politics in the first part of the twentieth century, particularly as the conversation developed before the rise of New Criticism that is taken to have poisonously formalized and depoliticized the term, rendering it a synonym for a quality of texts and individuals that plainly corrodes political action. I agree that "there may be no such thing as a typical or privileged form of modernist irony" and that irony as a term "may serve as a heuristic tool in severing the all too obvious links between 'high modernism' and a conservative political agenda."[40] My task here is both to compose and to employ the heuristic of "irony" to read widely and deeply through a variety of literary forms, contexts, and cultures to reveal how thinkers mobilized irony's multifarious and imprecise meanings as a political resource rather than as an unwieldy impediment to be overcome with definitional precision.

To do so requires that seemingly stable definitions of what qualifies as a political agenda—conservative, liberal, radical, or otherwise—are called into question, but it neither commences nor concludes with a definition of irony. I consequently follow mid-century philosopher and historian Morton White's observation that "a detailed study of a particular branch of mathematics need not wait upon clear and definite answers to the questions 'What is mathematics?' and 'What is deduction'" and proceed with a detailed investigation of what writers and thinkers in a variety of modernist milieus thought that irony could and should do to describe and to change literary and political culture.[41] Taken most broadly, it is indeed difficult to escape Colebrook's conclusion that "Irony is a point of view adopted toward meaning; it is a specific way of living one's language. It is, if you like, a form of life"; if irony is comprehensively understood as a "form of life," the writers in this study used "irony" to describe particular forms of life as they might be produced by irony's multiple referents in literary and political culture.[42] Thus, following the later Ludwig Wittgenstein, I commence with the basic premise that "the meaning of a word is its use in the language [*Die Bedeutung ist sein Gebrauch in der Sprache*]," and the examples I analyze are less an attempt to provide a compendium of idiosyncratic outliers than to establish a heuristic derived from a culture of dynamic use. It is established wisdom that "Although irony has long had its own secure niche within literary criticism, it was the New Criticism of the 1940s that gave it a particularly privileged position within Anglo-American critical discourse"; although New Criticism may have dominated educational institutions for many decades, it did not have a monopoly on the concept and practice of irony either within or after any definition of literary modernism other than the New Critical one.[43]

Because I am interested in irony not only as a literary or rhetorical mode but also as a subject and object of discourse, I have limited my analysis to writers who not only composed ironic texts but talked *about* irony and satire in their own work and in specific political contexts. This is emphatically not to make claims about authorial intention but to recognize that describing something as "ironic" or as "satire" fundamentally changes the interpretive dispositions and conclusions of readers toward those works and the world in which they appear. Again, I emphasize how a variety of modernist writers both recognized and mobilized the polysemantic instability of the concept "irony" and harnessed the multiple, slippery definitions as a rhetorical and political resource, rather than as a lexicographical stumbling block to be overcome. In doing so, I argue, these writers condition the reception of their literary production specifically *as ironic*—in all the various ways that the term denotes a dynamic, contingent, triadic relationship among texts, individuals, and political collectivities—and finally as politically active in a way that is adequately described neither by the New Criticism, by subsequent critical accounts, nor by party politics running from the CPUSA to the GOP. As writers themselves theorized politics by talking about irony and satire, the following pages are an attempt to think through the particular ways in which the concept of irony came to represent intersections between political and aesthetic practices in the first half of the twentieth century.

More than simply deriving the meaning of irony from its use, I proceed from the assumption that words have histories that precede and succeed both their users and their position within historical moments and discourses. There are *reasons*—political, etymological, social, and historical—why one word is chosen over another in particular literary and political situations, and why so many people have been moved to pronounce the "death of irony" instead of the "cancer of metaphor" or the "acne of skepticism." A detailed investigation of these uses reveals a desire for particular forms of life in ways that a lexicographical index does not.[44] Invocations of irony ineluctably bear the linguistic and conceptual traces of their many predecessors, and it is a sort of fantasy to imagine that there could or should be a cordon sanitaire erected among denotations or that language as it functions both in ordinary contexts and as a technical vocabulary might be cleansed of competing connotations. If Thomas Aquinas's judgment of whether or not irony is a sin (*"utrum ironia sit peccatum"*) predates any definition of Romanticism or modernism by eight hundred years, Ezra Pound warned in 1917 that "Irony is still set down as a 'sin' in manuals of devotion. The last heretic was burnt at the stake in 1758. We are not yet out of the forest."[45] The continuing debates around irony in literary studies and popular culture suggest that we are still not out of a literary-historical forest, wherein one imagines that one's crisis is discrete and recent and where the contingent values undergirding assumed definitions of politics frequently masquerade as empirical facts in the world.[46]

Wrestling irony within its muddling definitional field presents many challenges to clarity, and the difficulties multiply exponentially with the addition of equally contentious terms like "aesthetics" and "politics." To this end, I focus on a line of thinking in which "politics" depends upon a wider field of meaning known as "the political," wherein issues entailed by the various "differences" in irony and "differences" in a diverse nation are described by the representations of "differences" (or lack thereof) between facts and values. Adorno, after all, was not alone in choosing irony to name the difference between "ideology and reality" or to frame politically pernicious approaches to this difference as close kin to the "false inference that leads from the existence of stubborn facts to their erection as the highest value [*führt nicht von der Existenz der stubborn facts zu deren Installierung als höchstem Wert der gleiche Fehlschluß*]."[47] But neither was a positive conception of irony only attendant within conventional high modernism: in 1956, Walter Rideout's groundbreaking work on working-class radical fiction showed that "the chief ingredient of the proletarian writers' sensibility was a predilection for irony, that age-old defense developed by man to meet the disparity between what is and what ought to be."[48]

In the late 1930s, erstwhile radical Max Eastman worried that "the facts, even when known and molded to our desires, continue to say so much less and mean so much more than we do when we talk about them, that I am afraid their irony will never die."[49] The writers in this study are concerned with the role that irony could play not just in describing "ironic facts" but in staging the fact-value dichotomy as a function of aesthetic representation, wherein irony both describes and produces critical dispositions toward the values that facts always presume. Political philosopher Dick Howard, among many others, has emphasized the role of meaning in the fact-value dichotomy as central to the larger question of political praxis itself, and insists

> on the difference between the condition and that which it conditions—on the difference between the political and politics. This is not to deny that politics is about "who does what to whom," as Lenin famously put it. It implies that the dimension of meaning must be introduced in order to explain the dynamism that makes the "facts" appear to call for action—for politics.[50]

Following these terms, literary work is understood as praxis insofar as it is conceived to bring about, affect, and effect the field of "the political":

that is, the interpretive "conditions" under which nonideological, non-institutional forms of life may be imagined as a precondition for action. Thus one of my central concerns is highlighting irony's role in producing the very "dimension of meaning" that delineates parameters of public action and inaction. It has long been remarked that the "central problem in moral philosophy is that commonly known as the *is-ought* problem" and that political questions often descend from the question, "How is what *is* the case related to what *ought* to be the case—statements of fact to moral judgments."[51] The locus classicus for this problem lies in David Hume's *Treatise of Human Nature*, and philosophers and political theorists have been arguing about the subject in more or less explicit ways since the eighteenth century. I am less concerned, however, with whether or not one can logically, ethically, pragmatically, or delusionally move from statements of "fact" to statements of "value" as a means of understanding moral action, or in closely tracing the contemporary role of logical positivism as it inflected the conversation, or in rectifying the New Critical legacy of "removing the moral implications from the usage of the word [irony]" by reintroducing an aesthetic politics grounded in the category of the moral.[52] Rather, my story is more concerned with how the concept of irony has been imagined to play a key role in the formation of a specifically *amoral* and nonetheless ethical and activist politics predicated upon literary aesthetics changing individual and collective dispositions toward facts and values. I thus try to show how the language of the fact-value debate is echoed in, intersects with, and indeed structures much of the discussion about irony's good or bad, desirable or undesirable, inspiring or corrosive relationship with politics, and therefore militates against conventionally limited associations of irony with defeatist quietism. By deploying irony as a multivalent, unstable concept for describing the ineluctably value-laden nature of represented facts, the writers in this study understand irony as crucial to the aesthetic staging and reception of facts and values, and thus as political practice insofar as it strives to change the disposition of readers toward many different forms of information and action.

By "disposition," I have in mind what political theorist William Connolly means when he uses the word "sensibility": "a set of affectively imbued dispositions to judgment and action embedded in ideas set on different levels of body/brain complexity."[53] Irony has, at least since the early nineteenth-century opposition between Hegel and Schlegel, been a convergence point for discourses about rationality and affect and how each affects desirable or undesirable relationships among self, word, world, and democracy. By returning to the question of irony and embodied dispositions toward information and texts, I have no particular stake in past decades' notorious disputes about "aesthetic ideology." Nor do I try to emphasize or criticize understandings of modernist irony as essentially a rehashed version of Romantic irony manifested through different generic styles or forms. Rather, in the genealogy of irony and ironists I am composing, I find a constellation of writers who operate within a variety of conventional categories of affiliation—culture, gender, class, race, and nation, among others—who invoke irony as a term for staging and experiencing the dynamic interplay of aesthetic affect (variously rendered by them as "emotion," "sensibility," "feeling," etc.) and critical rationality. In their respective historical and rhetorical context, and with a long philosophical and rhetorical history behind them, they reveal an uncertainly pragmatic vision of irony that is focused not on the cultivation of self as either purely rational or purely sensual being but on the cultivation of dispositions: a form of political judgment that is beyond and outside of instrumental reason or aestheticist quietism.

For Connolly and other philosophers on the Left, dispositions such as these offer the hope of "a conversion from one ontological stance to another," which "involves intellectual arguments and affective movements entangled together and the potential of altering "the unconscious presumptions of everyday judgment."[54] Modernist irony in my story focuses as much on epistemology and aesthetics as ontology, and describes both dispositions and representations that acknowledge the ideological dangers of affect (e.g., as evidenced in propaganda or cultural habit) while also refusing to imagine that the embodied experience of individuals could or should be reduced—even as an ideal—to pure reason.

Consequently, I have frequent recourse to the pragmatist philosophers who most influentially articulated the political possibilities and liabilities of such socially disposed individuals as these, especially William James and John Dewey. The work of Jacques Rancière has risen to prominence in recent years for posing "the question of the relationship between aesthetics and politics" at "the level of the sensible delimitation of what is common to the community, the forms of its visibility and of its organization," and frequently invokes the fact-value dilemma to draw connections similar to the ones I've been discussing: "Politics and art, like forms of knowledge," Rancière writes, "construct 'fictions', that is to say *material* rearrangements of signs and images, relationships between what is seen and what is said, between what is done and what can be done."[55] Furthermore, he has in mind the facts and values of a specifically democratic politics, emphasizing that "Democracy is not a definite set of institutions, nor is it the power of a specific group" but rather—following late Derrida—understanding democracy as fundamentally grounded in self-negating paradoxes, a "democracy to come" that is "a promise that has to be kept even though—and precisely because—it can never be fulfilled. It is a democracy that can never 'reach itself', catch up with itself."[56]

Rather than taking up Rancière or his interlocutors in any sustained way, part of my project is to situate modernist writers within their own intellectual and political contexts; this again involves articulating the influence of pragmatism, especially as politically active ironists revised and opposed what they saw as pernicious political decisions made by its primary theorists. Thus, without claiming that pragmatists beat Rancière to theoretical punches, it bears repeating that these thinkers also saw how democracy can be reduced neither to self-development nor to a system of governance but should rather be understood—as John Dewey wrote in 1932—as "a postulate in the sense of a demand to be realized" where, "Like every true ideal, [democracy] signifies something to be done rather than something already given, something ready-made" such that "the desired harmony never is brought about in a way which meets and forestalls all future developments."[57] As a trope that pointedly relies upon and also produces communities of interpretation and disagreement, this modernist irony is invoked repeatedly as a descriptor for aesthetic practices that dynamically produce affiliation and disaffiliation while foreclosing an ideal of interpretive or political resolution. This is not to say that these thinkers sought what F. R. Ankersmit calls "aesthetic politics beyond fact and value," even though they frequently share his sense that "if one truly loves liberty, one should distrust liberalism," for "Liberalism has been the main agent in the process of the political domestication and emasculation of the individual, and has changed us into the nice and malleable people that we have become."[58] This is not necessarily because they hold quite different definitions of "aesthetics" in mind but because Ankersmit's analysis is, after all of his smart attention to irony, finally one focused on party affiliation and the creation of voter preferences via an emphasis on metaphor. Indeed, Ankersmit essentially agrees with Hegel, insofar as he predicts that in the "victory of Romantic irony over metaphor and with the reduction of the metaphorical distance between the state and the citizen, we will also lose our capacity to conceptualize social and political problems."[59] The writers under consideration in my study find precisely in public irony the hope of forming new capacities to conceptualize these problems and to disrupt the invisible metaphors that have constituted too-tractable and too-ideological publics.

It sometimes seems as if there is little left to say about this protean beast that started as a tricky, slippery character in Athenian drama and, at identifiable points along the way, became so vividly freighted with denotations and connotations—subsuming everything from urbane verbal style to relationships between individuals and the march of History—that it might not only live but die. Over the centuries, "irony" has come to describe a quality within a text, a process of recognition that arises in a reader who is invited to decide among competing voices, and also qualities of the world that texts render in varying degrees of adequacy. In this regard, irony has become a trope of tropes: not in the sense that de Man had in mind when he called irony the "trope of tropes" because it "includes all tropes"—that is, a "trope of tropes" in the sense that there could be a "King of Kings"—but "irony" as a repository for multiple discourses, a figure to describe how texts do or should represent a nexus of aesthetics and politics, and what the disposition of political agents is or should be.

In short, "irony" in popular and critical discourse has long been deployed as what political theorist Donald Schön calls a "generative metaphor" to figure a particular nexus of politics and aesthetics; like all generative metaphors, this one serves to obscure the fact that social and political problems are solved only as well as they are set. The problem of irony has been too frequently set in such a way that it falsely assumes what it should minimally set out to prove: the mistaken premise that effective political action relies upon rational individuals who seek collective solidarity to act within institutions and states and that pragmatically political literature provides either clear models for these actions or a mystical, infinitely receding horizon of possibility. Schön's argument has been particularly influential for social scientists and political theorists, and accords with Kenneth Burke's proposals about "terministic screens" in the 1940s as well as George Lakoff's arguments about "frames" in the twenty-first century. Schön argues that metaphorical figures are often viewed as "significant only as symptoms of a particular kind of SEEING-AS, the 'meta-pherein' or 'carrying over' of frames or perspectives from one domain of experience to another," and that this process should be known as a "generative metaphor."[60] The notion of the generative metaphor relies upon an understanding that the "essential difficulties in social policy have more to do with problem setting than with problem solving" and that "the framing of problems often depends upon metaphors underlying the stories which generate problem setting and set the direction of problem solving" (138). Schön's point is "not that we *ought* to think metaphorically about social policy problems, but that we *do* already think about them in terms of certain pervasive, tacit generative metaphors" (139). Because the narration of social and political problems constructs a "view of social reality through a complementary process of *naming* and *framing*," the hidden metaphoricity of narration serves conservative interests by making "the normative leap from data to recommendations, from fact to values, from 'is' to 'ought' . . . [and it] is typical of diagnostic prescriptive stories such as these that they execute the normative leap in such a way as to make it seem graceful, compelling, even obvious" (147). If democracy is to be understood as something more than participation in or maintenance of basically formal, proceduralist institutions manifestly serving a privileged minority of interests, tracing out the deep metaphors underlying our assessment of those problems has the potential to reframe basic assumptions about the possibilities of literature to effect individual and collective change in the material world. In U.S. literary culture, irony doesn't just help reveal those metaphors: the keyword "irony" *is* one of those metaphors.

A truly exhaustive account of irony in any literary epoch, genre, style, or mode would expand into an infinite number of pages, subject to a taxonomy more appropriate to Jorge Luis Borges than D. C. Muecke. Consequently, each of the following chapters takes a more limited view of the problem as represented by a variety of figures, each of whom presented themselves and were received as ironists, each of whom theorized their own work in terms of diverse political goals, and each of whose work continues to be contested politically. Over roughly the first half of the twentieth century, irony evolved as a figure for describing and revealing discourses around which power is constituted through acts of aesthetic representation and judgment; in terms of the story about irony that I've traced above, the figure of irony both describes and prescribes different ways of aesthetically representing the pragmatic facts and values of lived experience. What unites them all is that irony is the consistent term—a primus inter pares in a constellation of its best-known affiliates and nemeses, from satire to sentimentalism—to engage a variety of embodied political identities.

The first chapter traces the popular reception of Friedrich Nietzsche's work in the United States in the early part of the twentieth century: specifically, the influence of Nietzsche's irony among differently socialist and anarchist writers of New York in the 1910s. In this context, irony does not just describe particular aesthetic practices within democratic forms of governance but is a central term for reimagining the theory and praxis of democracy through the lens of a thinker popularly understood as virulently antidemocratic. The chapter offers a new reading of canonical essayist Randolph Bourne's "The Life of Irony" through the works of Nietzsche, pragmatist philosophers, theorists of visual aesthetics such as Lewis Hine and Alfred Stieglitz, and other sources ranging from government pamphlets to popularizing works such as H. L. Mencken's *The Philosophy of Friedrich Nietzsche*. The final portion of the chapter reintroduces the work of forgotten proto-Dada poet and journalist Benjamin De Casseres, who represented a competing reception of Nietzsche as a theorist of political aesthetics in order to decry what he described as an American culture crippled by that "Anglo-Saxon injunction: Thou shalt not commit irony!"[61] In different ways, De Casseres and Bourne figure Nietzsche's irony through the language of photographic and literary aesthetics: by restoring this conversation about irony to a dialectic—half of which has been omitted from consideration—I propose we read irony as a figure for reconceiving democratic action quite differently from the tradition that values private irony but banishes public irony and demands solidarity with liberal institutions or abstracted masses at the expense of collectivities formed by variously agonistic, publicly ironic individuals.

The second chapter moves from the turn of the century to the late 1920s, via G.W.F. Hegel's influential definition of women as the "eternal irony in the life of the community." The idea of modernist women "becoming" ironic can be understood as a broad cultural figuring of the particular challenges presented by preexisting discourses about the political role of art, which divided gendered particularity from the imagined universality of both political rights and literary value. On the one hand, "irony" would mean the capacity to conceive of relationships among gendered particulars and universals, to experience sensible pleasure without either surrendering to aesthetic rapture or reducing "beauty" to a mere symbol of "morality." On the other hand, it would simultaneously mean the subjective "impulse" to compose texts that were legible as a critique of the double bind in which postsuffrage women found themselves, enjoying formal equality under the laws of supposedly free electoral politics but neither experiencing a sensation of "freedom" nor seeing material changes as a result of exercising their franchise. After defining the chapter's central issues by reading a 1906 short story by novelist Katherine Holland Brown titled "The Birth of Irony," I situate Ellen Glasgow's immensely popular novel *The Romantic Comedians* (1926) in a cultural and political context that includes the pragmatism of William James and key episodes from F. Scott Fitzgerald's *The Beautiful and Damned* (1922) and Ernest Hemingway's *The Sun Also Rises* (1926). While irony reemerged as a central analytical term for 1990s feminist theorists,

Glasgow's repeated call for "Blood and Irony" as the "safest antidote to sentimental decay" offers a radical feminist riposte to the persistent myth of the "unironic woman" from within popular modernist culture itself.

My third chapter builds upon the second chapter's analysis of irony and sentimentalism to focus on satire in the 1930s, which Northrop Frye once defined as "militant irony." I demonstrate how widespread anxieties about the disappearance or impossibility of satire—appearing from the mid-nineteenth century to the present day but exploding in the first part of the twentieth century—echo parallel discourses about the disappearance of irony. They do much more than that, however: satire provides a key heuristic for understanding intersecting debates about rationality, aesthetic affect, and embodied responses to the defeat of journalism's Enlightenment and constitutional mandates by the rise of corporate and state propaganda. Drawing on sources ranging from U.S. Senate hearings and journalistic exposés to seminal debates about the nature of "the public" in the 1920s and 1930s, I read John Dos Passos's U.S.A. trilogy as a simultaneously new and old form of satire—what Dos Passos himself called "Satire as a Way of Seeing"—relying upon aesthetic affect to disrupt the interests of those who control the means of information production. In 1938, Mary McCarthy asserted that "You cannot produce trenchant political satire—at least not in America in this period—if your political horizon is the Wagner Act," explicitly repudiating both the venerable equation of satire with the normative sphere of law and the liberal equation of legislation with political action.[62] In this light, I argue that U.S.A. employs print satire to redefine the object of politics itself as the "indirect" distribution of aesthetic information: information that calls attention to its own means of aesthetic production and that oscillates between attempts to produce a naturalist-aesthetic, emotional response to cruel injustice and a critical awareness of how those effects are produced.

My final chapter examines the ways in which discourses of irony intersect with discourses of law, race, responsibility, and recognition in the period that saw the institutionalization of both modernism and the New Criticism. While establishing the historical and political context for relating "irony" to the work of "race"—ranging from Frederick Douglass's oratory to Langston Hughes's testimony before the House Committee on Un-American Activities—I draw on legal history, political theory, and formalist close reading to trace the ways that Ralph Ellison consistently invoked what he called a "gyroscope of irony" as a means of framing the political reception of his only finished novel.[63] While Invisible Man refuses to provide explicit instructions for resolving its irony, Ellison's prolonged engagement with the work of Kenneth Burke substantially clarifies how and why Ellison deployed the term, how sensitive he was to its possibilities, and how he alerts his own readership to the presence of non–New Critical irony as alternative praxis. *Invisible Man* and Ellison's exposition of it are not wholly discrete activities but work in combination toward providing a vision of democratic praxis that lies outside—but not in opposition to—more familiar means of action ranging from electoral politics to litigation and marches in the streets. For Ellison, this would be a praxis based not upon the rational exchange of information in a marketplace of ideas or of merely alienating effusion of irrationality: rather, what Ellison's use of irony reveals is a form of action that worked toward the goal of forming attitudes toward information and thus building forms of association that value agonistic disagreement as the means by which just decisions are reached in a democracy. Against attacks on the novel and on Ellison himself as retreating from political engagement, I argue that *Invisible Man* redefines and undermines definitions of politics that are limited either to direct action or to legislative formalism.

On the one hand, one wants to acknowledge that language is unstable, that we shouldn't resolve ironies rashly (or at all), that we should allow the free play of signification to produce pleasure and profit wherever it sees fit. On the other hand, politics of every stripe requires action at some point, and such action entails conventionally stable production and comprehension of language—at least for a transitory moment of interpretive decision. In many ways, the story of irony in the first half of the twentieth century is about the political implications of this double bind and about how irony might play a role in repositioning aesthetic abstractions of the nation-state and ethical politics themselves *as aesthetic double binds between fact and value* and thus undermine the foundational goal of consensus solidarity, required by political positions as widely varying as liberalism, communism, fascism, and progressivism. The writers in this study frame decision and consensus and participation in electoral politics as necessary and worthy goals but ultimately as politically chimerical when viewed as an end point, as a telos rather than as a pragmatic moment of transition. Thus the following pages are not intended to be the final, exhaustive word in a long dialogue, or necessarily to negate the positions of its many interlocutors. Rather, in composing an alternative story of modernist irony in the first half of the twentieth century, I aim to explore a salient thread of the conversation that is regularly in danger of being occluded, because implicit or truncated definitions of key terms are presented as the final word rather than the beginning of a constant series of engaged renegotiation.

1 / The Eye in Irony: New York, Nietzsche, and the 1910s

You will find irony treated angrily, as though it were an acid or a poison, where men love ease. And you will find it merely ignored when men have wholly lost the sense of justice.

—HILAIRE BELLOC, 1910

Amor fati is the core of my nature. This, however, does not alter the fact that I love irony, and even world-historical irony.

—FRIEDRICH NIETZSCHE, 1888[1]

Paul Fussell has claimed that there "seems to be one dominating form of modern understanding; that it is essentially ironic; and that it originates largely in the application of mind and memory to the events of the Great War."[2] In specifically literary terms, Fussell's influential assertion is agreeably consonant with the emergence of the New Criticism, high modernism, and canonical postmodernism, all of which are thought to be distinguished by the salient employment of different ironies. "Irony" simultaneously describes a form of consciousness, a rhetorical trope, a mode of aesthetic representation, a characteristic of historical events, and a disposition toward various modes of signification; if these are all imagined to emerge from the wholesale failure to flout laws of unintended consequences, then perhaps the notorious "rise" of irony really can be traced to the trenches of the Somme, whence it virally spread throughout the brains and books of the Anglophone world. What to make, however, of those years before "everything" putatively shattered into fragmented, disillusioned chaos; between the hopeful turn of the old century and the recognition that events in the new century might be more horrifying than any prediction? Was that period dominated by a single form of premodern, mid-modern, low-modern, mini-modern, or quasi-modern understanding? Are we to imagine that those years of apprehending, remembering, and representing the world were notably devoid of irony, either by definition or in comparison with prior and subsequent epochs?

There are obviously as many answers to that question as there are definitions of irony, and it's certainly easy enough to adduce all sorts of "modern" irony before 1914. Even in the moment, "irony" was used to describe the effects of the war, such as political theorist Harold Stearns's question in 1919: "when we look back now to the days before the war, did not the graceful sensuous satire, the slightly tired irony . . . seem best to typify the sophisticated anti-intellectualism of that era[?]"[3] In trying to assess just how irony "came to be what it is," the real question raised here is not whether irony was invigorated or exhausted by the war; rather, what was the cultural logic whereby such observations and propositions are coherent in the first place?

To approach the question of how we arrived at particular visions of irony in general, I want to suggest that the cultural deployment of "irony" as a term is best understood as a rhetorical staging area for the relationships between aesthetic and political problems. I'll do so by considering the work of two American theorists of irony in the context of irony's purported enemy: political praxis. In the space of a few years, and within a few miles of one another, American writers Randolph Bourne and Benjamin De Casseres used the word "irony" to describe multiple and competing intersections between aesthetics and politics. Bourne's concept of irony has been scrutinized and anthologized, explicitly championed or implicitly attacked, however, while the exclusion—not to say repression—of the equally prolific, more forthrightly individualist and avant-garde De Casseres reveals some of the aesthetic and political assumptions that structure both literary history and a particular political imaginary. Placing the two writers in dialogue with one another through the work of Friedrich Nietzsche, who influenced them in profound and different ways, suggests a more agonistic, pointedly conflict-oriented mode of discourse than the "Beloved Community" promoted by the Young Intellectuals of Greenwich Village and not coincidentally helps delineate the limits of how "irony" is frequently deployed in our own literary and political discourse.

Bourne himself advised that "Words are not invariable symbols for invariable things, but clues to meanings," and my concern is not to enumerate the multiple meanings of "irony" as classical trope, narrative mode, or dramatic recognition but to show how irony served as a central term for representing aesthetic-political action through intersecting contemporary discourses about photography, visuality, politics, and the philosophy of Friedrich Nietzsche as it circulated in the early twentieth-century United States.[4] This nexus of discourses does more than merely destabilize the conventional opposition between modernist and postmodernist ironies, and more than merely argue in favor of "irony" as a political disposition against its implied opposites of "sincerity" or "earnestness" or "commitment." In the New York Nietzscheans of the 1910s, I find in irony not just a term to describe particular aesthetic practices within particular democracies but a model for imagining and reimagining democracy itself. Bourne and De Casseres both figure irony through the language of aesthetics but in almost violently different ways: by restoring this conversation about irony to an actual dialectic, I propose we read irony as a figure for reconceiving democratic action quite differently from the legacy of "liberal democratic irony" of critics in the wake of Richard Rorty and Hayden White, who value private irony but banish public irony and demand solidarity with liberal institutions at the expense of agonistic, publicly ironic individuals.

Randolph Bourne is still fairly familiar to scholars of American literature and culture, and his paean to pluralism, "Trans-National America," can fairly be called part of an ever-expanding canon.[5] After achieving renown for his essays in publications as different as the decidedly bourgeois *Atlantic*, the markedly liberal *New Republic*, and the frequently radical *Seven Arts*, Bourne was famous by 1913 and dead by 1918, an underemployed victim of censorship and influenza, fired from *The Dial* by his erstwhile mentor John Dewey, blacklisted and harassed by FBI agents for loudly opposing American entry into World War I. A central figure in the prewar "Lyrical Left," by 1930 his fame had dwindled to the point where Lewis Mumford could plausibly claim that there "are many ways of establishing how old a person is, and one of them is to mention the name of Randolph Bourne."[6] This remained periodically true after John Dos Passos memorialized him in *U.S.A.* as the "tiny twisted unscared ghost in a black cloak . . . crying out in a shrill soundless giggle: War is the health of the state," but Bourne's figure has been resurrected repeatedly: when the League of American Writers gave Theodore Dreiser the 1941 Randolph Bourne Memorial Award in recognition of Dreiser's stance against American entry into World War II; during the early days of the Cold War, when anarchist-libertarian-socialist Dwight Macdonald invoked Bourne's image in his journal *politics*; when Noam Chomsky quoted extensively from Bourne's essay "Twilight of Idols" at the height of the movement against the war in Vietnam, finding in Bourne's essays "no program for action, but an injunction to seek such a program and create for ourselves, for others, the understanding that can give it life"; and more recently by opponents of the American invasions and occupations of Iraq and Afghanistan. Bourne's work (and beatification as a minor, secular saint of anti-imperialism) resurfaces both because he "rejected colonialism, bastard Anglo-Saxondom, and the cheap melting-pot American in favour of a transnational America," as his friend Paul

Rosenfeld wrote in 1923, and because his opponents "concentrated the whole of this powerful little man in a single resistant ironic point."[7]

Drawing parallels between the pre–World War I "Lyrical Left" and the 1960s New Left, Daniel Aaron remarked that "much of Bourne's philosophy of life is contained in 'The Life of Irony,'" and much of that philosophy emphasized how new forms of politics would aestheticize being and behavior, partially by cultivating a discursive politics of friendship.[8] "Good talk" among a community of like-minded friends, Casey Nelson Blake writes, "was the perfect example of Bourne's conception of irony, making intellectual exchange personal and yet objective, just as friendship itself united individuals in an emotional bond that still preserved their integrity as separate persons."[9] Most seem to agree that "Bourne's central argument in the essay was that irony was best understood not as a trope but as a lived experience that comes in accepting contradiction"; as Ross Posnock shows in drawing parallels between Bourne's work and that of Theodor Adorno, "Pivotal to Bourne's revisionary practice is irony, which he employs less as an aesthetic term than as descriptive of a quality of action that avoids crystallization by dissolving conventional oppositions, like passive/active."[10]

By displacing aesthetics in favor of personality and conversation, and by demarcating social performance, friendship, and embodied experience from aesthetics, the critical consensus on Bourne's irony isn't so much unjustified as it is symptomatically incomplete.[11] In his 1913 essay titled "The Life of Irony," Bourne does indeed figure irony as a modus vivendi that is partially distinct from aesthetic representation, and right away asserts that "we should speak not of the Socratic method but of the Socratic life. Irony is a life rather than a method."[12] With much more on his mind than a screed against Socratic rationalism, Bourne then expands his definition of irony to subsume an essentially discursive practice among acquaintances and friends, conducted with the express aim of expanding sociality, gaining new viewpoints on the world and formulating new approaches to the truth, and trusting that the moral category of the "good" will emerge from such interactive inquiry. Drawing on the figure of Socrates, Bourne describes irony as a

> pleasant challenging of the world . . . insistent judging of experience . . . sense of vivid contrasts and incongruities, of comic juxtapositions, of flaring brilliancies, and no less heartbreaking impossibilities, of all the little parts of one's world being constantly set off against each other, and made intelligible only by being translated into and defined in each others' terms. (102)

The idea that irony can "translate" one set of terms into another in order to arrive at a functional definition of justice, for example, is familiar to readers of Platonic dialogues. Yet for Bourne, irony is neither simply a rhetorical strategy to reveal an interlocutor's poor reasoning nor "a pose or amusement" (103) but is simultaneously "a life of beauty" (102) and "a critical attitude towards life" (103). The life distinguished by dissenting irony rather than agreeably complacent faith, Bourne writes, is a mode of conducting serious business without grave earnestness and as such provides a welcome "rival of the religious life," for "the life of irony has the virtue of the religious life without its defects. It expresses the aggressive virtues without the quiescence of resignation" (105). The ironist may be "at one with the religious man in that he hates apathy and stagnation, for they mean death," but "he is superior in that he attacks apathy of intellect and personality as well as apathy of emotion" (105).

Visions of Values, Envisioning Democracy

The significance of Bourne's pragmatism, his catholic openness to a shifting world of social relations, his prescient theorizations of ethnicity and gender as central loci for important political contests, and his legendary status as an opponent of bellicose American imperialism have been well established. The full significance of his irony, however, quite literally remains to be seen. In a passage that lies at the heart of the essay, Bourne presents his concept of irony in pointedly aesthetic terms:

> The ironical method might be compared to the acid that develops a photographic plate. It does not distort the image, but merely brings clearly to the light all that was implicit in the plate before. And if it brings the picture to the light with values reversed, so does irony revel in a paradox, which is simply a photographic negative of the truth, truth with the values reversed. But turn the negative ever so slightly so that the light falls upon it, and the perfect picture appears in all its true values and beauty. Irony, we may say then, is the photography of the soul. The picture goes through certain changes in the hands of the ironist, but without these changes the truth would be simply a blank, unmeaning surface. (110)

The initial comparison of irony to "the acid that develops a photographic plate" is both innovative and venerable: despite the relative novelty of photographic technology, the idea of irony as "corrosive" has a long tradition that includes the salt with which Horace and Ben Jonson rubbed the cheeks of their audiences, the acid invoked in 1910 by Hilaire Belloc,

Benjamin De Casseres's 1922 "Irony is an acid pity," and Northrop Frye's "irony is . . . an acid that will corrode healthy as well as decayed tissues."[13] Bourne's photographic metaphor of irony, however, develops into a full-fledged consideration of visual representation, visual apprehension, relationships among varying accounts of truth and realism, and an explicitly Nietzschean "transvaluation of values."[14]

In the 1910s, photography held forth the promise of accurately representing facts, and Bourne's conceit simultaneously emphasizes photographic images themselves, the means by which those images are composed, and the effect of those images on the aesthetic dispositions of percipients. Thus the ironist's life includes the literal, sympathetic translation of intersubjective points of view with the goal of winnowing out weak ideas, for "if an idea is hollow, it will show itself cowering against the intellectual background of the ironist like the puny, shivering thing it is. If a point of view cannot bear being adopted by another person, if it is not hardy enough to be transplanted, it has little right to exist at all."[15] Furthering this analogy between photographic and ironic processes, he acknowledges that meaning is produced through a complex interplay of subjective positions and aesthetic objects embedded in a social context and that there might be profound social implications if "perspectives" were exposed to the light of irony rather than the Enlightenment of reason: "Too many outworn ideas are skulking in dark retreats, sequestered from the light; every man has great sunless stretches in his soul where base prejudices lurk and flourish. On these the white light of irony is needed to play" (109). Thus the paradoxical result of expanding and multiplying perspectives on the world might actually be an aggregate reduction in total points of view; just as photography renders the multiplicity of vision into a few focused images, irony presents multiple views while framing a response to those views based on a system of values. After all, Bourne writes, the "dictum that 'the only requisites for success are honesty and merit,' which we applaud so frantically from the lips of the successful, becomes a ghastly irony in the mouth of an unemployed workingman. There would be a frightful mortality of points of view could we have a perfectly free exchange such as this" (109).

Bourne's reference to visual media pointedly invokes the Aristotelian metaphysical tradition that imagines vision as a privileged means of acquiring knowledge, which Claire Colebrook describes as "a desire to see or wonder of seeing [that] also allows the human soul to think beyond sensible knowledge to those principles that are not given to the senses," a characterization of perception that Bourne would wholeheartedly endorse: "the human eye is ironic," Colebrook writes, "capable of viewing this world from an unworldly perspective. The tradition of irony is a tradition that interrogates the essentially bifurcated possibility of the human point of view, at once within and beyond its own world."[16] This is a tradition that includes Kierkegaard's analysis of Socrates, who "elevates himself higher and higher, becoming ever lighter as he rises, seeing all things disappear beneath him from his ironical bird's eye perspective," and perhaps the first function of Bourne's photographic conceit is to emphasize the role played by vision in theories of mind and aesthetic dispositions toward the phenomenal world, as well as the historical characterization of such shifting perspectives within irony's ambit.[17] Bourne's metaphor of irony as photographic plate further revises the role played by aesthetic information in the development of new political imagination and emerges less from the empiricism of David Hume than from the "radical empiricism" of William James. In what James called the "rooted rationalism" of pre- or antipragmatic philosophy, experience meant the apprehension of discrete data that were connected, and thus made comprehensible, by a priori categories and concepts. In Bourne's highly pragmatic phrase, "Our minds are so unfortunately arranged that all sorts of beliefs can be accepted and propagated quite independently of any rational or even experimental basis at all. Nature does not seem to care very much whether our ideas are truth or not, as long as we get on through life safely enough."[18] Despite the fact that Dewey didn't take up art as an object of sustained critique until the mid-1930s, we thus arrive at one of the significant meeting points of turn-of-the-century American pragmatism and the aesthetic tradition as intercepted by Bourne: the notion that mental concepts themselves were not only produced but dynamically altered by encounters with new formulations of sensory data. As Bourne writes regarding the life of irony, "concepts are indispensable,—and yet each concept falsifies. The ironist must have as large a stock as possible, but he must have a stock" (114).

Indeed, James himself uses metaphors of visual representation to dismiss claims to a unified, essential truth. One may posit a truth "with no one thinking it," he writes, but "as well might a pencil insist that the outline is the essential thing in all pictorial representation, as chide the paint-brush and the camera for omitting it, forgetting that their pictures not only contain the whole outline, but a hundred other things in addition."[19] Such metaphors are strikingly common in this intellectual and political milieu, which further amplifies the significance of irony's acid on Bourne's photographic plate. For Bourne to declare that "irony is not a palliative so much as a perspective" is to associate the photographic figure of irony with not only a literal outlook but a specifically visual,

aesthetic disposition toward the world with ethical and political implications.[20] Indeed, Bourne argues that "the only justification of the aesthetic
attitude" is an ironic one, for "if taken provisionally, it sweetens and for-
tifies. It is only deadly when adopted as absolute" (120).

Significantly, Bourne identifies the ironic disposition with visual
stimulation toward action rather than inaction (contra the conventional
association of irony with withdrawal) and further identifies action itself
as a result of emotional feeling rather than rational contemplation: the
kind of "aesthetic irony" that is to be avoided is "the result not of exqui-
sitely refined feelings, but of social anaesthesia" (120). Photography thus
expresses irony's capacity both to adopt and to produce different perspectives; the shifting construction of those perspectives has political implications, Bourne argues, because irony can help the mind recognize the
fallacies of dogma. Bourne's colleagues and friends, such as Van Wyck
Brooks, denounced an American culture in which the "invisible government of self-interest, built up carefully from the beginning by maxim
and example, fills the vacuum a disinterested purpose ought to have
occupied";[21] Bourne, however, rejects this explicitly Kantian approach to
aesthetic objects, which requires disinterest (read: not "caring" at all),
and explicitly denigrates the "half-caring reflection on life" as quietism,
declaring that the "ironist has no right to see beauty in things unless he
really cares. The aesthetic sense is harmless only when it is both ironical
and social" (120).

Bourne's photographic conceit thus presents irony as a nonmethodi-
cal method, simultaneously enzyme and catalyst, working on the sub-
strate of truth in order to produce beauty. And, since the essay also states
that irony "should be a means to the truest goodness" (104), what we
have in the photographic conceit is a historical and social revision of the
Kantian triad of the good, the true, and the beautiful. Images are produced by the interplay of irony in different forms (light, acid, and active
process employing the two) and are produced not as unified totality but
as paradox. It is precisely through this slippery, polysemous, and openly
self-contradictory definition of irony, I suggest, that Bourne formulates
his nonmimetic, aesthetic politics of the social. In this account, actors
not only conceive of the need for a sort of Emersonian development of
the self in order to create a healthy social order but also recognize the
role of the aesthetic in developing social relationships that are salutary
to the polis. In the tradition of Kantian republicanism, of course, this
sort of sociality would be a partial function of reason working through
different forms of judgment to achieve an "enlarged" mentality via the
sensus communis. In the context of Bourne's pragmatism, this would

mean paying attention to the role of aesthetics and art as the antecedents of belief, and critically thinking through the ways that different forms of socially embedded representation produce habits of thought, rather than as the means by which thought adapts itself to material conditions.

Of course, the prospect of false representation relies upon the possibility of "true" representation, and Bourne considers this task an appropriate one for the camera. He writes:

> The photograph is a synonym for deadly accuracy. Similarly the ironist insists always on seeing things as they are. He is a realist, whom the grim satisfaction of seeing the truth compensates for any sordidness that it may bring along with it. Things as they are, thrown against the background of things as they ought to be,—this is the ironist's vision. (110–11)

Here, Bourne does more than emphasize irony as a staging area for conflicts between facts and values, and enters a debate that his contemporaries in the New York art world had not yet settled: whether or not photographs represent "facts" that could be called "true." On the one hand are arguments like those of the Mexican caricaturist and Dadaist painter Marius de Zayas, whose work was exhibited in New York's 1913 Armory Show. Writing in the January 1913 issue of Alfred Stieglitz's journal *Camera Work*, for example, de Zayas flatly states that photographs do not and cannot qualify as art, for "photography is the plastic verification of a fact" and in "this epoch of fact, photography is the concrete representation of consummated facts."[22] On the other hand, in Lewis Hine's seminal 1909 essay "Social Photography: How the Camera May Help in the Social Uplift," the great social protest photographer concludes the opposite: whereas "the average person believes implicitly that the photograph cannot falsify," Hine writes, "you and I know that this unbounded faith in the integrity of the photograph is often rudely shaken, for, while photographs may not lie, liars may photograph."[23] Bourne's metaphor hovers uncertainly between these opposing views. While he asserts that the "photograph is a synonym for deadly accuracy" and thus would seem to agree with de Zayas's characterization of the photograph as a "consummation of facts," he also points out that these facts are not discovered as preexisting data in the world but instead are produced both manually and aesthetically. After all, recall that the "picture goes through certain changes in the hands of the ironist, but without these changes the truth would be simply a blank, unmeaning surface."

This is a handy gloss on a historical moment in which photographers and philosophers acknowledged that photographic images of the world were dependent upon a photographer's mind. As Dewey wrote in his 1887 *Psychology*:

> There is no sense in which it is so necessary to discriminate between the simple sensuous element and the factor supplied by the activities of mind as in sight. Without consideration, it would seem as if the visual sensation were whatever we saw when we opened our eyes—the visible world of objects, of various kinds, at various distances. But in reality, this is a complex psychical product, formed by judgments which are the *interpretations* of the sensuous material and not the material itself.[24]

That is to say, experiences of the world that formulate the conditions for representation must include aesthetic experience as more than mere adaptation; the interpretation of given phenomena will constantly revise the perceiver's psyche, such that those same phenomena may be perceived differently at different times (according to what new phenomena have been encountered and interpreted in intervening periods). More important to this analysis, however, is how Bourne defines sound political and aesthetic judgment *as irony*. The principle of sense data may well be "given" on the photographic plate but still requires the hand of the ironist to translate in such a way that the data can be represented as "true"; further, this process would require not only irony but the opposite of disinterest. Thus the central metaphor in Bourne's definition of irony directly engages contemporary debates about the status of realism (the literary genre of "facts") through the language of values. Not only does the arrangement and depiction of facts depend upon the values of the ironist but irony itself has a distinct function in producing aesthetically "transvalued" facts: irony "brings clearly to the light all that was implicit in the plate before," and "if it brings the picture to the light with values reversed, so does irony revel in a paradox, which is simply a photographic negative of the truth, truth with the values reversed."

The full significance of the metaphor relies at least partially upon a pun that suggests Bourne's knowledge of both pragmatism and photography. The word "value" here indicates not only that which is desirable, worthy, or morally obligatory but the specific tonal qualities of photographs: it is in this sense that Alfred Stieglitz describes how photographers rely on the process of development (rather than the technology of the camera) to turn out a "plate whose tonal values will be relatively true."[25] At the same time, Bourne renders "truth" as a function of internally constructed and externally represented perspective. To construe irony as both an internal disposition and an external action that can reverse "values" is to suggest that irony and ironic aesthetic objects are not anathema to political engagement but rather a necessary condition for both individual and collective praxis. That is to say, Bourne figures irony as both representation and conception of the world, a means by which people can question—and re-value, trans-value, or de-value—received "truths." This is not simply the opposition of "fact versus value" that Hume formulated as the impossibility of deriving any "ought" from a given "is," and it is more than a central tenet of pragmatism contending that "there is no epistemological difference between truth about what ought to be and truth about what is, nor any metaphysical difference between facts and values."[26] Rather, irony here describes a means of representing the relationship between facts and values, in order to reveal that facts themselves are constituted aesthetically. Instead of the dichotomy between "fact and value," this is the opposition of "value versus value." Such an opposition is possible because "irony, the science of comparative experience, compares things not with an established standard but with each other, and the values that slowly emerge from the process, values that emerge from one's own vivid reactions, are constantly revised, corrected, and refined by that same sense of contrast."[27]

The political implications of this statement are significant if one considers the fundamental assumptions behind the social photography of Jacob Riis or Lewis Hine, the muckraking journalism of Lincoln Steffens, the literary naturalism that Georg Lukács characterized as "decadent" due to its "photographic authenticity of description," the "liberal irony" of Richard Rorty, or the social realism of Upton Sinclair.[28] All of these present political praxis as an endeavor wherein aesthetic objects effect political change by distributing factual information about the world, motivating people to devise institutions that cure social ills. If a novelist objects to the presence of rat turds in sausage, for example, he writes a factually realistic novel (e.g., *The Jungle*) about conditions in Chicago's meat-packing industry; readers learn of the problem, are moved by disgust and faith in liberal institutions until their elected representatives respond to their cries for reform. That same year (1906), a Pure Food and Drug Act will be passed, and an entire society may rest secure in the knowledge that their breakfast contains only legislated amounts of rodent feces.[29] The fact that it would take another twenty-nine years to pass federal legislation to protect collective bargaining (the National Labor Relations Act of 1935) and another thirty-two years to regulate child labor in the United States (the Fair Labor Standards Act of 1938)—and the fact that generations of readers know *The Jungle* as "the sausage" book rather than the "horrifying labor conditions under capitalism" book—is perhaps less comforting evidence of how reliably reformist literary realism produces observable changes in the social lives and political imaginary of readers.

Bourne was no opponent of either literary realism or of reform literature; he was personally acquainted with and promoted the work of Theodore Dreiser, and his literary criticism is generally considered to be in "substantial agreement with early Lukácsian aesthetics."[30] He was also by no means composing his critique ex nihilo; as early as 1908, Thorstein Veblen had called attention to the fact that the staging of the fact-value problem and positivist ideology not only had large moral implications but hinged upon the dimension of aesthetic representation:

> This Order of Nature, or realm of Natural Law, is not the actual run of material facts, but the facts so interpreted as to meet the needs of the taxonomist in point of taste, logical consistency, and sense of justice. The question of the truth and adequacy of the categories is a question as to the consensus of taste and predilections among the taxonomists; i.e., they are an expression of trained human nature touching the matter of what ought to be.[31]

That is, the "training" of human "nature" (which isn't "nature" at all) is a function of aesthetics insofar as the faculty of taste isn't a transcendental *sensus communis* (Veblen had written his dissertation on Kant's *Critique of Judgment*) but the by-product of either political deliberation or unreflective ideology: "consensus." This framing of the relationship between fact and value has long been the central problem not only of moral philosophy or postclassical cultural criticism of the kind practiced by Veblen but also to conceptions of political literature; as Lloyd Morris wrote in 1917, it is "in dealing with the everyday life of our democracy" that writers "are forced to take into account the disproportion between its basis in ideality and its functioning in actuality. Thus is it that contemporary literature . . . is expressing a social content."[32]

By calling attention to Bourne's emphasis on the facts and values of aesthetic irony, I want to highlight the recognition that "abolishing" the gap between fact and value merely by declaring it misguided or logically incoherent leaves little room for creating a new political imaginary, let alone for praxis. If "facts" are presumptively imbued with values, and values are composed aesthetically rather than rationally from the reception of "facts," how can one break free from a recursive cycle of conceptual schemas whereby the world-as-interpretation appears as world-as-given? This is the state of affairs that Adorno, in an explicit critique of Nietzsche's *amor fati,* calls "the same false inference that leads from the existence of stubborn facts to their erection as the highest value [*führt nicht von der Existenz der stubborn facts zu deren Installierung als höchstem Wert der gleiche Fehlschluß*]."[33] That Adorno nests the English "stubborn facts" in the midst of a German sentence suggests a sly critique of a misconception: that "facts" could somehow transcend the linguistic character of their production and reception in contexts laden with historical and political—not natural—values. Indeed, four years after "The Life of Irony," Bourne denounced precisely this tendency to idealize facts by naturalizing them. Sarcastically ventriloquizing those who voted for Woodrow Wilson as a man who "kept them out of war" only to demand American participation in that war, Bourne sarcastically declares "an end to the pain of trying to adjust the facts to what they ought to be! Let us consecrate the facts as ideal! Let us join the greased slide towards war!" Continuing sadly, he describes how this about-face resulted from process wherein "hesitations, ironies, consciences, considerations—all were drowned in the elemental blare of doing something aggressive, colossal."[34]

It remains a matter of some debate whether Bourne's blistering critique of John Dewey and other bellicose "New Republican" intellectuals was fundamentally an antipragmatic critique of pragmatists or a more thoroughly pragmatic critique of the demonstrable fact that pragmatism wasn't pragmatic enough. But here we may see both the aesthetic and political implications of Bourne's photographic metaphor: he understands that both writing and visual images produce conceptual understanding and that representations are part of experience. Thus, rather than presenting the gap between fact and value as either ineluctable or untenable, he posits irony as the means by which the gap may be represented in the service of a radical politics. For Bourne, irony reveals fact and value as both the source and product of aesthetics, and ironic representation thus becomes an articulating joint between aesthetics and politics. Understanding Bourne's essay on irony in these terms finally makes it possible to see what he meant in 1917 when he claimed that "only in a world where irony was dead could an intellectual class enter war at the head of such illiberal cohorts in the avowed cause of world-liberalism and world democracy."[35] Declaring irony's death at the very moment Fussell believes it is born, Bourne observes that valorizing mere literary "facts" (without attention to how those facts are constituted) obviates the possibility of new concepts for understanding and changing the world.

Bourne was neither photographer nor painter, and to my knowledge never mentions Stieglitz's Photo-Secession Gallery, the "291" that famously served as the central conduit for modern art into the American cultural scene. By considering the metaphor of irony as photographic plate and ironist as developer of photographs at such length, I am not characterizing Bourne as the unrecognized heart of the history of modern American visual arts. Rather, I am arguing that while "The Life of Irony" is recognized as central to Bourne's oeuvre, and by extension to the hotbed of influential prewar literary radicalism in the United States that anticipates many of the arguments about cultural politics made familiar by the New Left, critics have divested the essay of its engagement with both visual and textual aesthetics, both relying upon and reinforcing associations of aesthetic irony only with political withdrawal.

In fact, Bourne repeatedly associates irony with engaged politics. Throughout "The Life of Irony," he maintains that while the religious person is "essentially an aristocrat in his interpretation of values . . . the ironist is incorrigibly a democrat."[36] Furthermore, the ironist, "discovering unexpected vistas," creates "new insight into the world that he lives in" and that such "insight" is specifically not only visual but political: that such a "democratic, sympathetic outlook upon the feelings and thoughts and actions of men and women is the life of irony" (107), the distinguishing feature of which is "the broad, honest sympathy of democracy, that is impossible to any temperament with the aristocratic taint" (129). Like nineteenth-century social reform writers before him, Bourne views sympathy as crucial to democracy, but he also refuses the conventional understandings of irony and sympathy as anathema: indeed, it is precisely the "ironist, by adopting another's point of view and making it his own in order to carry light and air into it, [who] literally puts himself in the other man's place. Irony is thus the truest sympathy. It is no cheap way of ridiculing an opponent by putting on his clothes and making fun of him. The ironist has no opponent, but only a friend" (107).

The new perspectives that irony creates and the strong viewpoints that survive irony's attacks are not only individual but "imperishably founded in the common democratic experience of all men" (109). Bourne goes even further to assert that the "ironist is the great intellectual democrat, in whose presence and before whose law all ideas and attitudes stand equal" (115). And it is not just Bourne as a promoter of both irony and democracy who avers a connection between the seemingly dissimilar concepts of irony and democracy, for even in "the eyes of its detractors, irony has all the vices of democracy. Its publicity seems mere vulgarity, its free hospitality seems to shock all ideas of moral worth. . . . Irony, in other words, is thought to be synonymous with cynicism" (116). If the kind of socialist democracy that Bourne envisioned unsurprisingly "extends the ideals of democracy, equality, and fraternity from the political to the economic order, and adds the ideal of Justice," ironic democracy is especially attractive in that it "provides in addition that slight *aesthetic* appeal without which no complex ideal ever had dynamic force."[37]

For all his Platonic musings and invocation of Socrates as an ironist, Bourne's essay also roundly suggests a theory of anti-Socratic (but not-quite-Romantic) irony, in which passion and emotion rather than reason serve as the foundation for the "true" and "good" life: "Socrates made one mistake: knowledge is not goodness" (104), Bourne asserts pragmatically, suggesting that the ideal political subject acts not by rational contemplation or by amassing unproblematic facts but through "social intercourse of ourselves with others" (107). With this in mind, it must be recognized that the radical, visual, ironic brand of democracy that Bourne promoted in 1913 (and eulogized in 1917) is grounded in the work of a quite different ironist and a notorious antidemocrat: Friedrich Nietzsche. Nietzsche's conception and use of irony (as a rhetorical device and as a term) is as contentious and intentionally inconsistent as the rest of his philosophy. One may even go so far to argue, as Robert Guay does, that in works such as *The Genealogy of Morals* the "use of irony is so pervasive that it cannot be relied upon to report Nietzsche's views, even at the moment of writing, on a historical sequence of events or the causal sources of the phenomena that Nietzsche identifies."[38] For all of the close analyses of how ironic Nietzsche's texts are, however, his own use of irony as a concept is equally inconsistent and compelling: both proclaiming his "love of irony" in *Ecce Homo* and characterizing irony as the tonic especially for "men only of worn-out instincts, old conservative Athenians," suggesting that this particular "wicked Socratic assurance [*sokratische boshafte Sicherheit*]" equally indicates the strength of both the disease and the medicine.[39]

In *The Twilight of Idols*, Nietzsche specifies that people "must learn to think, and they must learn to speak and to write," but first "People must learn to see," "to accustom the eye to calmness, to patience, and to allow things to come up to it; to defer judgment [*das Urtheil hinausschieben*], and to acquire the habit of approaching and grasping an individual case from all sides"; Bourne echoes this sentiment with explicitly political overtones when he asserts that "the object of an education is to know a revolution when you see one."[40] As one might infer from Bourne's repeated language about irony producing "truth with the values reversed," the possibility of the "transvaluation of all values," his emphasis on gaining multiple perspectives, his call for a politics beyond good and evil, and the titles of some of his most potent essays ("Twilight of Idols" and "The Puritan's Will to Power"), Bourne avidly read and wrote about Nietzsche. In the early twentieth century, he was certainly not alone in this endeavor.[41]

Jennifer Ratner-Rosenhagen has recently described the ways that "Nietzsche offered the radicals [of the early twentieth-century United States] a method and language for critiquing an American life that they believed had not yet fulfilled its democratic promise" and gave politically active intellectuals new ways to "think about thinking in modern America."[42] The complete works of Nietzsche and many critical studies of those works were available in English by 1911, and even if the translations have not aged well (to put it mildly), the widespread dissemination of those translators' interpretive decisions was significant.[43] Helen Zimmern's 1907 translation of *Beyond Good and Evil*, for example, provides a lovely if significantly revised version of Aphorism 154—"Objection, evasion, joyous distrust, and love of irony are signs of health; everything absolute belongs to pathology" [*Der Einwand, der Seitensprung, das fröhliche Misstrauen, die Spottlust sind Anzeichen der Gesundheit: alles Unbedingte gehört in die Pathologie*]—by rendering "*die Spottlust*" as "love of irony" rather than the more conventional love of "sarcasm" or "mockery," and thereby expands the scope of the passage dramatically.[44] By 1913, H. L. Mencken introduced the third edition of his *The Philosophy of Friedrich Nietzsche* with the comment "that Nietzsche has been making progress of late goes without saying. No reader of current literature, nor even of current periodicals, can have failed to notice the increasing pressure of his ideas."[45] The November 1912 issue of Emma Goldman's *Mother Earth* advised that Nietzsche's complete works were available through the anarchist journal's bookstore, because "whoever wants to understand the history of the thought, of the art and literature of the last decades, should read Nietzsche, no matter whether his attitude is that of a friend or of an enemy," because "no one has had such universal influence as Nietzsche upon the human mind; no one has so mercilessly attacked the old values of religion and morality, literature and art."[46] The editorial goes on to identify Nietzsche as one of those "very rare cosmic characters of whom it may be said without exaggeration that they have given a tremendous impetus of incalculable value to the shaping of the modern consciousness."[47] Mencken was clearly not alone in claiming that "it must be manifest that the Nietzschean creed, in the long run, gives promise of exercising a very real influence upon human thought"; another article for the January 1913 *Mother Earth*, for example, expanded on the category of "thought" to include discriminating aesthetic judgment, for "to know [Nietzsche] will, in every case, redound to the enrichment of one's heart, mind, and *taste*."[48]

It wasn't only readers of anarchist little magazines who were directly exposed to Nietzsche's particular brand of modernity: "Friedrich Nietzsche was until recently almost unknown in America," wrote a columnist for a 1908 issue of *Current Literature*, "but nowadays his name constantly appears, in all sorts of connections. He is a peculiarly fascinating thinker, and those who have once fallen under his spell are not likely soon to escape it." By 1910 the question "Will Nietzsche Come into Vogue in America?" would be inspired by the observation that "The neurotic but strangely fascinating 'philosopher with the hammer,' Friedrich Nietzsche, has begun to invade this country." Even daily newspapers knew that "Nietzsche is in the air," as Joseph Jacobs wrote in the 1910 *New York Times*, recognizing that "much of the Pragmatism of Prof. James bears auspicious resemblance to doctrines of Nietzsche"; art critic James Huneker agreed in a book published in both 1913 and 1922, writing that "a wave of Nietzscheism is sweeping English-reading countries."[49]

In a review of New Humanist Paul Elmer More's 1911 book *Nietzsche,* Bourne argued that it was "natural that the man who translated all values should trail paradoxes after him" and that these paradoxes might themselves help people recognize some of the fundamentally ironic aspects of modern culture, such as the fact that "the supermen of today are practising and professing Christianity; while the most brilliant Socialists are preaching Nietzscheanism ... our industrial barons, our business geniuses, are practising an undiluted ethics of power and ruthlessness, and professing the mild and sacrificial ethics of Jesus."[50] And it was not only men who were inspired by the hammering philosophy; as Bourne wrote about a prominent American feminist in 1917, "Elsie Clews Parsons is one of the few Nietzscheans we have among us" because she had "the detachment of science without the aloofness of the impersonal. You feel in her an irony that is genuine sympathy," a fact that demonstrated how "one can interpret life in terms of the will-to-power and still be. . . . a non-resistant pacifist."[51]

Elsewhere—and more to my point here—Bourne argued that the problem with "mediocre" and "religious" interpreters of Nietzsche was a problem of confusing fact and value: it was precisely the "common mistake of confusing a diagnosis with an ethics," for the "common mind seems unable to keep from confounding Nietzsche's analysis of what is with his ideal of what ought to be."[52] Bourne identifies the Nietzschean political disposition as one where "fact and ideal must play freely back and forth, conspiring always against the staleness, the mechanicalness, of modern culture and morals and theories of knowledge."[53] In a culture that failed to recognize this strain of Nietzsche's thought, works like

Twilight of Idols might illuminate the moralistic mistakes of citizens, Bourne argued, for "Nietzsche has expressed perfectly the working philosophy of an age; some of his works read almost like a satire on modern industry looked at from the point of view of the masters. And yet he has inspired the social philosophy of some of the most resourceful of the leaders who are trying through Socialism to overturn that mastery."[54]

Nietzsche's expressions of "perspectivism" are perhaps as well-known as the will-to-power, and his call for the "transvaluation of values" is not only a process of creating new perspectives and shifting conventional perspectives on the world: it is also a process that Nietzsche describes in emphatically visual terms. As he writes in *Beyond Good and Evil*, the philosopher must be able to "traverse the whole range of human values and estimations, and that he may be able with a variety of eyes and consciences to look from a height to any distance" as "preliminary conditions for his task ... to create values [*Werthe schaffe*]."[55] Multiplying perspectives is not a task of sympathy—feeling another person's pain, seeing through their eyes—but a task of recognizing that "there is only a seeing from a perspective, only a 'knowing' from perspective, and the more emotions [*Affekte*] we express over a thing, the more eyes, different eyes, we train on the same thing, the more complete will be our 'idea' [*Begriff*] of that thing, our 'objectivity.'"[56]

Seen in light of antecedent theories of political subjectivity, the central role of concept-shifting perspectivism as a critique of reason appears to be not only epistemological but actively political. Political systems as different as classical liberalism and communism rely on (potentially) knowing subjects, who can rationally and intentionally act on the world after gaining enough reliable knowledge to be confident in their decisions. Nietzsche's rejection of *a priori* mental categories and his emphasis on the aesthetic formation of concepts highlights the twin questions of how the world is arranged in the mind and how the mind is arranged by the world. This is where irony in visual and verbal representations might be said to enter the picture, bearing the potential to change conceptual dispositions toward the world, and to acknowledge the role of aesthetics in constituting a resource where classical political theory sees only dangerous barriers. Nietzsche emphasizes the necessity of abjuring a notion of an "eye which *ex hypothesi* has no direction at all" in favor of an eye situated among "active and interpreting functions ... by means of which 'abstract' seeing first became seeing something."[57] Recall how John Dewey figured the sense of sight as "judgments which are the interpretations of the sensuous material and not the material itself," whereby what one sees affects how one sees (and vice versa).[58] Thus what one sees can reveal to us morals themselves; as Nietzsche argues in *Twilight of Idols*, "there are no such things as moral facts [*moralischen Thatsachen*]," for "morality is only an interpretation of certain phenomena: or, more strictly speaking, a misinterpretation of them." Continuing his revisionary engagement with Kantian judgment (*Urteil*), wherein beauty itself constitutes a symbol of morality, Nietzsche asserts that "moral judgment [*moralische Urtheil*] must never be taken quite literally: as such it is sheer nonsense. As a sign code [*Semiotik*], however, it is invaluable," for "morality is merely a sign language [*Zeichenrede*], simply symptomotology" for revealing "the most valuable facts concerning cultures and inner conditions," though "one must already know what it is all about in order to turn it to any use."[59]

Optical metaphors and eyes themselves pervade Nietzsche's work, an important point given the extent to which "physiological imagery forms a central component of [Nietzsche's] cultural critique."[60] We are more than foolish uncritically to trust our eyes any more than our words, Nietzsche argues, for in believing in the motion of the sun it was "our eyes that were wrong; in the matter of the concepts [of unity, identity, permanence, etc.] . . . it is our language itself that pleads most constantly in their favour";[61] we are thus forced into mistaking interpretive moral symptoms as objective "facts" about the world. This occurs because "when we speak of values, we speak under the inspiration, and through the optics of life [*der Optik des Lebens*]" (31 [80]), and we therefore miss the fact that the "'true world' has been erected upon a contradiction of the real world; and it is indeed an apparent world, seeing that is merely a moralo-optical delusion [*moralisch-optische Täuschung*]" (22 [72]). Moreover, it is not just a matter of misperceiving external phenomena, for of the putative "'inner facts of consciousness,' not one of which has yet proved itself to be a fact" (35 [84]), and even the "'inner world' is full of phantoms [*Trugbilder*] and will-o'-the-wisps: the will is one of these" (36 [85]). "To learn to see," therefore, "amounts almost to that which in popular language is called 'strength of the will'" (57 [102–3]).

Why should any of this matter in an historical critique of metaphors about political irony and irony as a metaphor for different intersections between aesthetics and politics? After all, even if pernicious moralism results from failing to achieve a perspective outside of the life as lived, we don't need ordinary-language philosophers to remind us that we usually have no trouble deciding between figurative and literal language: the Bible may well dictate that "'if thy eye offend thee, pluck it out,'" Nietzsche writes, but "fortunately no Christian acts in obedience to this precept" (26 [76]). It matters not only because readers frequently take

Nietzsche's ironic proclamations as sincere expressions but because the world of antiperspectival "morality" is construed as both a specifically linguistic and optical construct, and the notion of "seeing" life in one way or another, of developing a particular "outlook" on the world or a special "vision" for the future are optical metaphors that have themselves become divorced from their empirical and optical resonances. Furthermore, the hidden metaphoricity of these concepts becomes significant in the context of a literary aesthetics that was increasingly under pressure from technologies of photography to "document" the facts that are necessary for political action.

Thus, for both Nietzsche and Bourne, one might say that the whole point of philosophical and artistic inquiry, and the point of producing aesthetic objects that will provoke and assist that inquiry, is not to reveal or arrive at the telos of unitary political or moral truth, and especially not when moral, historical, and political truth are imagined to converge in the figure of the State (as in Hegel, himself a prominent denouncer of Romantic irony as conceived by Schlegel). Rather, the goal of such inquiries, criticisms, and representations is to reveal understandings of the world as the product of concept formation, a process predicated upon and brought about by the dynamic interplay of reason and feeling that was increasingly denoted by twentieth-century conceptions of irony in aesthetics. It is in this sense, I think, that by imagining political action to be a process of shifting not only one's own perspective but other people's conceptual and visual disposition toward the world of events as interpreted representations that radicals such as Bourne conceived of a genuine political potential for irony and aesthetics. It is in this sense that Bourne's friend Walter Lippmann (himself a reader of Nietzsche as well as a former teaching assistant for George Santayana) claimed in 1913 that "the goal of action is in its final analysis aesthetic and not moral—a quality of feeling instead of conformity to rule."[62]

Published in 1913, Lippmann's *Preface to Politics* is largely remembered as a naïvely juvenile, if brilliantly inventive, mélange of Nietzsche, Freud, and Bergson spiced with a dash of Fabian political philosophy: though positively reviewed in radical political publications such as the *Masses*, the book is considered a blip on the road toward Lippmann's long and increasingly conservative career of arguing for press reform and politics based upon scientific, rational technocracy. Lippmann was a member of one of the more illustrious literary moments at Harvard, where his classmates included T. S. Eliot and John Reed (the latter of whom would collaborate with Lippmann to organize the Paterson Pageant of IWW strikers in 1913), and his first book still provides a key articulation of how "cultural politics" might be understood as more than vaguely "subversive" and as the necessary antecedent to political action both within and without political institutions: "No amount of charters, direct primaries, or short ballots," he wrote, "will make a democracy out of an illiterate people."[63] Lippmann emphasizes the potential of philosophy, literature, and art to affect people's ability to recognize cultural and political influences that already existed: this was a necessary precondition for any fundamental, structural change in society, which argued against both liberal and moderate- to right-socialist conceptions of institutional political action, for it is "puerile to say that institutions must be changed from top to bottom and then assume that their victims are prepared to make the change."[64] Thus, against venerable liberal understandings of individuals as essentially static, desire-fulfilling units that rationally functioned in a marketplace of ideas to maximize personal good, the "education" of consciousness took an understanding of individual consciousness as malleable in the face not just of facts to be adjudicated rationally but representations to be judged aesthetically.

Bourne's work is signally consonant with Lippmann's assertion that political and social renewal would depend upon more than either disinterested, rational technocracy or spontaneous overflows of emotion: "Thoughts and feelings count," Lippmann wrote. "We live in a revolutionary period and nothing is so important as to be aware of it" (317). The function of irony as a means of aesthetic representation that subsumed both "thought" and "feeling" occupied a key role in a moment when "we picture political institutions" (16), and that therefore to "prepare a point of view . . . will engage a fresher attention . . . [to] see politics in a different light" (4) when "the invisible government is malign . . . [and] what is dangerous about it is that we do not see it, cannot use it, and are compelled to submit to it" (22). For Lippmann, Bourne, and others, there were serious political implications when "the gap between want and ought, between nature and ideals cannot be maintained" (113), and that not only was it a "very stupid prejudice of nineteenth century science" to assert "that the mental habits of human beings were not 'facts'" (175) but it "is impossible to leave this point without quoting Nietzsche, who had this insight and stated it most provocatively" (176).

The popular imagination is largely limited to the Nietzsche torqued into service of totalitarianism, on the one hand, or to the grotesquely laissez-faire hyper-egoist on the other: either the murderous inspiration for World War I and then German National Socialism or the self-satisfied conservative individualist described by Edmund Wilson in 1930 as one who recognizes the fact that the "the whole system is riddled with cruelties and abuses and absurdities" but is unconcerned, for "what should that matter to a resolute Nietzschean, who elsewhere refers to the unemployed as 'scum' and objects to paying taxes for poor relief."[65] Yet many anti-authoritarian, antitotalitarian thinkers and activists were equally inspired by the same works, and it is more than mere paradox that Jack London could describe *The Iron Heel*'s protagonist as "a super-man, a blond beast such as Nietzsche has described, and in addition he was aflame with democracy."[66] In the 1910s, when a bookstore in Pic-cadilly Circus advertised the philosophy behind the "Euro-Nietzschean War," it bears remembering that Nietzsche was defended by radicals as the war broke out and—amid rising tides of anti-German sentiment—Nietzsche's philosophy was adduced as evidence of Germanic barbari-ties and a purportedly natural tendency to express the will-to-power in military actions. As Emma Goldman wrote in 1914, "Many newspaper editors and other no less superficial readers of Nietzsche—among them some Individualist Anarchists—have savagely attacked Nietzsche as 'responsible' for the European war. The deeper students of the great poet-philosopher appreciate him as a bitter opponent of war who saw clearly the distinction between the spirit of culture and the spirit of empire."[67]

As Tracy Strong has written, what appealed to European and American feminists, progressives, anarchists, and socialists "was the unmasking trope, the ironic stance. Irony is the modern progressive mode. It conveys that things are not what they seem and, most especially, that anything that claims to be some thing is clearly not entitled to that claim."[68] These were the political and cultural actors who repeated Nietzsche's declara-tion that "culture and the state—let no one be deceived on this point—are antagonists: a 'culture-state' [*Cultur-Staat*] is merely a modern idea. The one lives upon the other, the one flourishes at the expense of the other."[69] Promoting the revaluation of values in social individuals was thus imag-ined to precede the revalued recognition and organization of broader political constituencies and associations, serving as a necessary first step toward destabilizing existing institutions that are deleterious to the free exercise of will (or even imagining that such a thing might exist). For this group of writers, the means of mobilizing and affecting individuals was not voter registration drives but the cultural work of literature (including magazines, newspapers, and visual art), which would work in concert with the militant direct action of the masses, whether seamstresses on the picket lines or those free-speech fighters from northwestern lumber camps, the Wobblies. The necessarily violent power exercised by certain institutions over individuals pervaded the cultural politics not only of anarchists such as Emma Goodman but even among liberals such as

Van Wyck Brooks and socialists like Lippmann, who envisioned a political possibility for art that was quite distinct from the sentimental and mimetic visions of conventional reform literature or photo-journalism. Lippmann's critique of pre-political life both assumes and argues that "literature in particular elaborates our insight into human life, and, therefore, enables us to center our institutions more truly," finding fatal flaws where the aesthetic and the political were imagined as belonging to separate de-eroticized spheres: "we in America have divorced them completely: both art and politics exist in a condition of unnatural celibacy. Is this not a contributing factor to the futility and opacity of our political thinking?"[70] These influences are most effectively pernicious when institutions and forms of life became both naturalized and concealed: when they become not only conceived as both inevitable and good but when people fail to see the "invisible government of self-interest."[71] Properly educated, however, the astutely perceiving mind could in Nietzsche's words see through the "morality of mediocrity"; confronted by such a mind, mediocre morality "will find it difficult to conceal its irony."[72]

The "I" in Irony: The Case of Benjamin De Casseres

One doesn't need deep archives to discover the Nietzschean ironist Randolph Bourne; he's in John Dos Passos's *U.S.A.*, Noam Chomsky's *American Power and the New Mandarins*, and the Heath *Anthology of American Literature*. Yet he remains far more well-known than another New York Nietzschean who wrote both popular and obscure pieces, for whom irony was a central organizing concept, term, and rhetorical practice in the 1910s and beyond: critic, journalist, essayist, proto-Dada poet, and proud collateral descendant of Benedict de Spinoza, Benjamin De Casseres. A prolific writer over four decades, De Casseres's career spanned a wide range of places and positions: he began as a copy boy on a Philadelphia newspaper and, after almost a year in Mexico City starting a newspaper entitled *El Diario*, he ended as a nationally syndicated Hearst columnist; he became known in the 1900s and 1910s for his wild mélange of Emerson, Nietzsche, Spinoza, Max Stirner, and F. T. Marinetti, and became better known in the 1940s as a disturbingly vitriolic Red-baiter. A regular contributor to publications ranging from the *New York Times* and Alfred Stieglitz's *Camera Work* to *The Reflex* and *The Bang*, he was a central figure in the production of *The Smart Set* (where his work included a series titled "The Nietzschean Follies"); indeed, H. L. Mencken told him, "You wrote some of the best stuff I printed in my time ... I know of no other contributor who was in it more, or who produced better stuff. You set its tone quite as much as I did."[73]

De Casseres's career is oddly bifurcated, however, as he achieved notoriety in mainstream publications while his avant-garde poetry and essays failed to achieve a significant readership. While in one public life he was a quirky drama critic and raconteur, in another he was "the muse of Job and Nietzsche, the voice of Walt Whitman and the echo of Max Stirner."[74] Before De Casseres wrote a vicious parody of *Days Without End* that brought their friendship to an abrupt and permanent halt, Eugene O'Neill described him as "that phenomenal ironist who does not want to be gentle, who must be supremely contemptuous and fiercely assertive."[75] At the same time, however, O'Neill also was prescient in describing it as "hardly likely that he will ever achieve wide public acceptance. Nor does it appear that he will be made the object of careful critical scrutiny by some small group of pedants who might get a thesis out of him as an American phenomenon. . . . He is looked upon, when he is discussed at all, as a freak who is exploding with metaphors."[76]

Perhaps O'Neill was able to predict De Casseres's fate correctly for basic reasons of literary fashion and style: the sentiment holds true for almost any Dadaist or Surrealist writer when it comes to public acceptance, after all, though perhaps less so for the theses produced by small groups of pedants. But one might also suggest a different reason for his obscurity: an aggressively individualist form of anarchist politics derived primarily from a discomfiting reading of Nietzsche. Moreover, De Casseres theorized and articulated these politics with and through a version of irony that is pointedly incongruent with the vision of "Beloved Community" distinguishing the more collegial cultural radicalism of Bourne, Lippmann, Stieglitz, or Millay. One can imagine any number of the Young Intellectuals claiming with De Casseres in 1917 that "Imagination, irony and the superb amoralism of Greece—that is what my work stands for, and it is that that I hope to see dominate the Coming Age in this country" after "a complete demolition of the stupidities and Puritanism that have ossified us and petrified us." It is more difficult to imagine Bourne describing himself as an "imaginative ironist and a mystical pessimist" or endorsing the following lines: "Today the symbol of American literature should be a teething ring; tomorrow I hope it will be two eagles ridden by Lucifer and Aphrodite."[77] Where Bourne wants irony to "annihilate the unoriginal and insincere" because "this delicious sense of contrasts that we call irony, is not a pose," De Casseres would "make a religion of the artificial, the insincere, the pose," for, he writes, "to live is to lie. To act is to pose. . . . there is no form of sincerity that in the last analysis is not interchangeable with stupidity."[78] Bourne championed Dreiser's fictional "pattern of life, sincere, wistful and unredeemed" and claimed that "irony . . . is no cheap way of ridiculing an opponent by . . . making fun of him."[79] De Casseres, on the other hand, described Dreiser—himself introduced to Nietzsche by Mencken—as "that illiterate sob-sister of American literature," arguing that "we should mock existence at each moment, mock ourselves, mock others, mock everything" for to do otherwise is to be "as stupid as a President or a college professor."[80]

Bourne read Plato to define irony as an unposed photograph of the sympathetic soul, whereas De Casseres claimed that "all seriousness is a defect of vision" and preferred to "look back to the Greeks [to] see that all they did was a pose. They seem to have decreed their own birth and evolved a civilization for the purpose of attitudinizing before the Kodak of posterity."[81] Where Bourne reported on the pragmatist educational reform of the Gary Schools, De Casseres advised that the "minds of literary America ought to be turned toward the heavens—the heavens of Imagination and Irony. Even Sinclair Lewis believes photography is satire, while Dreiser believes that reporting is creating. America cannot live by Pulitzer prizes alone."[82] Bourne called irony a "deep, anticipatory sympathy" by which the ironist is "kept clean from hate or scorn."[83] De Casseres claimed that "hate is ethical" and that "The root of nihilism in art is spite. 'Les Fleurs du Mal' is spite. 'Thus Spake Zarathustra' is spite. . . . All Futurism, Post-Impressionism, is spite. . . . All great movements begin with the gesture of hate, of irony, of revenge. This is as true in art as in social history" for irony "redistributes and revalues everything that comes to it for appraisal."[84]

For unsystematically individualist anarchists such as De Casseres, one problem with attempting to popularize a truly revolutionary art—that is, art that might accomplish something besides reinforcing or merely rearranging ossified liberal institutions—was not only a conservative publishing industry but the very literalist tastes of the American public. As he wrote in 1909, "a caricaturist, like a great novelist, a great painter, a great sculptor . . . has his message. But here in New York it so happens that this message carries at its core the one great sin, which is a violation of the Anglo-Saxon injunction: Thou shalt not commit irony!"[85] Twenty years later, relying upon the thinker whom he had long characterized as "that Viking of modern free thought, Friedrich Nietzsche," De Casseres expanded his attack to include the entire country: "In America, ironic invective, the brutal imagination, moral indignation that wears the face of hate and an unswerving and joyful adherence to the art of making enemies are anathema—in a country whose national anthem is O Be Joyful! Thumbs down on Bierce, then! He was inhuman-all-too-inhuman. Thou shalt not commit irony!"[86]

De Casseres was forthright about attenuating gaps between different modes of aesthetic representation and refusing easy distinctions between "high" or "low" cultural forms, and he found in caricature, such as those exhibited at the 1913 Armory Exhibition by de Zayas, an art form that was admirably ironic, pronouncing that "caricature is the art that is 'beyond good and evil.'"[87] De Casseres was perhaps only a debatably good Nietzschean; while he repeatedly and loudly claimed "I Dance With Nietzsche!" the editor of Nietzsche's complete works in English wrote "Nietzsche would dance with you, and not you with him."[88] He knew that being "beyond good and evil" was equivalent neither to rapacious disorder nor to apathetic self-indulgence; the deformed, antirealist grotesqueries of caricature were appropriate for the place and time he was writing not because they were vaguely modernist, and not because they offered light entertainment as opposed to the challenges of Cubism. Rather, it is because the United States is predicated upon contradictions, because "Irony is the logic of contradictions," because caricature "is like an eye of the retina of which holds only the ribs of action, the fleshless muscles of attitude. As irony is the supreme of philosophy, caricature is the supreme of art," and because "In literature irony is the touchstone of greatness. Only the story that ends ironically is true."[89] Furthermore, "truth" that could only be produced by narrative irony is analogous to the antirealist deformations of caricature that were both suited to and *mimetically representative of* the politics and culture in an ethically deformed nation and were thus almost a purer form of realism to depict political realities:

> America is a caricature of her own Constitution. She is a caricature of the spirit of the Declaration. Her politicians are caricatures of statesmen. Her culture is a caricature of the word culture. . . . Her plutocratic democracy is a caricature of Jeffersonian democracy. . . . Her financial grip on the countries of Europe is a caricature of Wilson's "we ask nothing in return."[90]

Much more than a mere withdrawal from the realities of contradiction, hypocrisy, imperialism, war, or laws, for De Casseres irony indicates something well beyond good and evil and well beyond simple individualism, and the *Übermensch* could not be further from the totalitarian blond beast: "The Superman?" De Casseres wrote in 1913. "He is the man who participates in life and watches his own antics with an indulgent irony. He is the man who is both actor and spectator at once."[91] And it was this version of the ironic Superman that led De Casseres to view electoral politics in the United States as a joke deserving scorn, mockery, and parody. Indeed, well before Hunter S. Thompson ran for sheriff of Aspen on the Freak Power platform, De Casseres ran for mayor of New York City on a "Smash It!" ticket that, appropriately, was both invented and wholly represented by him. Legalizing all voluntary sex work and substance abuse, his campaign was apparently limited to producing a stack of punning posters calling for "Absolute home rule for the City of New York. I am a secessionist, and I shall demand the erection of the State of Manhattan" and claiming that a mayor "should be impeached and removed the moment he attempts to regulate private morals."[92]

Where naturalists and social realists from Dreiser to Lukács might disagree about what kind of irony would bring power to the people, De Casseres was circumspect about whether such a goal was even worth achieving. After all the agitation and organizing, De Casseres writes, "at last the masses arrive at Democracy! The divine right of kings has become the divine right of the masses. The crown has been taken from the head of the ass and glued on the head of the ape. We pass from an assocracy to an apeocracy."[93] Furthermore, De Casseres not only championed irony as a mode of representation but contended that "irony is the supreme method of perception . . . the stealthy ghoul who creeps to the grave after the interment of the corpse. That is irony. That is the phase the intellectual and aesthetic worlds have reached." Indeed, it was just this form of perception that was necessary when producing aesthetic responses to conventionally political problems: describing a Futurist exhibit in 1919, he took consolation in the idea that "with a Winter ahead that is heavy with strikes, prohibition, and evictions it is good to know that there is a bunch of poets somewhere who are looking after our aesthetic needs."[94]

Recovering the work of De Casseres does more than exhume a once-popular writer who was squarely in the middle of an enormously influential moment in American literary and cultural history, but one needn't pretend that the addition of his work would dramatically alter the ambit of the increasingly large pile of new modernisms. Paying attention to the sheer breadth and weirdness of his work, however, does fatally complicate the widespread view of irony articulated by Sämi Ludwig in *Pragmatist Realism*: "Though irony seems to be the only acceptable attitude (as there is no representation without mask), this irony must be well intentioned, considerate, and supported by a positive attitudinal relationships. Otherwise, it is mere irresponsible 'play.'"[95] Neither "considerate" nor in possession of a "good attitude," the absurdist, violent, and vitriolic irony of De Casseres can hardly be dismissed as "unserious." Rather than a mere recovery operation, restoring the irony of New York Nietzscheans to dialogue rather than monologue suggests an historical, negative dialectical understanding of an irony that cannot be reduced to any of its constitutive parts, whether "cosmic" or "world-historical" or "verbal" or "modernist" or "postmodernist," and that makes it possible to understand irony as the first choice of the discontented instead of "the last resort of the desperate."[96] What emerges from a dialectical opposition among competing claims for interwar irony is an historical and philosophical understanding of how "irony" describes a critical nexus between politics and aesthetics, of social relationships that are simultaneously aesthetic, personal, and political, where all of these terms are placed into constantly agonistic replay. This is a genealogical politics of irony that aesthetically engages the problem of needing critically intelligent, fiercely ludic opposition to liberal institutions as a paradoxical condition of producing democratic institutions: not to exercise force in the name of preserving or eradicating individual liberties but precisely to provide the opposition that might prevent liberal institutions from becoming violently illiberal. That such a paradox might both emerge from and facilitate the "aesthetic advancement of the American people" comes straight from Nietzsche to democratic theorists of the present day, who recognize that the "irony of a tragically open, agonistic politics is that it need not 'infect' political life but in fact *spur* it toward the existential environments of its enactment," such that these politics would succeed in "precluding the silencing of any voice, something especially important when even purportedly democratic dispositions are comfortable with exclusions, thereby becoming susceptible to the most ironic and insidious form of tyranny done in democracy's name."[97]

H. L. Mencken pointed out in 1913 what theorists of radical democracy continue to argue today, that "a great many critics of Nietzsche mistake his criticism of existing governmental institutions for an argument in favor of their immediate and violent abolition," and it can be surprising to encounter so many early twentieth-century thinkers who saw no contradiction between Nietzsche's withering attacks on democracy and the achievement of genuinely and newly democratic forms of life.[98] Even Wilsonian Democrats in favor of World War I recognized that to understand Nietzsche as champion of state militarism required quirky reading indeed: the entry on Nietzsche in the *War Cyclopaedia* (a prowar propaganda guide produced by George Creel's Committee on Public Information in 1918) concludes that Nietzsche's "possible relation to the doctrines which produced the spirit of ruthless conquest in Germany is obscure" and that his "teaching seems to have been torn from its context by popularizing or political writers and to have been patched on to a wild theory of Teutonic race superiority."[99] Almost twenty years later, as the United States prepared for another war with Germany, De Casseres compiled and published his own bit of selective propaganda: a pamphlet of quotations from Nietzsche's collected works and correspondence titled *Germans, Jews and France*, wherein he described Nietzsche as both "the most independent, the most fearless thinker-poet-philosopher who ever lived" and as "the most uncompromising foe that Germany ever had, a German who was also pro-Semitic and pro-French."[100] The collection reads as a scathing riposte to Nietzsche's anti-Semitic editors and readers and a denunciation of the fact that "In Germany his universal doctrine of Will-to-Power and his ideal of Superman have been used by professors and mob-masters as a philosophy to excuse their atrocities, their sadism and their totalitarian state-crimes. But they have carefully concealed what you will find in this booklet."[101]

Indeed, for those who associate his philosophy only with the tragedies of totalitarianism, the Nietzsche who wrote that "liberal institutions straightway cease from being liberal, the moment they are soundly established: once this is attained no more grievous and more thorough enemies of freedom exist than liberal institutions!" is notorious. The subsequent lines from that work, however, seem less so: "The same institutions, so long as they are fought for, produce quite other results; then indeed they promote the cause of freedom quite powerfully."[102] Where Bourne famously claimed that "War is the health of the State," De Casseres echoes the difference between struggling for dynamic institutions as a political practice and hypocritically increasing the power of the state over individuals under the guise of liberty: for De Casseres and Nietzsche both, the state "is, therefore, always the enemy of the individual. And yet this enemy must not, cannot, be abolished. For, like all enemies, it breeds, by the law of menace and opposition, a more definite, a more militant form of Individualism."[103]

The recurrent emphasis on agonistic reevaluation of institutions rather than the sort of unreflective, consistently self-contradictory lionization of the individual that produces twenty-first-century Tea Party shouts of "Keep Your Government Hands Off My Medicare!" is nowhere to be found; for all his later pitched opposition to the New Deal and characterization of FDR as a Communist stooge, De Casseres nonetheless is working within a comparatively subtle political philosophy that concedes "Government is thus a necessary evil, but it is absolutely necessary. If it did not exist, the individual, in his present state of ignorance concerning what is his 'highest good,' could not survive; and no individual, no race."[104] And it was this vision of individuals and collectives, I would argue, that led De Casseres to write in 1931 that there was "one thing I like about [Upton] Sinclair: his militant, brutal, almost sadistic individualism. He's masked!" and Upton Sinclair to write a letter to De Casseres eight years later, claiming, "I think I am as much of an individualist as you are."[105] The relationship between individuals and collectives is far from schematically worked out anywhere in the prose or poetry of De Casseres, as his own work is much as he described Nietzsche's: "elliptical, broken, labyrinthine. He steps from the dome of St. Peter's to the pinnacle of the Matterhorn. In a single sentence he smashes the skull of Plato against the skull of Herbert Spencer. He tunnels, saps, undermines and then dynamites, but never reasons."[106] But in what may perhaps be the only similarity between Sinclair and De Casseres, it may fairly be said that they both consistently opposed what De Casseres characterized as "that pseudo-'Individualism' which is nothing but predatory greed wearing the mask of a great personal ideal."[107]

Envisioning the *Übermensch* as fiery democrat, or proposing the perpetual revaluation of values as a democratic practice, may be dismissed as the mistake of an undertrained socialist novelist such as London, or as the function of overheated rhetoric by a tendentious reader like De Casseres, or as overly close reading in the rarified hothouses of academia; it is rarely imagined as the impetus behind De Casseres's admirable political goal of "a LEGALIZED, LAW-ABIDING, WIDE-OPEN, PLEASURE LOVING, SANE, HUMAN CITY."[108] One cannot so easily dismiss the very pervasiveness of these ideas as mass misreading, and one must seriously consider the ways in which the intertwined categories of "irony" and "aesthetics" are mobilized to define democracy as the disposition to value paradox and to engage in a perpetual practice of redefinition: to redefine interpretation as reinterpretation, evaluation as reevaluation, consensus as dissensus, and conflict as a value to be nurtured rather than an unfortunate reality to be pragmatically overcome. This is a series of maneuvers to value constant renegotiation and reimagination of the possible and impossible, as politics. Chantal Mouffe and other radical-democratic theorists have shown that "liberal democracy results from the articulation of two logics which are incompatible in the last instance and that there is no way in which they could be perfectly reconciled," which produces a by-now familiar paradox: "Only by coming to terms with its paradoxical nature will we be in a position to envisage modern democratic politics in an adequate manner, not as the search for an inaccessible consensus—to be reached through whatever procedure—but as an 'agonistic confrontation' between conflicting interpretations of the constitutive liberal-democratic values."[109] Together, Bourne's and De Casseres's competing analyses of political aesthetics serve as a kind of crucible representing what Jacques Rancière "prefer[s] to call the democratic paradox"—that "democracy as a form of government is threatened by democracy as a form of social and political life."[110] In a different vein, Wendy Brown calls this a "paradox that Nietzschean philosophy helps us stage as political possibility rather than entrapment," and it may be that any conception of democracy that hopes to be more than the smugly hollow repetition of constitutional clichés will require openly—not cryptically—antidemocratic rhetoric as its interlocutor rather than its monstrous other.[111] Since Schlegel, irony has represented the form of paradox, and reducing irony from disposition to a position serves to resolve democratic paradoxes precisely when they should be highlighted. "Irony" both describes and demonstrably produces agonistic recontesting of how aesthetic representations help constitute forms of democratic individualism; if irony uniquely describes the irreconcilable, incommensurable frictions and fictions of democracy, it does so only when the critical terrain of "democracy" itself is allowed to be both pragmatic and antipragmatic, careful and wild, sympathetic and pitiless.

Gendering Irony and Its History:
Ellen Glasgow and the Lost 1920s

She has that rare gift among women—irony.
—BENJAMIN DE CASSERES, 1919

So let it be a merry jest . . . and let there be irony, that men may rock to
think of what I thought one night in fall, when I was but an oldish Girl,
and spreading at the end.
—DJUNA BARNES, 1928[1]

The curious fact that irony has periodically "died" over the course of the
twentieth century entails an equally curious question: exactly when and
how was irony "born"? There have been as many answers to this question
as there are definitions of irony, and the ability to conceive of this question in the first place is perhaps uniquely modern: despite the original
figure of the *eiron* in Greek comedy, there is no classical etiology for irony
along the lines of the birth of Eros (Love) or Eris (Strife). In searching for
a single origin of something as polyvalent as irony, the dangers of tautol-
ogy are both imminent and immanent: of course Socratic irony started
with Socrates, of course a Romantic writer originated Romantic irony,
of course the modernists, and so forth. What unites differing accounts
of irony's origin is the assertion of a genealogical narrative for what is
frequently invoked as a transcendental feature of language and thought
and the fact that each tacitly imagines "pre-ironic" times or practices
against which the contemporary moment can be opposed. If the various
deaths of irony reveal particular political anxieties about the ability and
desirability of language to represent and engage with cultural and political crisis, the rarer births of irony in the twentieth century illuminate
something else: that irony has not only a history but a gendered history
that is inextricable from the politics of gender in literary modernism.[2]

The most concise story of irony's origin appeared as a joke in a popular humor magazine, the January 1902 issue of *Judge's Library: A Monthly*
Magazine of Fun. Here is the full account:

THE BIRTH OF IRONY: *Adam* (to the serpent): "Come again."[3]

It is admittedly difficult to imagine this joke raising even a dry smile in 1902 or 1922 or today; nonetheless, the logic of the humor neatly and implicitly encapsulates a recurrent cultural desire for a prelapsarian form of language that once transparently conveyed the noncontradictory thoughts of a coherent subject in a comprehensible if unpredictable world. It's not clear what specific form of irony is born here: perhaps it was the first instance of verbal irony (Adam didn't *really* mean that the snake should return but rather that he *shouldn't* come again), emphasizing irony's ancient association with deception. Or perhaps it is the parturition of cosmic irony, a scene authored and overseen by a deity with a perverse sense of humor, who has both predicted and set into motion the unimagined consequences of an apparently innocent act of hospitality. It would certainly seem to involve dramatic irony, highlighting the difference between what players and audience know about action and dialogue on stage: "irony" would then simultaneously describe the difference between Adam's blissful ignorance and the knowledge of God and a twentieth-century magazine readership (both of whom know that this particular tragedy, however hilarious, does not have a comic ending). In the end, the joke represents irony as originating long before Socrates, when the immortal vacation in Paradise became the brutishly short labors of dying humanity and the unthinking pleasures of nudity became censorious strictures of shameful morality. Irony was born, it seems, in a moment of well-mannered deception, from an inability to predict the ultimate effects of individual acts. Setting aside the impossible empirical question of whether anyone actually laughed, the joke instantiates a common, salient characteristic of irony's continuing role in a more-or-less secular imaginary: the fact that Eve is at most a tacit subtext to the scene of this birth. There is indeed a woman involved, but invisibly and silently, out of the view of both actors and audience. Put plainly, in this drive-by account, irony came into the world precisely as the bastard offspring of (verbal) intercourse between two males.

If drawing such broad conclusions from such a brief joke suggests critical excess, consider what I believe to be the longest account of irony's origin in literary history: "The Birth of Irony," a short story by American novelist Katherine Holland Brown that appeared in the June 1908 issue of *Lippincott's Monthly Magazine*. The story is worth recounting at length, in that it expands upon the basic logic of the joke in the specific terms of idealist philosophy and consequently illuminates how "irony" denotes an expansive conceptual nexus for discourses about the roles played by reason, feeling, and gender in the formation of individual consciousness, political communities, and the state.

"The Birth of Irony" opens in the almost parodically prehistoric situation of a pre-rational protagonist: "Gund the Cave-Man squatted on the rippled sand outside his burrow door, thrust chin propped on hairy paws, and considered. His harsh yellow brows scowled peevishly; his slow beast brain fumbled in witless circles through his labyrinth of discontent."[4] As the narrative unfolds, the reader learns that the source of Gund's unhappiness is not his underdeveloped neocortex but rather a woman who is sleeping while the other Cavewomen of the tribe have gone to work in the fields: "the day was now half spent. And yet his mate . . . still she slept on. . . . stretched limp on [the] wonderful couch of aurochs skin" (750). The narrative then shifts to an account of who this sleeping figure is and how she arrived on Gund's lovely sofa: "She was not one of his own tribe. She belonged to the Painted Ones" and had been taken by Gund's chief as a prize of war. Gund became captivated by her beauty and seized her for himself despite the fact that "It was not lawful to snatch that which the Chief had already appropriated. Moreover, it was not wholesome. He who braved the tribe's unwritten law must establish his claims by brute strength. [. . .] However, this brown panther thing was worth a few bruises" (751). Gund defeats the chief and his followers in combat, happily winning the right to keep the Painted One despite the fact that "his mate was of little value; she fell far short of the women of his own tribe . . . in point of service. Her body was too light and thin for ploughing" and "where the other women yielded their patient days. She was always a thorn, a bewilderment" (751).

In fact, it turns out that not only is the captive woman both weak and lazy, she is also superficial: the only thing that truly ignites her passion is a gorgeously decorated robe that is the "supreme treasure of the Tribe itself . . . a miracle of labor; a triumph of their slow groping art." It's so beautiful and took so much work that "the Tribe, in clamorous unison, vowed it a sacred thing, and consecrated it, the crowning sacrifice, to the Great God of Harvests, their sovereign deity" (752). Gund also holds it sacred, but when his captured mate "darted forward, dark eyes ablaze. . . . pounced upon the royal robe, and clasped it tight in both soft arms, and pressed her pleading cheek" against it, Gund defies the tribe and gives it to her as a gift. After forcing her to dance to the point of exhaustion in order to propitiate the Harvest God, Gund decides to try to make formal amends but has to leave her on the altar wrapped in shell-jewelry when the "Painted Ones, that preposterous relic of their clan," join forces with a rival clan and attack them. After the war, he goes to find her with a host of treasures: elks' teeth jewelry, river stones, and feathers for her hair. He hopes that "Decked with these miracles, cloaked in the silvery deer-skins, she would be the envy of all the tribe. . . . And, joying in these treasures, perhaps she would forget his scarred face, his loose crippled limb" (756). Gund is shocked, however, when he arrives at the altar where he had left her and finds not his lovely brown panther but "a curious heap: a string of mottled rose and amber shells; an elks' tooth girdle; a little pile of silvery ashes and of bleached pearl bone." Wit-challenged in the best of circumstances, Gund is flatly stupefied:

> He stared from the one heap to the other; that curious Other,
> which, beneath the warm light wind, eddied and shifted and blew.
> [. . .] He gaped on, blankly. Presently he leaned forward, resting
> his elbows on both hairy knees. The rainbow feathers crumpled in
> his huge palm. And, shout on bellowing shout, his roars of laugh-
> ter echoed from the watching hills. And with that wail of rage, and
> mirth, and agony unspeakable, came Irony into the world. (757)

In short, irony in 1908 is born not from verbal intercourse between two males but from a bellicose blond-beast's interaction with his beautifully frivolous female slave. The pain of bringing a disembodied concept into the world is expressed somatically through the caveman's agonized laughter; the moment when irony becomes a figure of embodied, emotional thought is produced by the destruction of the silent female and by the male's painfully amused response to her reduction to ashes. As Brown's story teases out the logic of the Edenic joke—where irony is born from acquiring prohibited knowledge—it becomes clear that women neither "lack" nor "possess" irony. Rather, women's enervating effect on conventional masculinity and their subsequent destruction is what *produces* both self-critical-consciousness and the laughing, quasi-rational pleasures known as "irony." Finally, Gund's response to the self-sacrificial immolation of his dark-skinned, cosmetically enhanced captive—whose primary skills and interests are sleeping late and taking the community's fanciest clothes for herself—exemplifies the twisted condition of irony as a specifically gendered figure for the political constitution of modernist literary culture.

The Eternal Irony of Whose Community?

Barrels of ink have been spilled to criticize, to revise, or—more commonly—to reproduce Richard Rorty's use of "irony" to describe his preferred tactic for liberal politics. Irony here denotes a redescriptive disposition toward language and the world that relies upon a strict division between the public and the private spheres, relegates irony and the ironist to the private sphere, and consequently banishes irony from public spheres. For now, simply recall that Rorty chose "'ironist' to name the sort of person who faces up to the contingency of his or her own most central beliefs and desires" because "she can see, more clearly than the continuity-seeking historian, critic, or philosopher, that her *language* is as contingent as her parents or her historical epoch. She can appreciate the force of [Nietzsche's early] claim that 'truth is a mobile army of metaphors.'"[5] Rather than employing irony publicly in order to subvert or parody specific sexual mores, Rorty's "ironist spends her time worrying about the possibility that she has been initiated into the wrong tribe, taught to play the wrong language game," and nurtures her "private irony" to forfend cruelty and to fertilize "liberal hope" as an engine for political institutions to effect gradual change.[6]

That Rorty's ironist—like the Painted Other of Brown's story—might find herself passively initiated into the wrong "tribe" reveals a curious fact that even Rorty's best interlocutors don't discuss: while Rorty's irony initially claims to condition "his or her" beliefs, his ironist is subsequently and invariably a "she." His decision represents something much more than cheeky academic politeness and much less than forthright feminist praxis by pronoun. Indeed, any liberally antimetaphysical, world-redescribing ironist worth her salt, schooled in philosophy and distrusting language games in general and absolutist claims to truth in particular, would recognize that Rorty's "her" is situated within a much longer philosophical, cultural, and literary tradition: one that distrusts the corrosive effects of public irony, identifies women with and relegates women to the private sphere, and defines "womanhood" itself as an interruption and negation of masculine domains of natural law, politics, and the state. This is precisely the tradition that structures the mythologized logic of "The Birth of Irony" and that continues to circumscribe critical conventions for irony's politics in twentieth-century literature and culture.

More famously, this is the tradition of irony inaugurated by G.W.F. Hegel in the *Phenomenology of Spirit* and *Elements of the Philosophy of Right*, where he elaborates different forms of affiliation, obligation, morality, duty, and the conflicts between divine and human law within the family and the state. The Hegelian roots of classical pragmatism and Richard Rorty's neopragmatism are deep, contentious, and slightly beside the point; for both Hegel and Rorty, however, the division of public and private isn't merely incidental to the constitution of state and civil society but inextricable from the basic function of *Geist* and liberal politics.[7] What seems incidental in Rorty is fundamental to the tradition of political philosophy and cultural criticism, for what Hegel views as the particularity of the sexes in their proper milieus stands in constant tension with the universality of Spirit/Mind and consequently requires what appears as a fundamentally paradoxical (and misogynist) structure of negation underlying both family and civil society: "Since the community only gets an existence through its interference with the happiness of the Family, and by dissolving [individual] self-consciousness into the universal," Hegel writes, "it creates for itself in what it suppresses and what is at the same time essential to an internal enemy [*Feind*]—womankind in general [*Weiblichkeit überhaupt*]."[8]

Kimberly Hutchings recounts how the "masculine Hegelian story . . . is one in which the production of self-conscious selves requires the using up and incorporation of otherness, the domination of natural elements, of life by law."[9] In Hegel's analysis, this development is inextricable from women's "natural" association with feeling rather than intellect, for "Women may well be educated, but they are not made for the higher sciences, for philosophy and certain artistic productions which require a universal element. . . . When women are in charge of government, the state is in danger, for their actions are based not on the demands of universality but on contingent inclination and opinion."[10] Eradicating stylized feminine alterity—in Brown's story, literally named "Other"—constitutes masculine individuality and restores disrupted political community, where women's unfitness for labor, natural affiliation with the private sphere, and role as executors of divine law render them paradoxical, necessary impediments to the civilizing progress of history. When the dual status of "irony" in Hegel's thought is understood as a single signifier linking aesthetics and politics, Brown's etiological account of irony suggests how thoroughly the logic of his analysis had passed into ordinary language and thought about irony in the early twentieth century.

At least two definitions of irony function in Hegel: an "aesthetic" one that lies at the heart of his *Lectures on Fine Art* and a "political" one that plays a significant role in his elaboration of a political philosophy. At times, the two definitions bleed into one another in the very same sentence, such as when he describes how "Irony loves this irony of loss of character"; while the two don't converge precisely in the role that he assigns to women in the development of Spirit, the overlap is so pervasive as to make them inextricable from one another.[11] It is true that "Hegel rarely uses the word 'irony' except to criticize the views of others," and it is just one of those "rare" times that has become a central point of contention in debates about the role of gender in political philosophy.[12] If "irony" is the word that Hegel uses to encapsulate what he saw as the

worst excesses of a German Romanticism that led only to "absolute infinite negativity," in the *Phenomenology* he employs the word seemingly
quite differently: "irony" doesn't mean the "viewpoint" or "work" of
writers like Schlegel and Novalis, which Hegel views as deleterious to the
health of community and state. Rather, this is a word that both characterizes "womankind" (*Weiblichkeit*) itself as ironic and defines women
as irony, one of the more notorious word choices in political philosophy:

> Womankind—the everlasting irony [in the life] of the commu-
> nity [*die ewige Ironie des Gemeinwesens*]—changes by intrigue the
> universal end of the government into a private end, transforms its
> universal activity into a work of some particular individual, and
> perverts the universal property of the state into a possession and
> ornament for the Family.[13]

By claiming the robe for herself, Brown's Painted Other has performed just such a perversion of law, of duty, and of nature and must be
destroyed, narrating in miniature a story that has been taken up by feminist political philosophers reading Hegel and looking to the structure of
the dialectic as a resource for feminist praxis. From Simone de Beauvoir,
Julia Kristeva, and Luce Irigaray (who titled a section of *Speculum of the
Other Woman* "The Eternal Irony of the Community") to more recent
work by Seyla Benhabib, Kimberly Hutchings, and others, a fairly stable
consensus has emerged to describe the ways in which Hegel's account
symptomatically excludes women from both politics and history: "Hegel
'essentializes' woman's nature," Jocelyn Hoy writes, "relegating her to private life within the family, and denying her access to the public sphere"
because "woman 'feels' or intuits what she ought to do; she is insufficiently self-conscious to reflect on and understand the complexities of
her position in her community."[14] Men in Hegel's milieu and analysis are
inextricably linked to the universality of the state, rationality, and labor,
Seyla Benhabib writes, while women's "'substantial determination,' by
contrast, is in the family, in the unity and piety (*Pietät*) characteristic of
the private sphere. Hegel suggests that woman [*sic*] are not *individuals*,
at least, not in the same measure and to the same extent as men are," and
are thus primarily fit to serve the sexual needs of men and the reproduc-
tive needs of the nation.[15] Antigone's adherence to divine law and denial
of Creon's law results in her destruction and is evidence of the fact that
she cannot be wholly absorbed within the masculine dialectic, and thus
"irony" denotes both her relegation to the private sphere and the inability
of masculine logic either to expel or to subsume her completely. The fact
that she becomes "eternal/everlasting irony" is thus "not an expulsion of

gender from the story of spirit," Hutchings explains, "but a recognition of the gendered construction of the private sphere as a constant challenge to the extreme particularism of civil society and to the supposedly neutral, abstract authority of law."[16]

From the standpoint of literary modernism, one recognizes that the irrational, libidinal, and unbounded literary irony that Hegel attacks in the *Aesthetics* resembles the most putatively undesirable aspects of "womankind" in the development of "nonliterary" history. Yet as contentious scholarly debates continue "about Hegel's particular word choices, namely, his use of 'womankind' and 'everlasting' or 'eternal' irony of the community," the very lack of scare quotes around "irony" suggests a broader problem: that one of the most historically unstable and contentious terms in Hegel's formulation serves as the supposedly fixed conceptual point to anchor other, equally contentious concepts.[17] This is apparent even as Hegel relies upon its semantic instability to make arguments where the explicitly aesthetic and explicitly political collapse into one another. The dual status of "irony" as it functions in some feminist theory thus reproduces not only the essential duality of irony but the dual status of irony as it functions in Hegel's philosophy and as it bubbles up in recognizable forms throughout early twentieth-century discourse about relationships among literature, politics, and gender.

In other words, "irony" has long functioned as an organizing trope for the gendered imaginary of political philosophy and for the possibilities of literary work to alter the social conditions of individuals in collectivities. The concept emerges from and conditions subsequent cultural accounts of literature and gender politics, and provides the necessary background for illuminating what might otherwise appear to be either random cultural flotsam or the unique cultural production of either modernism or postmodernism. When Benhabib rightly claims that "Spirit may fall into irony for a brief historical moment, but eventually the serious transparency of reason will discipline women and eliminate irony from public life," the overtones of "irony" here demand that we pay attention to "irony" not only as the synonym for Romantic subjectivity and aesthetic production that Hegel gainsaid but as the term that works within modernism precisely because of its unruliness.[18] Ironically, women *are* irony because they lack the rationality that is necessary for "unromantic" irony and thus only *use* irony in its most rudimentary forms of self-interested sarcasm: "Woman in this way turns to ridicule/ sarcasm [*Spotte*] the earnest wisdom of mature age which, indifferent to purely private pleasures and enjoyments, as well as to playing an active part, only thinks of and cares for the universal."[19]

Feminist political theorists show how women hold a more than supplementary role in the very constitution of Enlightenment politics, wherein their expulsion is both necessary and impossible in order for history to progress and culminate in the form of the state. The influence of Hegel's critique cannot be overstated here, despite the fact that the central terms of the analysis are bound to be contested in perpetuity. The allegorical "birth of irony" also suggests the birth of reason, and the norm of the unironic woman is coextensive with the assumption of irrational women, for whom sympathy and sentiment are the proper aesthetic domains. While articulating an aesthetic politics of a certain literary history, emphasizing one particular constellation of terms and concepts in Hegel's political philosophy—women, irony, community, state, and so forth—serves as a sort of node in a genealogical wave of literary modernism that should give us pause. If dominant and revisionist definitions of modernism are oriented by notions of the male author whose irony is evidence of his alienation, whose ironic alienation and ironic aesthetic practices are a retreat from activist politics, and all of these reveal more fundamental anxieties about feminizing forms of mass culture, these terms frequently become tautologies rather than concepts to clarify the cultural work performed by a set of discourses or body of texts.

The gendered implications of Rorty's call for "private irony" are seemingly incidental, and the implicit misogyny is surely unintentional. Third-wave feminist philosophers such as Irigaray, Judith Butler, and Donna Haraway, however, deploy irony and parody forthrightly as politicized and gendered figures to describe a constitutive model of psychology and subjectivity within political philosophy, or a subversively performative model for the ways in which subjectivity and identity are enacted rather than inherited or inhabited.[20] As Lydia Rainford recounts, "Recent feminist writers have claimed or implied a special affinity between women and irony, and between feminism and irony on account of their 'double' relation to the prevailing order of things: both speak from within this order . . . and yet both remain 'other' to this order in some way."[21] In this line of thinking, irony is a uniquely apt figure for feminist work, for irony's "basic dictionary definition supposes an ambivalence or doubleness which may resist the subscribing force of the philosophical absolute," and thus "it might function as a form of 'negative freedom' for one who, like the figure of 'femininity,' is both contained by and excluded from the prevailing philosophical structure."[22] Debates over whether or not this negative freedom is a necessary adjunct to irony have arisen, Linda Hutcheon writes, "in feminist circles, where the suspicion of irony's instability is frequently countered by the realization of the power that lies in its potential to destabilize."[23] The multiplicity inherent in the figure of irony recurs as "both a reflection and a criticism of the position in which [women] find themselves," and thus feminist theorists "employ the figure of irony in different ways, and with different ends in mind, [as] the ironic mode is considered as a form of internalized agency for the feminist: as well as reflecting her double relation to the patriarchal structure, it turns her alterity to her advantage, by using it to negate the terms of the prevailing hierarchy."[24]

Where irony is drawn upon to denote formal models of gendered subjectivities tied to or expressed through different social positions as well as literary and philosophical styles, it seems to follow that those subjects would be able to employ "their" trope and "their" disposition strategically toward political ends. Thus, in many accounts, irony doesn't just describe women ontologically but describes a subversive rhetorical strategy uniquely suited to that subject-position, wherein women can *use* irony especially well because they already *are* ironic: since "women have also been granted privileged status vis-à-vis irony," women also "are said to be able to use irony as a particularly potent means of critique."[25] Even where critics agree that "irony" describes feminist subjects and feminist practices, larger debates persist about what *kind* of irony is most desirable. On the one hand, Haraway influentially asserts an oft-quoted, roughly "postmodern feminist" understanding of irony: "Irony is about contradictions that do not resolve into larger wholes, even dialectically, about the tension of holding incompatible things together because both or all are necessary and true."[26] This is for Haraway a fact to be drawn upon as a resource, for "Irony is about humor and serious play. It is also a rhetorical strategy and a political method, one I would like to see more honored within socialist feminism."[27] On the other hand, Naomi Schor has called for a revision of specifically modernist irony, which has nineteenth-century misogyny inextricably attached to it: she would prefer a "responsible feminist irony ... whose ultimate meaning—in contrast to that of the unstable irony of modernity—can be reconstructed," for a "politically engaged feminist irony. . . . would retain the destabilizing effects of modernist irony while rejecting its misogynistic libidinal economy."[28]

Yet to understand modernist irony as either male or misogynist *tout court* is to understand both "modernism" and "irony" in untenably limited ways. There is a history behind Haraway's implication that the "humor and serious play" of irony have *not* been "honored" by socialists and feminists, and it is a history that includes women who understood their writing as political instruments featuring irony as a defining quality. As Nina Miller writes, "[i]f women are more defined by tensions, it would follow that they also have special access to irony. Of course, such a gendering of 'irony' flies in the face of some key tenets of high modernism," yet insofar as many of those "key tenets" are retrospective projections, they are of varying usefulness for describing aesthetic practices and political semantics.[29] If the notion of women's "special access" to irony is a relatively recent one, the purported "duality" of irony in these critiques is itself more than dual and thereby destabilizes that which it supposedly denotes, radically decreasing the accuracy of the concept to describe literary and political practices from earlier parts of the century. Indeed, as a term to describe subjects and the aesthetic practices that emerge from that subjectivity, irony frequently serves as a sort of repository for the kinds of statements about gender that recursively echo the gender ideologies they attempt to subvert.

Men Without Women, Women Without Irony

By 1920, literary critic Frances Theresa Russell could observe that "whether in spite of its vagueness or because of it," irony had become "a term of great and increasing popularity. No phrase is at present more of a general favorite than 'The Irony of Fate,' no exclamation more frequent than 'How ironic!'"[30] While her observation might surprise cultural critics who understand irony's wide popularity to have emerged with *Seinfeld*, her analysis also unseats easy equations of popular irony with popular withdrawal from participation in matters of the republic. Indeed, for Russell and many others writing in her milieu, the fact that irony and satire were so popular was related to the fact that she was writing not only after the war but in an historical moment when "humanitarian democracy" was in the ascendant, and when "the scientific method has added reason to emotion, so that while the democratic ideal was conceived in a rationalized sympathy, the stress has [recently] slipped more and more from the sympathetic to the rational element."[31] There is no possible answer as to whether irony had become a popular term "in spite of its vagueness or because of it," but Russell's critique raises good questions about the presumed relationships among reason, emotion, sympathy, and democracy. In the context of the Hegelian legacy I have been describing, one sees that these questions lie at the heart of irony's gendered history.

In 2011, *Nation* columnist Katha Pollitt felt obliged to remind readers of the fact that "feminists have a sense of humor after all and grasp the concepts of irony, parody and appropriation."[32] As with many persistently pernicious myths, the roots of this particular discursive frame stretch back very far indeed, and the normative myth of the unironic woman is frequently visible as the object of satire, even by male writers.[33] In a 1922 story titled "If We Could Only See," for example, Don Marquis (best remembered as the owner of a typewriter on which the cockroach Archy and the cat Mehitabel composed popular poetry) skewered a protagonist named Ferdinand Wimple, a lazy philanderer who effuses demi-Romantic commonplaces to enraptured groups of wealthy women sighing at the names of Bergson and Nietzsche. This Wimple loves one of his pupils in particular, but for the fact that there was "only one thing that jarred upon" him about her personality: "a sudden vein of levity." Wimple is, for all his other merits, "vaguely distrustful of a sense of the humorous in women; whether it took the form of a feeling for nonsense or a talent for sarcasm, it worried him" so much so that he sometimes "in this thoughts, even accused her of irony."[34] Or consider John Galsworthy's *The Patricians* (serialized for American audiences in *The Atlantic*), in which it's difficult to identify clearly where exactly satire begins and where a cultural norm is reinforced rather than criticized. When an older aristocratic woman is confronted by an unexpectedly difficult conversation with a younger, less blue-blooded character, she is revealingly characterized: "Though occasionally employing irony, she detested it in others. No woman should be allowed to use it as a weapon! But in these days, when they were so foolish as to want votes, one never knew what they would be at."[35] Here, a younger woman's capacity to employ irony (understood as both a verbal style implying critique and humor as well as the unsympathetic and self-critical mind underlying such style as it apprehends an unpredictable cosmos) is tied inextricably to norms of manners and morals being disrupted by the threatened participation of women in the public sphere of electoral politics.[36]

Of course, the myth of unironic women was perpetuated more frequently than it was satirized. Benjamin De Casseres is a reliable source for a certain stripe of Nietzschean misogyny, but for the epigraph to this chapter (which comes from a blurb for the essayist Marian Cox) to be so widely legible as to be used in an advertisement requires its resonance with both literary tradition and dominant cultural assumptions. These discourses reveal the ways in which the multiplicity of irony's definitions works in conjunction with discourses about humor, to enforce a set of gendered norms around the propriety of reading and writing literature in a political context. In 1912 and again in 1918, for example, onetime *PMLA* contributor Florence L. Ravenel warned readers against the "fallacies of

Feminism," and warned feminists themselves away from writing that displayed "love of irony and paradox, [for] there is grave doubt that the feministic sense of humor would be adequate to the interpretive process required."[37] Emma Goldman employed the trope in a 1910 argument against what many saw as the misguided fight for women's suffrage: "a goodly number of our grandmothers had more blood in their veins, far more humor and wit . . . than the majority of our emancipated professional women who fill the colleges, halls of learning, and various offices," Goldman wrote, singling out for criticism the "exponents of woman's rights [who] were highly indignant" and "lacking humor."[38] Although not all writers articulated the putative fact as cogently and directly as the London reviewer who observed in 1894 that "Irony, wit, and satire are lost upon the majority of womankind," one frequently finds a dual movement encoded in this discourse that is the mirror image (in reverse) of poststructuralist feminist critique: that is, women naturally *lack* the ability to write ironically and humorously because they lack an ironic identity from which to write (which itself is figured as both cause and effect of an inability to recognize irony).[39]

As the story goes, even the most talented women writers rely upon the presumed emotional opposites of irony, such as sympathy and pity. As a 1903 column in *Harper's Weekly* described the case of a writer in whom "sympathy . . . is her most vital gift," sympathetic writing is symptomatic of sex: both the source and the consequence of the "natural shrinking of the feminine mind from the irony and cruelty of life."[40] It is not merely verbal irony, in other words, for which "true womanhood" is unsuited; indeed, women are frequently *too* suited to sarcasm, the limit case of unsympathetic verbal irony.[41] An 1856 conduct manual titled *The Lady's Guide to Perfect Gentility*, for example, explicitly warns women of a certain class to "Be careful also how you indulge in sarcasm. If you are constitutionally inclined to this, you will find that there is no point in your character which needs to be more faithfully guarded."[42] An 1891 column titled "Sarcasm Among Women" by Kate Tannatt Woods admits to readers of *Ladies' Home Journal* that she would "avoid a sarcastic woman as I would a contagion," for the "womanly woman dear to her own sex, and respected by men, is not sarcastic." This is not a mere matter of convention, moreover, but a transhistorical state of being, for the "habit of sarcasm grows upon men and women, but it finds its fullest and most disagreeable fulfillment in woman's nature."[43] As with Hegel's invocation of *Spotte*—and contra Nietzsche's identification of *Spottlust* as a sign of "health"—Woods understands the "nature" of women as particularly fertile soil for the "nature" of sarcasm, since the capacity of a wounding verbal style does not entail the ability to reliably evaluate relationships between world and word, between fate and fatality, and between a rational conception of a naturalistic universe and the mythological and theological systems that mystify and occlude the true nature of that universe.[44] Lest one dismiss this rhetoric as a relic of the mid-nineteenth century, etiquette manuals at least as late as 1910 advise women that "Words and phrases that have a double meaning are to be avoided," that "It is always silly to try to be witty," and to "Refrain from the use of satire, even if you are master of the art."[45]

On the one hand, irony since Quintilian has frequently been figured as a key quality of identity and thought as well as action. On the other hand, as the century progressed it became possible to imagine women's ability to practice irony despite the fact that an ironic subjectivity was reserved for men. This is how authors Helen Follett and Wilson Follett (the former a popular writer of young-adult fiction, the latter more famous as the author of *Modern American Usage*) characterized Edith Wharton in 1919: while the "masculine quality of Mrs. Wharton, her protective coloring against the merely feminine, is her tone of irony . . . this masculine tinge of irony or asperity, this habitual and determined skepticism which refuses to court illusions on any terms, is with Mrs. Wharton a secondary and incidental quality, not a primary or essential" one.[46] To perform irony is to perform masculinity but not to *become* male: as a woman, Wharton may inhabit "her role of ironist [as] her way of escape from the tyranny of intuition without criticism" (i.e., her close association with femininity) such that "Essentially, she is an ironist not at all." And yet the ability to perform irony—even if she cannot *be* an ironist—allows her to discard gendered literary baggage. The Folletts continue: "Her irony is a more or less conscious rejection of false gods and half-gods; but her full spiritual allegiance is to something beyond, that denies irony even as irony denies sentimentalism—the scientific spirit of modern realism."[47]

The unique position of the necessarily, essentially "unironic" woman writer who is nonetheless able to compose irony qualifies Wharton's writing for a kind of imagined universality, which is particularly suited to a disembodied, "scientific spirit of modern realism." This is a version of realism that might otherwise be infected by embodied sympathy and sentiment. Connecting the chain of associations shows how "irony" meant much more than masculine protection against shedding the tears of feminine sentimentality or the ability to bring about the painful tears of satire. Rather, the quality praised by the protagonist of Wharton's 1904 short story "The Descent of Man" as "So rare a sense of irony, so keen a perception of relative values" makes normative claims about gender and sex that are inextricable from evolving forms of literary production and aesthetic reception.[48] To practice a "technique" of irony was not only to possess and produce embodied emotional response and rational reflection upon that response but even to collapse the putative opposition between reason and emotion (well before the Frankfurt School) in such a way that the resulting "sexless" realism might exceed the presumed capacities and limitations of both gender and literature.

Consider a different, fictional account of the cultural phenomenon that so many literary critics had noted: the opening passage of F. Scott Fitzgerald's *The Beautiful and Damned*, a novel that moved John Peale Bishop to concede anxiously that he was "a little uncertain just what these young men mean when they hold themselves to speak ironically":

> In 1913, when Anthony Patch was twenty-five, two years were already gone since irony, the Holy Ghost of this later day, had, theoretically at least, descended upon him. Irony was the final polish of the shoe, the ultimate dab of the clothes-brush, a sort of intellectual "There!"—yet at the brink of this story he has as yet gone no further than the conscious stage.[49]

Writing in that notoriously wonderful modernist year of 1922, about that other notoriously wonderful modernist year of 1913, Fitzgerald's substitution of "Irony" for "Holy Ghost" echoes like a nondialectical version of Lukács's claim that "Irony, the self-surmounting of a subjectivity that has gone as far as it was possible to go, is the highest freedom that can be achieved in a world without God," wherein the fragmented skepticism of "irony" substitutes for a recently deceased deity.[50] In the philosophically informed rhetorical context of literary modernism that I have been elaborating, however, Fitzgerald's novel reveals less about a materialist analysis of class conflict than about the role of irony in articulating modernist gender politics.

In *The Beautiful and Damned*, readers are introduced to a protagonist who is at least "theoretically" visited by irony but whose quest for practical baptism by irony is consistently negated by the presence of beautiful, enervating women. In Fitzgerald's universe, "brains in a woman is . . . a smattering of literary misinformation," where a woman who is a "horrified democrat" is necessarily "oblivious to his irony."[51] After titling a particularly romantic episode in *This Side of Paradise* "Young Irony," by 1922 Fitzgerald's world had shifted to a point where marriage turns men into "no more than obsolete and broken machines, pseudowise and valueless, driven to and nursed within a ridiculous senility by the women they had broken." To be "more than that"—to be "more than" a henpecked, dissolute ruin—Fitzgerald's protagonist must resist the emasculating domestic sphere and therefore plans to achieve and evolve into a new, impregnable consciousness: after all, "He was Anthony Patch, brilliant, magnetic, the heir of many years and many men. This was his world now—and that last strong irony he craved lay in the offing" (47). This is true, at least, until Patch is overwhelmed by the gorgeous Gloria Gilbert, a beautiful, "practicing Nietzschean" who nonetheless sounds "overtones of profound sentiment" (135); who claims to have "a man's mind" but whom Patch knows to possess "a mind like mine. Not strongly gendered either way" (114). If Gloria is held semi-responsible for Anthony's dissipation, she is clearly held responsible for destroying his irony: "She was beautiful—but especially she was without mercy. He must own that strength that could send him away. At present no such analysis was possible to Anthony. His clarity of mind, all those endless resources which he thought his irony had brought him were swept aside" (98). Fitzgerald first appreciates irony as a "sort of intellectual 'There!'" and ultimately indicts Gloria as the force who sent irony "Where?" Gloria finally becomes the inglorious solvent of both irony and the rational political subject, the embodied means for dispatching mental clarity and creative activity, male production and female reproduction: Gloria's "sentimentality could cling fiercely to her own illusions, but her ironic soul whispered that motherhood was also the privilege of the female baboon" (324), leading her to have an abortion that the novel views as a tragic symptom of both Gloria's and Anthony's abrogation of humanity.

Fitzgerald's figuring of women as both possessing irony and being unnaturally corrosive to irony partially emerges from the complex connection between irony and reason that one finds instantiated in Hegel. In the 1920s, there may have been nothing particularly novel in satirizing the apotheosis of reason or of desiring a language so highly rationalized and logically positivistic that the threat of figuration could be eliminated once and for all: Swift had long ago visited the Laputans and the Houyhnhnms. Nor would employing "irony" to describe and theorize both the undesirable limitations of Enlightenment rationality and the insufficiency of pure feeling appear particularly new to readers of German Romanticism (or theorists who understand modernism as a rehashing of Romanticism): after all, "Irony is the other side of Romanticism," Gary Handwerk writes, "attuned to rationality rather than feeling, to calculation rather than sentiment, to self-reflection rather than self-expression."[52] In modernist literary culture, however, there was something new in how the concept of irony described a desirable relationship between reason and emotion, a new form of consciousness situated in social and historical subjects within an increasingly knowable universe, operating simultaneously in accordance with intelligence and feeling, with rational principles and irrational impulses.

In 1917, for example, Ezra Pound characterized "Delicate irony [as] the citadel of the intelligent" and further lamented that "The ironist is one who suggests that the reader should *think*, and this process being unnatural to the majority of mankind, the way of the ironical is beset with snares and with furze-bushes."[53] In 1922, popular literary critic Joseph Wood Krutch affirmed irony's association with reason in "A Note on Irony" in *The Nation*, where he argued that irony was "the highest form of literary expression" and that this value was partially an effect of living in an historical moment when "sciences of which evolution is the type have condemned us to inhabit henceforth an ironic cosmos." The formulation's "henceforth" is crucial, for the ancient "irony" was increasingly embedded in popular discourse not merely as a transhistorical, formal quality of nature or literature but as a progressive characteristic that originated via new forms of information, recognition, and knowledge: indeed, Krutch writes, "This point of view is peculiarly modern, because former ages knew but half of the ironic predicament in which man finds himself."[54]

If the cosmos had *become* ironic as a result of the recognitive effects of rational inquiry, then this universal irony would necessarily and unsurprisingly affect criteria of literary value and literary language, including the denotative and connotative value of "irony" as a term.[55] In the emergence of this constellation associating irony, shifting forms of rationality, and literary representation of women with more body than soul, one sees more than a post-Romantic, pre–New Critical stipulation of irony as the supreme literary value: irony now represents a nexus of new forms of consciousness, both producing and apprehending new literary values in the context of scientific information with explicitly social and political effects. This is particularly true in early twentieth-century communities seeking to imagine new forms of political and aesthetic praxis appropriate to emerging forms of consciousness and subconsciousness, which themselves clashed with the presumed rationality of classical liberal and conservative political theory. Jennifer Bajorek describes how the "principal interest of irony in a political context is that it limits our ability to conceive of man as a rational subject or purposive actor, and thus as a political agent, at least insofar as this agent has been conceived by traditional models."[56] Yet the long association of irony with the ability and capacity to reason seems to fly in the face of this "principal interest," especially when it comes to the presumed incapacity of one half of the

population to act rationally, an incapacity that long served as one justifi-
catory narrative for the exclusion of women from electoral politics.

It has always been a mistake to associate modernist irony purely
with the explicitly conservative logopoeisis of Pound and Eliot, with
the casual gendering of both reader and writer as male that pervades
Krutch's analysis, or with the more controversial political implications of
New Criticism. Paying attention to the gendering of irony as a social and
literary value highlights the implications of this mistake.[57] Russell and
others emphasize the relationships among irony, satire, and the shifting
roles of reason and sympathy in the formation of democratic ideals, and
the complicated relationship of irony to rationality and emotion emerges
from Anglo-American literary culture in a way that both precedes and
exceeds the retrospective definitions of theoretical modernisms. Indeed,
irony has long signified an external relation to certain kinds of feeling;
as Lewis Campbell remarked in 1879, "the word 'irony' in ordinary use
and to the common apprehension implies the absence or suppression of
sympathy, and it cannot therefore be applied indiscriminately to every
kind of dramatic contrast."[58] If irony and sympathy are incompatible,
however, neither is irony reducible to a merely unreflective anesthesia
because it requires both rational evaluation and knowledge: "The *studied* absence of emotion," J.A.K. Thomson wrote in 1926, is "but another
name for Irony."[59] By the early twentieth century, it is precisely the rela-
tional convergence of knowledge, reason, and emotion that is subsumed
by irony, "because irony consists in a certain *relation* of feeling to expression."[60] Moreover, this is a form of mental activity that is simultaneously
a form of action modeled on language: "by a 'practical irony' we can
only mean a course of action which, taken as an expression of feeling, is
analogous to ironical language."[61]

Comedy and irony also indicate a retreat from unreflective human
sentiment, an opposition to literary sentimentalism, and even a preference for reason and realism: "if the comic idea prevailed with us,"
George Meredith wrote in 1877, "There would be a bright and positive,
clear Hellenic perception of facts. The vapors of unreason and sentimentalism would be blown away before they were productive."[62] There is an
unfortunate tendency to view this opposition as a mere function of the
New Criticism and therefore by extension as congruent with the conservatism of critics who were beginning to formulate their own accounts of
irony in the 1920s.[63] Yet the imagined relationship among the concepts
has a longer and broader history that does not promote disembodied
formalism as a mere means to suppress pragmatic realities about the
lived experience of various identity formations. While debates continue

about the precise politics of the New Negro movement as codified by Alain Locke, for example, it would certainly stretch credulity to associate his literary politics or philosophical pragmatism with the openly racist Southern Agrarians. Yet in 1925 Locke claimed that "reason and realism have cured us of sentimentality: instead of the wail and appeal, there is challenge and indictment. Satire is just beneath the surface of our latest prose, and tonic irony has come into our poetic wells." Furthermore, the realistic irony that clarified Locke's literary waters was not merely pleasant but was understood as "good medicines for the common mind, for us they are necessary antidotes against social poison." Neither can antisentimental, pro-rational irony be reduced to antipolitical quietism; despite the successes of *Uncle Tom's Cabin*, the reformist possibilities of literature lay not in the tears of a sentiment that degenerating bourgeois culture had relegated to the private lives of women but within the transvaluing spikes of irony and satire: "And so the social promise of our recent art is as great as the artistic."[64]

Seth Moglen observes that "Much of the irony for which American male modernists are justly famous is, in fact, a defense against the sentimentality, the 'prettiness,' of thinking that what one had lost (personally and collectively as a culture) could ever be retrieved."[65] Irony is understood as a salient, if not necessarily laudable, literary value (not just well-known but "justly famous") and simultaneously a defensive gesture: a "hard-boiled retreat" from potentially traumatic nostalgia and from psychological and literary sentimentality.[66] But the fact that sentimentality has long been gendered as female is likewise essential to understanding the characterization of irony as masculine: after all, for *The Sun Also Rises'* Jake Barnes it could never be "*handsome* to think so."[67] If irony denotes the "detachment" of Hemingway from his protagonist, as well as the "detachment" of Barnes from the emotional dangers of his traumatized world, the symptomatic analogue to this detachment is supposedly legible in the form of verbal irony: readers who have witnessed the internal and external ugliness of Barnes's world know that it is quite the opposite of "pretty" to think that he and Brett "could have had such a damned good time together" but that the genders of "handsome" and "pretty" are only opposed within a set of aesthetic and social values. These values are themselves legible in the novel's interplay between verbal and dramatic irony. When Bill Gorton learns that the sole function of a steer is to be gored by bulls, he says that "It must be swell being a steer." The reader, of course, knows too well that the war has transformed Jake not into Wilfred Owen's "men who die as cattle" but into just such a castrated steer for whom life is most un-swell.

If such moments represent the emblematic "irony" of male modernist fiction, what of the most famous exchange *about* irony in the 1920s, if not all of American fiction? In chapter 12 of *The Sun Also Rises*, Jake has returned to the hotel room after digging for fishing worms, whereupon Bill Gorton gets out of bed, "step[s] into his underclothes," and commands Jake to "Work for the good of all . . . Show irony and pity." Bill then repeats the command in the form of a question: "Aren't you going to show a little irony and pity?" Jake thumbs his nose, which prompts Bill to inform him "That's not irony," before singing—to the tune of "The Bells Are Ringing for Me and My Gal"—"Irony and Pity. When you're feeling [shitty], Oh, Give them Irony and Give them Pity."[68] In case adequate context for the highly gendered and semi-sexualized subtext isn't provided by Bill's parody of a popular love-and-marriage song, the subsequent exchange is worth quoting at length:

> "What's all this irony and pity?"
> "What? Don't you know about Irony and Pity?"
> "No. Who got it up?"
> "Everybody. They're mad about it in New York. . . ."
> The girl came in with the coffee and buttered toast. Or, rather, it was bread toasted and buttered.
> "Ask her if she's got any jam," Bill said. "Be ironical with her."
> "Have you got any jam?"
> "That's not ironical. I wish I could talk Spanish." (114)

Like most ironic discussion about irony, this passage is invariably quoted rather than analyzed, for the opaque centrality of "irony" to cultural and literary discourse allows the passage to serve as conceptual premise precisely where it should be taken up as text; "irony" is relied upon as stable synecdoche rather than recognized and approached as destabilizing object of scrutiny.[69] Intersubjective connections and disconnections are invariably entailed by the linguistic and epistemological qualities of irony—some interpretive community is constituted, or at least imagined, in every such utterance—but Hemingway's scene is no mere abstraction of subjects, for it is precisely irony that indicates a particular *form* of social connection: between men of the same linguistic community and without the woman whose presence threatens their intimate connection. Indeed, Bill's insistence that Jake "be ironical with her" (and Jake's inability to be ironical with her, despite the fact that he speaks the Spanish that Bill doesn't) embodies the gender dynamic of irony, inherited from and redacted through the nineteenth-century idealist tradition that modernist irony is so frequently taken to oppose.

Though the pairing of "Irony and Pity" itself is taken from Anatole France, Hemingway's social and narrative context reveals the terms as more than supposedly obverse sides of the same coin or as mutually opposed terms that form a total and totalizing disposition toward the world.[70] If "irony and pity" is read as a revision of the "fear and pity" of Aristotelian tragedy, for example, the terms and their mocking invocation suggest more than the idea that laughing comedy is the proper response to impotent mutilation: the illusions of unity and cathartic aesthetic experience within classical tragedy can be avoided so long as modern "Irony" replaces "Fear" as the response to be aroused in the audience. If there is a subtle "fear" in this modernist irony, it is precisely of the women's threats to creatively homosocial pleasures, for female irony would disrupt the necessarily chaste bonds between Bill and Jake just as surely as returning to the United States would: "I'm fonder of you than anybody on earth," Bill says two pages after his irony song. "I couldn't tell you that in New York. It'd mean I was a faggot."[71] In Hegel, woman's irony and unreasonable interruption of history results from her unfitness for "real" work; in Hemingway's scene, Bill explicitly rejects work "for all" and the only labor performed is in domestic service of the male cohort. As historian John Pettegrew has argued about the relationships among various forms of masculinity, individuality, and historiography, "irony has a corrosive effect on masculinity and its reliance on what it takes to be instinct," but—in a seeming paradox—"Irony is often built into the subject position of masculinity itself."[72] Pettegrew is talking specifically about recent "postmodernist" forms of masculinity, and by "irony" he means a certain self-estrangement and distancing. The same can be said, however, of the specifically literary irony attached to the weirdly fragile masculinity of Hemingway.

I have recounted competing discourses about gender and irony and tried to show how that language emerges from intimately related questions about reason and feeling. I have emphasized the enduring legacy of the fact that Hegel's "eternal feminine" ("womankind—the eternal irony in the life of the community") is "eternal / everlasting [ewige]" precisely because her labor is both necessary and disposable, her negation is the precondition for the historical progress from which she is excluded, and her irrational presence in the face of masculine law threatens to derail reason into Romantic irony: what Hegel (and Kierkegaard after him) understood as the "absolute infinite negativity" of irrational egoism, deleterious to the ethical life of individuals and the state. The irony of this split stands as a figure for dueling traditions in Anglo-American cultures, wherein women are imagined as incapable of—even threatening to—the masculine ironies of modernity and simultaneously as so defined by structural irony that they are equipped with psychological irony that serves as a resource for a literary and social irony. As theoretical propositions, of course, these are nonfalsifiable, or perhaps *too easily* falsifiable. Depending on the definition at work, one can obviously point to particular instances of irony in women's writing just as soon as one can find writing by women, or point to particularly unironic (or "literal" or "earnest") writing of other particular women, but invariably reaffirm untenable distinctions between "resolved" modernist irony and "irresolute" postmodernist irony as ontological categories rather than what they are: strategic stipulations that mistakenly rely upon the categories of "woman" and "irony" as stable, consistent, transhistorical figures.

Socratic, Romantic, or New Critical conceptions of irony are plainly inadequate for the social critique in poetry like Edna St. Vincent Millay's *A Few Figs from Thistles* or novels like Anita Loos's *Gentlemen Prefer Blondes*. At the same time, the assumed stability of modernist irony clashes with arguments about how writers such as Dorothy Parker present the "imperative of cutting sentimentalism with irony, the scalpeling out from under the hand of recognition through a concision that will not resolve" owing to the fact that "Irony necessitates living with the alien, with the irresolute, for what will not resolve or capitulate to the known."[73] Elizabeth Francis describes the "politics of nostalgia and irony that characterized both modernist and feminist thought in the twenties," and Susan Rosenbaum reminds us that "conventions of irony work toward varied ends in sentimental culture," but even if one chalks these inconsistencies up to evolving definitions of what qualifies as "modernism," the curious fact remains that feminist ironists such as Parker, Millay, and Loos don't really talk *about* irony.[74] Any approach to feminist, modernist irony as historical and rhetorical practices stumbles upon the dearth of women writers who make irony a central component of their critical and creative vocabulary, at least before third-wave feminist philosophy and literary criticism. To recognize this fact is to recognize how exemplary rarities—seemingly accidental outliers or mass-cultural ephemera like Katherine Holland Brown's story—must be understood as visible genealogical nodes in the transmission of discourses that continue to structure our thinking today. The fact that women writers are infrequently understood primarily as ironists (or at least invoke irony relatively infrequently) is often explained by recourse to authority and marginality: irony is a subtle weapon that relies upon power that is culturally and institutionally denied to women, the story goes, so the privileging of irony as a critical hermeneutic has been perforce a symptom of male privilege: as Eileen Gillooly writes, "if irony is 'masculine,' being a direct, negative response to the Law, then 'feminine irony'—impeded by the feminine position from active rebellion—can only, as Cordelia famously demonstrated, be expressed as silence," with Hegelian "intrigue" outside of history.[75]

What then to make of women who proclaim their irony as the animating spirit of and hermeneutic for understanding their literary work, who create the conditions for their works to be received through the lens of irony and for themselves to be understood as ironists, who imagine literary work as political work, and who profess individualist political positions that are directly opposed to conservative forms of capitalist individualism and openly dubious about the powers of liberal institutions to serve as engines of freedom? What to make of a character named Cordelia who lies in her grave at the beginning of a comic novel rather than at the end of a tragedy? What of that rare beast, the modernist comedy that announces itself as comedy (as opposed to the tragic novel that ironically announces itself as comedy, such as Jessie Redmon Fauset's 1933 Comedy: American Style)? The answer lies partially in a feminist, comic, and emphatically public irony that is openly opposed to literary sentimentalism and philosophical idealism, which resists the narrative closure familiar to both comedy and to dominant understandings of modernist irony. In short, the answer lies in the "blood and irony" of Ellen Glasgow and a best-selling novel from 1926 titled *The Romantic Comedians*.

Blood and Irony

In the words of her biographer and best critic, Glasgow was "An almost singular case in American letters": winner of the 1942 Pulitzer Prize for fiction, a member of the Academy of Arts and Letters, and Book-of-the-Month-Club selectee who became rich and famous from almost five decades of writing, who traveled internationally and lived in New York City for several years, but is inextricably associated with Richmond, Virginia, site of her ancestral home and most of her novels.[76] In 1905 she replied to the question "What does the South need now?" with the epigrammatic response "blood and irony," a quip she would grind into a hermeneutic lens in subsequent decades and that would eventually become a sort of a critical epitaph. Despite the fact that the "most trumpeted dimension of Ellen Glasgow's literary career has been the campaign of 'blood and irony' she conducted as a realist and feminist against the nostalgic fiction . . . dominating Southern writing in the 1890s when she began to publish," the basic question of what "blood and irony" actually *means* has been left almost wholly unaddressed and consequently an entire mode of cultural politics obscured.[77]

In announcing a program of "blood and irony," Glasgow was following ordinary language use in opposing "irony" to "sentimentality," associating the former with "thinking" and the latter with "feeling," satire and sentimentalism with—as one critic put it in 1916—"criticism and sensibility, the will to analysis and the will to sympathy."[78] In a critical essay published in 1938, she emphasized this aspect of irony and its relationship to the war: "The First World War, though actually I had been well out of it, had drained me of feeling," and "because I had had enough of tragedy, and enough too, of pity, that for the moment . . . my mind needed to bite down on some hard substance, on some core of life that was impervious to sympathy." In short, "I wanted amusement tinctured with irony. I wanted a faintly sardonic laughter."[79] Yet, as suggested by the fact that she had repeated "blood and irony" for more than thirty years, this antisympathetic irony was not solely born of the war. The protagonist of her 1913 novel *Virginia*, for example, is a young woman whose rationality and viewpoints are characterized exactly in these terms: when Jenny's mother presents her with a putative fact about the world— that "men are different, darling. One doesn't expect them to give up like women," Jenny replies as a distinctively modern and perhaps modernist woman can: with "sweetness [that] had borrowed an edge of irony. It was Science annihilating tradition, and the tougher the tradition, the keener the blade which Science must apply."[80] Glasgow was also obviously concerned with the specific sentimentalism of Southern literature and culture that she saw persisting from Reconstruction through the 1930s of *Gone with the Wind*; as she explained in a 1928 essay for *Harper's Magazine*, she objected to the decay of the Southern novel into "sentimental infirmity," a weakness because the "emotions with which they deal are formal, trite, deficient in blood and irony, and as untrue to experience as they are true to an attitude of evasive idealism."[81] (As a confirmed Darwinian, she was also concerned with antiscientific, antirational religious fanaticism in the South after the 1925 Scopes Trial.)

Yet this is not merely to affirm old narratives about the strict separation of gendered public and private spheres of masculine irony and feminine sentimentality, wherein the old powers of aesthetically elite patriarchy would triumph over the degraded feminization of American culture. In 1938, Glasgow proclaimed her "subject, the ironic perversity of human nature," and revised a series of essays from the 1920s into critical prefaces for a presentation edition of her best novels, where she specifically employs "irony" to describe her evolution as a novelist with a keen sense of aesthetic politics.[82] Semi-dismissing her conventionally realist, politically progressive early novel *The Voice of the People* as juvenilia composed when "Revolt had not yet been subdued to the civilized uses of irony," she holds "civilizing" to a particular political valence.[83] For Glasgow and many other feminists, the proper object and engine of political change was socially situated, individual consciousness, the root of institutions that produce social, political, and economic inequality as experienced by the mass of people. "Civilized" indicates the achievement of that consciousness: "I believe in social justice [and] . . . that the approach to a fairer order lies, not without, but within," she wrote in 1933, "and the only way to make a civilized world is to begin and end with the civilizing of man."[84]

This "civilized" world is emphatically not to be understood as the genteel separation of spheres or the conservative perpetuation of exploitation under the guise of personal responsibility. After all, Glasgow simultaneously argues for personal renewal and that "the private ownership of wealth should be curbed; that our natural resources should not be exploited for individual advantage; that every man should be assured of an opportunity to earn a living and a fair return for his labor." She sounds more like a Communist critic of the National Recovery Administration than a New Deal champion when she adds "that our means of distribution should be readjusted to our increasing needs and the hollow cry of 'overproduction' banished from a world in which millions are starving."[85] And it is precisely through internal renewal as a means toward achieving specific political and economic objectives that she recalls and expands upon her early epigram, in language that invokes both the "embodied intelligence" of pragmatism and what she thought of as a brand of modernist realism wherein the "whole truth must embrace the interior world as well as external appearances":

> When all is said, the arteries in the intellect are as essential to literature as the arteries in the body are essential to life. Of this I was thinking many years ago when I said that the South needed blood and irony. Blood it needed because Southern culture had strained too far away from its roots in the earth; it had grown thin and pale; it was satisfied to exist on borrowed ideas, to copy instead of create. And irony is an indispensable ingredient of the critical vision; it is the safest antidote to sentimental decay.[86]

In calling for "blood and irony," one first notes a witty Southerner's postbellum and post-Reconstruction pun on "blood and iron," Otto von

Bismarck's famous defense of German militarism and national unifica-
tion. More important, Glasgow is articulating the primary hermeneutic
for understanding how to undermine discursive codes that both relied
upon and reproduced normative political ideals of "pure womanhood"
via sentimentalism.[87]

This was not mere posturing against a fashionable or unfashionable
genre, however, much less what she perceived as a "feminine" mass
culture to be corrected by the masculine irony of high modernism.[88]
For Glasgow, the errors of both modernism and sentimentalism were
pragmatic and ethical. In a classic ironist's move, she includes herself as
the object of critique, for the South's aesthetico-political wounds were a
matter of her own subjectivity as well as of other novelists and readers.
Indeed, she felt a chthonic relationship to the region and culture that
produced atrocities: "if I could criticize," she recalled later, "it was not
because I had escaped from the elegiaic tone that surrounded me. . . . I
had been brought up in the midst of it. . . . Underneath my revolt there
was, I believe, an uprising of that old hatred of inhumanity. I revolted
from sentimentality, less because it was false than because it was cruel.
An evasive idealism made people insensitive; it made people blind to
what happened."[89] In the longer context of gendered irony and European
philosophy, Glasgow's motto proclaims not a retreat from politics but
an active disposition toward subjective states, agonistic conflicts among
states (the psychological states of the South), and the political negotia-
tion of literary aesthetics as they both reflect and inflect embodied conventions of behavior.[90]

Glasgow's contemporary critics understood her and promoted her
specifically as an ironist, suggesting that she successfully produced the
felicity conditions for her public persona and her irony to be understood
as actively political. In 1926, for example, the liberal chair of the Vanderbilt English Department (and soon-to-be enemy of the Southern Agrarians) Edwin Mims admired what he called "the social philosophy" of
Glasgow's novels, claiming that "No one has written with more penetra-
tion and discrimination about the forces of reaction and progress that
have been for a half century contending for supremacy in the South" and
marveling that "she is even possessed of irony and other forms of humor
in dealing with sentimentalism and false romance."[91] In 1939, the editor
of the liberal *Virginia Quarterly Review*, James Southall Wilson, claimed
that "She spoke the language of irony and irony was not then one of
the ways of Southern speech," while Henry Seidel Canby described her
in 1941 as "a realist of the old South, when Southern writers were still
sentimentalists. She was an ironist when irony was rare in American

literature."[92] In 1942, Alfred Kazin affirmed her primary artistic identity in terms of "irony, a crisp and epigrammatic irony that could verge on farce—or an inclination to the despair that is beyond all understanding," and obliquely connected this to the fact that her literary fortunes were somehow connected with an aesthetic politics that stood outside of conventional left-right distinctions: she had become a political "martyr to American criticism," Kazin wrote, when "Radical critics ignored her because they could not place her; conservative critics praised her blindly because they could use her as a lesson to irreverent modernists."[93]

Kazin overstated the case of Glasgow's martyrdom—that same year, she won the Pulitzer Prize for her novel *In This Our Life*—and the difficulty in classifying her politics was at least partially a symptom of 1930s literary-political battles over different forms of realism. Yet the task of unpacking her politics seems scarcely easier with a "modernism" explicitly defined by its emphasis on reason and antisentimental formalism, eschewing "politically committed" art (narrowly defined via allegiance to political party, whether Communist, Fascist, Democratic, or Republican) and averring irony as a central term of literary value. These are, after all, precisely the terms used to understand New Criticism, which is thought to rest "on deeper underpinnings in the Southern Agrarian platform for an elite 'squirearchy' of cultural domination."[94] The case is particularly risky for a writer from Virginia, given her proximity to the formalism whose irony not only retreated into the genteel studies of the Vanderbilt faculty club but did so as an explicitly conservative gesture that is imagined to be complicit with lynching and other atrocities of the twentieth century: "It is no accident that the rise of New Criticism," Walter Kalaidjian writes, "witnessed in works such as Brooks's *Modern Poetry and the Tradition* in 1939, is coincidental with the signing of the Soviet-German Nonaggression Pact that same year."[95]

Although Glasgow was no more fond of proletarian realism than she was of postbellum sentimentalism, repulsed equally by Mike Gold and Margaret Mitchell, her modernism was neither T. S. Eliot's nor Robert Penn Warren's. She enjoyed a much longer friendship and correspondence with Radclyffe Hall and Hall's partner Una Troupridge than she did with Allen Tate; she visited Vita Sackville-West in 1927, hosted Gertrude Stein and Alice B. Toklas at her home in 1935, publicly and privately admired Virginia Woolf, and openly proclaimed herself as one among those who "are and have been always in accord with the artistic impulse we are pleased to call Modernism."[96] Unlike more famous modernists, she aligned herself neither with Mussolini nor William Z. Foster nor the Anglican Church, and was more personally connected with Republicans running for office in Virginia than Republicans fighting Franco's troops in Spain. Consequently, deriving something like a practical politics for Glasgow's literary project remains tricky business, especially given that even her best critics discreetly pass over her more radical propositions.

Despite her emphasis on irony as both an aesthetic and ethical value, despite the fact that she identified as a writer in the South who desired to amend degenerating Southern culture as a citizen of the world, despite the efforts of some critics and the fact that she explained her own motto in terms of the "earth" of Southern culture, she is emphatically not to be associated with the Fugitives, the Southern Agrarians, or the reactionary politics that attended the cultural and literary criticism of books such as the 1930s *I'll Take My Stand*. The interconnected grammars of reason, gender, and politics are illuminated by philosophical, fictional, and critical narratives about irony and suggest that Glasgow's "blood and irony" repudiates a mistakenly dominant set of influentially reductive associations: irony with New Criticism with quiescent formalism with the horrific racism and antiprogressivism of the American South. While she did not "like the twin curses of modern standardization and mass production," she openly liked "even less the hookworm and pellagra and lynching of the agrarian scene, the embattled forces of religious prejudice and the snarling feature of our rural dry-nurse prohibition," and her choice of that particular synonym for "rural" can be no accident.[97] This is not to claim that she was secretly attending the American Writers Conference instead of holding teas at her Richmond manse, but she was emphatically and consistently politically active if one recognizes connections between literary reception and self-development in order to understand how this might be so.

Glasgow was no stranger to conventionally organized political action: she helped found the Equal Suffrage League of Virginia and marched through the streets of London with English Suffragettes Emmeline Pankhurst and May Sinclair in 1909. In 1913, she argued in the pages of the *New York Times* that "there is not a single valid reason that I have ever heard against giving votes to women," but her fundamental political convictions and assumptions are nonstatist, more pointedly radical rather than liberal or Fabian: "we have been talking of suffrage for dear knows how long," she continued, "when the really important thing to talk about is the feminist movement as a whole. I think that the ballot itself is a very small and unimportant factor in the whole movement to emancipate women."[98] And it is here that liberal critics tend to founder, staging a common and false dilemma to find that "Her ideas on feminism were always philosophical rather than political," thereby ignoring and obviating an entire strain of nonelectoral politics.[99]

Clearly Glasgow didn't take an openly anarchist oppositional stance toward what Emma Goldman called "The Tragedy of Woman's Emancipation"—nor did she arbitrarily separate gender politics from the larger struggle for social justice in which it was situated: "by means of the feminist movement and the effort for equal suffrage," she continued, "we are wiping out class distinctions and class prejudices."[100] Yet it is in the means of eradicating those distinctions and prejudices that one finds an articulating joint between aesthetics and politics via the engine of irony. The identification of irony with intellect and a critical attitude toward aesthetically produced emotion—running from Pound to Glasgow—is especially germane to a diagnosis that claims "Opposition to suffrage, in this country at least, is all emotional. It does not exist—certainly not in the average run of cases—where its judges have troubled themselves to think."[101] Mere preference for "thinking" over "feeling" is only a part of her critical program; what is required to make her platform of irony coherent as a political disposition is the context of radical Anglo-American feminism in the early part of the century and an understanding of its necessarily comprehensive sphere of praxis. Consider Glasgow's claim in another 1913 editorial that "what we call the woman's movement is a revolt from a pretense of being—is at its best and worst a struggle for the liberation of personality."[102] Nor was this youthful indiscretion: in the very different political moment of 1942 she proclaimed, "I was always a feminist, for I liked intellectual revolt as much as I disliked physical violence."[103]

The emphasis on "liberation of personality" seems opposed to the more familiar political action of marching through the streets or petitioning legislators for reform. As an immensely influential philosophical structure for radical politics, however, it is far more compatible with forms of anarchism circulating in Glasgow's New York and London with more familiar lines of Emersonian (or Horatio Algerian) individualism. As historian Lucy Delap has written, "other strands of individualist thought also focused upon self-emancipation through will, personality or character," but the strain of what she calls "avant-garde feminism" paid close "attention to internalised constraints (emotional and psychological) on self-realisation" and contended that "self-reliance or self-development should be motivated by the desire to help others and be of service. This was even more influential upon feminism than the liberal/libertarian stress on equal rights and freedom from external constraints which is more usually associated with women's emancipation."[104] This was a strain of feminism, moreover, that was closely associated with aesthetic forms of modernism.[105] Glasgow's cultural politics remain remarkably consistent over the years and express a dying faith in the capacity of electoral politics to produce a revolutionary structural effect on democracy or on the lived experience of those who were granted the ballot. As she wrote in an article for *The Nation* some eight years after the ratification of the Nineteenth Amendment to the U.S. Constitution, "I should like to think that a fairer social order might be attained in an orderly way, through some third party with high principles; but is it probable, I ask myself, that the selfishness and greed of political parties can be overthrown by high principles and an appeal to right reason?"[106]

For thinkers like Glasgow, participation in electoral politics was desirable but neither a sufficient nor necessary condition for bringing about something like "social justice," and by 1926 this was a sentiment increasingly shared by a generation of American activists who had placed their political hopes in the goal of expanded suffrage. Regardless of how unlikely the political bedfellows were before and during legislative struggles, the aftermath of legislation that was passed certainly helped many children drink cleaner milk and many women enjoy citizenships that weren't tied to their husbands; such legislative victories did not, however, necessarily translate into an experience of freedom. As radical feminist Victoria McAlmon wrote anonymously in 1927, "I feel no need for more freedom, but I want a world in which the freedom I now have can be used. We women are free, but free for what? . . . my adventurous and questing mind was never so thwarted as it has been since I got my citizenship."[107] As many progressive constituencies have recently discovered, legislative victories can produce only a certain kind of fleeting satisfaction, and the disillusion that many feminists felt in the 1920s might be likened to a sort of inverse, if not ironic, victory: the satisfied desire for a formal recognition of "equality" via electoral politics does little to sate other, more embodied desires. As Lorine Pruette wrote in 1927, "If I were building a Utopia, I would take away our memories, so we would start fresh every day, and then I would endow each of us with strong, lusty desires, and I would give us strong, eager feet with which to run swiftly and determinedly after our desires. I would leave principles out of my Utopia, even feminism; in place of principles I would give us all a magnificent and flaming audacity."[108] And it is precisely this experience of embodied freedom—libidinal or otherwise—that Glasgow represents as the real object of personal and political development.

The erosion or denial of desire isn't wholly distinct from the problem of rationality, of course. As political scientist Ann Towns has shown in a transnational context, late nineteenth-century women were figured as more than merely "unfit" for prominent roles in statecraft. Drawing directly upon the evolutionary biological analysis that viewed male's active struggle for reproduction as a salutary force in advancement of the species, wherein the "physical strength and intelligence of men were allegedly constantly improved and developed by means of sexual competition for women, while women's capacities remained quiescent," women found themselves figured as "vestigial beings of passions and little reason, [such that] it was critical that women not be entrusted with deliberating law and other forms of civilization's creation and maintenance."[109] Paradoxically, then, "the exclusion of women from the political sphere was widely represented as an elevation of woman and a characteristic effect of a state having reached an advanced stage" (74). Thus women found themselves enmeshed by the perverse logic whereby they were not naturally or habitually unfit for public roles in the state but the state was unfit for women: "By the end of the nineteenth century," Towns writes, "the following norm was evidently in place: *civilized states exclude women from politics*" (79).[110] Under such conditions best described by the figure of irony, a nineteenth-century reform politics relying upon sentiment, sympathy, or pity for marginalized subjects would be inadequate to the task of emancipation, as would a documentary impulse of mimetic realism allied with virtues of detached objectivity. Instead, for writers like Glasgow, irony held the promise of political action that focused on changing "habits of mind" rather than formal claims to the law and the negative liberties putatively enforced by the Constitution. What she calls "social justice," then, would require not just voluble personalities, moral rectitude, ideological demystification, or sheer force of concentrated effort but a complicated and fractured subjective power called "Will," the acquisition of which is strangely allied with irony: the figure that uniquely subsumes the aesthetic disposition toward the pragmatic judgment of emotional and rational experience.[111]

The Will to Personality

Glasgow was well read in both the European philosophical tradition and American pragmatism (though both her library and her vocabulary indicate that she preferred William James to John Dewey and George Santayana to Josiah Royce). Bored and distracted on vacation in 1906, she wrote a friend: "I've even detached myself from metaphysics—Kant and Bradley stand half read on my desk, and my best beloved Fichte I haven't dared open for a month."[112] Later she would recount how "the German philosophers, especially Schopenhauer . . . possessed more of the hard truth I required—more, too, of that intellectual fortitude I was seeking. . . . I read Kant and (though I could never read Hegel) the whole wide group of idealists, which included Fichte and Schelling. Of the German philosophy, only *The World as Will and Idea* stayed with me, until, by pure accident, I discovered the great prose-poem, *Thus Spake Zarathustra*."[113] She singled out Hegel for criticism, repeating, "Hegel, I could not read. It may have been that his stiff and involved German style defied translation. It may have been that I was irritated by vagueness even in metaphysics. Or it may have been that I was reading from the wrong motives," and Santayana and Schopenhauer for praise: "alone among modern philosophers, if we except the incomparable Santayana, who was then a stranger to me, Schopenhauer has a style that can survive, not only translation, but critical violence."[114] In this light, it's worth noting that her "earth" metaphor for "blood and irony" more properly belongs in the vein of American pragmatism rather than American Agrarianism: the metaphorical account of psychology as rooted and situated within a specific environment and social system ranges from John Dewey's praise of post-Darwinian scientific realism as "a necessity to bring the Antaeus of humanity back to the mother soil of experience" to William James's warning that "if we treat all this abstraction literally and oppose it to its mother soil in experience, see what a preposterous position we work ourselves into."[115] That preposterous position, of course, was a premodern, inflexible conception of morals and morality, a monistic and pre-Nietzschean conception of sociality wherein "Good was good, and bad was bad" and where "values showed no hollowness and brooked no irony."[116]

Indeed, an interwar politics of literary irony that anticipates third-wave feminism's fragmented, performative subjectivity becomes visible in moments when Glasgow invokes James, a philosopher who recognized that human subjectivities are embodied, performative, malleable (up to the age of thirty, at least) "bundles of habits."[117] "Regarding the freedom of the will, and regarding that doctrine alone," Glasgow wrote in 1938, "I suppose I may call myself more or less of a pragmatist," but as early as 1917 she had sounded a politically rich philosophical note that resonated strongly with the Young Intellectuals' reading of pragmatism: "true democracy consists chiefly in the general recognition of the truth that will create[s] destiny," she wrote, because "Democracy . . . consists in the knowledge that all people should possess an opportunity to use their will to control—to create—destiny, and that they should know that they have this opportunity. They must be educated to the use of the will, and they must be taught that character can create destiny."[118] Lest one falsely reduce this stance to a conservatively voluntarist individualism, she clarifies that "environment inevitably has its effect on the character, and, therefore, on will, and, therefore, on destiny. You can so oppress and depress the body that the will has no chance. True democracy provides for all equal opportunities for the exercise of will."[119]

These terms are all richly overdetermined, of course, and bear their own political connotations: it can be difficult to hear admonitions to improve "character" via "acts of will" and not suspect a reactionary recourse to individual responsibility and moral rectitude as distinct from socially situated individuals who suffer and thrive individually through their collective attachments and interactions. But these pronouncements must be understood in terms of the specific milieu in which they were uttered and received: for James, "character" doesn't equal a disembodied moral category roughly akin to true grit but is a function of contingent and malleable experience that denies the dyad of disembodied volition and active bodily experience: "character," he writes, "consists in an organized set of habits of reaction. . . . Our volitional habits, depend, then, first, on what the stock of ideas is which we have; and, second, on the habitual coupling of the several ideas with action or inaction respectively."[120]

Glasgow's 1926 turn from realism to comedy, her lifelong promotion of "irony" as the lens through which to read her fiction, and her political debts to avant-garde feminism converge to suggest that "blood and irony" describe more than a vague rebuke to "evasive idealism." Irony instead comes to offer a means of instilling new habits by helping subjects evade what James described as identical-twin errors of sentimentalism and rationalism: on the one hand, "The 'sentimentalist fallacy' is to shed tears over abstract justice and generosity, beauty, etc., and never to know these qualities when you meet them in the street."[121] On the other hand, the rationalist's fallacy is to claim that truth stands as a unity outside of experience and that therefore "Reason is deformed by experience. As soon as reason enters experience it becomes contrary to reason." Yet even to describe the problem as existing on separate hands is to commit a dualistic fallacy, for "The rationalist's fallacy here is exactly like the sentimentalist's": each commits the error of denying the contingent actualities of lived, embodied experience. It is the identically obverse side of this same coin that provides the object for Glasgow's literary politics, which take fundamental pragmatist critiques and advance them in directions that are sometimes radical, sometimes progressive, but invariably outside the sometimes conservative political agendas of their early exponents.[122] This is a dual task that has explicitly aesthetic causes and effects, with irrationality and rationality standing in mutually constitutive relationship to one another. As Glasgow's "beloved Santayana" wrote in 1922, "Reason cannot stand alone; brute habit and blind play are at the bottom of art and morals, and unless irrational impulses and fancies are kept alive, the life of reason collapses for sheer emptiness."[123] Glasgow thus turned to a form of irony that offered the possibility of disrupting the pernicious political habits of readers: comedy.

Habits, Duties, and *The Romantic Comedians*

In the same year that Hemingway published *The Sun Also Rises*, Glasgow turned away from decades of realist novels to produce *The Romantic Comedians*, a modernist comedy of manners that sold more than 100,000 copies in just a few months.[124] Benjamin De Casseres praised it as her "masterpiece" on the same grounds that poet Dorothea Lawrance Mann considered it "her most brilliant" novel: because "her irony is fathomless" producing what Carl Van Vechten described as "high spirited . . . social satire" featuring not only irony but the "rare quality. . . . of malicious, feminine wit" from a writer who is "Always feminist in her point of view."[125]

The Romantic Comedians concerns a May-December "romance" between an aged widower and a young woman, thereby situating itself in a venerable literary tradition running from "The Miller's Tale" to *Middlemarch*. Judge Gamaliel Bland Honeywell is a wealthy and successful widower, "a conservative character, as volatile as a judge, as adventurous as a vestryman," "who respected print and had done his duty by contemporary literature, [and thus] could not have escaped the knowledge that women suffer from strange delusions and are often the victims of their sacrificial virtues."[126] He is "tolerant of any views that were not brought into vocal conflict of his own" (*RC* 155) and "disposed to encourage liberty of thought as long as he was convinced that it would not lead to liberal views" (*RC* 4). His main interests include work, golf, mourning his dead wife, Cordelia, and the occasional glass of Prohibited bourbon; like his father before him, "If there is anything wrong with the Episcopal Church or the Democratic Party," he "would rather die without knowing it" (*RC* 8).[127]

Gamaliel's name associates him with Warren Gamaliel Harding (the first American president elected by actively seeking women's votes) and the biblical Pharisee, and his profession as judge emphasizes the allegorical association with the masculine domain of authoritative Law. His worldview remains deeply rooted in the waning years of the nineteenth century, when women "had known how to suffer in silence. What an inestimable blessing was this knowledge, especially when it had passed into tradition!" (*RC* 40). Above all, Gamaliel is a man of habit: "after years of renown in his profession, mental concentration had become an inflexible habit" (*RC* 34), and ever since "the eighteen eighties, when his opinions were formed" (*RC* 4), he "had never acquired the new habit of thinking of women as detached beings" (*RC* 141). If even he can recognize that "It is strange the hold habit gets over you" (*RC* 150), mere recognition of these habits isn't enough to change his views, since "the confirmed habit of a lifetime was stronger even than passion" (*RC* 175). Thus he remains "far from convinced that the modern mind, with its mastery of vital problems, was an improvement upon the sentimental Victorian one, which, when all was said, had had its own way with sex" (*RC* 117).

Honeywell's mental habits have a linguistic basis, such that his expressions as well as his impressions are formulaic: attempting to express the grief that is expected of him as a widower, he sighs, "'I am a bird with a broken wing' . . . as he had sighed so often into other ears since the day of his bereavement." Glasgow reveals this sentiment as hollow convention by calling attention to its hyperconventional language: "while this classic metaphor was still on his lips, he felt an odd palpitation within the suave Virginian depths of his being, where his broken wing was helplessly trying to flutter" (*RC* 3). Two pages later the Judge concedes with classical pragmatism that "Yes, the phrase slipped more easily than the thought in the groove of his mind, he was as helpless without Cordelia as a bird with a broken wing" (*RC* 5). Language is not merely constitutive of thought here but coextensive and emphatically pragmatist in its maintenance of a Jamesian social stability: "like most lawyers and all vestrymen, he was able to believe automatically a number of things that he knew were not true. It was owing, indeed, to his proficiency in this exercise, which conservative people called 'right thinking,' that he had achieved his enviable position in an epoch when faith and facts did not cultivate an acquaintance" (*RC* 175).

Where critics have described the irony of the novel as pointedly attacking the gap between "manners and morals," positioning the novel within a broader aesthetic-political program and philosophical tradition reveals an entirely different aspect of Glasgow's irony: her sustained critique of the ways in which embodied habits of misogynist mythologies are perpetuated. As early as 1913, Glasgow attacked literary sentimentalism in general (and Richardson's Clarissa in particular) as "the most convincing of the feminine prigs with which the imagination of man has enriched the pages of literature" that contributed to the perniciously "evolving masculine ideal of women."[128] She repeatedly attacked the sentimental literary tradition not for failing to achieve disinterested aesthetic standards of an emerging modernism but for elaborating a mythical "true womanhood" that was nothing more than projected and elaborated masculine fantasies about women that had become habitual: "It is the peculiar distinction of all woman myths," she wrote in 1928, "that they were not only sanctioned but invented by men."[129] Literary genres both rely upon and engender ideas that become culturally dominant as myth; myth is then internalized as habit, something much more difficult to shake: "Ages of false thinking about her on the part of others have bred in woman the dangerous habit of false thinking about herself," Glasgow argued, "and she has denied her own humanity so long and so earnestly that she has come at least almost to believe in the truth of her denial."[130]

For James as for Glasgow, the notion of habit is much more than the Aristotelian cornerstone of ethics or a synonym for ideology; it is the neurologically embodied means by which subjects act both individually and collectively, a "material law" they must follow, and precisely what *prevents* social or political change. In one of his most famous passages, he writes that "Habit is thus the enormous fly-wheel of society, its most precious conservative agent. It alone is what keeps us all within the bounds of ordinance, and saves the children of fortune from the envious uprisings of the poor."[131] Furthermore, for James this is emphatically not an impediment to be overcome but a robust feature to be preserved in individuals for the good of the stable collective: "it is best he should not escape. It is well for the world that in most of us, by the age of thirty, the character has set like plaster, and will never soften again."[132] Taking James's diagnosis of the "conservative flywheel" as a political problem to be dislodged rather than a machine to be kept running smoothly, Glasgow represents habitual gender ideology as a problem inculcated by both sentimental fiction and its legacy within misogynist modernism and figures her own irony as a means of advancing an explicitly feminist political "freedom" by dislodging habits of reading and thinking.

Glasgow diagnosed a literary history wherein women were subdued by a literary and cultural mythology that reduced them to fonts of romantic and Romantic "inspiration." Only later, when the dominant myth of women as inspiration for male creativity and activity "encountered all the sad young men and the Freudian perils of the postwar years was it overthrown and replaced by the bold modern myth of woman as an impediment," a move that rendered woman "public property" after "they secured permanent habitation in that sheltered area of the mind where superstitions reside and they have long been embodied in innumerable rubrics and rituals."[133] In the Lost Generation male mythology, "Even a feminine inspiration does not persist in getting in the way of adventure after the unfortunate habit of a feminine impediment," and so Glasgow sets herself the task of composing not just a comedic countermythology but an intervention in that tradition that would harness irony: not to formally defamiliarize or simply distance herself from the characters she created but to disrupt readers' habitual understanding of gender and character in misogynist terms.[134] Dislodging these habits thus expands the possibilities of imaginative self-production and expands the definition of "political action" to include such production. Anticipating Hannah Arendt by a few decades, Glasgow observed that "the trouble with all modernism is not that it is young, not even that it is strange, but that it must soon grow old and decrepit. When that happens and the method ceases to shock, when it becomes as familiar as Victorian aesthetics, it will be thrust from the limelight by some more nimble or more imprudent performance."[135] This is to state what is by now fairly obvious to anyone who has read *Ulysses* without being scandalized or viewed a Cubist painting without becoming nauseously disoriented or socially adrift: that transformative literary politics can't rely for long upon the shock of disrupted formal conventions to destabilize ideological habits. By ironically employing the familiar literary form of the comic novel of manners, Glasgow stages the problem of gendered habits so that readers are forced to do so themselves.

Narrated with heavy irony and salient free-indirect discourse, the basic plot of *The Romantic Comedians* concerns Honeywell's relationship to a number of women and a number of women's relationship to an economy of material and sexual satisfaction. As ever, the Judge's thinking about these matters is equally habitual and conservative. The novel opens as he attempts to mourn his dead wife, Cordelia, trying "with all the strength of his decorous will to remember her features and mourn for her as sincerely as she deserved" (*RC* 3). Cordelia is the perfect Victorian woman whose name associates her with older, more tragic forms of silent female devotion: "For thirty-six years" she "had sacrificed her appetite to his digestion" (*RC* 3), had "been a perfect wife . . . and worn out herself in [his] service" (*RC* 6). He misses her "rather in the capacity of a ministering angel than of a wife" (*RC* 123), and even his nostalgic longing for her presence is misogynist and subjunctive: "If only she had had a dozen children instead of the two . . . her life, he felt, might have been as abundant and as satisfying as she had deserved" (*RC* 6). He is visited and regularly needled by his good-humored but ill-reputed twin sister whose name continues the Shakespearian punning: "Edmonia Bredalbane, an intrepid woman of liberal views and loose behaviour" who "had indulged herself through life in that branch of conduct which was familiar to ancient moralists as nature in man and depravity in woman" and, worst of all, "declined to remain a picturesque ruin in company with other damaged virgins of quality" (*RC* 7). There is also the faded Victorian beauty Amanda Lightfoot, briefly loved by Gamaliel in his youth and presumed by "public opinion" to be Cordelia's successor: "grave, stately, self-possessed, confirmed in queenliness, wrapped in her Victorian reserve as in a veil of mystery" (*RC* 40), she is "Serene, unself-ish, with the reminiscence of a vanished day in her face and figure," and "belonged to that fortunate generation of women who had no need to think, since everything was decided for them by the feelings of a lady and the Episcopal Church" (*RC* 101).

When the Judge meets the beautiful young Annabel Upchurch, she revivifies an "inarticulate longing to protect, to be generous, to give presents, to fondle gently" in the "petrified forms in his mind" (*RC* 45); there is indeed something dislodged in his body, but not in the "slow but honourable processes of [his] judicial mind" (*RC* 3), for Gamaliel never loses the conviction that "the traditional feminine virtues—patience, gentleness, moderation, reserve, especially reserve—were excellent things in woman" (*RC* 41). Annabel is recently heartbroken, bereft of both money and her first lover, Angus, and thus at first is happy to accede to the Judge's sly offer of material support, since she is "not looking for joy" but would "like, if it isn't asking too much, to have a shop in its place" for she would "rather have money than anything in the world" (*RC* 50). Her physical charms are intoxicating, and "the only defect he had ever found in her was her failure to be amused by his jokes" (*RC* 56). She rejects warnings about his increasingly matrimonial—and randy—designs on her, and in fact declares her preference for a man past his physical prime: "'So long as he is old,' Annabel declared, 'I don't care how old he is. It is this horrible poverty that I can't bear,' she continued passionately. 'It's bad enough to be poor when you're happy, but to be poor when you're unhappy is too much to endure'" (*RC* 90).

With Honeywell's growing recognition that Annabel is finding all sorts of happiness with a younger, less judicious man, Glasgow's feminist critique emerges in Annabel's twin assertion of happiness and freedom and rejection of disembodied duty and embodied desire. If she is at first willing to deny her own sexual desires in order to enjoy the material wages of marriage, sustained interaction with Honeywell—no matter how well intentioned he is, no matter how kind, no matter how doting—awakens her to the fact that his material support (in a labor economy from which she is largely excluded) is an insufficient substitute for his corporeal shortcomings: "'Do you know, I am really fond of you?' she said, smiling down on the bracelet. Yet, with the words on her lips, she was thinking how different old arms were from young ones, how different Judge Honeywell's embrace was from the embrace of Angus, who was both impetuous and violent in his tenderness" (RC 110), and she therefore concludes about her marriage that "there's too much fondling in it" (RC 134). As the novel proceeds and she is forced to confront her visceral disgust at physical intimacy with the generally kind but senescent judge, Annabel reaches a startling conclusion that marriage under these conditions isn't just distasteful but something much worse: "I didn't know how *immoral* marriage can be. . . . When you dislike a person. When you simply can't bear to have him near you. [. . .] as soon as he comes into the room, I can't think of anything except the fear that he will want to be affectionate" (RC 198, my emphasis). Far from the self-abnegating morality of an earlier generation, Annabel will not subordinate her own sexual desires to more abstract imperatives: even her mother reluctantly (and temporarily, since she expresses no consistent viewpoint) concedes the fact to Annabel, for these days "You can't bring moral pressure to bear upon a physical aversion" (RC 208).

Annabel's revision of sexual morality precisely as a libidinal aesthetic stands in direct contrast with that of her mother, Bella, who is "by instinct rather than by theory, a pragmatist" and who had "found that few acts and still fewer reactions were either good or bad in general, but merely moral or immoral when applied to a particular circumstance" (RC 178). Yet as an ironic inversion of Annabel's growing recognition, the reader sees in Bella one who judges the Judge *too* pragmatically, motivated by the fact that she depends upon him financially: she sees him as physically "withered and parched and brittle as a dead leaf; yet, when estimated by moral values, which are of course the only permanent values, a most wonderful man" (RC 234). This is why ten years later Glasgow would describe how that "invincible good sense of Mrs. Upchurch was stirred if not shaken away from its anchor of pragmatic morality" (RC xii): pragmatism, she might have said, could not be pragmatic enough when it came to the means by which gender ideologies might be dislodged rather than perpetuated. It emphasized embodied adaptation without recognizing just how distasteful pragmatic adaptation might be when forced to sleep next to particular bodies. The threat that modern women pose to Honeywell's psychological security lies not in their irrepressible sexuality but in their willing ability to assert that sexuality, so he understands women as the passive creatures of their own libidinal impulses unrestrained by reason: "There are women," he recalls, "(having a wide theoretical knowledge of character) who, though virtuous by instinct recognize no ultimate authority beyond emotion" instead of a "balanced mind where sober reason was in the ascendent" (*RC* 152).

The now familiar belief that women destroy rational and creative abilities recurs throughout the novel: reminded by Amanda that Honeywell "never wrote the great book on law we used to talk over," the Judge thinks, "What long, what unconscionable memories women had for emotion!" and blames his failure on the pleasures of women: "'I've had two of the best wives in the world,' he added dutifully, 'and they have made me too comfortable'" (*RC* 141). Indeed, "that is one of the reasons I didn't write my book. I doubt if a great book, even on law, was ever written by a really happy man" (*RC* 141). By openly articulating the implicit gender ideology at the heart of a literary tradition stretching at least to the eighteenth century, Honeywell is finally incapable of judging his own failed judgment; simultaneously, the reader is forced to recognize the pitifully unreasonable insufficiency—and physically distasteful—implications of his worldview as the basis for either a physical relationship or ethical culture.

Freedom, Morality, and the Duty to Be Sexy

The insuperable structural irony of the novel in its framing of law's relationship to politics and experience appears in the final scenes, wherein the Judge persists in his delusion that "freedom" is merely a contingently embodied set of negative restrictions to be removed. What Glasgow calls irony, the novel stages as a critique of both disembodied reason and unreflective physicalism: this is a cutting critique of Kantian morality and duty as a means to happiness and proffers instead the idea that the recognition and indulgence of sexual desire are preferable to "duty"—ethically, morally, and as a component of lived experience, even aesthetically—as the justification for women's moral or ethical action. The value of duty is, after all, the central point of contention between sexually conservative and sexually radical actors in the novel: the Judge first agrees to support Annabel and her mother not because he's attracted to her but because he claims "'It is my duty to think of Cordelia's relatives, in whom she took a motherly interest. It is my duty,' he repeated earnestly" (*RC* 18). For Edmonia it is just this emphasis on duty that grates uncomfortably with her bodily desires: "That is the trouble with all of you in Queenborough, especially the women," she tells Gamaliel. "You look as if you had lived on duty and it hadn't agreed with you" (*RC* 59). When Annabel leaves him for a more vigorous and youthful partner, he laments that "The world has found nothing to take the place of duty, especially in a woman's life" (RC 182), and despite the fact that neither Bella Upchurch nor the Judge fits the role of sentimentally moustache-twirling villain or evil stepmother, Annabel's mother agrees: she wants her daughter be happy but also feels that Annabel "ought to have sacrificed feeling to duty, as women used to do when we put religious principles before personal emotions" (RC 235). This recalls, of course, the good old days when "many girls had married men old enough to be their fathers or grandfathers, and yet nothing disastrous had come of it, nothing, at least, with which husbands, aided by duty or the fear of living, had not been able to deal. Women had known then how to live without love, just as they had known how to live without beauty or happiness" (RC 207–8). This is a sentiment with which Annabel's mother not only agrees but attributes precisely to the animating spirit of the novel: "It all came back, Mrs. Upchurch decided, to the lost idea of duty. 'The judge was right,' she thought despondently. 'You can't hold people in when you take the sense of duty away.' And not duty alone, but remorse also, which she had found even more efficacious in unlawful love, appeared to have flown on wings of levity and ridicule" (RC 199). Indeed, Bella "had considered the disadvantages, in man or woman, of an incurably amorous habit of mind," and concludes that "even the insidious irony of the modern point of view had scarcely damaged the popular superstition that love and happiness are interchangeable terms" (RC 187).

Readers recognize that Bella is once again incorrect because it is precisely the "irony of the modern point of view" that Annabel has adopted, simultaneously distancing herself from habitual modes of thinking and enabling her to recognize that her own somatic desires and aversions are just as important as the rational evaluation of her circumstances. Her point of view evolves and develops to the point where the novel might be understood as an anti-Romantic, feminist Bildungsroman, as Annabel recognizes her own relationship to longer gendered traditions: "So many women chain themselves to their own fears, and pretend they are being noble. They call the chain they have made duty; but, after all, they are not noble; they are only afraid of life [. . .] courage to be yourself is the greatest virtue of all" (RC 224). Annabel reframes the very category of morality from Kantian adherence to duty and law to the rejection of that law in favor of somatic desire and pleasure; "love" and "happiness" do indeed become interchangeable terms, so long as "love" is understood as a contingent set of dispositions toward pleasure under the aegis of "freedom," and so long as the decision is one made in accordance with individual desire. If the sorrows of young Werther could only be ameliorated by suicide, Annabel's sorrows can be rectified rather less drastically by hopping a train with her lover.

In *The Romantic Comedians*, "happiness" is narrowly construed as series of libidinal attachments that have become constrained by the intersection of ideology and economy: for the women in the novel, "freedom" to achieve "happiness" is composed of recognizing the extent to which rational autonomy—a precondition for "maturity" in the public world of Kantian enlightenment—is itself preconditioned by social and economic networks and embodied desire. When Glasgow and so many others propose irony as an antidote for sentimentality, they are suggesting an aesthetic means for achieving a political end: that is, in Glasgow's case, a recognition of the impediments to women achieving an embodied experience of "freedom" as opposed to an emphasis on purely formal "equality" under the law. The novel should be read neither as an antipragmatic reassertion of idealism—"evasive" or otherwise—nor as the promotion of a determinist materialism under which the possibility of independent judgment or freedom is rendered moot by biology and economy. If anything, *The Romantic Comedians* criticizes a triadic relationship among morality, duty, and happiness as the practical gender inequalities that persist under the guise of liberal universalism.

Glasgow knew well the prominent place this triad held in the philosophical tradition. As Kant wrote in the *Groundwork of the Metaphysics of Morals*, duty rather than desire or pragmatic results must be the engine of moral actions, for "duty is the necessity of an action from respect for law," and "an action from duty has its moral worth not in the purpose to be attained by it but in the maxim in accordance with which it is decided upon, and therefore does not depend upon the realization of the object of the action but merely upon the principle of volition in accordance with which the action is done without regard for any object of the faculty of desire."[136] Furthermore, "a free will and a will under moral laws are one and the same," and thus an assertion of "free will" is the denial of desire with no reference to results, and happiness itself is a pure function of acting in accordance with "a law, namely to promote his happiness not from inclination but from duty; and it is then that his conduct first has properly moral worth."[137] Glasgow's purpose is not to represent the pursuit of happiness stipulated as an inalienable right in the Declaration of Independence but rather what we might call a feminist Declaration of Interdependence: a recognition that normative claims to equality relying upon purely procedural, constitutional, or statutory guarantees reduce politics to the mere affirmation of preexisting narratives and thus become blind to how those narratives pragmatically function in terms of the daily lives of individuals in collectives. In opposition to the transcendental idealism of Kant or the evasive idealism of Southern sentimentalists, the joyously romping Edmonia remarks to Gamaliel with more than a hint of anarchist pleasure: "I never approved of the sour kind of duty you pretend to enjoy. On the contrary, I've always believed that happiness, any kind of happiness that does not make someone else miserable, is meritorious" (*RC* 158).

After Annabel has decamped to another city, claiming only her old clothes and leaving behind all of the expensive accoutrements of her marriage with Gamaliel, he first tries to bring her home with promises of expensive vacations and gifts. Annabel, however, has recognized her own capacity for choice, her own preference for embodied pleasures of love rather than the pleasures of shopping; moreover, she has recognized the extent to which imperatives of "morality," "duty," and "happiness" had been very narrowly defined according to the masculine prerogative represented by the Judge's legal sense of the world. She thus reframes the very category of morality from Kantian adherence to duty and law to the *rejection* of that law in favor of somatic desire and pleasure. When Honeywell finds her in a rundown hotel room waiting for her new partner, he judiciously attempts to blame himself but in the process only reveals his continued sense of the world as one in which legal and moral authority rest entirely in the world of masculine logic that he denies to Annabel: "I shall assume responsibility," he claims, failing to understand that he is speaking with a newly emancipated Annabel, who replies, "You can't. You are kind and generous, but you can't do that" (*RC* 224).

After confronting the fact that Annabel is not only happy but neither guilty nor remorseful over her actions, he attempts to take a sort of elderly high road that is another version of moral responsibility, only to be confronted with perhaps his largest shock of the novel. With paternal magnanimity he says, "Of course I shall give you your freedom," to which Annabel again replies with the kind of pleasure that Emma Goldman would approve: "I *am* free" (*RC* 226). In the face of both "internal tyrants" and "public opinion," Goldman insisted that "The right to vote, or equal civil rights, may be good demands, but true emancipation begins neither at the polls nor in courts. It begins in woman's soul. . . . It is necessary that woman . . . realize that her freedom will reach as far as her power to achieve her freedom reaches" and that "Until woman has learned to defy them all, to stand firmly on her own ground and to insist upon her own unrestricted freedom . . . she cannot call herself emancipated."[138] Annabel's "freedom" comes not from acting in accordance with a moral duty originally framed or perpetuated by Honeywell or

Hegel or Kant or anyone else but by acting in accordance with a combination of reason and desire known as "irony."

Framing the conceptual and historical tension between different forms of feminism and their relationship to different accounts of particularism and liberal universalism in this way achieves more than an intriguing critique of the role that the conventionally masculine tool of "law" should play in a feminist project. By explicitly framing this political question as a question of aesthetics, Glasgow evokes what Drucilla Cornell has recently called "somatic freedoms" outside the institutions that regulate such desires and explorations: "It is the pathos of freedom and the intensive feeling of self-empowerment arising from it that [keep] many of us going in progressive politics even when we know we cannot prove this freedom," Cornell writes, and the realm of the aesthetic may well provide a staging ground for imagining "a world in which nature and freedom can be reconciled."[139] This reconciliation won't occur in the delicate counterpoise between phenomenal necessity and noumenal freedom presented in Kantian aesthetic judgment but in the resolutely desiring body of the pragmatist feminist subject. Glasgow proposes an irony that emphasizes embodied reason of a pragmatic type: the employment of rational thought toward indeterminate outcomes, the progressive critique of regressive mythologies about women and desire. Glasgow attempts not merely to expand preexisting institutional norms (voting) or promote a version of liberal universalism that fails to account for the particularities and even generalities of experience. These are, after all, gender mythologies that "though subject to decay from within, are equally invulnerable to time and chance, enlightenment and the Darwinian hypothesis."[140]

Ellen Glasgow called attention to, deployed, and became famous for a pointedly antinostalgic irony that pronounced the welcome decay of gender codes undergirding concepts of duty, character, personality, sexuality, and identity. If Jake Barnes lost his "manhood" in the war, the Judge of *The Romantic Comedians* lost his manhood to history, and it is an occasion for comedy rather than tragedy; Gamaliel Bland Honeywell is thwarted from consummating his desire for Annabel not because he has been castrated by the war but because Annabel is in a position to refuse him and choose another lover who doesn't physically repulse her. In the end, despite all of his powers of intellect and learning, he's left to suffer in a self-recursive tailspin of negation and egoism that his legal rationality is unable to rectify: "Everything was driven out of his mind by this desperate craving for physical comfort, for the inestimable consolation of habit" (*RC* 228). His conscious mind slips in and out of a curious admixture of nostalgia for past codes of "true and pure womanhood" while his actual libidinal comfort comes not from Annabel's body or memory but from the presence of his old scientific male friend: "the doctor's urbane presence hovered over him like an embodied image of congenial habit" (*RC* 233). Despite what he has been taught over the course of the novel about the dated inappropriateness of his gender ideology in the twentieth century, he retains the central understanding of gender that has driven the society for which he is nostalgic and which has proven more resilient than suffrage advocates had hoped: "Any one with an ounce of logic would recognize that as pure paradox; but the truth was, he supposed, that paradox, not reason, was the natural law of her being" (*RC* 174).

When Annabel asserts her sexual freedom to the shocked Judge, she enacts that which Hegel found most objectionable about the Romantic ironists and Schlegel's novel *Lucinde*. But Annabel isn't Lucinde, *Lucinde* isn't *The Romantic Comedians*, and Glasgow composes a set of conclusive ironies with a very particular sort of resolution. This is not the irony in fiction valorized by Cleanth Brooks and Robert Penn Warren, who "would not endorse an irony which precluded resolution."[141] Rather, Glasgow's irony offers an unstable irresolution, which highlights the futile egoism of the protagonist and his dearest convictions. If "irony" for Hemingway and Fitzgerald indicates detached mockery and sophisticated alienation, respectively, it also indicates for both of them that which is dissolved by the presence of women, the creative energy that women dissipate and the form of social masculinity that is enervated and disrupted by the intrusion of women into the community. The Judge is enraptured by the very sight of Annabel from his first meeting and never stops perceiving her specifically as a literary figuration rather than an embodied subject: he is first struck by her beauty "as if, he found himself thinking sentimentally, she had walked straight out of allegory" (*RC* 14), and much later "he felt, with sudden anguish, that she was a symbol, not only of his lost paradise, but of all the burning desire of the world" (*RC* 167). If his pleasure and his pain are a function of perceiving Annabel as tropes, neither compares to the psychological dissonance occasioned by Annabel's ironic, modernist disruption of his sentimentalism: he begins to recognize his own inadequacies and her rising powers when he comes across her "with her eyes raised to a futurist sunset of black and red" with "Some poetic rhythm in her attitude" (*RC* 171); there is no hope in classic metaphors in the face of new subjects, and he is "tormented, without intermission, ever since the afternoon when he had stolen upon his young wife while she watched the futurist sunset" (*RC* 185).

For Glasgow, irony indicates something much different from either futurist fragmentation of the body or New Critical coherence of texts and bodies. Simultaneously "Modernist" and political in the firmly nonelectoral, nonproceduralist sense of the word, she presents irony as a formal quality of texts and a disposition of mind and feeling that can be produced in aesthetic experience, and which can consequently serve as an engine of political reform via the reform of the libidinal individual. As Edmonia remarks to Gamaliel, who remains scandalized by her sexual freedoms, "you could have forgiven my committing a sin if you hadn't feared that I had committed a pleasure as well," and the remedy for this collectively dogmatic opposition to women's freedom and pleasure is both coded and, in the context of Glasgow's critical remarks, quite clear: "America is an anæmic nation," Edmonia continues, "and the danger with national anæmia is that it runs to fanaticism in the brain" (*RC* 159). Anemia is a malady distinguished by a shortage of both blood and iron, which can be cured collectively only by curing individual bodies. Glasgow moves from iron to irony (and back in her 1935 novel *Vein of Iron*), girded by the recognition that the road to individuality runs first through both sociality and universality. It is also emphatically an irony that is both public and feminist, pragmatic in a way that counters a vein of perceived conservatism within philosophical pragmatism itself.

Richard Rorty writes that he "cannot go on to claim that there could or ought to be a culture whose public rhetoric is ironist. I cannot imagine a culture which socialized its youth in such a way as to make them continually dubious about their own process of socialization. Irony seems inherently a private matter."[142] This is a sentiment to which Ellen Glasgow might reply: "Yes, it is precisely your inability to imagine that culture that ironic fiction and a feminist rhetoric of irony should address."[143] Glasgow insisted that "the concluding paragraph of *The Romantic Comedians* echoed the keynote of the book, and reflected the ironic mood," and the irony here lies in a recognition of the relationship among habitual language, habitual thought, and the inability to escape ideological habits pertaining to gender.[144] Gamaliel lies desiring his young nurse—who reminds him of his mother, not of the young Annabel who has learned irony—and foundering in "No slow judicial process; no firmly drilled reasoning; no logical necessity" but "Merely a shimmering void of sensation into which his spirit sank as a wounded bird sinks in the afterglow" (*RC* 232). Glasgow's free indirect discourse returns via the wounded bird to the beginning of the novel, and one recognizes that Annabel has developed a mode of consciousness promising something that all of the alienation and stern true words of Hemingway couldn't have imagined:

a form of emancipated feminist freedom for an embodied mind. If, as Glasgow wrote in the preface to *The Romantic Comedians*, "The comic spirit [is] an enemy to unreason in any form" and "its irony was suddenly spiced with malice," this is a malice that is reserved for those who lack the iron to get the irony.[145]

Irony and the End

Political theorists and literary critics frequently arrogate a variety of powers to "irony" in the service of feminist democratic action, but it is just as frequently ambiguous how "irony" distinctively serves to connect philosophical and literary practice. When Seyla Benhabib writes that "What women can do today is to restore irony to the dialectic, by deflating the pompous march of historical necessity," it's clearly a direct riposte to Hegel; it is less clear what precisely might be restored, even if the concept is subsequently redeployed in explicitly postmodern literary contexts.[146] In suggesting new ways of adjudicating a putative split between reason and emotion, "intellect" and "feeling," a feminist modernist irony entails much more than mere masculine alienation as a hard form of antisentimentalism that, like the electoral franchise itself, had recently been opened to and practiced by women. Rather, "irony" suggests an inextricably linked mode of aesthetic production and a means of aesthetic reception, structured by highly gendered philosophical and literary figuring of reason and desire, which pragmatically reject the obverse ideals of "disinterest" and aesthetic rapture as a means of both individual and even national renewal.[147] The idea of modernist women "becoming" ironic must be understood as a broad cultural figuring of the particular challenges presented by a preexisting discourse about the political role of art, which split gendered particularity and the imagined universality of both political rights and literary value. On the one hand, "irony" would mean the capacity to conceive of relationships among gendered particulars and universals, to experience sensible pleasure without either surrendering to aesthetic rapture or reducing "beauty" to a mere symbol of "morality." On the other hand, it would simultaneously mean the subjective "impulse" to compose texts that were legible as a critique of the double bind in which women found themselves, enjoying formal equality under the laws of supposedly free electoral politics but neither experiencing a sensation of "freedom" nor seeing material changes as a result of exercising their franchise.

It may seem ideologically quaint that Fitzgerald's characters could sneer at the sexual codes enforced by mass culture, wherein the boys

intend to watch a play "tersely called 'The Woman'" and they ironically "presume that she will 'pay,'" while a coterie of Harvard men won't
"complain about conventional morality" but will "complain rather of
the mediocre heretics who seize upon the findings of sophistication and
adopt the pose of a moral freedom to which they are by no means entitled by their intelligences."[148] Yet at this late date, some critics still implicitly imagine irony as a dangerous or vexed achievement for modernist
women writers: where "Poetry by women need not protect itself with
irony or modesty of indirection" and where "the pervasive moral confusion in early-twentieth-century women's writing—the hard edge, the
bitter cynicism of a Djuna Barnes or a Mina Loy—was the ultimate price
that women writers paid for using irony as their instrument of choice."[149]
If my formulation sounds like an explicitly post-Kantian, post-Hegelian
account of aesthetic judgment that promotes irony as a disposition to
both analysis and pleasure, this is no mistake. But rather than taking
my word for it, consider an exchange between Amelia Ryder and her
husband's mistress, Kate-Careless, in Djuna Barnes's raucous faux-Eliz-
abethan satirical novel *Ryder*: "'I smell irony,' said Kate. 'You smell judgment, 'tis the same thing,' said Amelia, 'to the common nose.'"[150]

3 / The Focus of Satire: Public Opinions of Propaganda in the *U.S.A.* of John Dos Passos

Irony is perhaps democracy's best instrument.
> —PUBLIC OPINION QUARTERLY, 1938

You cannot produce trenchant political satire—at least not in America in this period—if your political horizon is the Wagner Act.
> —MARY MCCARTHY, PARTISAN REVIEW, 1938[1]

Parody, humor, caricature, and satire all have long literary histories, all are theoretically vexed, and all rely upon some version of irony. At the same time, the connotation and function of each of these terms produce a particular understanding of irony, until all of the terms begin to circulate as a mutually constitutive constellation of denotations and connotations. While adding yet another term into the already unruly account of irony risks obscuring rather than clarifying the individual terms and their relationship to one another, the case of satire is particularly central to the modernist literary aesthetics of facts and values. As the last chapter's account of gendered irony suggests, the political implications of this aesthetic problem are particularly pointed when it comes to irony and satire as purported antidotes to sentimentality and other politically contested forms of aesthetic affect.[2]

The close affinity between satire and sentimentality poses a series of problems concerning the rapidly evolving cultural and individual experiences of modernity. In 1857, one might plausibly describe a century-long tradition wherein "Satire and sentiment represent the extreme opposite poles of conversation and authorship"; by 1911, however, the *Encyclopedia Britannica* could observe that "It is indeed exceedingly difficult to define the limits between satire and the regions of literary sentiment into which it shades" and that therefore "One remarkable feature of the modern age is the union of caricature (*q.v.*) with literature."[3] Setting aside the taxonomic difficulties inherent in distinguishing caricature from other varieties of satire, the problem here comes down to "feeling." As

Jonathan Greenberg has recently argued, "it is precisely the difficulty of the distinction between sentiment and sentimentality that is at issue" in many accounts of modernist affect: "Once feeling is understood as potentially sentimental," he writes, "all appeals to feeling run the same risk" of being aesthetically, ideologically, and politically suspect.[4] With this in mind, trying to account for the political function of satire—real or imagined—within a genealogy of political irony raises a thorny paradox: while irony is a central component of modern satire, and modern satire produces aesthetic responses that are nigh indistinguishable from those produced by sentimentalism, irony is frequently figured as an anesthetic, the "safest antidote to sentimental decay" and the "studied absence of emotion."[5] The seemingly paradoxical movement, where aesthetic irony both produces bodily sensations and wards them off, raises another question: how does one reconcile the putative dissolution of sentimentalism under evolving canons of modernist literary value, with what Steven Weisenburger has described as "One of the remaining, unchallenged shibboleths of formalist New Criticism": Northrop Frye's 1944 claim that "the satirist cannot 'speak for the twentieth century' because satire itself has allegedly 'gone stale and mouldy'"?[6]

The first step in unraveling this knot is to situate Frye's proclamation about satire—which he most succinctly defined as "militant irony"—in a line of other proclamations about the disappearance of satire, for the claim is neither uniquely Frye's nor uniquely bound to New Criticism or to any other brand of formalism.[7] Like the "end of irony," the putative "end of satire" has a history, which suggests how all of these terms serve as capacious rhetorical repositories for the figuration of broader cultural and political norms: in particular, for expressing anxieties about the change or disappearance of norms themselves. In the first century CE, surveying the state of social and moral decay occasioned by the transition from republic to empire, Juvenal famously found that "difficile est saturam non scribere."[8] While Juvenal's situation rendered it difficult to write in a mode other than satire, a few millennia later Theodor Adorno inverted what he called "Juvenal's Error" to indict a late modernity, wherein the collapse of ideology and reality made it "difficult *to* write satire [*Schwer, eine Satire zu schreiben*]."[9]

Adorno was not the first to diagnose this definitively modern but not exclusively modernist condition: as early as 1854, a British writer observed that "we are told sometimes, that the day of Satire is past."[10] The title of an 1899 column in the *Atlantic Monthly* asks "Why Have We No Satire?"—a question that *Life* magazine would later refine as a problem of audience by asking, "Why is it that America will not tolerate satire?"[11] Ambrose Bierce defined the mode in *The Devil's Dictionary* as "An obsolete kind of literary composition" because "In this country satire never had more than a sickly and uncertain existence."[12] Satire classically and conventionally is understood as a literary mode that both relies upon and disrupts stable social and political norms, thereby maintaining a recognizable moral—and frequently conservative—aspect. Therefore responses to the rapidly shifting parameters of cultural, social, political, or moral norms would inevitably include literary symptoms such as obsolescence of the mode that most relied upon those norms. When it comes to the disappearance of satire in a social and political "situation, which needs it more than any ever did," the reasons that are adduced for satire's disappearance reveal a concomitant anxiety about the disappearance of publics that either want satire or would be capable of recognizing satire when they saw it.[13]

In 1913, for example, a San Francisco protégé of Bierce named Herman Scheffauer attributed what he called "The Death of Satire" to the fact that "the modern mind is not in sympathy with the means of satire," due to "the commercializing and effeminatizing of taste" wherein "the potent masculine product of satire would meet with no sympathy or toleration" and thus "Reform, the true end of all satire, is slowly to be brought about by reason, and not by flagellation."[14] Doubts about the health of the genre and the public appeared even in notably self-aware, ironic political publications such as the *Masses*, which observed in 1912 that "in profit-ridden capitalistic America Dame Satire has fallen into disrepute" and "editors no longer cultivate her . . . writers and artists shun her."[15] By 1915, Van Wyck Brooks followed the same logic by asserting that it was "perhaps just as well that Cervantes lived and died in Spain three hundred years ago. Had he been born an American of the twentieth century he might have found the task of satire an all too overwhelming one."[16] The writer for *Atlantic Monthly* lamented that satire was on the outs because "nothing is powerful enough to centralize all our thoughts. Our conduct shows that we are looking for a thought capable of dominating us" and because "The tendency of modern life is to reduce all mankind, externally, to rigid similarity."[17] Expanding his dictionary definition into a brief, comedic philosophical dialogue, Bierce in 1909 satirically diagnosed similar reasons for what he called "The Passing of Satire": "Satire cannot co-exist with such mollycoddle sentiments as 'the brotherhood of man,' 'the trusteeship of wealth,' moral irresponsibility, tolerance, socialism and the rest of it."[18] In a different issue of *Life*, another writer observes that "the experts appear to be of the opinion that the American public is not up to it," asserting that

"The real reason why satire is not understood by Americans of the present generation is that events take place and conditions change so rapidly that they do not become fixed in the public mind long enough to furnish a basis for satire. Another reason is that so many Americans are satires in themselves. Prohibition is real satire on humanity. So is war. So is theology."[19] These differing analyses share the common anxiety about the interplay of changing material conditions producing a homogenous public whose primary characteristic combines degraded literary sensibilities with desire for unanimity, while the last few sentences neatly encapsulate a dilemma in accounting for satire's contested possibilities as an engine of political change: on the one hand, writers express a sense that the experience of modernity is simply too fast and dynamic to sustain or ascertain the stable norms upon which satire and a capable audience for satire would rely; on the other hand, the collapse of ideology and reality into one another obviates the very idea of cultural or ethical norms as a reliable guide for praxis.

As with the broader case of irony, one must resist the temptation to adduce an empirical response to what is fundamentally a theoretical question; although dactylic hexameters had lost their appeal to both readers and writers of satires, a wide variety of satires were and are still produced. If satire's disappearance is evident only by proclamation rather than by bibliography, what remains interesting is the cultural logic that undergirds descriptions of that supposed disappearance. Perhaps satire, like other formal critiques, was difficult because the world itself had become so familiarly grotesque, the definition of folly and vice so absurdly inverted that their correction and punishment were more worthy of ridicule than the infractions themselves. At the same time, perhaps the treasured American myth of universalism was itself a lie no longer robust enough to structure supposed common sense. If it had never really been the case that rationality and stable national norms of consensus ruled the day, with disagreements neutralized via the state (with federalist factions or with liberal recourse to the ultimate authority of natural law), by mid-century it also seemed increasingly plausible that the political tragedy of American life was due to *too much* rather than *not enough* agreement among factions. If so, proclamations of satire's demise are necessarily bound to the question of how to find a stable point of ethical and aesthetic adjudication in a world where morality was decreasingly imagined to be a transhistorical, transnational, or transideological phenomenon, where recourse to mere convention or tradition was recognized as a poor source of either ethics or etiquette.

Phrased this way, the problem of satire and irony in the twentieth century seems inextricable from the problems diagnosed by both Frankfurt School theorists and the consensus historians who had learned so much from them. These are thinkers who, in the words of James Livingston, proposed that the "titanic struggles of the past had typically (not always) taken place within a cross-class ideological agreement, or rather a cultural system, which *pacified* social conflict by *naturalizing* possessive individualism and liberal capitalism."[20] Adorno seems to reject the position of earlier critics, claiming that

> The impossibility of satire today should not be blamed, as sentimentality is apt to do, on the relativism of values, the absence of binding norms. Rather, agreement itself, the formal *a priori* of irony, has given way to universal agreement of content. As such it presents the only fitting target [*Gegenstand*] for irony and at the same time pulls the ground from under its feet. Irony's medium, the difference between ideology and reality, has disappeared.[21]

Yet Adorno's very phrasing—ironically, echoing the earlier critics in culture-industrialized *Life* magazine—suggests that the two positions are not quite as opposed as they might seem and rather represent the structural definitions of irony and satire themselves, which always exceed their merely literary incarnations: reality was never *not* ideological and always admitted the presence of *disagreement* as both the formal *a priori* and the inevitable reception of irony and satire.[22]

Thus anxieties about the disappearance of traditional—or even reliable or desirable—norms for reconciling individual desire with collective goods gradually combine with anxieties about the disappearance of a rational public capable of understanding and evaluating information; together, they form a kind of logically circular whole accounting for the role different forms of information play in the liberal political imaginary. It is not simply that potentially "political" information requires stable social norms to be comprehensible but that rational publics exist because of that information. At the same time, however, the existence of those publics is one of the norms that precedes the information that creates them. And it is into this nearly tautological totality that different kinds of information and different kinds of publics intersect: newspapers, novels, and satires. As early as 1925, sociologist Frederick Elmore Lumley included a chapter titled "Satire" in his *Means of Social Control*, arguing that those who claim "newspapers, with their swift and infallible readiness, make [satire's] use unnecessary" fail to recognize the newspaper itself as a means of social control.[23] Even if the postwar "age is more sentimental and takes less joy in the agonized writhings of those stung by satire," and even if "satire fails against the gigantic and lurid evils of the age," nonetheless "Satire is not dead; it may have changed its dress. These two facts—the quantity of satire and the universal fear of it—when put together yield something akin to certainty that this device has been a powerful social control agency."[24]

This confluence of news, satire, and novels appears not only in popular journalism and sociology but within literary texts themselves. Consider, for example, a section in Ruth McKenney's 1939 novel *Industrial Valley*, titled "Satire, February 24, 1933." The brief episode describes a group of rich Republican supporters of Herbert Hoover who throw a country club party "understood to be a clever satire on the Inauguration Ball in Washington to be held the same night. No further news of bank closings."[25] Here, where journalistic "news" focuses on the convivial fripperies of the rich rather than causes and effects of economic collapse, the absurd burlesque of democracy seems to exceed the conventional hyperbolic tools of satire, so satire targets the collective disposition toward the information (and lack thereof) bolstering the elite beneficiaries of monopoly capitalism. That is, when it becomes impossible to distinguish among actions of people, news of those actions, and literary modes that ridicule those actions, satire describes a mode of absurd life as much as the literary mode intended to reflect upon how different representations lead publics to think and feel about that situation. In the context of a long crisis of democratic publicity, the satire of John Dos Passos's *U.S.A.* trilogy engages a problem much more profound than the correction of folly and vice: in short, the problem of how to provide individuals and collectives with the kinds of information that are necessary preconditions for democratic judgment, for adjudicating the positions and possibilities of individuals in collectivities.

1938 and Before

In 1938, the publication of *The 42nd Parallel*, *1919*, and *The Big Money* as a single novel provoked a flood of essays debating how John Dos Passos's *U.S.A.* related socially, aesthetically, and politically to the U.S.A.[26] While assessments of the novel's literary politics ranged from Lionel Trilling's ambivalent judgment that it was "the important novel of the decade" to Mike Gold's bald declaration that the novel and Dos Passos himself were full of "merde," reviewers recognized the trilogy not only as satire but as both a new form of the novel and a novel form of news. Jean-Paul Sartre, for example, observed that "John Dos Passos reports all

his characters' utterances to us in the style of a statement to the Press";
two months later, the poet and critic Delmore Schwartz echoed and
expanded Sartre's seemingly self-evident assertion:

> If we think . . . of the newspaper as a representation of Ameri-
> can life, we get some idea of the basis of John Dos Passos' enor-
> mous novel. It is not merely that one of the devices of this novel is
> the "Newsreel" and consists of an arrangement of quotations from
> newspapers of the past thirty years; nor that another device is the
> "Camera eye," and still another consists of biographies of Amer-
> icans who have for the most part been prominent in the news-
> papers. It is in its whole sense of American life and in its formal
> character . . . that Dos Passos' novel seems to . . . derive from the
> newspaper.[27]

For all of *U.S.A.*'s aesthetic debts to modernist cinema, it is worth recalling that *U.S.A.* is a novel in print that is not only formally marked by
its invocations of "the news" but thoroughly about journalism and the
degraded masquerade of journalism known as "public relations." The
famously fragmented Newsreel sections comprise real and imagined
newspaper headlines, several characters in the novel are journalists, and
several others routinely influence the press as public relations agents.[28]
The *political* implications of this intermingling of novel and news, print
and visual culture, have always been more contentious.[29] Whereas
Schwartz considered *U.S.A.* to be a political disappointment—"the greatest monument of naturalism because it betrays so fully the poverty and
disintegration inherent in that method"—Sartre found that the novel
instilled a "revolutionary" spirit in him and famously regarded Dos Passos as "the greatest writer of our time."[30] In the context of the pitched
political battles about aesthetics and politics among the 1930s Left, there
are many reasons why a novel would frustrate *Partisan Review* critic
Schwartz while invigorating Sartre. Like many fellow-traveling reviewers of *U.S.A.*, Schwartz objected that the novel emphasized the negative
"facts" of political oppression without delineating the positive "values"
that might help readers envision the goals of political praxis. Sartre,
meanwhile, found revolutionary potential in the novel's presentation
of value-laden facts and in Dos Passos's refusal to compose artificially
hopeful blueprints for action.[31]

Perhaps discouraged by these contradictory political stances, critics
tend to read the facts and values of the different sections as a totalized
fragmentation of individual and situation: "Like Dos Passos," Jacques
Rancière writes, the "revolutionary painter or novelist . . . will represent

a shattered reality: fragmented stories of erratic individual destinies that translate, by their illogicality, the logic of the capitalist order."[32] This is a kind of data explosion that mimetically represents a national consciousness shattered by World War I, that sketches historical context for the more conventional aspects of the narrative, or that resembles modernist montage in order to express a kind of alienated disgust at new media technologies.[33] Dos Passos's apparently chaotic juxtaposition of song lyrics, speeches, and incomplete chunks of news copy is thus understood to exemplify a multigeneric staging of "is" and "ought," an irony that has itself become curiously emblematic of both high-modernist and high-postmodernist literary practice.[34] When combined with the aesthetic critique known as "satire," this fragmentation produces an affective irony that "merely focuses our gaze sharply upon the contrast between things as they should be and as they are"; as Donald Pizer concludes, the "underlying motive for [Dos Passos's] distortion of the 'factual' lies in Dos Passos' powerful ironic and thus satiric vision of the immense distance between verbal construct and actuality in twentieth-century America. *U.S.A.* is thus throughout, and not merely in the Newsreels and biographies, the work of a satiric moralist."[35]

These critiques represent a broader disposition toward the last century of American literary politics: that "irony" is the literary mode best suited to reproducing the violently maintained "distance" between the facts of American existence and the values articulated in foundational American political documents (e.g., the Declaration of Independence and the Constitution). In other words, when contradictory "facts" and "values" are represented in close textual proximity to one another, critics frequently name the representational tactic and the hermeneutic effect "irony"; when a stable element of moral critique or ridicule is recognizable (especially with the stylistically heady admixture of the comic, the burlesque, the grotesque, or the painfully profane), one finds satire.[36] That Dos Passos is perceived specifically as a moralist is perhaps responsible for Michael Denning's perception that "the book no longer lives for American readers."[37]

Indeed, for critics writing in the decades immediately following *U.S.A.*, it is just this sort of reversal-revelation model of irony that was understood as a political limitation of naturalism in general and of Left 1930s fiction in particular. As Alfred Kazin influentially asserted in 1942, one of the fundamental problems with both social-realist and naturalist fiction was that the muckraking aspirations to "accuracy" precluded more politically and semiotically complicated forms of representation: that "the greatest creative irony the reportorial mind of the thirties could establish" was "a picture of Negro farmers wandering on the road, eating their bread under a billboard poster furnished by the National Association of Manufacturers—'America Enjoys the Highest Standard of Living in the World.'"[38] This is only part of the story of American irony in *U.S.A.*, however, when the novel is understood as engaging and revising prominent 1920s and 1930s debates about the relationship among politics, publics, news, and the aesthetics of visual and print information. Until the relatively recent popularity of *The Onion* and *The Daily Show* as sources of political information, the distortions of satire and the instability of verbal irony were anathema to the assumptions behind the function of the news, which is not to say that satirical undoing of the news is a recent phenomenon. Amber Day has recently described "the newer forms of irony, parody, and satire" as possessing a "striking seriousness of purpose, where irony is put to use in the service of real political aims, pointing to flaws in the existing political discussion and gesturing toward possible solutions," but we might also look to earlier modernist interventions into the tradition holding that useful political information requires words to "mean what they say."[39] As Bliss Perry observed in 1912, irony had become "less often used by pamphleteers and journalists. It is a delicate rhetorical weapon, and journalists who aim at the great public are increasingly afraid to use it, lest the readers miss the point. . . . it might not be understood, and the crowd must not be left in doubt."[40] Yet it is precisely doubts produced by irony that provide a vital heuristic for *U.S.A.*'s engagement with political journalism and an aesthetics of information that can account for satire. Here again, "aesthetics" refers not only to the conventional, formal study of art and beauty but in the full etymological sense as those kinds of sensory, corporeal responses to certain representations, signs that do not just fall upon but actually constitute embodied perception: this is the sense in which Rancière has argued that "aesthetics can be understood in a Kantian sense—re-examined perhaps by Foucault—as the system of *a priori* forms determining what presents itself to sense experience. It is a delimitation of spaces and times, of the visible and the invisible, of speech and noise, that simultaneously determines the place and the stakes of politics as a form of experience."[41]

Reading the novel through the focused constellation of irony and publics produces a particular view not only of *U.S.A.*'s political significance but of the possibilities for satire to play a central role in activist literary aesthetics that the newspaper should have played.[42] The Enlightenment political ideal running from Kant (e.g., in "Pax Perpetua" and "What Is Enlightenment") through the authors of the *Federalist* and beyond relies upon a polity of citizen-readers publicly using reason to evaluate information circulated via a free press; as Dos Passos and many of his contemporaries recognized, however, the rise of professional "public relations" around World War I starkly revealed the extent to which reading publics did not preexist such information but were manipulated and even constituted by it. Dos Passos's novel does more than merely document the increasingly prominent role that aestheticized information plays in political decision making: it articulates a pointed riposte to the increasingly dominant discourses of corporate- and state-sponsored propaganda and repurposes the lessons of advertising and public relations into a novel distinguished by what we should understand as a decidedly activist form of aesthetic irony and satire. In short, Dos Passos deploys satire as a mode of activist irony to educate readers' aesthetic sense of print, image, and text in the age of public relations and hopelessly corrupt information.

New Problems, the Problem of News, and Problems with Publics

U.S.A. narrates the merger of mainstream journalism and public relations, on the one hand, and corporate and state power, on the other, showing how the mergers are not only related but mutually constitutive. As Mark Wollaeger has shown in a British context, the distinction between modernism and propaganda is vexed, to say the least, and the two constructs are "Neither uniformly antithetical nor identical," for "modernism and propaganda were sometimes agonistic, sometimes allied, and sometimes nearly indistinguishable."[43] Both Dos Passos and his characters understand that propaganda seeks to identify, constitute, and manipulate a unified, tractable public; by contrast, *U.S.A.* neither depicts nor strives to produce the kind of political consensus required of party politics running from liberalism to fascism. This is not simply because the ironies of *U.S.A.* represent and reproduce the tragic gap between American democratic theory and highly antidemocratic American practice. Rather, the trilogy offers an ironic, interpretive pluralism that is radically at odds with conventional understandings of what it means to produce useful political information: the ironies of *U.S.A.* seek to depict and produce the interpretive conditions for politics and information to be reimagined through the embodied individual. Put plainly, Dos Passos's fiction doesn't simply inform readers about the material facts of American life that determine the behavior and delimit the choices made by individual political agents. Rather, *U.S.A.* deploys what we might call a postnaturalist satire, using the form of the novel to present information as a sensible *aesthetic* exchange, a recognition that Dos Passos thought would be necessary for new political communities to emerge and for extant, marginalized political communities to be recognized.

After witnessing the lynching of the Wobblies and the suppression of both the *Masses* and *Seven Arts*, Dos Passos had a keen sense of what happens when one is able to use unstable language to provoke determinate courses of action. He also suggests, however, that a programmatic element *is* necessary for revolutionary change, lest the infinite negativity of unresolved irony produce no praxis at all: like Walter Lippmann, Jürgen Habermas, and Richard Rorty after him, he requires a hand to steer the political vanguard, a situation in which the aesthetic becomes a mere instrumental subdivision of politics, but employs irony to dispose readers toward contingent, temporary stabilizations of meaning rather than toward a final linguistic or historical truth. *U.S.A.* is precisely about the political implications of this double bind, and Dos Passos's engagement with this problematic suggests that genuine praxis will be preceded by repositioning the aesthetic abstraction of the nation-state itself *as an irresolvable double-bind between fact and value*. Rather than relegating irony to the realm of the private and calling for public discourse to remain sincerely rational, and rather than banishing embodied interpretation to the realm of the purely ideological, Dos Passos shows how radical politics requires information framed by and filtered through the rational feelings of a very public irony. The novel's disposition toward the public, toward nations, and toward individuals actively resists resolution to produce a definition of the United States *as* lack of resolution, *as* the unstable position between discourses of "fact" and discourses of "value." To redefine the nation thusly is to identify a fundamental tension between individual rights and collective decisions and to compose a pointed critique of the state under conditions described by Kenneth Burke's "essential paradox of federalism" or Chantal Mouffe's or Rancière's "democratic paradox."[44]

Newspapers have long been considered to play a central role in defining national identities and public consciousness, but from his earliest days as a novelist Dos Passos had reminded readers that a putatively "free" press does not entail the free circulation of ideas or unbiased information. In *One Man's Initiation—1917*, for example, a soldier attributes the devastation around him to "this new particular vintage of lies that has been so industriously pumped out of the press and the pulpit," eagerly consumed by "stupid damn-fool people" who believe "that the Bible was written in God's own handwriting and that the newspapers tell the truth."[45] Waving flags isn't enough to produce bellicose obedience: "the

gradual unbaring of teeth, gradual lulling to sleep of people's humanity and sense" is produced by both waving flags and "the phrases, the
phrases. . . . America, as you know, is ruled by the press. And the press
is ruled by whom?"[46] If it took a disillusioned soldier to ask that question
in 1920, by 1925 even a drunk thespian in *Manhattan Transfer* knows the
answer: the newspaper as the "fountain of national life is poisoned at the
source" by the "interests of advertisers and bondholders."[47] In *The 42nd
Parallel*, the public distribution of ideas is more overtly hindered: When
the young Chicago boy Fenian "Mac" McCreary attempts to distribute
his uncle's Socialist pamphlets, he is accosted and chased away by a
policeman who demands a "permit to distribute them handbills."[48] Later,
when Mac arrives in Nevada to help print an IWW newspaper during a
miners' strike, he poses as an itinerant bookseller—drawing on his early
occupation as peddler of pornography, knowing that mine owners are
threatened by newspapers but not by "literature"—and is allowed to pass
by private soldiers whose orders are to detain "goddamn agitators, the I
Won't Work outfit."[49]

Dos Passos understood the danger that such overt censorship posed
to democracy: he had witnessed the U.S. government directly and indi-
rectly suppress Socialist and radical information during World War I,
activities wearily described in *1919* as "indictments, the Masses trial, the
Wobbly trial, Wilson cramming the jails."[50] As Lippmann had pointed
out in 1920, censorship of the American press was a venerable tradition
dating to the very first days of the colonies: "Volume I, Number I, of
the first American newspaper was published in Boston on September 24,
1690. It was called *Public Occurrences*. The second issue did not appear
because the Governor and Council suppressed it."[51] As Dos Passos
and Lippmann well knew, the importance of a "free press" was hardly
incidental to conceptions of American democracy but was explicitly
addressed by the earliest theorists of American federalism, from James
Madison and Alexander Hamilton to Alexis de Tocqueville, who imagined that the press would distribute objective "facts" to help rational citizens form judgments about affairs of state; these judgments would then
be mimetically reflected in the decisions made by their political representatives. This is not to claim that the degraded faith in newspapers was
a distinctively twentieth-century phenomenon or that early theorists of
democracy in the United States were laughably naïve: Thomas Jefferson
knew that "Nothing can now be believed which is seen in a newspaper.
Truth itself becomes suspicious by being put into that polluted vehicle."[52]
Nonetheless, as historians remind us, even early twentieth-century
muckrakers addressed their exposés to "a reading public that had been

socialized to regard public opinion as the outcome of a town-meeting-like process of thoughtful deliberation and to view communication as a technical process for the transfer of information."[53] Despite long-running evidence to the contrary, this early twentieth-century reading public had been socialized to believe in the existence of what Jürgen Habermas would call a half century later the "public sphere"; not incidentally, this is also the rational readership and literary "factuality" that people like Delmore Schwartz denounced as the defining characteristic of politically exhausted, resigned literary naturalism.

By the early decades of the twentieth century, a polity based upon the "public opinion" of rational citizen-readers had long occupied a central conceptual place in the imagination and theorization of American democracy but was beginning to be shaken by increasing recognition of covert and overt censorship of the press. Censorship, however, presented only one problem for democratic readers hungry for information on which to base their political decisions. As even the authors of the *Federalist* had recognized, when it came to a "free" press, legal and institutional protections would be wholly secondary to the popular mandate on that freedom: a mandate that would emerge from the amorphous engine of "public opinion." As Alexander Hamilton wrote in *Federalist* 84:

> What is the liberty of the press? Who can give it any definition which would not leave the utmost latitude for evasion? I hold it to be impracticable; and from this I infer, that its security, whatever fine declarations may be inserted in any constitution respecting it, must altogether depend on public opinion, and on the general spirit of the people and of the government. And here, after all, as is intimated upon another occasion, must we seek for the only solid basis of all our rights.[54]

These were fine and enormously influential sentiments, of course, but events in the early twentieth century revealed a tragically circular logic to his argument. For Hamilton, freedom of the press would depend entirely upon public opinion, but public opinion would itself depend upon information distributed by that same press. As events throughout the twentieth century would show, one fatal flaw in the system is that the flow of information is controlled by the people whose actions are supposed to be held accountable by that information.

In contrast to this dominant understanding of informative news represented by Hamilton and other framers of American democracy, and consonant with journalistic exposés like those of Lippmann and George Seldes, which flourished in the 1920s and 1930s, *U.S.A.* provides numerous instances in which news reports concerning inconvenient "truths" are suppressed by vested economic interests.[55] In *The Big Money*, when journalist Mary French is assigned to report on striking steel-workers, her editor plainly tells her what kind of information he wants: "what part of Russia they were born in, how they got into this country in the first place . . . where the money comes from . . . prison records, you know."[56] French fails to grasp the editor's unsubtle suggestion that she depict the "agitators" as immigrants, Communists, and criminals (read: un-Americans) and either naively or bravely reports "the things she'd seen, the jailings, the bloody heads, the wreck of some family's parlor, sofa cut open, chairs smashed, chinacloset hacked to pieces with an ax, after the troopers had been through looking for 'literature'" (883). Predictably, her editor refuses to run the story: "Well, young lady. You've written a first-rate propaganda piece for the *Nation* or some other parlor-pink sheet in New York, but what the devil do you think we can do with it? This is Pittsburgh" (882). The scene pointedly illustrates the maddeningly circular character of the "news" and the "public" that informs the novel: the public remains unreceptive to information that might disrupt its political convictions because it is never presented with such information in the first instance.

Elsewhere in *U.S.A.*, the government directly censors newspapers under the auspices of war powers. In *1919*, an interior decorator and war volunteer named Eveline Hutchins begins spending time with Jerry Burnham, an increasingly dissolute war correspondent working for the United Press in Paris. With the right amount of cognac burning in him, Burnham admits to Eveline how badly the "free" press is serving the American public:

> how his work disgusted him, how a correspondent couldn't get to see anything anymore . . . he had three or four censorships on his neck all the time and had to send out prepared stuff that was all a pack of dirty lies every word of it . . . a newspaperman had been little better than a skunk before the war, but . . . now there wasn't anything low enough you could call him. Eveline would try to cheer him up telling him that when the war was over he ought to write a book like *Le Feu* and really tell the truth about it.[57]

These lines do more than simply remind readers that governmental pressure and corporate profit motives impede the clear-eyed empirical integrity of the "news"; they suggest that the novel—like Henri Barbusse's *Le Feu*, the first antiwar fiction to emerge from World War I—might intervene precisely when newspapers fail to "really tell the truth" (544).

Yet *Le Feu*—and, for that matter, *One Man's Initiation—1917*—adheres to recognizable conventions of the naturalist novel in a way that *U.S.A.* strikingly does not. Why, then, does *U.S.A.* look so radically different from *Le Feu*, and what are readers today to make of this difference? For that matter, why does it look so different from Left satires in the classical vein, such as those published by Charles Erskine Scott Wood in the *Masses* (and collected in the best-selling 1927 volume *Heavenly Discourse*)? What kind of "truth" could Barbusse's novel tell in 1916 that was no longer possible when Dos Passos invented a radically new novelistic form in the 1930s? Why would Dos Passos choose to *reproduce*—rather than openly denounce or expose—many of the patently false newspaper headlines that were printed under the dictates of various censorships? After all, whether guided by the rational and institutional dictates of liberalism or communism, politically useful "truth" would be served by rationally describing how the American and European publics were misled by such headlines, not by mimicking them. Dos Passos, however, understood that public opinion was "educated" not only by putatively objective facts but by the very way that information is experienced aesthetically. He further understood that public opinion was "educated" not only by newspapers and magazines but by other sources of cultural information such as films, radio, and novels. With the emergence of professional "public relations" around World War I, it became increasingly apparent that public opinion depended not just on *what* facts were distributed but on *how* those facts were distributed; not just "how" materially or economically but "how" aesthetically. And it is in recognizing the background to this "how" that we can understand the political motivation behind the formal innovations of *U.S.A.*: to deploy satirical irony in order to force readers to recognize the aesthetic conditions under which new means and ends of politics might be possible.

The Rise of Public Relations and the Fall of the Public

In the early years of the century, American business concerns realized that they could influence legislation much more cost-effectively by manipulating public opinion than by the older, more traditional means of bribing legislators outright. When labor legislation such as the 1935 Wagner Act outlawed—among other things—the venerable practice of hiring private armies of strikebreaking "private police" such as the Pinkertons, corporate concerns realized that they could just as effectively suppress strikes and quell dissent with information: by convincing a pliable public that strikers and dissenters presented a clear and present danger to their communities, families, and country the convinced publics would exert their own pressure, even if they didn't form the active vigilante groups of earlier decades.

A key episode in *The 42nd Parallel*, for example, takes place in a New York bar at the beginning of the war. People are overheard saying, "A few days ago I was sittin' at the Cooper Institute listening to Eugene Victor Debs, and what was he sayin'? . . . 'What is this civilization, this democracy that the bosses are asking you workers to give your lives to save, what does it mean to you except wageslavery, what is . . .?'" The response comes neither from police nor soldiers nor Pinkertons—that is, neither from the realm of law nor from its various arms of violent enforcement—but from anonymously "average" citizens: "'Hey, shut up, youse. . . . If you don't like it go back where you came from,' came voices from the crowd" (355). The initial discouragement is followed by the physical violence that threatens all such suppression of dissent, in the form of "cops two policedepartment cars with big searchlights were charging the crowd. Arms, heads, hats, jostling shoulders, riotsticks rising and falling stood out black against the tremendous white of the searchlights" (355). When a "plateglassindow" breaks, the American police and their citizen-supporters are immediately and ironically identified not as representative "American" servants but as counterrevolutionary agents of Russian feudalism: as somebody shouts, "Look out for the Cossacks" (355).

When nation-states produce information that causes such crowd reactions, it is popularly known as "propaganda." The profession that perfected the distribution of such influence for the private sector called it "public relations," and during World War I, the relatively new "science" of public relations was put to a most serious test. Woodrow Wilson had, of course, been reelected to the presidency on his ability to keep the United States out of war, so he knew that getting the United States *into* the war presented a formidable task. In 1917, he thus authorized the creation of what he described as "A Division of Advertising for the purpose of receiving and directing through the proper channels the generous offers of the advertising forces of the Nation to support the effort of the Government to inform public opinion properly and adequately."[58] The report suggests just what qualifies as "proper" and "adequate" information by defining its goals as "building morale, arousing the spiritual forces of the Nation, and stimulating the war will of the people."[59]

George Creel, former muckraker and eponymous chairman of the new Committee on Public Information, boasted a few years later that the committee was an innovation in the history of warfare. He reflects in his suggestively titled 1920 memoir, *How We Advertised America*:

> It was the fight for the *minds* of men, for the "conquest of their convictions," and the battle-line ran through every home in every country. It was in this recognition of Public Opinion as a major force that the Great War differed most essentially from all previous conflicts. The trial of strength was not only between massed bodies of armed men, but between opposed ideals, and moral verdicts took on all the value of military decisions.[60]

To achieve this goal, Creel drew freely (almost literally, with partici-pants known as "Dollar-a-Year-Men") on the talents of Madison Avenue advertising executives, as well as on the skills of journalists and cultural critics like Lippmann. The committee was hugely successful, and as Dos Passos sardonically reports in *U.S.A.*, "the war was great fought from the swivel chairs of Mr. Creel's bureau in Washington."[61] Here Dos Passos presents his readers with verbal irony in its most familiar form, remind-ing readers that the "Great War" was a war that was "great" only for those who fought with words and ideas rather than machine guns, artil-lery shells, and poison gas and that the devastation of the war far out-stripped any possible rhetoric of glory that motivated citizens to support the war. Although the activities of the committee were hugely influen-tial, the experience of fighting the war this way was hardly like living in the trenches. It is in this sense, of course, that Paul Fussell claimed "the Great War was more ironic than any before or since."[62]

The production and comprehension of verbal irony, understood at least since Quintilian as "saying one thing while meaning another," destabi-lizes ostensibly reliable linguistic reference; throughout this section of *U.S.A.*, including a biography of the great anti–Great War critic Randolph Bourne, Dos Passos shows how effective propaganda similarly depends not only on institutional regulation of particular information but on the semantic deregulation of language. His solution to the problem, however, is not positivist language stripped of potential polysemy but more irony. While relating what happened when Bourne dared to oppose the war publicly, Dos Passos formally enacts the subtle semantic shifts that would prove to be so effective at mobilizing and manipulating public opinion:

> in the crazy spring of 1917 he began to get unpopular where his
> bread was buttered at the New Republic;
>   for *New Freedom* read *Conscription*, for *Democracy*, *Win*
> *the War*, for *Reform*, *Safeguard the Morgan Loans*

> for Progress Civilization Education Service
> Buy a Liberty Bond,
> Straff the Hun,
> Jail the Objectors.[63]

In Dos Passos's biography of Bourne, the explicit substitution of slogans is first indicated by typefaces and punctuation: "for *New Freedom* read *Conscription*, for *Democracy*, *Win / the War*," and the enjambment begins to meld apposite words. Terms are offset in italics and by the line break, and the disappearance of the verb "read" intensifies both the visual and semantic effect: while the act of reading is commanded ("for *New Freedom* read *Conscription*"), it is the disappearance of precisely that word—"read"—that haunts the subsequent litany of propaganda.

The passage offers much more than familiar modernist literary fragmentation mimetically reflecting social and psychological fragmentation: after the removal of visual semantic markers and the simultaneous persistence of the semantic substitutions, what remains is critique semi-passing as reportage, an ironic novelistic mode calling attention to itself via the imperative mood. The ironic *coup de grâce* occurs when Dos Passos suggests how public consensus about the war was formed by "educating" citizens via propaganda masquerading as fact. He continually reminds his readers how susceptible public opinion actually was to the manipulation of language and how actions sanctioned by that opinion could produce results that were (with irony both "tragic" and "cosmic") opposed to what was intended. In doing so, Dos Passos reveals the notion of a rationally formed and informed public opinion not just as hopelessly naïve but as actively harmful: a disposition toward the world of ideas that would invariably favor the interests of those who control the means of information production.

Dos Passos's Bourne biography continues, "force to the utmost, thundered Schoolmaster Wilson" (449). Woodrow Wilson had been a professor and president of Princeton University before he was president of the United States, and his characterization here as "Schoolmaster" implicitly characterizes Wilson's followers as puerile students, undermining the neutral claim to an "education" of the public made by the Creel Committee and other champions of government public relations. In relating Bourne's harassment by government agents after he publicly opposed the war, moreover, Dos Passos further inverts and reframes the entire notion of a public "educated" by aesthetic information: Bourne was "cartooned, shadowed by the espionage service and the counter-espionage service; taking a walk with two girlfriends at Wood's Hole he was arrested, a trunk full of manuscript and letters was stolen from him in Connecticut" (449). Wilson's pedagogical "Force" that was putatively intended to crush "barbaric Huns" pragmatically necessitated the crushing of domestic dissent, and Dos Passos understands this simultaneous inversion and perversion of democratic, journalistic discourse as specifically ironic: as *1919*'s "Newsreel XXXVII" reports, "the irony of the situation lies in the fact that the freedom of speech and the press for which the social democrats clamored is now proving the chief source of menace to the new government" (698).

In his memoir about the service of the Committee on Public Information, Creel reflected that "In all things, from first to last, without halt or change, it was a plain publicity proposition, a vast enterprise in salesmanship, the world's greatest adventure in advertising."[64] Meanwhile, both the official Creel Report and other sections of Creel's memoir maintain that the task was simply one of transmitting data to a rationally capable public, who could be trusted to arrive at the same conclusion that President Wilson had: "Our effort was educational and informative throughout," Creel wrote, "for we had such confidence in our case as to feel that no other argument was needed than the simple, straightforward presentation of facts," an apology that itself counts as propaganda. Despite such blithe protestations, the Creel Committee plainly realized what Hamilton had not anticipated: that the creation of a public "war will" would occur not through the Enlightened processing of transparently factual information but by rendering information via the emergent techniques of industrial psychology, advertising, and public relations.[65] Furthermore, the committee realized that their goal was not only immediate victory in World War I but the formation of a public consciousness favorably disposed toward unrestrained corporate interests. In their own suggestively metaphorical characterization, written in the 1918 report to the National Association of Manufacturers (NAM) and included as an appendix to the U.S. Senate's La Follette Committee report, the "public educational movements" that inculcated patriotic fervor in citizens would first help win the military conflict in Europe, and had the "secondary purpose of arming American industry for the trade conflict to follow the conclusion of the war."[66]

The pedagogical language of both the Creel Committee and the NAM was standard among public relations experts, and Dos Passos parodically echoes the language throughout every appearance of the "public relations" counsels in the novel.[67] When labor unions and industry come to increasingly frequent loggerheads, what is required (from the perspective of industry) is not the equitable distribution of wealth among workers or the improvement of unsafe working conditions: rather, as Dos Passos writes in *The 42nd Parallel*, "What was necessary was an entirely new line in the publicity of the industry. It was the business of the industry to educate the public by carefully planned publicity extend ing over a term of years."[68] The conflicts are generated not by manifest inequalities between owners and operators of the means of production but by "the lack of properly distributed information," which "is the cause of most of the misunderstandings in this world" (236). To recognize this, advises the public relations counsel, is to recognize that the "time for an educational campaign and an oral crusade that will drive home to the rank and file of the mighty colossus of American uptodate industry is right now, today."[69] The passages weigh the realities of corporate communication against an ideal of the unbiased, unfiltered, neutral sphere of information.

The explicitly pedagogical language that Dos Passos parodies here demonstrates how the term "educational" was redefined by the Creel Committee and others to refer to the aesthetic means by which the public was persuaded to support the policies of a given presidential administration or business concern. Indeed, pronouncements like the one above describing the "educational" efforts of the Creel Committee make manifestly clear what war supporter Thorstein Veblen—whose critiques were "etched in irony"—claimed in 1920: that "A more far-reaching department of the educational system, though not technically rated as such, is the periodical press, both newspapers and magazines."[70] The "education" referred to by both Creel and Veblen is not the mere transmission of information but transmission of information in a way that instills in readers, viewers, and auditors a particularly unskeptical, unironic disposition toward the world.

Dos Passos was well aware of just how successfully the government had educated public opinion to its own will and just how central the role of aesthetics had been in the formulation of public policy both during and after the war, and not only because the successes of the Creel Committee were publicly celebrated rather than concealed: Dos Passos conversed with Ivy Lee, one of the founders of the field of public relations, when they were staying at the same hotel in Moscow in 1928.[71] In *The Big Money*, the field of "public relations" is represented by J. Ward Moorehouse, whom one character describes as having "done more than any one living man, whether you like what he does or not, to form the public mind in this country."[72] Moorehouse rises from the rank of proletarian newspaper reporter to become the wealthy confidante of presidents and corporate barons. He starts his career by "resolving" conflicts between

labor and industry, "keeping the public informed about the state of relations between capital and labor and stemming the propaganda of sentimentalists and reformers, upholding American ideas against crazy German socialist ideas and the panaceas of discontented dirtfarmers in the
Northwest."[73]

Moorehouse accomplishes this task not only by "publicizing" the common or competing interests of management and labor but by inventing
new ways of rendering mundane commodities more desirable to consumers through a combination of creative brainstorming and research
into the published work about public relations. Moorehouse "read
Crowds, Jr. and various books on psychology, tried to imagine himself a
hardware merchant or the executive of Hammacher Schlemmer or some
other big hardware house, and puzzled over what kind of literature from
a factory would be appealing to him"; he then "draft[ed] the literature to
be sent out."[74] When the war breaks out, Moorehouse offers his services
to the fictional equivalent of the Creel Committee; working under their
auspices, the principles of his advertising business remain the same.
When advertising the Wilson administration, however, the product
isn't just hardware, real estate, or the vision of corporate America as a
benevolent creator of prosperity and liberty; the product is loyalty, conformity, patriotism, and enthusiasm for American entry into World War
I. Late in the novel, Moorehouse makes his point plainly while describing his "product" to the allegorically named U.S. senator Planet, with
whom he is engaged in business: "'The force of public opinion, Senator,' . . . 'That is what we have to offer.'"[75] That Dos Passos characterizes
Moorehouse's products specifically as "literature" emphasizes a punning
gesture toward the political aspirations of his own novelistic project: the
creation of a public opinion that is trained and attuned to recognizing
paradox and irony and may thus read corporate and novelistic "literature" with a critical eye that inculcates resistant skepticism rather than
tractable credulity.[76]

Throughout the trilogy, Dos Passos repeatedly returns to this task by
focusing on the role of representation, information, and "the public." In
1919, for instance, J. Ward Moorehouse's companion, Eveline Hutchins,
is drinking and dining with Moorehouse and Mr. Rasmussen, an engi-
neer with Standard Oil who keeps "talking about Baku and Mohamma-
rah and Mosul, how the Anglo-Persian and the Royal Dutch were getting
ahead of the U.S. in the near East." While colonial and corporate interests
are carving the region into Iran, Iraq, and other countries, Moorehouse
is concerned that "We stand to lose our primacy in world oil production"; the only hope for establishing U.S. colonial interests where British

colonial interests are preparing to be established, as Moorehouse sees it, lies in the fact that "public opinion can be aroused."[77]

While dancing with Rasmussen, Hutchins tries to sell Moorehouse's services. When Rasmussen angrily remarks that "if [Woodrow] Wilson now was going to let the British bulldoze him into giving them the world's future supply of oil when we'd won the war for them, he was through," she responds with a remedy that echoes the supposedly rational language of both the Creel Committee and the public-relations industry: "But can't you do something about it, can't you put your ideas before the public, Mr. Rasmussen?" (617). As the novel has repeatedly demonstrated up to this point, a unified media campaign distributing aesthetically effective "scientific" information is just the strategic ticket. Yet Rasmussen's response reveals a key shift in the understanding of what is meant by "public" relations in the postwar period:

> That's Moorehouse's job not mine, and there isn't any public since the war. The public'll damn well do what it's told; and besides like God Almighty it's far away. . . . What we've got to do is make a few key men understand the situation. Moorehouse is the key to the key men.[78]

The fact that Rasmussen simultaneously denies the existence of the public and asserts that it will "do what it's told" suggests an ironically doubled definition of "public." First, he means the conglomeration of citizens that exists at least enough to take orders, whose concerns as individuals are putatively congruent with "private" industrial concerns. This is a public identified by the U.S. government and by the NAM first and foremost as comprising rationally willing participants in the sphere of market economics. Indeed, the NAM itself proposed that "the public—which in the industrial sense of the word comprises employer, employes [sic] and the consumer—is capable of understanding the folly of curbing and crippling industrial enterprise, and that the dissemination of truthful information on this score will result in the substitution of harmony for discord."[79] This is a consuming public that needs only positive "facts" in order to be guided to the same conclusions as government and industry.

Second, and more important, we understand that the "public" Rasmussen identifies as having disappeared during or immediately after the war designates a pluralist collectivity capable of making choices that might be at odds with the desires of industry and capital: a public capable of recognizing the difference between the rhetoric and the actuality of multinational industry and capital, destroyed by the information campaigns rather than the trenches of World War I. Consider that

Rasmussen's definition of two different kinds of "publics" resonates first with industry's and second with the definition shared by both Lippmann and John Dewey: a public that disappeared because, in Dewey's words, the "creation of political unity has also promoted social and intellectual uniformity, a standardization favorable to mediocrity. Opinion has been regimented as well as outward behavior. . . . Mass production is not confined to the factory."[80] In typically ambiguous fashion, Dewey here both reinforces and revises a Marxian conception of ideology: that it first may seem to emanate from the means of production but—*pace* Marx, Engels, or Mike Gold—might also be produced beyond the economic base. Either way, the key characteristic shared by both kinds of public is its uniform reception of information and the uniformity of action that results from that information.

The Painful Information of the Aesthetic Counterpunch

When Rasmussen says of the public that "like God Almighty it's far away," he blithely reveals an important feature of representative democracy: that the relation of individual citizen to government representative (senator, congressperson, president, etc.) is not unlike that of investor to the stock market or of supplicant to God. As economist Kenneth Arrow would later show in *Social Choice and Individual Values* (1951), when presented with more than two choices, there is no system that can convert the individual preferences of voters into a systemic set of results that meet consistent criteria. All are at least theoretically free to submit their opinions to the appointed representative, whether in the form of a monetary vote for a particular stock or a ballot for president; no particular outcome is guaranteed, however, and no valid causal relationship is attributable to a particular choice. Genuine unanimity among the electorate would obviate the necessity for any representation whatsoever; my senator is free to vote for war whether or not this expresses my will or the will of my neighbor who disagrees with me; the fact that I pray for something doesn't guarantee that I will receive it; fervently collective hopes for a bull market may well be greeted by the Crash of 1929; and so forth. In this sense, the means by which a political representative actually "represents" a constituent must be understood as a fundamentally aesthetic relationship that is most effectively depicted in and altered by aesthetic terms.[81] In contrast to this reality for the novel's readers, however, for Rasmussen, the most effective—if depressingly undemocratic—political tactic is to build up enough power and prestige that one has access to the "few key men" who make decisions for the rest of the country and world:

"What we've got to do is make a few key men understand the situation. Moorehouse is the key to the key men."[82]

Scenes such as these might seem to provide a bleak example of just how resigned and fatalistic the politics of Dos Passos's novel actually are: as practical political advice, "gain power, prestige, and unmediated access to Congress" is hardly an answer to the perennial question of "what is to be done?" The idea emerges in other parts of the novel as well. For example, when Moorehouse becomes mortally ill, Richard Ellsworth Savage—his right-hand man, at least partially based on Dos Passos's own life—upbraids his friends for deigning to take Moorehouse's illness lightly. As he scolds them in *The Big Money*:

> Whether you like it or not the molding of the public mind is one of the most important things that goes on in this country. If it wasn't for that American business would be in a pretty pickle. Now we may like the way American business does things or we may not like it, but it's a historical fact like the Himalaya Mountains and no amount of kidding's going to change it. It's only through publicrelations [*sic*] work that business is protected from wildeyed cranks and demagogues who are always ready to throw a monkeywrench into the industrial machine.[83]

The passage reasserts the fact-value dichotomy as a central problem of the novel, but by acknowledging the extent to which the "molding of the public mind" is a process occurring in the present tense ("goes on in this country") and by asserting that "no amount of kidding is going to change that," Dos Passos here steers his readers away from mere "kidding" as a response to the political and informational crisis his novel represents: in particular, the sort of "kidding" that distinguished the "gentle satire" that Dos Passos decried as the distinctive feature of American literature.[84] Instead of gentle satire that would enlighten readers to conditions but do nothing to change them, Dos Passos models for his readers a particular hermeneutic disposition: a way of reading not only his own novels but society as a social text and of processing cultural information in such a way as to form a new, politically viable public.

The key to the strategic identification of this public is to be found not only in the novel itself but also in a letter Dos Passos wrote to *The New Republic*, published six months after *The 42nd Parallel*. Dos Passos's letter was titled "Wanted: An Ivy Lee for Liberals," and the context that I have delineated thus far suggests how the letter can serve as a sort of exegetical manifesto for the political coherence of *U.S.A.* The letter sets out to consider two relatively straightforward questions: "Can anything

be done to avert a bitter nationwide persecution of Communists and sus-
pected Communists?" and "What sort of an appeal would be effective?"[85]
It proceeds to consider precisely the question of what kind of "public"
would be necessary to prevent the sorts of abuses that dissenters had
been suffering since the beginning of the war. The question emerges as
particularly poignant for Dos Passos, since those abuses were directed
at the minority of people who were to be admired for resisting the patriotic propaganda of the Creel Committee. Moreover, having witnessed
the manifest successes of the Creel Committee in identifying dissenters
with Communists and Communists with evil, Dos Passos had no faith in
the efficacy that muckraking presentations of "factual" abuse had once
offered: "I doubt if even the secure sub-aristocratic liberal fringe that is
occasionally moved by the thought of starving babies, or little children
getting T.B. working in textile mills, will get anything but pleasure out of
the knowledge that Communists are being beaten up, imprisoned, shot
or deported."[86]

If the "liberals" were just as susceptible as anybody else when it came
to propaganda justifying violence against Communists, who was to be
the object of the appeal, and what was the nature of the appeal to be
made? Dos Passos suggested a solution where rank-and-file Communists
of the New Masses variety (with whom he had an increasingly strained
relationship) located the problem: "the business class, from high-salaried
management experts to the white-collar poor who have sufficient technical education to make a living without working with their hands." It
was not only that electoral numbers were on his side because "This class
bulks large numerically." Even more important than sheer numbers, Dos
Passos followed Veblen to find in the business class "the source of that
mysterious force, public opinion, of which so much was hoped in the old
reforming days before the War."[87] The task at hand was not just to get this
class to recognize itself as a "public" distinct from its broader self-identity
as "Americans," but to get it to recognize itself as a public to whom the
massive structural shifts represented by a more-or-less Socialist revolution posed no threat. Thus, unlike more conventional models of political
organization—wherein one convinces individuals and groups to join in
collective solidarity with a positive program—Dos Passos suggests that
the task at hand is to convince people to withdraw from antagonisms:
not because harmony and consensus would thus be achieved but because
it would reformulate the numbers of the metaphorical "armies" of ideological warfare to the advantage of the workers. Although it was to be a
battle, this battle would be distinguished by its comparatively humane
conduct, for "Once you could convince these people that it wouldn't hurt

them to be neutral, it ought not to be hard to make them feel that atrocities on either side in a war lower the general level of humaneness for everybody concerned."[88]

If the "business class" represents the source of renewal for a poisonously manufactured "public opinion," how would this class be aroused to the paradoxical "action" of becoming neutral? For Dos Passos, the answer would emerge not in cognition but precisely in *ironic pathos*: not the rational evaluation of information about market economics or competing political theories, and not in the reasoned argumentation of seasoned rhetors, but in the reflective experience of corporeal *feeling*. As the language of the above lines indicates, the task of the politically engaged writer is to convince people that neutrality won't "hurt," to help them "feel that atrocities" are wrong, and thus to discourage the "pleasure" they might otherwise get from hearing that Communists are being abused. With the right appeal, they might well be "the people who can be made to *feel* that police persecution of Communists and the bitter sadism with which judges impose maximum sentences for political offenses are crimes."[89] The task is literally one of establishing "aesthetic sympathy" in the etymological sense of both words: a "feeling with" the victims of state persecution. But the sympathy thus established is not intended to produce single-minded identification with a greater cause but the kind of broader outlook that can result in a position of neutrality; this is what distinguishes Dos Passos's model of reading from the successes of wartime propaganda that instills blind obsequious patriotism in viewers and readers, and what leads the novel to qualify as satire.

In *U.S.A.*, the reactionary goal of public relations is to create such a blind, single-minded, reflexive response from reading to acting. When Moorehouse arrives in Paris to train "information officers" and oversee the propaganda efforts, he delivers a rousing speech to his staff that produces the desired somatic response in his listeners. At the end of Moorehouse's speech,

> Major Wood leaned back in his swivelchair and it let out a squeak that made everybody look up with a start and several people looked out of the window as if they expected to see a shell from big Bertha hurtling right in on them. 'You see,' said Major Moorehouse eagerly, his blue eyes snapping, 'that is what we must make people feel . . . the catch in the throat, the wrench to steady the nerves, the determination to carry on.'[90]

Such effects are clearly the first step of "sympathetic" propagandizing, which results from figuring out what "type of fear-stimulus in the mass mind would have to be played on," by puzzling "over an analysis of that automatic putting yourself in the other fellow's place that is at the bottom of the horror of cruelty."[91] If the process were to stop here, Dos Passos suggests, one would remain in a sort of Foucauldian reverse discourse that would do nothing to alleviate the fundamental cruelty to individuals practiced in Wilson's U.S.A. and Stalin's U.S.S.R.: reproducing the "pathic" discourse of propaganda might well appropriate the tools of the oppressor and achieve temporary "victories," but would fail to change any of the fundamentally oppressive mechanisms that crush individuals and groups. In the crucial next step, however, Dos Passos indicates what would distinguish his "liberal Ivy Lee" from the reactionary real one: the "good" counsel "would work on these motives, at the same time trying to kid people out of the fear that was at the bottom of the cruelty impulse."[92]

In precisely this vital second stage of *removing* the fear that has just been instilled, Dos Passos distinguishes his fictional aesthetics from propaganda. Perhaps it is true, as he suggests, that "if by propaganda you can make women wear corsets and everybody believe cigarettes good for the voice, it's conceivable that by propaganda you can make them hate cruelty or tolerate the idea of change." Yet, as he has already indicated, merely instilling fear may create a unified and tractable public, but it does not create a public that can be counted on to avoid cruel oppression of dissenting opinion—quite the opposite. But herein the business class also offers a great opportunity; although Dos Passos admits that "By education and training they are unfitted for political action," he also avers—in the conventional language of visual aesthetics—that "as the molders of ideas they are supremely fitted to color events. And it is just on that coloring of events that the humane values depend."[93]

The business class, then, has the capacity to "color events"—that is, aesthetically represent and interpret selections of the world—in such a way as to draw their relation to "humane values." Beginning with G.E. Moore, philosophers refer to one version of the impossibility of deriving "values" from "facts" as the "naturalistic fallacy." Dos Passos' new naturalism (as sketched in the "Wanted" letter and instantiated throughout *U.S.A.*) echoes a position that runs throughout twentieth-century critiques of philosophical pragmatism: that rational, factual, and pragmatic discourse efficiently satisfies objectives, but that literary aesthetics remain the proper realm for generating the values that allow individual agents to choose among objectives. The task of literature, then, is not so much to delineate a blueprint for future action, nor simply to model mimetically the successes and failures of certain attempts at praxis, but to present "facts" within a visible field of symbolic exchange that calls attention to its own manipulation of readers. What would result, Dos Passos hoped, is much more than a plan of attack that, by the time it was formulated and executed, would necessarily be overtaken and rendered obsolete by continually evolving material conditions. Rather, what was needed was the generation of a new set of aesthetic "values"—and a readership capable of recognizing those values—that would be able both to conflict and to resonate with material "facts." Since the "whole structure of the political ideas of the people who are neither members of the Communist party nor pro-capitalists is built of rotten timber," Dos Passos found that it was an entire disposition to the world of "the political" that must "be replaced by something more in accord with the historical facts. Until that is formulated, any appeal to 'humanity,' 'civilization,' 'mercy,' must necessarily be on pretty shaky foundations."[94]

Key to the political-informational strategy in the "Wanted" letter is the sense that the identification and constitution of various publics is a process of recognition; thus, the task of politics might well lie in using literary aesthetics to help publics to recognize themselves. That is to say, Dos Passos realized with his reactionary counterparts in the fields of public relations and advertising that "publics" can be not only targeted, but *constituted* by various forms of representation—including literature, news media, and film—and that consequently aesthetics might play a crucial role in helping certain publics recognize themselves (a process that redefines the task of "constitution" as "recognition"). The point here is that the kind of readerly response Dos Passos hopes to inculcate is complex, polysemous, ironic: it always depends on readers being aware of the processes by which that response is being provoked. This is not so far from conventional understandings of "ironic distance," but where this kind of irony is usually figured as a liability to politics—a quiescent retreat or abrogation of responsibility of individuals to collective sociality—Dos Passos figures this distance as a precondition for the distribution and reception of effective political information.

Dos Passos came to believe that the particular "public" that needed to be identified wasn't only an oppositional "counter-public" in Michael Warner's sense, but one that would actually remove its counter-revolutionary opposition to the positive changes as represented, for instance, by the Bolshevik revolution (with subsequent Soviet governments not yet fully recognized as being even more adept at brutal suppression of a populace).[95] The political task of the writer, then, was to facilitate the self-recognition and subsequent emergence of a public that wouldn't feel threatened by radical political change, and which thus wouldn't oppose such change, whose members would need simultaneously to be viscerally horrified by the indisputable economic and physical violence (it is always both, Dos Passos reminds us) of unrestrained capitalism. With the twin actions of these two forces—one asking them to dis-identify from the objects of revolution and the other asking them to identify with victims of violence—a public might emerge that would serve as a focus of revolutionary energy.

The idea that such de-identification would take place in order that a public might more fully and corporeally empathize with the pain of the oppressed is more Dos Passos than Brecht, and flouts conventional wisdom about the form and goals of political organization. The next step is to make that public feel and think the complex rational and emotional stimuli to action, a process that would occur via the distribution of aesthetic information. Working in the realm of the novel rather than the theater—after his own deep involvement in the aesthetically avant-garde and politically radical Playwrights Project, where he worked as director, playwright, and scene painter—Dos Passos moves even further beyond the narrative questions of "what" and "when" events will occur to "how." That is, in composing a novel that is equal parts history, biography, and conventional naturalist fiction, the novel poses the question of how to represent events so that the difference would be not just generically radical but politically radical. The answer lies in how *U.S.A.* employs satire to reevaluate supposed facts according to revalued values. The task of such education—to establish readers' relationships to themselves as individuals and to each other as members of a community—was one of simultaneous identification and distantiation, what we might call empathy and anesthesia, while the form of address is recognizable irony within a satire. Irony as a critical concept subsumes the simultaneous corporeal identification and distance necessary for authentic political action, and simultaneously foregrounds the central role that visual and literary representation play in such praxis. It is just this seemingly paradoxical movement among text, reader, and environment that Dos Passos would take up not only in the context of individual readers, but in collectivities of individuals: that is, in the context of publics.

Problematic Publics

In the early twentieth century, press outlets that dealt in the "written word" certainly played their part in the success of both newsreels and feature films: as the Creel Committee reported, newspapers "cooperated splendidly with local theaters on these features by timing the publication of this matter just preceding and concurrently with the local play dates of the Government features."[96] More important than such organized collaboration or formal collapse, the manifest failures of news media produced two different approaches to the "problem of the public" that intertwine "practical" and "aesthetic" solutions. The full import of Dos Passos' engagement with the language of journalism and "the public" emerges from the context of the defining statement on the subject, which not incidentally emerged in the years leading up to the publication of *U.S.A.*: the 1920s exchange between John Dewey and Walter Lippmann, which offered both institutional and aesthetic solutions to the problem of a public decreasingly capable of engaging in politics.[97]

On the "institutional" hand, erstwhile radical journalist Lippmann published three books that directly addressed a crisis in democracy: *Liberty and the News* (1920), *Public Opinion* (1922), and *The Phantom Public* (1925).[98] Pleading for a quasi-positivist, objective journalism that would return the country to the wise hands of rational political agents, Lippmann asserted that "Liberty is not so much permission as it is the construction of a system of information increasingly independent of opinion."[99] The ideal newspaper and newsreel would transmit "facts" to a discriminating public, Lippmann argued, and the failure of both media to do so had profound political implications:

> Now, men who have lost their grip upon the relevant facts of their environment are the inevitable victims of agitation and propaganda. The quack, the charlatan, the jingo, and the terrorist, can flourish only where the audience is deprived of independent access to information. [. . .] The whole reference of thought comes to be what somebody asserts, not what actually is.[100]

If a situation wherein thought refers merely to language qualifies as a political ill, Lippmann's proposed remedy was an independent, global news organization staffed by expert readers, writers, and observers: a sort of non-profit, transnational, positivist network, which would ensure that unbiased information was impartially and globally distributed. This is precisely the sort of classically liberal, institutional remedy for polit-ical-structural defects in which Dos Passos had little faith; he makes it abundantly clear that, even if information could ever be transmitted and distributed with positivist transparency, media magnates like "*POOR LITTLE RICH BOY*" William Randolph Hearst would ultimately control the transmission of such data, so that the struggle for political change would simply be deferred to a different theater.[101]

Dos Passos's take on the crisis of information was closer to that of Dewey, who replied directly to Lippmann in the form of *The Public and*

Its Problems (1927).[102] His conception of the role that aesthetics played in distributing information substantially differed from Lippmann's. Essentially agreeing with Lippmann at first, Dewey wrote that "The smoothest road to control of political conduct is by control of opinion. As long as interests of pecuniary profit are powerful, and a public has not located and identified itself, those who have this interest will have an unresisted motive for tampering with the springs of political action in all that affects them" (182). Yet Dewey shared none of Lippmann's faith in an unproblematically transmissible fact. Whereas Lippmann's "facts" would fight "terrorists," Dewey responded that one should "realize the distance which may lie between 'facts' and the meaning of facts," for even though "[m]any persons seem to suppose that facts carry their meaning along with themselves on their face . . . the power of physical facts to coerce belief does not reside in the bare phenomena" (3). Ironically, Dewey thus found his solution to "the problem of the public" precisely where Lippmann found the source of the problem: the aesthetic free play of information.

As early as 1922, Dewey was pointedly aware that the gap between "news" and "propaganda" was theoretical at best, and that both of these organs of information were means of social control. In an essay titled "Education as Politics," he wrote that:

> Doubtless the régime of propaganda brought on by the war has had much to do with forcing upon us recognition of the dominant role in social control of material put in circulation by the press. The bulk and careful organization of propaganda are testimony to two outstanding facts: the new necessity governments are under of enlisting popular interest and sentiment; and the possibility of exciting and directing that interest by a judiciously selected supply of 'news.'[103]

Whether or not the need of governments to excite popular interest was new, the institutional recognition *by* governments that popular sentiment was something to be created and manipulated rather than merely reflected or followed seemed to be, and this remained true throughout *The Public and Its Problems*. Contra Lippmann, Dewey proposed that "[o]nly when the facts are allowed free play for the suggestion of new points of view is any significant conversion of conviction as to meaning possible."[104] Where Lippmann held that a team of positivist technocrats could provide the informational means to both inform and control an incorrigible audience, Dewey suggested that art might play a crucial role in first forming, then informing, publics. Because a reformed vision of the world was necessary for information adequately to be processed, Dewey thought that the "freeing of the artist in literary presentation . . . is as much a precondition of the desirable creation of adequate opinion on public matters as is the freeing of social inquiry," for "Poetry, the drama, the novel, are proofs that the problem of presentation is not insoluble. Artists have always been the real purveyors of news, for it is not the outward happening in itself which is new, but the kindling of it by emotion, perception and appreciation."[105] The emphasis that Dos Passos placed on aesthetic, bodily sensation and response in "Wanted: An Ivy Lee for Liberals" is echoed when Dewey remarks that "The level of action fixed by *embodied* intelligence is always the important thing."[106]

To distinguish provisionally between Dewey's and Lippmann's arguments is not to obscure the fundamental similarities they shared. Like Dewey, Lippmann asserts in *The Phantom Public* that public-political processes are essentially processes of symbolic manipulation; moreover, that political manipulation of signs is a fundamentally "aesthetic" activity that produces bodily feeling:

> The making of one general will out of a multitude of general wishes is not an Hegelian mystery . . . but an art well known to leaders, politicians, and steering committees. It consists essentially in the use of symbols which assemble emotions after they have been detached from their ideas. Because feelings are much less specific than ideas and yet more poignant, the leader is able to make a homogenous will out of a heterogeneous mass of desires. The process, therefore, by which general opinions are brought to cooperation consists of an intensification of feeling and a degradation of significance.[107]

Whereas for Rousseau the task of the legislator is to ascertain and enact the general will (to the extent that Rousseau conceived of the general will as a practical proposition), Lippmann shifts the discussion to understand how something as amorphous as the general will can be ascertained, but only after it has been *constructed*.[108] That process of construction is equally a process of recognition and instruction, and aesthetic symbols are the pedagogical means by which the "will of the people" is formed.[109] As Michael Warner formulates oppositional counterpublics, "the perception of public discourse as conversation obscures the importance of the poetic functions of both language and corporeal expressivity in giving a particular shape to publics."[110] In *U.S.A.*, we find a "counterpublicizing" Dos Passos instructing readers in the art of recognizing,

THE FOCUS OF SATIRE / 133

and thus shaping, a symbolic order at the heart of any "public," the self-conscious formation of which can be called "irony."

In a novelistic contribution to such emerging conceptions of the public, Dos Passos's aesthetic-political task is not simply to inform people that the media is corrupt, or that this corruption is directly related to an increasingly corrupt democracy: it is to tell us that simply "knowing" that the media is corrupt provides little protection against its influence. In one telling instance in *The 42nd Parallel*, the Merchant Marine Joe Williams knows that his sister Janey "works for J. Ward Moorehouse, the public relations counsel, you know . . . he does propaganda for the Morgans and the Rockefellers. . . . He runs pro-war stuff through a feature syndicate. And they call this a free country."[111] Nevertheless, a few hundred pages later, Williams succumbs to the putative opportunities for individual and national success recommended by the papers, knowing full well that the papers are controlled by the same propaganda machine that employs his sister: he first tells a friend that "Anyway if you believed the papers the heinies were getting licked, and it was a big opportunity for a young guy if you didn't get in wrong by being taken for a proGerman or a bolshevik or some goddamn thing. After all as Janey kept writing civilization had to be saved and it was up to us to do it" (560).

The irony here functions at several levels. First, of course, Dos Passos presents a comic pun: if one believes the propaganda of the newspapers, then one not only believes that "heinies were getting licked" (i.e., that Germans are being defeated) but one also becomes a sycophant who has figuratively "licked the heinies" of moneyed interests. The irony expands and contracts in the very next line, when "Joe started a savings account and bought him a liberty bond," for the reader realizes that Joe's supposed decision to help "save civilization" is precisely the act scripted by a public relations representative just thirteen pages earlier: Moorehouse has stipulated, after all, that government "publicity ought to have two aims, to stimulate giving among the folks back home and to keep people informed of the progress of the work" (547). The scene doesn't so much characterize Williams as an egregious sap as imply how particular forms of information herd readers toward particular forms of action; whether or not one has privileged access to contradictory information, one still reads a newspaper and still purchases a war bond. Reading stimulates action, Dos Passos suggests, at a level beyond rational contemplation—a level best designated in the context of an aesthetic disposition of the world. But Dos Passos's novel works to instill an aesthetic model of reading-to-action that is thoughtful, aware, and self-conscious, as opposed to the reactive model of reading-to-action associated here with newspapers and public relations. And this is precisely why, the novel suggests, one must learn to read anew, and novelists must work to change readers' aesthetic response to information.

Seeing Irony, Feeling Satire

Where a sympathetic *Dial* reviewer of Dos Passos's early, naturalist novel *Three Soldiers* claimed the "author does not need to be ironical. He sits still, and the unforgettable idiocy of everybody in sight supplies the irony," by 1936 Horace Gregory would remark about *The Big Money* that "only the most unresponsible reader would fail to appreciate the humor which is the force behind the keen stroke of Mr. Dos Passos's irony."[112] Even reviews that felt *The 42nd Parallel* "falls short of being sheerly creative" claimed that, the "book being satire, Mr. Dos Passos has 'interpreted' his people in terms of irony" and thus published "very effective social castigation."[113] Yet Dos Passos's own statement on satire's aesthetic effects on bodies has been largely ignored.[114] In a 1937 preface to a book of drawings by George Grosz entitled "Satire as a Way of Seeing," Dos Passos puzzles over the relationship among radical politics, emotional empathy, and modes of literary and visual representation. Indeed, he goes so far as to identify a wholesale cultural shift in the hermeneutic habits of Americans based on the interplay of word and image. His parents' generation, visually trained by the conventions of realist Victorian painting and drawing, when "enjoying a view from a hill, say, were stimulated verbally, remembering a line of verse or a passage from Sir Walter Scott, before they got any real impulse from the optic nerve."[115] With the rise of film technology and evolution of non-realist styles of painting, however, "In the last fifty years a change has come over the visual habits of Americans as a group . . . From being a wordminded people we are becoming an eyeminded people."[116]

Central to this piece, as in the earlier "Wanted: An Ivy Lee for Liberals," is the sense that the diagnosis of a diseased body-politic must occur at the intersection of language and visuality, and that a literary "treatment" must emerge from the directed irony of an allopathic satire: "The satirist in words or visual images is like the surgeon who comes with his sharp and sterile instrument to lance some focus of dead matter."[117] Given *U.S.A.*'s obsession with the interplay of visuality and literality, and the role the two play in the "education" of publics, Dos Passos's metaphor that equally suggests wounds, cameras, and eyes—the noun "focus," the OED tells us, refers both to a concentration of light through a lens and to the epicenter of disease in a body—can hardly be understood as accidental, and in fact points toward the rhetorical interplay of irony and satire and its presumed bodily effects that Northrop Frye theorized a few years later: "irony is not simply the small man's way of fighting a bigger one: it is a kind of intellectual tear-gas that breaks the nerves and paralyses the muscles of everyone in its vicinity, an acid that will corrode healthy as well as decayed tissues."[118]

"Satire as a Way of Seeing"—like *U.S.A.*—suggests that effective political aesthetics would have to inspire not only cognitive or informational interest (the interest of new "facts") but visceral and emotional "feeling." Crucially, Dos Passos identifies the capability to inspire just this sort pain as the particular talent of the satirist:

> A satirist is a man whose flesh creeps so at the ugly and the savage and the incongruous aspects of society that he has to express them as brutally and nakedly as possible to get relief. He seeks to put his grisly obsession into expressive form the way a bacteriologist seeks to isolate a virus. Until that has been done no steps can be taken to cure the disease. Looking at Grosz's drawings you are more likely to feel a grin of pain than to burst out laughing. Instead of letting you be the superior bystander laughing in an Olympian way at somebody absurd, Grosz makes you identify yourself with the sordid and pitiful object. His satire hurts.[119]

Rather than a standard-issue "alienation" to prevent empathic audiences, Dos Passos proposes a sort of diagnostic empathy in which the visual or verbal artist employs irony to engage a higher form of embodied realism: that is, an ironic hyperrealism that depicts and evokes an empathic sense of the object's pain while simultaneously establishing a distance between the object and its representation. Satire uniquely describes this form of irony, and Dos Passos was not alone in imagining the creation of an alternative aesthetic politics: as WPA graphic artist Mabel Dwight wrote in 1936, "Satire implies the presence of disease in the social organism; it can exist only in an unhealthy society. Utopia would have no place for it. A militant satirist sees a sick world and tries to operate on it with his rapier . . . His healthy satire is intellectual, but the fire of his emotion forges his weapons" in an age where "propaganda and satire are popular forms of expression."[120] In literature rather than painting or caricature, the novelist's task is not to construct objective correlatives to emotional states, but to employ the distortions of irony in order to capture a distorted world and to introduce such distortion into readers' perceptive capacities. At the same time, the distance between object and representation must not be the sort that could be reconciled or resolved without moving through the field of meaning, the space that is too often ignored, occluded, or erased under the conventions of realism or naturalism.

The fact that Dos Passos starts his critique by noting how Americans have transmogrified from "wordminded people" to "eyeminded people" is crucial to his sense that both verbal and visual irony ("in words or visual images") might be representational tonics for an ill democracy, and he powerfully employs both in the shaped prose of U.S.A. As with his penchant for redefining terms, Dos Passos was following the public relations industry in his recognition of the importance of visual media on par with print media.[121] The year 1937 witnessed the birth of the academic journal Public Opinion Quarterly, though professional study of public opinion was already thriving: according to the editors, "A recently published bibliography of public opinion studies lists more than five thousand titles; but the attack has not much more than begun."[122] In describing their object of study, the editors again invoke the conventional language of "education" to remark that "More than ever the press must be reckoned the Fourth Estate, but two new agencies of mass impression—the radio and the motion picture— have appeared. Motion picture and radio alike stamp the mind with vivid flashes, and the full educational effect of this bombardment has yet to be experienced."[123] It was no secret that the Creel Committee had effectively "educated" the public using films, posters, and radio spots to supplement more traditionally literary propaganda distributed throughout the nation in 1917. And it is precisely in this context that U.S.A. attempts much more than the mere documentation of this new force in politics. The 1918 report to the NAM asserted that "In all public educational movements there are three main or leading channels through which to work; namely, the press, the public and private speaking forum, and the moving picture screen," and Dos Passos contributes a "fourth" mode of address to the American public that lacked a decent Fourth Estate: fiction that explicitly accounts for and includes the other three.[124]

In 1919, when Moorehouse first begins to develop the techniques of what he later calls the "modern campaign of scientific publicity," he tells a potential client that "There's got to be a word to catch your eye the minute you pick it up."[125] It is no accident, then, that the first word in the first novel of the trilogy—the word that first catches one's eye— is "Newsreel" rendered in large italic print.[126] The film newsreel, of course, was a visual medium that functioned precisely through its ability to "catch one's eye," and it's unsurprising that the film newsreel was a crucial means by which World War I was sold to a skeptical American audience.[127] As the Creel Committee reported, "the three great agencies of appeal in the fight for public opinion were: The Written Word, the Spoken Word, and the Motion Picture."[128] Though they are all rendered in prose, these sections of the novel represent precisely the three forms of communication that were employed to sell both Ford Model T's and imperialist war. Because the headlines come from actual newspapers and refer to actual events, and the song lyrics are actual songs (some of them parodies), Dos Passos's Newsreels surely aren't well described by contemporary or subsequent New Critical accounts of irony: their referents are too plainly material to be of great use to the putatively disinterested world of poetic irony. Nonetheless, in their fragmentation at the levels of sentence, line, and page, the Newsreel sections don't attempt the sort of first-person, "humanized" account of events that distinguishes the Left reportage of writers such as John Reed or Meridel Le Sueur (or, for that matter, the "Camera Eye" sections of U.S.A. itself) or the exploded grammar of Gertrude Stein's 1935 lecture where she described how "Newspapers . . . want to write that happening as if it was happening on the day the newspapers are read that is not as if the thing was happening on the day the newspaper is read a little but all the same but as if the writing were being written as it is read."[129]

In the U.S.A. biography of John Reed, for instance, Dos Passos says three times of the author of Ten Days That Shook the World that "Reed was a westerner and words meant what they said."[130] It should first be noted that Reed qualified as a "westerner" because he was from the more overtly Progressive Portland, Oregon—not as a resident of the hemispheric "West"—and that consequently Reed was imagined to have come by his radicalism as a territorial birthright in a way that most Masses writers could not. More important, it is both the ideal journalistic and the ideal social-realist conceptions of language—the language of reportage, wherein words more or less "mean what they say"—that the Newsreels reveal as increasingly problematic. The Newsreels, after all, don't even pretend to "mean what they say" but rather invite readers to "see what they mean." Understood as a response to the success of "informational campaigns" during and after the war, and in the context of a "nation beaten by strangers who have turned our language inside out who have taken the clean words our fathers spoke and made them slimy and foul," the Newsreels don't so much represent certain mental, social, or nation-states by mimetically reflecting cultural ephemera, such that "circumstances" surrounding "events" are rendered "accurately" (371). Rather, the Newsreels highlight the aesthetic and ideological presentation of putative "facts" that masquerade as "news" and thus call attention to how facts themselves always presume, occlude, and function within a theory of meaning.

For instance, the first words of *1919* are "Newsreel XX." Like all of the other Newsreels, this one mixes newspaper headlines, song lyrics, and copy from news stories. In the representative first half, we see:

Oh the infantree the infantree
With the dirt behind their ears
ARMIES CLASH AT VERDUN IN GLOBE'S
GREATEST BATTLE

150,000 MEN AND WOMEN PARADE

but another question and a very important one is raised. The New York Stock Exchange is today the only free securities market in the world. If it maintains that position it is sure to become perhaps the world's greatest center for the marketing of

BRITISH FLEET SENT TO SEIZE
GOLDEN HORN
The cavalree artilleree
And the goddamned engineers
Will never beat the infantree
In eleven thousand years
TURKS FLEE BEFORE TOMMIES
AT GALLIPOLI

when they return home what will our war veterans think of the American who babbles about some vague new order, while dabbling in the sand of shoal water? From this weak folly they who have lived through the spectacle will recall the vast new No Man's Land of Europe reeking with murder and the lust of rapine, aflame with the fires of revolution. (363)

What begins as a simple soldiers' parody of a patriotic song moves immediately into what appears to be a relatively unproblematic statement of fact: the battle of Verdun was, after all, indisputably one of the largest and most devastating battles that the world had ever seen. Yet the smaller font of the subsequent lines and the decentered, even smaller text of the newspaper story about the "free" market, begin to suggest that the reader is also a *viewer*, that there is an aesthetic performance of the "fact" that inflects the transmission of "information." Indeed, the first snippet of news copy and the second large headline can hardly be said to exist in mere juxtaposition. The seemingly incomplete assertion that the New

York Stock Exchange is "sure to become perhaps the world's greatest center for the marketing of" becomes a complete sentence, which hypotactically indicates precisely what the Stock Exchange's public-relations branches would be "marketing:" the imperial aspirations of both the U.S. and the "BRITISH FLEET SENT TO SEIZE GOLDEN HORN" of the Middle East. As the sentence is completed, the word "free" is retrospectively ironized as well, leading astute readers to suspect that Wilson's "New Freedom" refers more specifically to the violently enforced freedom of "markets" rather than of "peoples."

The fine line between a "lie" and "irony" emerges from the final headline, for it requires historical knowledge on the part of the reader to recognize the extremely limited validity—if not outright falseness—of the newspaper's report (that Australian soldiers caused Ottoman soldiers to flee, when in fact it was the Allies who were defeated in the Dardanelles Campaign). Although more commonly known to American readers in 1938 than today, we can distinguish the kind of historical knowledge required to recognize the progression from "true statement" (armies fight at Verdun) to "false" statement (Turks flee at Gallipoli). By contrast, the purely formal, aesthetic distinction between the facts is immediately recognizable. The different typefaces emphasize that individual lines are to be read not only in juxtaposition but as complete semantic units in their own signifying right: this formal figuration drives home the extent to which reading Dos Passos's novel is a specifically visual activity, and the specifically visual component of the novel foregrounds the degree to which "facts" on film or paper are by no means transparently transmissible.[131] The larger font emphasizes the glory of battle, while the news copy suggests the reason behind the battles—a distinction that doesn't detract from but rather adds to the layers of ironic recognition. Readers are being "educated" to recognize how meaning is not only produced but—visibly or invisibly—manipulated by the interests of those who compose the text.

Teaching us how to "read" newspaper headlines that appear in a novel next to song lyrics that themselves are parodies, Dos Passos places the reader in the ironic position of "student" for his particular brand of education, and to understand the Newsreels this way is to emphasize the significance of the line uttered by Mac's guide in revolutionary Mexico. When Mac hears singing in the Mexican village where he has just arrived, his guide explains, "They sing about the murder of Madero. . . . It is very good for the education of the people . . . you see they cannot read the papers so they get their news in songs" (115). As readers of *U.S.A.*, we also get our "news" in "songs," but the news we get is that newspapers and newsreels under the control of corporate and state interests are only serving up a parody of "facts."

That ostensible "facts" always presume a theory of meaning (even if that theory is occluded) is hardly a new suggestion, of course, insofar as it might describe Nietzschean (and pragmatist) aesthetics in shorthand. Yet it flies in the face of a series of conventional understandings of what it means for a novel to be "political," especially when the "politics" at stake are conceived in the scientific terms of those Marxists who decried the novels and the politics of John Dos Passos. At the same time, Dos Passos submits his novel as an aesthetic corrective to the diseased realm of cultural hermeneutics by refiguring politics through "the political." As political philosopher Dick Howard describes, the stipulated difference between "politics" and "the political" is itself central to questions of aesthetic praxis:

> The philosopher insists on the difference between the condition and that which it conditions—on the difference between the political and politics. This is not to deny that politics is about "who does what to whom," as Lenin famously put it. It implies that the dimension of meaning must be introduced in order to explain the dynamism that makes the "facts" appear to call for action—for politics.[132]

By amending Howard's sentence to read "the philosopher and the novelist," the most ironic literary production can be considered as an active engagement with politics insofar as it affects the interpretive conditions ("the political") for praxis ("politics"). In U.S.A., Dos Passos uses the ironic presentation of "news" precisely to highlight the "dimension of meaning" that had proved so influential in dictating the parameters of public action and inaction.

Conclusion: Novel News

U.S.A. paratactically and hypotactically juxtaposes newspaper and filmic information that serves to prevent figurative symbols from being understood as literal ones; the irony that pervades the novel further reveals the private interests that create unreflective social cohesion in place of pluralist disagreement about the generation of political values. This is the ironic rendering of the problem of aesthetic democracy. Dos Passos presents apparently "factual" information subsumed under the broader rubric of a new literary aesthetic: a new form of representation that thematizes the act of reading as an ironic interchange and evaluation of information, which produces dissensus rather than consensus. The novel is thus reframed not as "Art" to be viewed and evaluated with Kantian disinterest but as an alternative media for political education that prevents the illusion of disinterest by including long, autobiographical, purely subjective sections of "The Camera Eye." Like Russian filmmaker Dziga Vertov's *Man with a Movie Camera* (which includes shots of the filmmaker and editor making the film), the novel announces its own sign-system as the production of a controlling authorial presence. It does so, however, within print that lionizes and redefines nationhood itself as "the speech of the people," emphasizing the linguistic basis of persuasion, inviting movement backward and forward throughout the book where film proceeds relentlessly forward. In Dos Passos, we find the attempt to instruct readers in the art of recognizing and manipulating a symbolic order: one that is the very nature of any "public," the self-consciousness of which is called "irony."[133]

Dos Passos understood that it is precisely when "the reference of thought comes to be what somebody asserts," as Lippmann had written—that is, when language is the object of contemplation—that politics looks less like an exercise in empirical research, grassroots organizing, or legislative reasoning and more like an exercise in literary production and evaluation. When the press is understood to constitute and direct the actions of a public that it is meant to inform, Schwartz's and Sartre's analogies between newspapers and Dos Passos's novel finally assume a politically "pressing" significance: the possibility that the crucial gaps left by a failed press might be filled by the novel.

Lippmann and Dewey partially agree that "the problem at the present time [is] that of securing experts to manage administrative matters."[134] For his part, Dos Passos certainly indicates a need for expertise in the political management of informational affairs; this was ever more urgently the case when individuals and crowds were faced with rapidly evolving technology to manipulate corporeal responses to signifying phenomena. In yet another proleptic review of how presidential conventions relied more upon visual imagery than upon rational argumentation or moving rhetoric, Dos Passos wrote in the same year that *1919* was published that

> history, or the mass mind, or whatever you want to call the solution
> of forces and urges and hindrances we live our lives in, is becom-
> ing more and more involved with the apparatus of spotlights, radio,
> talking pictures, newsprint, so that the image-making faculty,
> instead of being the concern of the individual mind, is becoming a

social business. The control of radio waves is externalizing thought
and feeling to a hair-raising degree. . . . Who's going to be man
enough to stand at the switchboard?[135]

In some sense Dos Passos envisioned himself as that man "at the switchboard," yet unlike Dewey, Lippmann, Habermas's referee in the sphere
of communicative rationality, or Rorty's liberal ironist, Dos Passos also
conceived of his role as removed from the day-to-day management of
informational affairs. His role was to contribute to the aesthetic education of the populace and then absent himself from the role of political
manager while newly forming and adjudicating publics evaluated the
possibilities and liabilities of "selfgovernment." In this view, it is individuals and collectivities themselves—and not the consolidated, institutional power of magnates and managers—who become "expert" in
the recognition and subsequent management of political affairs. Satiric
irony in *U.S.A.* presents a parabasis wherein not only the author and
the text are conceived as speaking directly through the narrative but the
reader is forced to hold such a conversation simultaneously with author,
novel, and other competing information systems.

The year after the publication of *U.S.A.*, the La Follette Committee
reported that the NAM had

blanketed the country with a propaganda which in technique has
relied upon *indirection of meaning*, and in presentation of secrecy
and deception. Radio speeches, public meetings, news, cartoons,
editorials, advertising, motion pictures and many other artifices
of propaganda have not, in most instances, disclosed to the public
their origin within the Association.[136]

Wisconsin senator Fightin' Bob La Follette—who earned a glowing
biography in *U.S.A.*—decried the "indirection of meaning" that distinguishes corporate propaganda. We might say, however, that effective
propaganda relies precisely upon the meticulous *direction* of meaning
in order to produce more or less determinate results in public opinion
and subsequent behavior. Ironically, in fact, it this supposedly "plain-
spoken," *directed* meaning that constitutes the linguistic ground shared
by the admirable Progressivism of Fightin' Bob and the reactionary cor-
poratism of the NAM.

One thus suspects that Dos Passos's novel is politically controversial
at least in part because its politics—roughly and revisionally anarchist
in the vein of the Spanish anarchism he had described in 1922 as "an
immensely valuable mental position"—fall outside the discursive bounds

delineated by any number of familiar party politics.[137] The same year that
U.S.A. was published, Mary McCarthy asserted that "You cannot produce trenchant political satire—at least not in America in this period—if
your political horizon is the Wagner Act."[138] In doing so, the novelist and
critic explicitly repudiated both the venerable equation of satire with the
normative sphere of law and the liberal equation of legislation with political action: specifically, legislation such as the Wagner Act that served to
de-radicalize an increasingly powerful labor movement. *U.S.A.* redefines
the object of politics itself as the "indirect" distribution of aesthetic information, which calls attention to its own means of aesthetic production to
oscillate between attempts to produce a naturalist-aesthetic, emotional
response to cruel injustice and an ironic awareness of how those effects
are produced. In "Camera Eye (46)," Dos Passos relates how he goes
home and reads Martial's epigrams to "ponder the course of history and
what leverage might pry the owners loose from power and bring back (I
too Walt Whitman) our storybook democracy."[139] If Dos Passos admits
that, like Whitman and Langston Hughes, "he too" can "sing" America,
we should perhaps take him at his word and understand his novel as a literal "storybook democracy": not as the jingoistic fairy-tale fantasies sold
to schoolchildren but as a literal "storybook" that attempts to instantiate
aesthetically a new democratic order. Early in *The 42nd Parallel*, a young
Moorehouse gives a real-estate pamphlet—what he calls his promotional
"literature"—to a potential client, saying: "I thought maybe you might
like to glance at it as . . . as something a bit novel in the advertising line"
(177). By the end of *The Big Money*, readers have indeed been consuming
something "novel in the advertising line": a novel called *U.S.A.*, which
advertises an impossibly old and radically new version of the U.S.A.

4 / Visible Decisions: Irony, Law, and the Political Constitution of Ralph Ellison

At a time like this, scorching irony, not convincing argument, is needed.
—FREDERICK DOUGLASS, 1852

... irony is not something that most Negroes understand, especially the ones who write for the papers.
—CARL VAN VECHTEN, 1960[1]

Invisible Man famously commences and concludes with a Prologue, an Epilogue, and an ironic paradox. The anonymous narrator inhabits a cavernous apartment beneath the streets of Harlem, where he has retreated after a series of disillusioning encounters with leading white citizens of the Jim Crow South, a university for African Americans, the corporate philanthropists who endow it, and a more-or-less Communist political organization working to supplant all of these groups. For some time, the narrator has inhabited this warm, bright hole: not as an ascetic but as a reflective "thinker tinker" who enjoys a hyperilluminated world of jazz, smoke, and ice cream slathered with sloe gin. The narrative frame presents a number of propositions about the relationship between reflection and action, which produce the apparent paradox: after stoutly asserting that "I believe in nothing if not action," he eventually proclaims, "I took to the cellar; I hibernated. I got away from it all."[2] These apparently opposite responses to stark injustice—withdrawal versus direct action, "to the cellar" versus "to the barricades"—have long disappointed critics who want "clear blueprints for ... later conduct," or at least legible narrative models for confronting the continuing sickness of American racism.[3] As Houston Baker laments, the "grassroots resistance and organization—the utter determination for 'freedom now'—that were bedrock for the Civil Rights Movement in America make no appearance" in the novel written by "the conservative Ralph Ellison."[4]

Ellison was keenly aware of the extent to which his novel produced equally committed champions and detractors and famously debated one critic who was both. Irving Howe had served as judge on the committee that gave *Invisible Man* the National Book Award for Fiction in 1952, but in 1963 he argued that the novel's "literary" achievements were a "political" shortcoming: that the committed naturalism of Richard Wright and *Native Son* was aesthetically inferior but politically superior to the subsequent fiction of fellow African American writers James Baldwin and Ralph Ellison. For Howe, *Invisible Man* not only was an individual political failure but metonymically exemplified the "ideological delusions" of the 1950s in its "esthetic distance" and extreme violations of realism. Especially "troublesome" to Howe was "the sudden, unprepared and implausible assertion of unconditioned freedom with which the novel ends. [...] Though the unqualified assertion of self-liberation was a favorite strategy among American literary people in the fifties, it is also vapid and insubstantial."[5]

Howe's "Black Boys and Native Sons" exemplifies the increasingly conservative literary convictions of the postwar anticommunist Left, which eschewed the putative detachment of modernist aesthetics and disavowed "the determinism of the thirties." Finally, though, the essay is best remembered for Ellison's scathing riposte: "The World and the Jug" was subsequently read as both manifesto and conceptual lexicon for decoding the aesthetic complexities of *Invisible Man*, though one especially significant line has been overlooked.[6] In a slyly devastating combination of ventriloquy and obloquy, Ellison remarks that "Ellison also offends by having the narrator of *Invisible Man* speak of his life (Howe either missing the irony or assuming that *I* did) as one of 'infinite possibilities' while living in a hole in the ground."[7] In Chapter 2, I traced ways in which "irony" helps make assertions of freedom both qualified and legible, and here I argue that it is precisely Ellison's invocation of irony that renders the activist political aesthetics of *Invisible Man* both coherent and plausible.

This is not to say that Ellison's personal political commitments didn't change dramatically or that there aren't plausible alternative explanations for his language. As Barbara Foley has shown, by 1963 Ellison had long been engaged in a project of distancing himself from his deep and early involvement in Left politics of the *New Masses* variety, such that he "customarily disparaged the left but remained evasive regarding the novel's relationship to his own political history."[8] One might thus dismiss Ellison's invocation of irony as a mere renunciation like Langston Hughes's 1953 friendly testimony before the House Un-American Activities Committee. There, Hughes successfully disavowed his own 1930s communism and justified "Goodbye Christ" by patiently explaining the concept of persona to the senators, claiming that it was "an ironical and satirical poem."[9] Despite the fact that both Hughes and Ellison were accusing audiences of failing to perceive irony, Red-baiting persecution and relatively friendly literary exchanges are quite different from one another: not simply because Hughes was charged with being insufficiently Right, while Ellison is alternatively attacked for being insufficiently Left or insufficiently liberal, but because Ellison forthrightly and consistently claims irony to describe rather than to disavow *Invisible Man*'s activist politics.

Old Stories About the New Criticism

A more common critical tactic is to reduce Ellison's use of "irony" by locating it within a limited, retrospective reading of New Criticism. Howe himself suggested as much when he claimed that "to write simply about 'Negro experience' with the esthetic distance urged by the critics of the fifties, is a moral and psychological impossibility."[10] Here "esthetic distance" partially refers to the literary echoes of philosophical existentialism, an association that supposedly taints both Ellison's novel and the entire decade surrounding its publication. Yet "esthetic distance" also suggests the quarantine of literary production and reception from "real" political literature, an ostensibly necessary distance articulated by the diverse set of thinkers roped together as the New Critics. "[L]ike a New Critic," Foley writes, "the invisible man cherishes the ambivalence that enables him to oscillate between the poles of antinomy and avoid the dull certainties of political commitment."[11] As with other erstwhile radical authors in the United States, Ellison's later rightward political migration has served as a means of stabilizing the highly unstable ironies of his novel. Indeed, while the novel itself remained unchanged, over the course of the 1950s and 1960s *Invisible Man* allegedly followed its author and larger institutional trends by steadily becoming depoliticized; as Lawrence Jackson writes, "underlying this transformation in the meaning of the novel *Invisible Man* was the widespread adaptation of the New Criticism in American colleges and universities," ostensibly because "New Critical methods investigated tropes of paradox, irony, and ambiguity and exclusively confined their analyses to the printed artifact."[12]

These critiques typically conflate "irony" and "New Criticism," render "irony" and "ambiguity" synonymous, and thus make irony—particularly as it functions in modernist fiction—so pervasive as to become paradoxically invisible. The arguments both rely upon and propound a sort of transitive logic, which acknowledges irony as a key term for New

Criticism, tacitly assumes a definition of politics in order to stipulate that New Criticism produced an "apolitical" evaluation of literature, takes "New Criticism" as synecdoche for formalist literary evaluation writ large, and therefore concludes that "irony" indicates a retreat from politics for both individuals and society as a whole.[13] "[T]he emerging valorization of qualities such as myth, irony, and alienation as the markers of great literature and art," Foley writes elsewhere, "cannot be fully understood apart from the 1950s cultural establishment's disaffiliation from, and disparagement of, the socially committed representations of the 1930s."[14] The opposition of "social commitment" to irony here is typical, even if Foley does (with deft irony, it should be noted) concede that such ostensible retreat from responsible literary practice may not have been intentional, exactly, for "clearly it would be reductionist (and, God forbid, 'vulgar Marxist'!) to posit that the elevation of irony and paradox as the defining qualities of literary value was all part of a ruling-class conspiracy."[15] Again, Foley exemplifies a much broader discourse, echoing an analysis made by Daniel Bell as early as 1960: that a generation of disillusioned radicals including Lionel Trilling, John Dos Passos, Reinhold Niebuhr, and Richard Wright were "after the Moscow Trials and the Soviet-Nazi pact, disenchanted and reflective; and from them and their experiences we have inherited the key terms which dominate discourse today: irony, paradox, ambiguity, and complexity."[16]

This transitive logic must ignore a good deal of evidence to the contrary, and my previous chapters have argued that irony was a central and popular term for representing a nexus of radical social, literary, and political values long before the institutionalization of American New Criticism. Indeed, even African American Communists writing for other writers and readers on the Left had employed irony as a desirable criterion of value long before publication of *The Well-Wrought Urn*: "the poetry of Sterling Brown has become progressively more realistic and proletarian," Black Communist theorist Eugene Clay wrote in the proceedings of the 1935 American Writers' Congress. "Not only is the handling of his material more deft, but his irony has become more trenchant, the revolutionary implication surer, the humor more Olympian and the perspective wider."[17] "Let Negro writers write about the irony and pathos of the *colored* American Legion," a still-radical Langston Hughes wrote in that same volume.[18]

None of this is to deny that Ellison was indeed an avid reader of the *Kenyon Review, Sewanee Review*, and other organs of New Criticism. It is furthermore true that Albert Erskine, who had helped Cleanth Brooks found the *Southern Review* (one of the major organs for second-wave

American New Criticism), worked closely with Ellison to trim hundreds of pages from his manuscripts. It is finally unclear, however, how illuminating it is to assert that "ultimately [Erskine's] saturation in the New Criticism made him an apt match for Ellison's project," even if the reductive version of irony is symptomatically commonplace.[19] Yes, New Criticism emphasized form and content, structure and texture; such emphasis departed from differently ideological systems of interpretation advocated by proletarian critics like Mike Gold or reactionary New Humanists such as Irving Babbit. Furthermore, the strain of New Criticism that emerged from the Agrarian South was frequently, indisputably, unapologetically racist; in these terms, it makes more sense to think of Ellison's irony as an agonistic intervention in and repurposing of the literary-critical discourse that he is too frequently taken to exemplify.

Deciphering what exactly Howe failed to see when he "missed the irony" of *Invisible Man* requires a more comprehensive account of what irony signified in these years, though an exhaustive account of the role played by irony within New Criticism—itself an almost impossibly unwieldy category of diverse work—would require several separate books (one task of which would likely be to disentangle irony as a distinct term from paradox and ambiguity). While the paradox of a narrator who advocates action while seemingly refusing to act is the most obvious of the novel, and the conclusion of the novel emphasizes rather than clarifies the ambiguity that has distinguished the frame, the narrator does state, "The hibernation is over. I must shake off the old skin and come up for breath," and now "having tried to give pattern to the chaos which lives within the pattern of your certainties, I must come out, I must emerge." In the next paragraph, he repeats himself by reminding the reader that "as I said before, a decision has been made. I'm shaking off the old skin and I'll leave it here in the hole. I'm coming out, no less invisible without it, but coming out nevertheless."[20] If one difference between "irony" and "ambiguity" is that irony relies upon the presence of narrative information while ambiguity relies upon the absence of that information, the fact that the narrator is "coming out" in the present rather than the future tense indicates that it is the process of writing and producing his memoir/novel that qualifies as an emergence into the world of political action. While the novel *constitutes* a "coming out," it nevertheless fails to *depict* his "coming out" and doesn't describe what the narrator plans to do once he ceases hibernating.[21] The novel does, however, provide the necessary information to connect disparate strands of narrative such that by the end of the epigraph, "irony" accurately describes the absence of narrative events.

Indeed, the novel's refusal to depict the narrator's emergence is a refusal to resolve those ironies that Ellison repeatedly emphasized. And it is this lack of resolution, this resistance to depicting the emergence of the narrator that is read as an endorsement of withdrawal: a situation in which representation is equivalent to advocacy and a direct denial of the most widely distributed New Critical emphasis on resolved ironies. This lack of resolution is something that at least two leading exponents of the New Criticism would frankly identify as a failure; they would, however, describe this failure in political terms that qualify the Prologue and Epilogue as exercises in irony. In the "Letter to the Teacher" preface to their hugely popular 1943 textbook *Understanding Fiction*, Cleanth Brooks and Robert Penn Warren unambiguously described what role irony played in their critical system. A crucial function of irony, they wrote,

> is to indicate an awareness of the multiplicity of options in conduct, idea, or attitude—an awareness of the full context. This suggests one of the objections which may be brought against the emphasis on irony; the objection that such an emphasis ends in the celebration of a smug and futile skepticism which is at variance with the actual effect which most successful literary compositions leave upon the reader. The editors would hope that, by this time, the grounds upon which they would answer this particular objection are clear. They would not endorse an irony which precluded resolution but they would endorse an irony which forced the reader to take stock of as full a context as possible. The reader wants the resolution, but he does not want it too easy or too soon.[22]

Opposing "smug and futile skepticism" with both feeling and social commitment, they simultaneously stipulate that irony is inextricable from choice in both thought and action; they also portend decades of objections not only to both Ralph Ellison and to *Invisible Man* but to an entire strain of modernist aesthetics.[23]

Ellison also clearly shared with many New Critics the sense that "irony" signified the complication of mere "facts." More broadly, the salient opposition of literary language to scientific language that appears in such works as *The Well-Wrought Urn* casts useful light on the role played by facts and values within literature engaging the politics of race in the United States. After all, "it is the scientist whose truth requires a language purged of every trace of paradox"; if the distinctively "literary" features of language were to be excised (e.g., by paraphrase), then "deprived of the character of paradox with its twin concomitants of irony and wonder," Brooks writes, the poem "unravels into 'facts,' biological, sociological, and economic."[24] In this account, the critic distinguishes scientific language (wherein words ideally function as transparent data that are independent of their location in a semantic system) from literary language, wherein "irony is the most general term that we have for the kind of qualification which the various elements in a context receive from the context."[25] This emphasis on ascertainable, objective, and unambiguously transmitted facts as the basis for predictable political action is shared by those with a wide range of organized political sympathies. By 1945, when Ellison started working on *Invisible Man* in earnest, critics like Alfred Kazin were already asking, "Why is it that so much of a literature of the thirties and forties must seem in retrospect a literature of Fact . . . the chief effort of many writers seemed bent only on reporting, reporting; on running not too far behind the phenomena of the times?"[26] In 1946, Ellison was likewise asserting that "our naturalistic prose—one of the most vital bodies of twentieth-century fiction, perhaps the brightest instrument for recording sociological fact, physical action, the nuance of speech, yet achieved—becomes suddenly dull when confronting the Negro."[27] Later, in his 1953 acceptance speech for the National Book Award—for which Kazin was also on the jury—Ellison remarked that the "explosive nature of events mocks our brightest efforts. And the very 'facts' which the naturalists assumed would make us free have lost the power to protect us from despair."[28]

As I have argued over the past three chapters, facts are frequently understood as aesthetic objects; "irony" is regularly invoked as that which posits and describes the collapse of the fact-value dichotomy, and politics illuminates an attendant rejection of "mere fact" in favor of a representing a dynamic interplay of "values." While James Baldwin felt that the success of *Native Son* gave "proof that Americans were now able to look full in the face without flinching the dreadful facts," Ellison imagines political praxis to emerge not from merely amassing "dreadful facts" but from the inculcation of a particular disposition toward facts with the awareness that facts are already representations: a specifically literary politics anathema to sociology, for example, or legal positivism.[29] As Ellison wrote in 1957, novels "form the ground of assumptions upon which our social values rest; they inform our language and our conduct with public meaning, and they provide the broadest frame of reference for our most private dramas."[30] In short, the "ground of assumptions" among critics who talk about irony frequently conflate the beliefs of a supposedly apolitical author and his supposedly apolitical narrator, and it has long been difficult to disentangle the two objects of criticism. Irony refers both to embodied life and to disembodied representations of that life, and Ellison's critics frequently reproduce a limited logic wherein the presence of irony in one reciprocally taints the other: that an ironic life may produce a too-ironic novel or—worse—that a too-ironic novel will produce an author, and readers, who view politics with "mere" irony.[31]

When it comes to reading *Invisible Man*, "verbal irony" is obviously inadequate as a conceptual hermeneutic, even in its most satirical or sarcastic flavors, but of course the text doesn't explicitly explain what specific forms of irony are at work. A century earlier, explaining the language of his Fourth of July oration that serves as an epigraph to this chapter, Frederick Douglass clearly specified what *he* meant by irony: "biting ridicule, blasting reproach, withering sarcasm, and stern rebuke."[32] While indicting both hypocrisy and slavery on a public holiday dedicated to celebrating liberty, the idea that verbal irony was a decorous response to situational irony would have been apparent to Douglass's audience (not only to those schooled in the tenets of classical rhetoric). And yet, whereas Douglass confronted the outright denial of humanity to those of African descent, Ellison confronted a different, if no less peculiar, situation: almost eighty-five years after the end of the Civil War, African Americans were acknowledged legally as fully human and yet frequently denied both procedural protection as humans under the law and recognition as humans within the dominant culture. For Ellison, this fundamental contradiction between principle and practice—between ideal and action, value and fact, "ought" and "is"—constituted "a stave so deeply imbedded in the American *ethos* as to render America a nation of ethical schizophrenics. Believing truly in democracy on one side of their minds, they act on the other in violation of its most sacred principles; holding that all men are created equal, they treat thirteen million Americans as though they were not."[33] It is this glaring chasm between fact and value that irony was long imagined to be able uniquely to represent; as Douglass and Ellison confronted fundamentally different historical and rhetorical situations in 1852 and 1952, they also appealed to fundamentally different values of irony.[34]

While irony indicated the opposite of unproblematic "facts," Ellison also knew that the term resonated with a number of values that he was at pains to transvalue, including the dominant American logic of race. If New Critics such as Brooks and Robert Penn Warren were only some among many who regarded irony as a touchstone of literary value, for example, they also imagined an ideal reader to account for a text's full complications and implications. Note that the New Critic's ideal reader is almost by definition disembodied but nonetheless was assumed to resemble the white "man in the street (of whom the average college freshman is a good enough replica)."[35] Ellison conversely envisions the reader as not only embodied but quite specifically racialized. As he remarked in a 1955 interview, "There is a kind of ideal reader and that ideal reader would be a Negro who was in full possession of all the subtleties of literature and art and politics."[36] Ellison's stipulation of such an embodied reader dramatically complicates his relationship to New Critical positions and emphasizes the fact that Ellison didn't simply advocate the unreflective, deracialized universality at the heart of liberalism. Indeed, as Ellison explained to Kenneth Burke in a 1945 letter, "all the 'felt experience' which being a Negro American entails" made it impossible to sign on to either a disembodied universalism or the reactionary idiocy attending some American versions of formalism: "I certainly agree with you that universalism is desirable," Ellison wrote, "but I find that I am forced to arrive at that universe through the racial grain of sand, even though the term 'race' is loaded with all the lies which men like [Agrarian New Critic Donald] Davidson warm their values by."[37]

This is all to emphasize that the ideal reader of much New Criticism was inevitably imbricated by a pernicious racial and economic logic, and so too were the values of "irony" as a central term of that criticism. Since "irony" has long served as a commodious repository for different intersections of social, cultural, political, and aesthetic discourses, the term was inevitably freighted with racial logic long before ninety-four million people visited the blog listing irony as #50 of "Stuff White People Like."[38] Ellison detractor Jerry Gafio Watts, for example, has described a tradition that had "long rendered black people one-dimensional, dominated by racial concerns, and most importantly, void of irony," which is evident in curiously homologous ways by Carl Van Vechten's epigraph to this chapter and by aesthetic theorist Clive Bell's 1922 assertion that

> Not by irony and sarcasm, but by jeers and grimaces does Jazz
> mark its nobility and beauty. They are the products of the cultivated
> intellect, and Jazz cannot away with intellect or culture. Niggers
> can be admired artists without any gifts more singular than high
> spirits; so why drag in the intellect?[39]

As I have argued in earlier chapters, the strong association of irony with intellect and recognitive abilities dates at least to early modernism (if not early Romanticism), so Bell's and Van Vechten's off-handed racism is more representative than esoteric. Indeed, the specifically racialized aspect of the language lends an unnerving but symptomatic subtext to

Alain Locke's 1953 review of *Invisible Man*, where he expressed relief that "At last . . . here is a Negro writer capable of real and sustained irony."[40]

The contextual logic of an assumed "white irony" reframes Ellison's frequent, salient invocation of irony to describe the interpretive conditions in which his novel was received. This is the context in which he asserted that "We Negroes are the most ironic observers of the American scene," simultaneously inverting and gainsaying the tradition that denied irony to African Americans.[41] Ellison's assertions about African American irony can be positioned within a broader twentieth-century dialogue about the famed duality of African American consciousness, yet the notion of ironic duality itself is a contentious proposition. For Marxist critics such as Russell Ames, writing in *Science & Society* in 1950, irony is both a nonvolitional condition and an aesthetic practice that, in the case of African Americans, is further evidence of injustice and inequality: "the American Negro, more than most people, has had subtlety and irony forced upon his art."[42] James Baldwin, on the other hand, understood ironic double-consciousness quite differently in 1951, claiming not only that "no American Negro exists who does not have his private Bigger Thomas living in the skull" but that it is precisely the *recognition* of this double-consciousness that can lead to a political liberation of consciousness described by irony: "Only this recognition sets him in any wise free and it is this," Baldwin writes, "which lends to Negro life its high element of the ironic."[43] That is to say, in a moment where irony can describe a deplorable condition and a practice foisted upon members of a disempowered group, thinkers like Ellison and Baldwin draw upon an alternative tradition wherein irony describes the subjective process of recognizing and ameliorating this condition. In this respect, Baldwin revises the New Critical formulation wherein "irony is our most general term for indicating . . . recognition of incongruities" and establishes a recognizable background for Ellison's rearrangement of irony's unstable equipoise of perspective, subjective condition, and artistic practice: "segregation is far more than a negative social condition," Ellison wrote in 1989. "[I]t is also a perspective that fosters an endless exercise of irony."[44]

The "Real" Politics of Irony

And thus, at long last, I return to the question with which this chapter started: why would Ellison invoke irony as a defense when it seems to be the crime of irony with which he and his novel were being charged?[45] As always, irony's multiplicity provides many answers depending on how and where the critic decides to stabilize the term; that is, whether one chooses "verbal" or "dramatic" or "New Critical" or "Romantic" or "modernist" of the high-, late-, or post- variety. As is also frequently the case, the definition of "irony" one chooses to employ is a useful masquerade for stealthily stipulating equally contentious definitions of "politics." Evaluations of the novel's politics frequently rely upon the same tacit definitions of "real" politics—especially liberal politics—and imply that these limitations are shared by both the novel and the author. As Kenneth Warren argues, Ralph Ellison's contention that the "problem of race . . . was the problem of the novel" was "wrong, because the problem of race . . . is at bottom a problem of politics and economics—of constitution making and of wielding power legislatively and economically in order to mobilize broad constituencies to preserve an unequal social order."[46]

Perhaps these critics are right, and "real" politics—and, by extension, the adjunct of "real" political literature—is to organize constituencies into coalitions that elect and then influence their legislators to pass laws that are more just and equitable. In this view, the role of literature is to depict the reprehensible in unequivocally reprehensible terms and then construct characters whose responses can serve as models for readers who will presumably become organizers or direct actors, if not voters, legislators, and judges: a mimetic chain whereby the author is a middle term in an unbroken series of imitations running from life to text and back into life. On the other hand, as a still-radical Walter Lippmann wrote in 1913, progressive laws "are a symptom and an aid but certainly not the cause" of progressive actions. "Constitutions do not make people; people make constitutions. So the task of reform consists not in presenting a state with progressive laws, but in getting the people to want them."[47] Lippmann would argue that "getting people to want" good laws is a job for both propaganda and literature. While many critics claim that *Invisible Man* is the wrong kind of literature for political praxis (how useful for building would an ironic blueprint be, after all?), to recognize what Ralph Ellison meant by "irony" is to recognize how the novel still serves as a model for reflecting upon extra-institutional politics; these can only be read as a failure if one denies the possibility of individual politics in the first instance and (impossibly) quarantines aesthetic activity from the "real" political action whose purview and definition are already assumed. And to recognize Ralph Ellison's irony is to recognize one of the most interesting theorists of irony in the twentieth century as one of Ellison's key interlocutors: Kenneth Burke.[48]

Mastering Tropes Beyond the New Criticism

All literary criticism may be said to exist in a dialogue with its literary object, but in the case of Ellison, something like a "trialogue" has developed among his novel, his critics, and Ellison himself. Since Ellison published many more words in interviews and essays than in his novel, it is perhaps not surprising that his criticism—like "The World and the Jug" or "The Little Man at Chehaw Station"—has provided the most widely employed interpretive framework for reading his novel.[49] Ellison's frequent invocations of irony in this body of work can't be said to provide explicit instructions for decoding the irony of his novel but do clarify the ways in which he used the term, suggest how sensitive he was to its possibilities, and serve to alert his own readership to the presence of irony in ways that fundamentally alter the felicity conditions for meaning to be produced and understood.

In point of fact, Ellison so frequently invokes "irony" as an interpretive key to *Invisible Man* that it contributed significantly to the symbolic and interpretive economy in which the novel was received, serving as what Kenneth Burke calls a vital "terministic screen" for reading the novel.[50] In *Language as Symbolic Action*, Burke writes:

> Not only does the nature of our terms affect the nature of our observations in the sense that the terms direct the attention to one field rather than to another. Also, *many of the "observations" are but implications of the particular terminology in terms of which the observations are made*. In brief, much that we take as observations about "reality" may be but the spinning out of possibilities implicit in our particular choice of terms.[51]

Here, Burke helps us see why Ellison might have pointed his readers to "irony" so frequently and consistently over almost fifty years; why Ellison was drawn to "the nature of the term" irony, not just the "use" of irony; and what "possibilities" literary irony possessed for him as a means for understanding aesthetics and politics.

Bryan Crable has recently analyzed the "intimate connections between Ellison's project and his friendship with Burke," expanding upon what Ellison scholars have known for years: that it was Burke, perhaps more than any other single writer, who influenced *Invisible Man* and its underlying theory of how literature might have social and political impact.[52] In the preface to *Shadow and Act*, for example, Ellison expressed "special indebtedness" to "a community of ideas and critical standards for two decades, and to Kenneth Burke, the stimulating source of many of these."[53] The collection of essays and interviews is filled with Burke's name and conceptual vocabulary, as when Ellison asserts in the "Art of Fiction" interview that "The three parts [of *Invisible Man*] represent the narrator's movement from, using Kenneth Burke's terms, purpose to passion to perception."[54] Ellison felt strongly that Burke had provided a "Gestalt through which I could apply intellectual insights back into my materials and my own life."[55] In a letter of gratitude he wrote to Burke in 1945, he asserted that "the one stable thing I have in this sea of uncertainty is the raft of your concepts on which I lie as I paddle my way towards the shore."[56]

Ellison's interest in Burke went back as far as June 5, 1935, when Ellison heard Burke speak at the New School for Social Research. As editor of the journal *Directions* in 1941, Burke published Ellison's essay "Richard Wright and Recent Negro Fiction" and approvingly quoted "the Negro intellectual Ralph Ellison" in his 1935 *Permanence and Change*. In 1943 Ellison wrote the first of many letters to Burke—which eventually ranged from coherent theoretical exchanges to equivalents of hung-over, post-party text messages sent via U.S. Postal Service—to request a copy of Burke's 1931 book *Counterstatement*. As he wrote to Burke on November 23, 1945:

> if in the little things I write from time to time you observe anything of value, then to that extent am I able to express concretely my appreciation for what you have done. That is a debt I shall never stop paying and it begins back in the thirties when you read the rhetoric of "Hitler's Battle" before the League of American Writers, at the New School (I believe you were the only speaker out of the whole group who was concerned with writing *and politics*, rather than writing as an *excuse** [*for politics].[57]

Ellison continued to cite Burke in interviews, to quote him extensively in essays, and to use Burke's unique vocabulary for describing the relationship between writing and action. In "The Little Man at Chehaw Station," for instance, Ellison virtually plagiarizes Burke to assert that

> principles in action are enactments of ideals grounded in a vision of perfection that transcends the limitations of death and dying. By arousing in the believer a sense of the disrelation between the ideal and the actual, between the perfect word and the errant flesh, they partake of mystery. Here the most agonizing mystery sponsored by the democratic ideal is that of our unity-in-diversity, our oneness-in-manyness.[58]

For Ellison, in this passage, the word "mystery" does not invoke a resigned obscurantism in the face of magic, as in the term's theological incarnations, but rather designates a certain inability to describe analytically how "values" and "facts" are intertwined and how attempting to deduce one from the other performs the "naturalist fallacy."

Today Burke appears as perhaps the most strikingly original (if discursive and occasionally maddening) theorist of irony publishing in English in the twentieth century, which makes the relative absence of "irony" as a key term for understanding Ellison and Burke all the more striking. Indeed, when reading *Invisible Man* with Burke in mind, irony emerges as one of the strongest logs in the Burkean "raft of concepts" that bolster *Invisible Man* as a political document seeking to produce dispositions toward information rather than prescribing particular actions. Burke devoted much of his career to arguing that "Every book embodies a set of values—and implicit in every set of values there is a social attitude, or program of conduct"; if how one acts in the world is preceded and inflected by how one perceives the relationship among meaning, action, and outcome, then to inculcate an "attitude" in a reader is to fulfill a necessary precondition for any other action.[59] As it turns out, "irony" describes the values of both the book and the reader who "acts in the world."

Ellison often related the story of how he had learned to hunt by reading the novels of Ernest Hemingway, because Hemingway "wrote with such precision about the processes and techniques of daily living that I could keep myself and my brother alive during the 1937 Recession by following his descriptions of wing-shooting; because he knew the difference between politics and art and something of their true relationship for the writer."[60] If Hemingway could write novels that taught Ellison to hunt, critics seem to ask, why couldn't he write a novel that *combined* politics and art to teach readers how to engage in political action? How could Ellison actually believe that great art could teach people how to shoot pheasants but not Klansmen? Or that it could model the organization of a fishing trip but not of a broad-based coalition of community activists, leaders of national foundations, and congressional representatives? Was it not an irresponsible contradiction (corrupted by a faint whiff of aestheticism) for Ellison to claim that "protest is an element of all art, though it does not necessarily take the form of speaking for a political or social program," and that the "protest is [in *Invisible Man*] . . . because I *put* it there . . . in the belief that the work of art is important in itself, that it is a social action in itself?"[61]

No, because to recognize how irony as a concept functioned in a larger grammar of late modernist literary and political culture is to recognize that "getting" the irony is finally a necessary (but not sufficient) political condition. It is necessary not only to redress some enduring misconceptions about Ellison and *Invisible Man* but also to understand significant relationships between "public" and "private" forms of literary and political practice, particularly when literary and cultural critics began—as they did in mid-twentieth-century U.S. culture—to associate irony with terms like "responsibility," "recognition," "decision," and "law." While irony is often considered to be a merely mimetic formal device for reflecting what Ellison called "the irony implicit in the dynamics of American democracy," irony's broader discursive history suggests how literary practice and political practice are related in aesthetic, but distinctly *nonmimetic*, ways.[62] *Invisible Man* and Ellison's exposition of it are not wholly discrete activities but work in combination toward providing a vision of democratic praxis that lies outside the parameters of electoral politics. This would be a praxis based not upon rational exchange of information in a marketplace of ideas, to be deliberated upon with the aim of forming consensus, but the fostering of an attitude toward information and community that would value agonistic disagreement as the means by which just decisions are reached in a democracy. In this respect, Ellison participates in a tradition of American politics that is neither specifically Marxian nor classically liberal nor remotely conservative, a tradition locating in "impractical" narrative and even "impractical practice" the possibility of effecting change in the "practical" realms of law and politics (as opposed to the other way around, wherein literature is a product of economic and institutional relationships). By emphasizing moments of decision and the importance of reflecting upon individual and collective responsibility, *Invisible Man* inculcates habits of awareness in readers rather than prescribing specific courses of action.

The conventional wisdom about irony generally bears an uncanny similarity to the more familiar opposition between the literary naturalism represented by Wright and the late modernism represented by Ellison: as Ellison and *Invisible Man* are understood to share irony as a salient characteristic, *Invisible Man* is figured as a palinode to *Native Son* that also spelled the beginning of the end of the friendship between Ellison and Wright. This is emphatically not to characterize *Native Son* as somehow devoid of irony but to point out that Max's speech and Bigger's imminent death conclude the novel and figuratively resolve any hanging ironies in the narrative as a whole. As long as political action seems synonymous with earnest promotion of institutions and authorized actions to reform those institutions—such as states, political parties, or various nongovernmental associations—then these discourses reiterate the assumption that irony (as a quality of both personal and literary character) is anathema to serious political commitment. This is as true for critics like Foley today as it was true in 1947 for Charles Humboldt, the literary editor for the Communist journal *Mainstream*, lamenting the presence of "agents of doom" in novels, for such agents "teach us first, that nature works in a mysterious way to punish us for our civilized futility, and second, that the realm of action, of politics, is ruled by irony. Thus there is no escape."[63] It was still true when Louis Menand remarked that "The kind of racism that figures in most of *Native Son* . . . is not tragic, and it is not an occasion for irony. It is simply criminal."[64]

If we accept Humboldt's assumption that literature plays a role in forming or encouraging worldviews and heed his admonition that the responsible stance of an activist reader is to fight against a worldview wherein "politics are ruled by irony," then Menand's idea that depicting horrific racism is anathema to both irony and tragedy makes sense. In this reading, Bigger's obscene poverty and the murders he commits are traceable to a common cause of systemic and individual racism, and all three are imagined to be adequately and responsibly represented only by confessional polemic, unironic naturalism, or gritty social realism. For the moment, set aside the important question of what kinds of racism *would* provide an "occasion for irony." Rather, focus on the curious fact that the conflict in both Menand's and Humboldt's formulations is not simply between irony and racism but between irony and criminality; irony, in other words, is defined in opposition to what is—or should be—defined and controlled by the domain of law.[65]

Irony, when used to denote a publicly expressed worldview or a belief that action is incongruous with expectation or intention, is imagined as corrosive to political praxis because democratic politics supposedly reside within and emerge from law, a linguistic realm in which obvious tropes are manifestly unwelcome.[66] If Ellison's critics object to the failures of *Invisible Man* to get to the real politics of lawmaking, Burke's vision and version of "irony" describe a relationship between literature and law such that a novel can itself be understood to serve as a sort of nonstatist "constitution" to form attitudes in readers and consequently guide their actions. Identification of those conflicting "principles" and "practices" is no simple matter, especially when one asserts—as Ellison consistently did—that pluralistic disagreement rather than consensus unanimity is a political value to be nurtured rather than an uncomfortable fact to be pragmatically overcome. The idea that the sole course for rectifying antidemocratic practice resides within the law or within mass-organized, direct action is depicted with no small amount of irony in *Invisible Man*; Burke's theory of how irony relates to both law and political representation explains how this can be so. The connection reveals not only that recognizing the fundamental paradox in constitutional democracy is a necessary precursor to healthy democratic practice but also that if "irony," "law," and "political action" exist in mutual exclusion, they are excluded as much by bad reading as by bad writing.

Burke's conception of language is somewhere between the Nietzsche of "On Truth and Lies in an Extra-Moral Sense" and the Wittgenstein of the *Philosophical Investigations*. While he asserts that "language develops by metaphorical extension, in borrowing words from the realm of the corporeal, visible, tangible and applying them by analogy to the realm of the incorporeal, invisible, intangible; then in the course of time, the original corporeal reference is forgotten," he is finally concerned with how language functions in shaping individuals' attitudes and dispositions toward the world.[67] For example, in "Key Words for Critics," a short review essay about New Criticism that he wrote for the *Kenyon Review* in 1942, Burke extends John Crowe Ransom's comparison of exegetical practice to democratic practice; Burke recounts how Ransom "calls the unitary interpretation of a poem 'Hegelian,' and 'mystical'" and "likens the poem instead to a 'democratic' organization that gives a distinctive measure of local autonomy to the details, or 'texture' of the work."[68] It is significant, but hardly surprising, that a politically committed critic such as Burke would pick up on a distinctly political rhetoric in criticism that is popularly understood to be apolitical. More interesting is how Burke expands Ransom's analogy to compare the organization of states and poems by inverting a standard articulation of the American political motto: "Were I to suggest a slogan for his version of the poetic state," Burke writes, "it would be not *e pluribus unum* but *ex uno plura*."[69]

While "language as symbolic action" is probably Burke's most famous legacy to literary studies, the imagined relationship that he gleans from Ransom's work—between literary organization and federal organization—occupied a substantial amount of Burke's attention in his post-communist years. Indeed, part of what attracted Ellison to Burke's work was Burke's focus on "the old problem of unity and diversity," the paradox at the heart of democratic organization that Ellison redacted as that "most agonizing mystery sponsored by the democratic ideal . . . that of our unity-in-diversity, our oneness-in-manyness."[70] Burke's rendition of irony in particular bears directly on how the novel might help individual agents relate to the central paradoxes of American democracy: not only that supposedly universal values of the Constitution and the Declaration of Independence were denied to a large portion of the American population but also that the tension among popular sovereignty, minority rights, and individual autonomy itself constitutes an irreducible paradox.

In "Four Master Tropes"—which accounts for metaphor, metonymy, synecdoche, and irony—Burke's primary concern is "not with their purely figurative usage, but with their rôle in the discovery and description of 'the truth.'"[71] For Burke, distinguishing among the tropes—that is, distinguishing precisely how "irony" functions as opposed to any of the other tropes—is itself a provisional exercise, for "the four tropes shade into one another."[72] That the tropes are finally inextricable, however, does not mean that engaging any given text (or the very concept of textuality itself) via one of the tropes is useless; rather, Burke asserts that any such investigation can be undertaken if one is cognizant that strict isolation of categories is more than misguided when it comes to linguistic enterprises. Such strict isolation characterizes the method of "scientific realism," which is anathema to the "poetic realism" that can produce genuine insight into such realms as human motivation, attitude, action, and *decision*; the reasons why tropes must be banished from the language of science are thus the very stuff of "poetic realism."[73]

So far, this account of tropes may seem like a familiar discussion of figurative language as such. In the historical moment anticipating Gunnar Myrdal's sociological compendium *An American Dilemma*, however, and several years before such sociological data would be submitted as *amici* briefs in *Brown v. Board of Education*, the question of how best to "represent" humanity and the conditions in which humans live had a particularly pointed resonance. The question of what type of knowledge—"aesthetic" knowledge or "scientific" knowledge—would most likely produce real effects in the real world was of more than passing theoretical interest. When Burke refers to "the widespread belief that the mathematico-quantitative ideal of the physical sciences can and should serve as the ideal of the 'social sciences,'" he is calling for an alternative, nonquantitative means of representing both individuals and large groups of people.[74] In this emphasis on value-oriented aesthetic inquiry as a means of social-individualist political resistance to an increasingly oppressive state (and emphasis purely on mass action), Burke's politics sound very much like the mid-century libertarian socialism of former Trotskyites like Dwight Macdonald.[75]

Here Burke's work achieves a pointed utility for reading *Invisible Man*. Ellison, like many of his postnaturalist contemporaries, believed that positivistic representations of human life inevitably reduced those lives to pure products of conditions. This was "unfortunate," in Ellison's view, because "many Negroes have been trying to define their own predicament in exclusively sociological terms, a situation I consider quite short-sighted. Too many of us have accepted a statistical interpretation of our lives and thus much of that which makes us a source of moral strength to America goes unappreciated and undefined."[76] In Burke's terms, such representations as one might find in a sociological account of human relationships are bound to reduce humanity to such qualities as can be measured and calculated by census takers; as a false reduction, they fail to serve as a "representative anecdote" through which genuine insight can be gained. This sense, of course, fueled much of Ellison's critique of Wright, which was consonant with Burke's assertion that Wright's "role as a Marxist critic transcended his role as a Negro novelist."[77] If, for Burke, "any terminological approach to the analysis of human acts or relationship that is shaped in conformity with an unrepresentative case" would patently fail to illustrate problems of motivation and action, the obvious question arises: what sort of textual data would provide such a "representative anecdote"? Burke's reply is succinct, for it is precisely that question "that takes us into the fourth pair: irony and dialectic."[78]

Burke doesn't taxonomically distinguish among different forms of irony.[79] Rather, he keeps all these definitions of irony simultaneously in play, unexpectedly employing the term in opposition to "relativism," which occurs in "the fragmentation of either drama or dialectic. That is, if you isolate any one agent in a drama, or any one advocate in a dialogue, and see the whole in terms of his position alone, you have the purely relativistic. And in relativism there is no irony" (512). Burke's version of "relativism" is the "reduction" of any given situation to just one viewpoint, which the reader (or spectator, or viewer) is necessarily forced to adopt. This is not just aesthetically degraded, he argues, but socially and politically pernicious and anathema to pluralistic society because "relativism sees everything in but one set of terms" (512). Irony, on the other hand,

> arises when one tries, by the interaction of terms upon one another, to produce a *development* which uses all the terms. Hence, from the standpoint of this total form (this "perspective of perspectives"), none of the participating "sub-perspectives" can be treated as either precisely right or precisely wrong. They are all voices, or personalities, or positions, integrally affecting one another. (512)

To define irony in these terms is to revise radically the idea that politically engaged fiction must mimetically describe a series of events or situations and predict or instruct how the reader might react within them. Rather, with Burke's interjection of ethical language ("right" and

"wrong") into his definition of irony, we understand that irony simultaneously describes both the linguistic action of a text and the weighing
of perspectives faced by a reader of that text. Because perspectives cannot be "treated as either *precisely* right or *precisely* wrong," Burke avoids
the absolutist tendency that he understands as anathema to both irony
and democracy; for pluralistic democracy can only exist within a society
wherein no agent grants prima facie privilege to one "voice" or "perspective" over another.

This conception of irony has profound implications for understanding
the polyphony of voices and perspectives that pervade *Invisible Man*, as
well as Ellison's critical description of his narrator's "ironic, down-home
voice."[80] This is a narrator who, as Ellison reflects in the 1981 introduction to *Invisible Man*, "had been forged in the underground of American
experience and yet managed to emerge less angry than ironic." He is "a
blues-toned laugher at wounds who included himself in his indictment
of the human condition."[81] Ellison's indictment of his narrator, or his
narrator's indictment of himself as well as the world in which he lives,
suggests that Ellison's narrative voice is neither superior to nor disengaged from the society that he is describing. By including his narrator
in the indictment of the world and yet engaging that world critically,
Ellison constructs the kind of readers that he didn't find in Irving Howe:
the kind who, as he wrote to Howe, "will come to view this exchange as
an act of, shall we say, 'antagonistic co-operation.'"[82] Such readers are
attuned to Burke's own definition of "true irony": "irony that really does
justify the attribute of 'humility,' is not 'superior' to the enemy. True
irony, humble irony, is based upon a sense of fundamental kinship with
the enemy, as one *needs* him, is *indebted* to him, is not merely outside
him as an observer but contains him *within*, being consubstantial with
him."[83]

Individual instances of irony obviously pervade *Invisible Man*, but
irony as a conceptual political schema requires more broadly formal
reading; it becomes visible by juxtaposing crucial scenes of "action" in
the terms that Ellison and Burke used to theorize the constellation of
irony, politics, law, recognition, and responsibility. Both scenes occur
in Harlem: one depicts the fight against an eviction, which begins the
narrator's career in political organization, and the other depicts the
burning of a tenement building by its residents. To recognize irony in
these scenes, I suggest, is to recognize Ellison's critique of legal formalism, consensus, and heroic models of politics as insufficient conditions
for genuine change. To understand *Invisible Man*'s irony specifically as
non-New-Critical, non-Romantic but resolutely Burkean and Ellisonian

irony—as a "parliamentary development" of terms with a telos of reevaluation rather than conclusion—suggests more than simply another definition of irony for the taxonomic heap. It suggests models of aesthetic representation and politics, which discourage reliance on institutional action in order to promote a model of recognition, ethical information, and decision making based upon an ideal of "sub-certainty."

Direct Action, Ironic Action, and the Law

Despite all the focus upon his putative failure to "act," Invisible Man actually does spend much of the novel engaged in recognizable politics. There is, first of all, the fact that the narrator's underground residence is itself supported by a form of direct action: his life isn't subsidized by a trust fund or a wage but by a "battle with Monopolated Light & Power." He has rerouted power into his hole, "wired the entire ceiling, every inch of it. And not with fluorescent bulbs, but with the older, more-expensive-to-operate kind, the filament type" in order to "carry on a fight against them without their realizing it . . . I use their service and pay them nothing at all, and they don't know it."[84] While more current notions of environmental responsibility might not favor this particular action against corporate monopolies, the narrator doesn't conceive of his enlightened squatting as mere theft; rather, he likens his actions to a long tradition of radical resistance to oppressive organizations: taking the power is "An act of sabotage, you know" (7).

Ellison was no Wobbly, but the "sabotage" exemplifies the novel's refusal to provide customary, comfortable models of liberal political action for readers to emulate: none of the characters is seen voting or lobbying for a Voting Rights Act, and only the march to Tod Clifton's funeral seems familiar. None of them marches on Washington, boycotts businesses with discriminatory hiring practices, or campaigns for a constitution that guarantees the rule of law without reference to race, gender, or creed. The narrative does indicate that such actions have been taken in the past: Barrelhouse the bartender explains to the narrator why Harlem has grown disillusioned with the Brotherhood, "things are tight and lots of folks who got jobs through you people have lost them" (426), by which the reader understands that action had been taken to secure employment for residents of the community. Whatever specific tactics used while "you people was fighting for 'em" (426), however, occur beyond the sight of the reader and are thus putatively unusable as a guide to future action in the "real" world. The types of direct action that *are* represented, nonetheless, delineate a relationship between "action" and "represented action" and suggest how the ironic representation of action in a novel might be imagined to lead to "real" action in the "real" world. Models of direct action contrast the concept of law with heroic models of leadership and history, where the possibility of collective action is thought to reside in a particularly charismatic, intrepid, or strategic individual; when read as parodic parataxis, the two scenes embody the circulation of multiple voices—as opposed to the one voice of a leader—that characterizes Burkean/Ellisonian irony.

Right before the eviction scene, for example, the narrator finishes the roasted yams he purchased from a street vendor and experiences a revelation: he will no longer deny himself what he understands as his authentic desires, whether or not their fulfillment is socially acceptable (he has previously associated yams with the life he left behind in the South). This momentary assertion of individual will is followed by a dilemma of collective action. Suddenly coming upon a "rapidly growing crowd" and piles of worn furniture that he mistakes for refuse, he realizes that he is witnessing the forcible eviction of an old couple from their apartment, and he is filled with "a sense of foreboding . . . a quick sense of uncleanliness" (267). The assembled crowd objects to the eviction, too: several believe that somebody "ought to beat the hell out of those paddies" (268) because "they got no business putting these old folks out on the sidewalk" (269). But nobody raises a voice or hand to stop them. When one man opines that "'Sho, we ought to stop 'em . . . but ain't that much nerve in the whole bunch,'" his interlocutor's response is significant: "'There's plenty nerve,' the slender man said. 'All they need is someone to set it off. All they need is a leader. You mean *you* don't have the nerve'" (268). The response is significant because it invokes the primary model of leadership that the narrator has heretofore desired to emulate and which he has experienced in the form of the corporate leader Mr. Norton and the corrupt head of the college, Dr. Bledsoe. The implication is that the narrator's longstanding desire to be a heroic "leader with nerve" will be fulfilled in this scene and perhaps throughout the remainder of the novel.

The crowd does mobilize collectively but pointedly *not* because of leadership on the part of the narrator or anyone else. Rather, they begin to move when the evicted woman tries to force her way back into the apartment with a family Bible and is physically prevented from doing so by the marshal. When he warns that "'You can't go in, lady,'" "'I want to pray!' she said. 'All we want to do is go in and pray,' she said, clutching her Bible." Her demand inspires the crowd's first comment to the marshal: "Sure, let them old folks pray," while others shout, "That's what's wrong with us now, all this damn praying" (274). As the tension begins to escalate and the policeman warns the crowd back with his pistol, the narrator is filled with physical revulsion and a desire to help with the attack on the police. "Beneath it all," however, "boiled up all the shock-absorbing phrases that I had learned all my life" (275), and he launches into a speech that reveals his "shock-absorbing phrases" to be the language of law: "'No, no,' I heard myself yelling. 'Black men! Brothers! Black Brothers! That's not the way. We're law abiding. We're a law-abiding people. [. . .] Let's follow a leader, let's organize. *Organize*" (276). Engaging in repartee with a crowd that is increasingly agitated but momentarily diverted, speaking "without thought but out of [his] clashing emotions" (275), he asks and conservatively answers Lenin's revolutionary question: "'*What is to be done?* I propose we do the wise thing, the law-abiding thing'" (277).

He proceeds, however, to engage in rhetoric and action that redefines "law-abiding." Pointing toward the marshal who is holding the crowd at bay, he says, "Look at him, standing with his blue steel pistol and his blue serge suit. . . . *Laws*, that's what we call them down South! Laws! And we're wise, and law-abiding" (278). This shifts the rhetorical register within which he is organizing the crowd such that "laws" no longer refers to a constitutionally mandated system of legislation, articulating wise or just principles intended to direct and regulate behavior. Instead, the narrator uses a vernacular idiom, "Laws," to describe the violently embodied enforcement of that system. This is not about the law of rent, he reminds the crowd, but the law of force. As the marshal says, "'I got my orders, Mac,' . . . waving the pistol with a sneer. 'You're doing all right, tell 'em to keep out of this. This is legal and I'll shoot if I have to'" (279). The narrator-turned-orator responds by addressing the crowd again and juxtaposing two forms of legal code—the divine biblical code and civil code elided into and embodied in the cop—that are proving useless in resisting or rectifying manifest injustice: "All we have is the Bible and this Law here rules that out" (280).

At this point, the narrator seems to exemplify the fundamentally conservative function of law in order to pacify the unruly crowd: if law serves to perpetuate certain relationships, principles, and forms of behavior, and to prevent other relationships, principles, and forms of behavior, this is how he means to prevent his "law-abiding people" from attacking the policeman. The scene opposes a "conservative" function of law, as much as a "liberal" function of law, having as it does an historical precedent in openly *radical* resistance to eviction and foreclosure that occurred in New York, Chicago, Detroit, Cleveland, and other cities in the early 1930s. Organized by Communist-led Unemployed Councils, riots like the one that became known as "The Battle of the Bronx" saw thousands of supporters shower police with bottles and sticks—not petitions or laws or pleas for mercy—at least temporarily halting the eviction actions.[85] The function of law in American history, of course, was particularly visible in how African American people had their social and economic status codified in both the national Constitution and in individual statutes that varied by state and region. As Ellison wrote in a 1976 essay titled "Perspectives of Literature," African Americans "could obey or break laws, but not make or interpret them."[86] Therefore, when considering forms of social action to ameliorate the condition of oppressed populations, Ellison "saw no hope in the law. It was to be obeyed in everyday affairs, but in instances of extreme pressure, it was to be defied, even at the cost of one's life."[87] Of course, when *Invisible Man* was published in 1952, segregation had been upheld by *Plessy v. Ferguson* for almost sixty years, the first *Brown v. Board of Education* decision was two years away (enforcement more than a decade away), and just a year earlier Willie McGee had been executed in Mississippi for having a consensual sexual relationship with a white woman (an impossibility under Mississippi law and custom). Ellison knew too well that African Americans' relationship to the law was one almost frequently characterized by grotesque force along with the covert force that undergirds the concept of law itself. This aspect of embodied force is reflected in the eviction scene and clarified by Ellison's essay: "In our common usage, law was associated more with men than with statutes. Law-enforcement officers in our usage were 'Laws,' and many were men with reputations for being especially brutal toward Negroes."[88]

In Ellison's novel, however, when the gun-toting "Law" prevents the couple from reading their tattered copy of Divine Law, the crowd finally surges forth and begins brutally stomping him. The narrator reports that he "saw a woman striking with the pointed heel of her shoe, her face a blank mask with hollow black eyes as she aimed and struck, aimed and struck, bringing spurts of blood, running along beside the man who was dragged to his feet now as they punched him gauntlet-wise between them."[89] When the enforcer of one law (pay rent or face eviction) is violently removed, however, the narrator shifts his speech in order to urge the crowd to enforce a different law, against littering: "Take it all, hide that junk! Put it back where it came from. It's blocking the street and the sidewalk, and that's against the law. We're law-abiding, so clear the street of the debris. Put it out of sight!" (281). The crowd follows the narrator's directions, and the narrator concedes that he was "no longer struggling against or thinking about the nature of my action" (281). What results from such unreflective action is justice, in a sense—the couple is returned to their home, no doubt temporarily—but, absent reflection, the action also parodies praxis: nothing fundamental is changed in the consciousness of the individuals comprising the crowd or in the structural relations that produced the situation in the first place. Instead, the appearance of change (putting broken belongings in a rented tenement) serves as a palliative for continuing direct action.

The eviction scene denies the opposition between "irony" and "law" and instead reframes the relationship between them as dialectical. On the one hand, the narrator's rhetoric would seem to be a fairly straightforward use of verbal irony: over the course of the scene, the shifting meaning of "law-abiding" allows the narrator to endorse breaking the law (which evicts people who can't pay their rent) by urging people to follow the law (against things blocking the sidewalk). On the other hand, the scene points to a more complicated conception of law than the mere linguistic articulation of transcendent precepts that gain their power either from ideology (the Bible) or force (the gun). Indeed, the shift in the narrator's speech suggests that judicial interpretation is not a matter of uncovering the "true" principle articulated by a law but a matter of choosing among conflicting principles that constitute a hierarchy of desires. Of all the "laws" at work in the scene—the law of rent, the law against blocking the street, the "Law" in the blue suit, and the divine law represented by the Bible—none works together to constitute a unified perspective. The law is a cacophony of voices whose efficacy rests upon the possibility of violence: much like the "illegal" crowd itself.

Ellison repeatedly emphasized what he saw as the sacred importance of constitutional ideals (not practices) of equality and freedom as guides to action, representing them as both sources and objects of faith in a distinctively American version of democracy. For Ellison, such principles "exert the compelling force of the ideal, of the sublime; ideas that draw their power from the Declaration of Independence, the Constitution, and the Bill of Rights," even though "instead of the single democratic ethic for every man, there now existed two: one, the idealized ethic of the Constitution and the Declaration of Independence, reserved for white men; and the other, the pragmatic ethic designed for Negroes and other minorities, which took the form of discrimination."[90] At the same time, he also exhibited a profound awareness that the ostensibly transcendental principles of the Constitution were linguistic assertions that are consequently subject to interpretive revision and material violence. These were, he wrote, "principles that were conceived linguistically and committed to paper" amid "contention over political ideals and economic interests," "principles that were enshrined—again linguistically—in the documents of state upon which this nation was founded."[91] Ellison felt that Americans must "recognize that behind the Constitution which we say rests in principles that lie beyond the limits of death and dying, are really man-made, legal fictions. . . . We must be able to express our dissent, especially when the members of the bench fail to do so for us."[92] This recognition of how social and political hierarchies were legally maintained and codified could result, in Ellison's view, from a public's increased attention to language, for "ironically, the nation's recognition of the new problems of its hierarchy was coeval with its increasing concern with its language, with its linguistic style": a series of statements that virtually deny foundational legal documents' imagined status as transcendental philosophical principles and instead emphasize their linguistic contingency and validity only as a function of interpretation."[93]

Invisible Man's self-deprecating depiction of his own unreasoned response to the unjust eviction may not serve as Richard Wright's "Blueprint for Negro Writing," let alone as a blueprint for effective political action. Nevertheless, the scene demands, by way of irony, a recognition of the polyvocality of "the law." By advising the crowd to return the old couple's furniture to their apartment, Invisible Man employs "basic" verbal irony, encouraging resistance to the eviction by invoking a general concept of law-abiding. He is not simply advising the crowd to break one law (against interfering with an eviction), he is advising them to uphold good law (mandating clear sidewalks) by breaking bad law (that puts old people on the street). Here the reader's approach to the text becomes much like a judge's as theorized by Burke and Ellison: judges read the laws, which feature conflicting commands to be adjudicated and subsequently enforced by interpreters.

Even the most recalcitrant judicial originalist would have to concede that documents may articulate any number of transcendent ideals but that the articulation of such ideals requires adjudication and cannot possibly ensure that those ideals will harmonize rather than conflict. After all, as Burke writes, "when, in the realm of the practical, a given case comes before the courts, you promptly find that this *merger* or *balance* or *equilibrium* among the Constitutional clauses becomes transformed into a *conflict* among the clauses—and to satisfy the promise contained in one clause, you must forego the promise in another."[94] This is, of course, where the work of judicial interpreters comes into play, for it is precisely the conflict among linguistically enacted principles that must be adjudicated—and at least temporarily resolved—before any given textual law can function to enable or limit given behaviors. These relationships among different principles and the injunction to adjudicate them "impose a new kind of command upon the Court: a command not simply to see that the wishes of the Constitution are fulfilled, but rather to decide which wishes shall be given preference over others."[95] The narrator in the eviction scene has practically functioned as a judge outside of the state, and the scene places the reader in a similar position of judgment: he has interpreted two conflicting wishes in the law (one protecting private property, one protecting public right-of-way) in favor of the general public and the particular members of the public who wish to have adequate housing.

According to both Burke and Ellison, however, such adjudications are not made on the hermetic hermeneutic of a discrete textual document: such is the oppressive fiction of legal positivism, which Burke excoriated and which gives the illusion that its interpretive activities are—as in some New Criticism—purely textual.[96] Instead, Ellison and Burke show, the interpretation of both laws and novels is a social-linguistic act. Here, legal positivism emerges as the counterpart of literary naturalism: both purport to offer facts requiring no interpretation, whereas Ellison and Burke emphasize that the reader of novels and the reader of laws can never escape the responsibility of interpreting language within an embodied social context. As Burke wrote, any act, including a court's act of judgment, "must be derived from substance in its total scope, not merely in the restricted range laid down by the document—and it is from this wider area, rather than from the document, that the Court must draw its motivations for arbitrating contradictions within the document."[97] In the eviction scene of *Invisible Man*, it is from the wider area of the social public that the narrator draws his conclusion that the furniture must be replaced.

In this nexus of two different kinds of interpretation—legislative and literary—both Ellison and Burke gesture toward a conception of literary documents wherein artistic production may afford an avenue of praxis for those who are denied access to institutional power. Ellison was hardly naïve on this point; in 1957 he admitted that "I would be on dangerous ground if I tried to trace too closely a connection between documents of state and literature."[98] Yet recall how novels can also approach the status of state documents in that they "form the ground of assumptions upon which our social values rest; they inform our language and our conduct with public meaning, and they provide the broadest frame of reference for our most private dramas."[99] As Ellison would clarify twenty years later, both constitutions and novels should be understood as conditioners of attitudes toward language and action that collapse distinctions

between private and public: "Perhaps law and literature operate or cooperate . . . in their respective ways these two systems, these two symbolic
systems, work in the interests of social order. The one for stability—that
is, the law is the law—the other striving to socialize those emotions and
interests held in check by manners, conventions, and again, by law."[100]
Because conditions inevitably change, Burke writes in a revolutionary
spirit derived from Thomas Paine, "no document that did our willing for
us more than a century and a half ago can will the point at which our
representatives today shall draw the line."[101] Therein lies fiction's potential ability to serve as a "calculus of motives" that works immanently
within the historical situation in which it is produced. One of the novel's
merits as social praxis is that it serves as a nonbinding enactment of contingently produced wishes; unlike law, a novel produces no obligations
or duties backed by force but rather produces hermeneutic dispositions
toward the linguistic practices that *do* produce and enforce such obligations, and to the aesthetic processes by which values are adjudicated
within a hierarchy of both volition and power. Read this way, the eviction
scene teaches readers that "the law" is embodied, violent, and linguistic;
its enforcement and effects are nothing if not relative, local, and inconsistent. The crowd's violence toward "the Law"—that is, the policeman—
expresses the inaccessibility of all other manifestations of the legal. The
narrator's resistance to violence does not make him the exceptional hero
of the scene but puts him in the position of a liberal reader: he comes to
understand both the limitations and the possibilities of "law" through
witnessing its bloody collapse and its linguistic manipulation but fails to
recognize his own mystified framing of the action.

Ellison had read his Freud, and one recognizes here the psychoana-
lytic overtones anticipating Gilles Deleuze's claim that "The first way of
overturning the law is ironic, where irony appears as an art of principles,
as ascent towards the principles and of overturning principles."[102] Yet
there is also something much more pragmatic at work. As legal historian
Michael Klarman has shown, shifting social attitudes and public opinion
had as much (or more) of an effect on the lived experience of African
Americans as judicial decisions such as *Brown v. Board of Education* (a
fact that should require some serious reflection today, when American
schools are actually *more* segregated by race than they were when Martin
Luther King Jr. was assassinated).[103] Sounding much like Burke, Klarman
writes that "in the absence of determinate law, constitutional interpretation necessarily implicates the values of the judges, which themselves
generally reflect broader social attitudes."[104] With these reminders that
judicial interpreters are culturally and socially conditioned by literature

and arts as much as any other member of a given society, it is tempting to derive a chain of causation from the fact that Supreme Court Justice William O. Douglas was on the dais when Ellison delivered his acceptance speech for the National Book Award and that he received the award just as Douglas and the Supreme Court were considering the arguments of *Brown v. Board of Education*. This was the speech in which Ellison explained that "to see America with an awareness of its rich diversity and its almost magical fluidity and freedom, I was forced to conceive of a novel unburdened by the narrow naturalism which has led, after so many triumphs, to the final and unrelieved despair which marks so much of our current fiction."[105] As Burke asserted throughout his work, however, it is just this fallacious temptation to confuse correlation with causation that produces confused thinking about the relationship between literary and political practices.

The narrator's use of irony in the eviction scene invites comparison between the interpretive act of reading with the interpretive realm of "laws" and reminds us that constitutional law serves a conservative function insofar as it depends upon the principle of *stare decisis*. It also clarifies Burke's otherwise semi-cryptic assertion in the conclusion to "Four Master Tropes" that "irony, as approached through either drama or dialectic, moves us into the area of 'law' and 'justice' (the 'necessity' or 'inevitability' of the *lex talionis*) that involves matters of form in art (as form affects anticipation and fulfillment) and matters of prophecy and prediction in history."[106] The *lex talionis*, the "law of retaliation," refers of course to the biblical injunction to demand "an eye for an eye." Imagine, then, that the origin of both "law" and "state" can be found in an originary moment wherein the primal attempt to regulate violence produces an impersonal, putatively disembodied ground of action that stands outside of an economy of justice: indeed, like money or language, the law in such a case is the tertium quid that allows for any symbolic economy of "justice" to function. In this sense, the proverbially harsh injunction of "an eye for an eye" actually regulates relationships that would otherwise devolve into unrestrained cycles of escalating violence.

Ellison himself suggests as much in *Invisible Man*, when the narrator's Rinehart disguise allows him to overhear a discussion about how to respond to the murderous police shooting of Brotherhood activist Tod Clifton: "'What we need is some guns,' one of them said. 'An eye for an eye.' [...] 'Wasn't for that Sullivan Law this here New York wouldn't be nothing but a shooting gallery.'"[107] Here the 1911 gun control law is understood to be the force that prevents violence, both retaliatory and otherwise; it is also *misunderstood*, as subsequent episodes insist that

New York is a shooting gallery where the police hold most of the tokens and the targets are black men. A liberal account of both law and justice requires figurative blindness and literal impersonality, for the regulation of violence and justice must reside somewhere outside of the relationship between disputants. This is just one reason why it is so horrifying (if unsurprising) when the police officer—the Law—first taunts and then shoots Clifton: not only because the cop represents the state and putatively embodies the principles of equality under law enshrined in the Constitution but because murdering Clifton exceeds any reasonable economy of retaliation for the punch he threw. Furthermore, in the narrator's eulogy for Clifton, he reminds the audience (as he did in the eviction scene) that laws and Laws are historical subjects rather than transcendental concepts and as such depend upon the fact that aesthetic interpretation and rational adjudication are opposed in a false dilemma. Thus the eulogizing narrator recounts the shooting in literary-critical language at Clifton's funeral: "There was a cop and a waiting audience but he was Tod Clifton and cops are everywhere. The cop? What about him? He was a cop. A good citizen. But this cop had an itching finger and an eager ear for a word that rhymed with 'trigger,' and when Clifton fell he had found it. The Police Special spoke its lines and the rhyme was completed" (457). Tod Clifton's world ends, one might say, with an ironic bang, which indicates not only that state violence is both enacted and resisted by individual, embodied citizens but that it is precisely this violence that makes these structural relationships visible.

Later in the novel, a second "eviction" scene occurs, which both parodies the first eviction scene and employs irony to build a formal critique of political representation and heroism. The scene begins when the narrator learns from a cab driver that riots have started, that "they're taking the joint apart" in Harlem (532). In a local reenactment of his bus journey to New York City from his college in the American South, he first takes a city bus and then runs north toward Harlem until he hears the sound of gunfire, which he describes in politically evocative language: "the shooting sounded like a distant celebration of the Fourth of July" (535). When the gunfire—coming primarily from police rather than from rioters—grazes the narrator, he is helped up by a group of men whom he subsequently joins in a sort of parodic shopping spree, what police and newspapers call "looting." Unlike other rioters, however, who confine their acquisitions to television sets, hats, whisky, and other objects of conspicuous consumption, the narrator's group also enters a hardware store, where they acquire equipment to burn down the infested tenement where they reside. (They specifically *reside* there rather than *live* there, as

Scofield rhetorically reminds the narrator when he inquires where they will "live" after the building burns down: "You call *this* living?" [545].) As the scene proceeds, the narrator has a hard time believing that he is actually participating in the arson. It is significant, however, as with the previous scene, that he does not reflect upon the action as he helps it unfold because "It didn't occur to me to interfere, or to question. . . . They had a plan" (546).

At this moment, what the narrator identifies as the reason not to interfere—that the leaders have a plan—is also identified as a symptom of the narrator's political immaturity. Indeed, for all the narrator's supposed growth and development from the naïve youth who came to Harlem, the moment reveals that his longstanding, habitual relationship to the world of action is one wherein a plan is formulated (by somebody else) and then followed (by him and others). When the leader begins to remove what is apparently his own family, a pregnant woman pleads with him not to continue: "'Please, Dupre,' she said, '*please*. You know my time's almost here . . . you *know* it is. If you do it now, where am I going to go.'" Dupre's insurrectionary response is immediate and admits of neither debate nor disagreement: "'Why you have to start this now? We done been all over it and you know I ain't go'n change. And lissen here, the resta y'all,' he said, reaching into the top of his hip boot and producing a nickel-plated revolver and waving it around, 'don't think they's going to be any *mind*-changing, either. And I don't aim for no arguments neither'" (546). The figure of the pistol-wielding Dupre overseeing the removal of old, prayerful people from their homes echoes with the image of the pistol-wielding marshal who oversaw the novel's first eviction, with the primary difference between them being that one serves the authority of the state (the marshal embodies what Bledsoe has described as "rich white folk's power, the nation's power—which means government power" [142]). This is not, however, an unsympathetic portrait of a mad gunman; Dupre explains, "My kid died from the t-bees in that deathtrap." Rather, he embodies a model of leadership wherein one man rises up and leads his community into resistance, and the bolder among his community follow: as one of his comrades describes the situation, "Listen to ole Du lay it down—he's a bitch, ain't he, buddy? He always liked to lead things" (543). His friend will continue to follow him, even though he stipulates that Dupre is "always leading me into trouble" (543).

Such adherence to predetermined courses of action is not only the motto of the country youth who, recently arrived in Harlem, revealed his naiveté to Peter Wheatstraw—a man with a shopping cart full of scavenged architectural blueprints—by saying, "You have to stick to the plan" (175). It is also the feeling inspired in the narrator when the first eviction is stopped by overwhelming the policeman and moving the furniture back inside, wherein he can lead a crowd with shouts of "'Come on, men,' dashing down the steps and seizing a chair and starting back, no longer struggling against or thinking about the nature of my action" (281). Such a model of action, for all its emphatically unscientific pragmatism and the extent to which it requires nonreflective followers, bears a striking resemblance to the emphasis on conformity and obedience demanded by the more scientifically minded Brotherhood. At this point in the novel, the Brotherhood has essentially abandoned Harlem residents because their historical analysis has dictated that "the people" (read: "the Negroes") are moving more quickly than scientific materialism, a rationally and predictably progressive History, should allow. As Hambro, the Brotherhood's theoretician, says, "We don't have to worry about the aggressiveness of the Negroes. Not during the new period or any other. In fact, we now have to slow them down for their own good. It's a scientific necessity" (503).

It is therefore unsurprising that upon witnessing Dupre's leadership, the narrator repeats the name of the Brotherhood's leader three times: "What type of man is he, what would Jack say of him? Jack, *Jack!*" (547). Note the ambiguity in the very name that springs to the narrator's mind, for one of the first commands of the narrator to the reader was to "Call me Jack-the-Bear, for I am in a state of hibernation" (6). The ambiguous referent of "Jack" here thus reminds the reader that the narrator "Jack-the-Bear" is writing his memoir, is in a position to relate and evaluate his own past actions in his own terms, but that those terms might well be uncontrollably inflected by the terms of the Brotherhood. This is not only because Ellison had remarked of language that "the essence of the word is its ambivalence, and in fiction it is never so effective and revealing as when both potentials are operating simultaneously, as when it mirrors both good and bad, as when it blows both hot and cold in the same breath"; it is also implicit in the fact that the narrator himself has "become acquainted with ambivalence."[108] Thus the question "what would Jack say of him?" simultaneously suggests to the reader that Dupre be evaluated not only in the terms laid down by the Brotherhood—who "seemed able to say just what they felt and meant in hard, clear terms" (317)—but also in the terms established by the reflective, ambivalent, retrospective narrator. We might thus understand Jack-the-Bear's name as an invitation to mimetic action as expressed in the last three words in the Prologue: his punning imperative that the reader "Bear with me."[109]

As the narrator moves through the tenement, "filled with a sense of Jack's outrageous unreality," he "slopped the kerosene about, upon an old mattress, along the floor; then moved into the hall, using the flashlights. From all through the building came the sounds of footsteps, of splashing oil, the occasional prayerful protest of some old one being forced to leave" (547). Rhetorically, the sound of "prayerful protest" here evokes a number of the novel's earlier depictions of frustrated attempts at self-improvement. Immediately following the Battle Royal, for instance, one of the town's prominent white onlookers describes the combatants, who are aligned around an electrified carpet to fight for their wages: "These niggers look like they're about to pray" (127). After he has arrived in New York and is awaiting a reply from the various trustees to whom he has sent letters, the narrator "remained about the building for three days awaiting an answer. But the letter brought no reply. Nor, any more than a prayer unanswered by God, was it returned" (170). After he has suffered the explosion in the Liberty Paints factory, the surreal hospital scene is punctuated by an overheard conversation between two of the scientists who are "curing" him of his delusions: "And in this case especially, with this, uh . . . background, I'm not so sure that I don't believe in the effectiveness of simple prayer" (235).

At first blush, this repeated invocation of prayer may seem like an ironic critique of the ways in which organized religion has often served to mitigate revolutionary sentiment and action. As noted earlier, during the novel's first eviction scene, one member of the crowd remarks, "That's what's wrong with us now, all this damn praying" (274). But an ironically comparative relationship is established within the text between the ineffectual, perhaps even counterproductive, linguistic "action" of prayer and instances of inflammatory "direct action," both of which effect uncertain change in social conditions: the elderly couple's furniture is carried inside (no doubt to be evicted the next day) and the diseased tenement is burned down, leaving the residents homeless (but devout) after they have prayed not to be delivered from their oppression but to be allowed to remain within it.

On one level, this is very similar to how Linda Hutcheon formally defines modern parody, as "extended repetition with a critical difference."[110] On another level, we see the narrator ironically progress from someone who speaks out to defuse collective violence to someone who actively participates in such violence. The scenes represent actions that are materially similar, yet functionally and politically different, in such a way that one simultaneously foreshadows and retrospectively echoes the other. They provide not a mythic repetition of ritual violence but a parodic parataxis, inviting a multiperspectival comparison of agents, actions, and scenes. There is certainly a version of New Critical formalism that could describe such symmetries as harmonious tensions resolved narratively; at the level of content, however, such juxtaposition either entirely beggars received wisdom about New Critical irony or requires that "irony" be understood not as Brooks's, not as Schlegel's, but as Ellison's and Burke's. I've shown how Ellison and Burke both associated such multiplicity of perspectives and voices with irony and democratic pluralism, and this is the way in which Ellison's novel uses irony to encourage radically democratic, pluralistic perspectives on individuality and collectivity: as the narrator states in the Epilogue, "diversity is the word. Let man keep his many parts and you'll have no tyrant states. [. . .] America is woven of many strands; I would recognize them and let it so remain" (577).

In the burning of the tenement, for example, both the Brotherhood and the liberal democratic consensus into which the novel was published would understand the narrator as having regressed rather than progressed, although the spectators in the scene assume that he has fulfilled his promise as a heroic leader: "Brother, ain't it wonderful," an unseen voice yells. "You said you would lead us, you really said it" (549). The question for the reader becomes whether we should agree or disagree with Invisible Man when he describes the burning building as the effect of autonomous agency: "They've done it, I thought. They organized it and carried it through alone; the decision their own and their own action. Capable of their own action" (548). The novel here asks the reader to reflect quite specifically on the empirical bases of political (as well as aesthetic) judgment as it pertains to causation and responsibility: has the building burned down because of the Brotherhood, because of the misguided violence of its residents, or because of the racist conditions that produce such gross inequalities between black and white lives? "If only there was some way of getting the Jungle condemned," the liberal reader is tempted to lament along with the narrator in a line that was excised from a draft of the novel.[111]

To read the narrator's belief that the men are "capable of their own action" literally is to understand (and perhaps agree with) his suggestion that the black men burning down their tenements, evicting their friends, neighbors, and family, *are* responsible for "the decision their own." To do so, however, is to decry the action they took, and—if we are disposed to agree with political critics of *Invisible Man*—to read this scene as a conservative allegory of the violent shortsightedness of African American political agency (or, more broadly, what we might call "agency of the oppressed"). If we decry the scene, then we must further decry Ellison himself for refusing to depict an affirmative blue-print for effective social action and only depicting stereotypical images of drunken rioting, looting, and burning members of a community. On the other hand, to suggest that the men *are not* responsible for the burning and riots—that is, to read *ironically* the narrator's assessment that they are "capable of their own action" with his own "fierce sense of exaltation" (548)—risks paternalistically pathologizing the rioters and thus participating in a long, racist tradition of reading African American men as without genuine agency, tools of their own puerile passions. Such a reading would legitimize the Brotherhood's predictive, manipulative science of action and history and would affirm the logic of scientific and literary naturalism that Ellison was so clearly at pains to disavow.

More problematically, from both narrative and political perspectives, to assent to this position critically is to agree with the narrator, to assent to the narrator's own diagnosis of the situation:

> I could see it now, see it clearly and in growing magnitude. It was not suicide, but murder. The committee had planned it. And I had helped, had been a tool. A tool just at the very moment I had thought myself free. By pretending to agree I *had* agreed, had made myself responsible for that huddled form lighted by flame and gun-fire in the street, and all the others whom now the night was making ripe for death. (553)

To read the narrator's acceptance of responsibility for both the living and the dead as an earnest, authorially legitimated voice is to read the novel as a fairly straightforward Bildungsroman occasionally punctuated by and intercalated with the aesthetic influences of sur-realism and high modernism. It is also to agree that the narrator is "responsible" for the evicted people and the subsequent destruction of property and thus to agree with a particular assessment of causation. Neither social nor economic conditions "made" the cadre burn down their own homes, the narrator implies; nor was it a rational, strategic assessment of how best to protest or to rectify unsafe living conditions. Rather, what caused the burning of the tenements was the fact that the narrator had formally acquiesced to the Brotherhood's desire to "sacrifice" Harlem. By retreating from direct opposition, the narrator suggests, he had rendered himself complicit in any action that he failed to oppose.

Irresponsible Reading

To isolate this moment of accepting responsibility is to ignore how it represents just one instance of the narrator's vacillating relationship to responsibility as a concept. It is also to ignore the narrator's and others' misjudgments about responsibility throughout the text. Recall that the narrator almost suffers mob violence himself when his speech after the Battle Royal briefly substitutes "social equality" for the acceptable "social responsibility" (31). Early in the novel, when Trueblood tells the white college trustee Norton the story of how he impregnated his own daughter, he begins in good naturalist fashion by attributing his actions to environmental and economic conditions: "You see, suh, it was cold and us didn't have much fire. Nothin' but wood, no coal. I tried to git help but wouldn't nobody help us and I couldn't find no work or nothin', It was so cold all of us had to sleep together; me, the ole lady and the gal. That's how it started, suh" (53). When the story so upsets Norton that they end up in a brothel patronized by insane veterans, the narrator first attributes responsibility to somebody else ("Damn Trueblood. It was his fault" [98]) and then squarely accepts a purely individual responsibility: "though I still believed myself innocent, I saw that the only alternative to permanently facing the world of Trueblood and the Golden Day was to accept the responsibility for what had happened" (147). When Clifton is murdered, the narrator's first assessment is that he "felt responsible. All our work had been very little . . . no great change had been made. And it was all my fault" (444). Scant pages later, however, he retracts this line of thought and asserts, "I could only accept responsibility for the living, not the dead" (447). A little later, when he dons his Rinehart costume and almost gets in a fight with a friend who doesn't recognize him, he is quick, like Trueblood, to externalize responsibility: "Here I'd set out to test a disguise on a friend and now I was ready to beat him to his knees— not because I wanted to but because of place and circumstance" (489).

This tendency to obfuscate or denigrate responsibility is equally and explicitly the case within the Brotherhood as a whole. After Clifton is murdered, the narrator organizes a funeral march "on my personal responsibility" (463). Brother Jack responds scathingly to the very idea: "'His personal responsibility,' Brother Jack said. 'Did you hear that, Brothers? Did I hear him correctly? Where did you get it, Brother?' he said. 'This is astounding. Where did you get it?'" (463). In the Brotherhood, after all, one doesn't "decide" to start or stop action but externalizes any given decision, either to the Committee, to History, or to scientific rationality itself, for "at the proper moment science will stop"—and take responsibility for—a given action (505). Moreover, to repress reflection concerning action characterizes those in the novel who discount the element of individual decision in any given situation. Just as they externalize the entire notion of responsibility, they imagine the law as an external space for the regulation of collective behavior.[112]

With all of these ironically conflicting perspectives on the possibility and failures of individual responsibility—and with the overarching specter of reactionary rhetoric that demands "personal responsibility" for criminal behavior in the face of overwhelming systemic pressures to engage in that behavior—how could Ellison accept the National Book Award by stating that the "chief significance of *Invisible Man* as a fiction" was "its experimental attitude, and its attempt to return to the mood of personal moral responsibility for democracy which typified the best of our nineteenth-century fiction"?[113] As the narrator informs the reader at the end of the Prologue, he considers himself

> one of the most irresponsible beings that ever lived. Irresponsibility is part of my invisibility. . . . But to whom can I be responsible, and why should I be, when you refuse to see me? And wait until I reveal how truly irresponsible I am. Responsibility rests upon recognition, and recognition is a form of agreement.[114]

Here Ellison's language resonates strongly with Hegel's notion of recognition (*Anerkennung*), in the context of a narrative that does not seem to come down firmly on either side of the dilemma in political philosophy—what should be the primary engine of producing a more just and equitable society?—succinctly captured in the titular opposition of Nancy Fraser's and Axel Honneth's *Recognition or Redistribution*.[115] As the sustained and recurring narratives about responsibility in the novel attest, ideas of responsibility are inextricably related not only to recognition but to causation, for one can only be responsible for an event to the extent that one is implicated in its genesis or execution. Yet questions of causation are notoriously sticky in narratives characterized by irony, especially of the cosmic variety. Ellison thus presents multiple perspectives on action, causation, and responsibility in a form that is named "irony"; this irony delineates ethical ties between reading and responsibility and emphasizes that such ties depend upon interpretive decisions. Further, Ellison stages such decisions among numerous, multiple perspectives on action, asserting that interpretive recognition is tied to political recognition. Ultimately, the reader's shifting relationship to the novel is made coherent—but not resolved—by what Ellison in 1945 called "a gyroscope of irony" representing a "racial situation [that] has become like an irrational sea in which Americans flounder like convoyed ships in a gale."[116]

The twin scenes of eviction thus do much more than model particular forms of action, some of which were employed during the 1943 Harlem Riots that Ellison covered for the *New York Post*.[117] They also do much more than comment ironically on the delimited forms of action available to residents of ghettos who wish to protest their living conditions but who have access only to the material conditions themselves rather than to the various causes for such conditions (and, moreover, who are held criminally and morally responsible for actions while being denied any reasonable facsimile of recognition that is a precondition for democratic participation). Indeed, it is precisely the notion of causation that the narrator invites the reader to engage by repeatedly emphasizing the concept of responsibility. The novel suggests that the very possibility of deciding between options—the possibility of authentic "choice"—is a necessary component of political action but that emphasis on a single narrative perspective occludes the possibility of identifying those choices in a literary context. As the narrator reflects upon how to adjudicate among options (in this case, represented by the unlikely figure of roasted yams), "it involved a problem of choice. I would have to weigh many things carefully before deciding and there would be some things that would cause quite a bit of trouble, simply because I had never formed a personal attitude toward so much. I had accepted the accepted attitudes and it had made life seem simple."[118] Finally, we see in the novel a dialectical definition of responsibility evolving, wherein neither the wholesale acceptance nor the wholesale denial of responsibility is viewed as an adequate "attitude" toward democratic practice. What is required is not only direct action but the sort of reflection upon one's relationship to causation and action that the novel encourages; such reflection on causation is understood by both Burke and Ellison to be necessarily ironic and aptly described by the socially and politically engaged word "irony." Indeed, this dialectical approach toward responsibility and democracy is precisely where we can see what is perhaps Ellison's most striking expansion, if not revision, of Burke's critical thinking into the realm of fiction. The fact that it is described by "irony" serves as one of the salient focal points in the evolution of twentieth-century critical terminology and cultural history.

How it is possible to convey this dialectic relationship among so many perspectives within a novel that is narrated through one voice? After all, a first-person account such as *Invisible Man* presents a univocal articulation of the narrator's experience and thus is a literary form seemingly anathema to Burke's crucial account of conditions where politically desirable irony emerges and where literary irony is required. Recall how Burke proposes a particular form of "relativism" in which views of the world are reduced to that provided by one term alone. In contrast, he provides a definition of irony as a moment when

> terms are . . . encouraged to participate in an orderly parliamentary development, [and] the dialectic of this participation produces (in the observer who considers the whole from the standpoint of the participation of all the terms rather than from the standpoint of any one participant) a "resultant certainty" of a different quality, necessarily ironic, since it requires that all the sub-certainties be considered as neither true nor false, but *contributory*.[119]

Note that "parliamentary" development requires a vastly different symbolic economy than, say, a "Federalist" development of terms. If part of Ellison's political goal is to write a novel that instantiates the democratic and pluralistic value of multiperspective polyvocality—and thus establish difference as a value to be nurtured rather than a fact to be accepted—then why not write a novel with more than one narrator?

In any literary or social situation, Burke wrote, "there is usually some one character that enjoys the rôle of *primus inter pares*. For whereas any of the characters may be viewed in terms of any other, this one character may be taken as the summarizing vessel, or synecdochic representative, of the development of the whole."[120] Ellison's narrator appears as "summarizing vessel" and "synecdochic representative" in both the Prologue and the Epilogue to the novel, when he emphatically "decides" to go back aboveground (at the very least, to publish the novel that we are holding in our hands). But by relating the narrator's experiences through so many ironic inversions, the question "synecdochic of *what*?" forcefully emerges. The ending is also the moment where, after falsely declaring himself to be "responsible" for so many actions, the narrator is able to recognize himself as "implicated and partially responsible."[121] This is the point at which Ellison invites the reader, like the narrator, to reflect upon the possibility that she or he is necessarily implicated in the situation of Invisible Man and to reflect upon the very condition of "responsibility" itself. This is a profoundly ethical moment of literary reflection for both narrator and reader. Summoning Burke's account of prophetic irony, this is "the point at which different casuistries appear (for fitting these 'general laws of inevitability' to the unique cases of history)."[122] The novel has moved (not "progressed") from a moment when Trueblood's incestuous actions are understood to be "caused" by a lack of coal to a point where the narrator literally "falls" into a room full of nothing *but* coal; where his figurative "Enlightenment" comes from literally igniting a series of supposedly "personal" documents that establish his bona fides as a state citizen: "I started with my high-school diploma," Invisible Man says, "applying one precious match with a feeling of remote irony."[123]

Ellison and Burke believed that "it is important that we try to see around the edges of our customary perspective, if we would understand the part that motivational assumptions play in implicitly or explicitly substantiating human decisions"; this metaphor of "seeing around edges" of perspective recurs throughout *Invisible Man*.[124] In all of these examples, "seeing around a corner" is not simply a figure for going beyond empiricism by accomplishing the empirically impossible, but neither is it simply a figure for mantic abilities; rather, it describes a disillusioning expansion of perspective that greets a given character when events overtake expectations, when experience collides with prediction. In the Prologue, the narrator swears off smoking "reefer" because "to *see* around corners is enough (that is not unusual when you are invisible). But to hear around them is too much; it inhibits action."[125] Similarly, when he stares at the old couple's belongings strewn about in the snow of the eviction scene, he looks "inwardly-outwardly, around a corner into the dark, far-away-and-long-ago" (273); and when he delivers his first speech for the Brotherhood he admonishes the crowd to "peep around the corner, there's a storm coming" (344). When he realizes that the Brotherhood intends to abandon Harlem, it "was though I'd learned suddenly to look around corners; images of past humiliations flickered through my head and I saw that they were more than separate experiences" (508), and he "looked around a corner of my mind and saw Jack and Norton and Emerson merge into one single white figure" (508).

Burke wrote about the ways in which agents could assess responsibility for past actions and attempt to predict what actions would lead to certain historical developments, and he argued that the multiply interrelating perspective known as "irony" could assist in such prediction:

> We may make such prophecy more precise, with the help of irony, in saying that the developments that led to the rise will by the further course of their development, "inevitably" lead to the fall (true irony always, we hold, thus involving an "internal fatality," a principle operating from within, though its logic may also be grounded in the nature of the extrinsic scene, whose properties contribute to the same development).[126]

Only toward the end of the novel, however, are the narrator's glimpses "around the corner," or expansions of individual perspective, related directly to irony: as the narrator attempts to derail the Brotherhood's Harlem policy and listens to how "the program was correct, events were progressing in their predetermined direction, history was on their side," he relates that "incidents of my past, both recognized and ignored, sprang together in my mind in an *ironic* leap of consciousness that was like looking around a corner."[127] Here Ellison clarifies Burke's own notion of "prophecy" as that which is simultaneously reflective and prospective; it is the condition under which decisions are made with equal attention to contingent pasts and futures and the individual's relationship to events in both.

These intersections between Burke's and Ellison's thinking reveal the crucial role of Burkean irony as a "terministic screen" not only for reading *Invisible Man* but for the ways in which prior accounts of both modernist and postmodernist irony obscure the imagined political pos-sibilities of formalist reading. For both Burke and Ellison, irony precisely describes *both* the reader's process of arriving at sub-certain aesthetic judgment (as opposed to conceiving of stabilization of ambiguity as final decision) *and* the reader's search for principles of causation and respon-sibility. The narrative demands that decisions be made by both character and reader. In this decisive recognition of a responsibility to decide—and the concomitant question of how to "share" responsibility—the novel itself qualifies as political action: it not only functions within a cultural "scene" (and by definition changes that scene) but ideally changes the habits of readers. This is obviously a disposition that is different from what Chantal Mouffe has described as "the Kantian-inspired model of democracy which envisages its realization under the form of an ideal community of communication" and instead begins to sound much more like what Mouffe calls

> a conception of democracy that, far from aiming at consensus and transparency, is suspicious of any attempt to impose a univocal model of democratic discussion. Aware of the dangers of rational-ism, this is a view that does not dream of mastering or eliminating undecidability, for it recognizes that it is the very condition of pos-sibility of decision and therefore of freedom and pluralism.[128]

In the attempt to compose literature that is neither pure reflection nor purely revisionist historical memory, neither idealistic nor utopian in its prediction of a hopeful future, Ellison has constructed a political plat-form of a divergently new sort.

What makes the use of the term "irony" so important for literary study in this context is that "irony" describes not just the reader's search for responsibility and desire to engage in what it might mean to be "responsible" for injustices (both systemic and particular) but also the aesthetic literary practices and conventions that demand this sort of engagement on the part of the reader. As ever, "irony" describes a quality within the text, a process of recognition that arises in a reader who is invited to decide among competing voices, and a quality of the world that a text can render in varying degrees of adequacy. This production of meaning is explicitly conceived as a trialogue among critics, text, and reader. Ironic hermeneutic practices exist neither in the ideal reader of New Criticism nor in the ideal text of poststructuralism; neither in the putative withdrawal of modernist aesthetics nor in the mythological seasons of Northrop Frye: rather, irony is both situated in and dependent upon a text that functions simultaneously as a self-referring artifact and an artifact to be decoded as a part of a larger "scene" of history, in what political theorists call a "situation." The logic of irony in *Invisible Man* doesn't simply strive for or enable the mimetic reproduction of a society built upon contradictions; in these terms, a Fourth of July celebration in the antebellum United States was no more and no less "ironic" than a Reign of Terror conducted under a banner of fraternity, liberty, and equality; neither more nor less ironic than a conservative Democratic president in a supposedly postracial society being denounced as a Maoist because he identifies as mixed-race; neither more nor less ironic than Tea Party activists who demand that "Government Stay Out of Medicare!" Rather, the logic of Ellison's irony relies upon the process of seeking out and testing the possibilities of assessing responsibility for unjust practices, as well as constructing reflective and evolving definitions for both "justice" and "practice."

The end of *Invisible Man* not only depicts but *enacts* Burke's conception of irony and action by both representing "the point where one tries to decide" and inviting the reader "to decide"; to decide with the full knowledge that decisions about both interpretive and political practice must be made with the disposition of a "sub-certainty," particularly when examining historical relationships and asserting, for instance, a causal relationship between one form of political action (say, marching and boycotting) and positive change, while denying the same causal relationship to another form of political action (say, writing a novel like *Invisible Man*). If there is a mimetic function in Ellison's Prologue and Epilogue, it lies in ironically representing a mimetic relationship between the embodied reader and the disembodied narrator. At precisely the point when the narrator announces that "the very disarmament has brought me to a decision," that "a decision has been made" to emerge from his hole, the reader must decide *what that decision will look like*.[129] Of course, the reader knows that this isn't the first moment for the narrator to emerge from his hole: vanilla ice cream, lightbulbs, joints, sloe gin, Louis Armstrong records, and powerlines presumably do not come to him magically, and in the Epilogue the narrator says that he has been searching for an answer to the question "what *is* the next phase?" and that "over and over again I've gone up above to seek it out" (576). But to recognize the moment as adequately described by the "irony" that has been established within the text (and emphasized in the world wherein the text is circulating) is to recognize that there is no simple "opposite" to "inaction."[130] The reader must simultaneously confront the fact that the reader's own inaction may be a part of the "internal fatality" of responsibility for the narrator's condition. Furthermore, to establish the narrator's *representative* function—the fact that, in the political sense of representation, "what frightens" the narrator is that he does "speak for" a "you" that is both "me" and "us"—is to consider the conditions under which the narrator's particularity may be expanded to a larger community, to engage the question of who is and who should be represented in both literary and legislative bodies.

The Beginning of the End

In the conclusion to the long section of *Grammar of Motives* titled "The Dialectic of Constitutions," Burke quotes "one passage much to our purposes" from the political theorist Denis de Rougemont in order to address what Rougemont called "the essential paradox of federalism, which means taking seriously the expression 'union in diversity.'"[131] Sounding very much like an unacknowledged source for the work of radical democratic theorists a half century later, he asserts that "a 'system,' presumably, would require some kind of 'educating and organizing hegemony,' which is precisely what the idea of federation must avoid."[132] Keeping Burke's vocabulary of irony in mind, and reading Ellison's use of literary aesthetics as a means to encourage readers to reflect upon their own responsibility for the situation in which the narrator finds himself, we can understand precisely what Ellison meant when he recast Burke's "essential paradox of federalism" specifically as "the irony implicit in the dynamics of American democracy."[133] It is this reflective disposition toward responsible decisions that underpins the Epilogue of *Invisible Man*, which can therefore be read as a "representative anecdote" about the need for reflective decisions upon conditions of effective political and literary representation.[134]

The proper attitude toward politics for both Burke and Ellison is not the elimination of conflict but a disposition that allows citizens to embrace the fundamentally unstable interpretive nature of politics; one that seeks only a Burkean "sub-certainty," particularly when regarding a hierarchy of principles circulating in unresolved paradoxes of fact and value. Today it seems decreasingly far-fetched to point out that even the most violent social and political hegemonies tend to masquerade as consensus, and political consensus conceals its own violently exclusionary character under a veil of stability and resolution: "Hence the need to relinquish the illusion that a rational consensus could ever be achieved where such a tension would be eliminated," Mouffe writes, "and to realize that pluralist democratic politics consists in pragmatic, precarious and necessarily unstable forms of negotiating its constitutive paradox."[135] This form of pragmatic interpretation, which seeks to construct and to expose the aesthetics of decision making, is a form of interpretation that is radically at odds with the rule-based, principle-guided form of bureaucracy that Burke had identified in opposition to "freedom."[136]

Finally, irony emphasizes the central role of hermeneutic and aesthetic practice within and as political practice. Irony describes the function of and disposition toward law, justice, and attendant concepts of causation and decision making; it describes the aesthetic arrangement of narrative and the world as well as aesthetic responses to and actions upon and within that world. Via his emphasis on "choice" and "decision," Ellison enacts such a use for irony in *Invisible Man*. Simply recognizing incongruities is not enough to alter those incongruities, of course, and that is why the novel and Ellison's criticism simultaneously emphasize the need for an attitude toward agonistic disagreement and the agents with whom one might disagree: not as an enemy to be speared (like Ras the Destroyer) or lynched (like the narrator's dream self in the conclusion to the novel) but as an antagonist whose very disagreement serves as the foundation for democracy itself. The ideal, though emphatically not guaranteed, result of such an ironic disposition is the possibility of adjudicating a hierarchy of contested principles (such as "equality" and "freedom").[137]

To argue for political ends achieved by inculcating skepticism may seem to render literature merely instrumental, simply another talking head of a multimedia hydra that roars enforcement of standardized public opinion. But the abiding ferocity of some Ellison criticism should attest to the fact that Ellison's use of irony produces—and has been producing for more than half a century—manifestly more than the unanimity of acquiescence that is the end goal of propaganda. The novel suggests, indeed, a condition of thought wherein unanimity of opinion in one person—much less several—is nothing less than irrational: "There is . . . an area in which a man's feelings are more rational than his mind, and it is precisely in that area that his will is pulled in several directions at the same time."[138] It is perhaps because Ellison produces feelings of unresolved antagonism—toward the narrator for not giving us blueprints for action, for example—that *Invisible Man* encourages us not simply to move but to act: not simply to choose arbitrarily among equally valid courses of action but to *decide* to act in newly imaginative ways rather than simply to respond to injustice with familiar exhortations.

Beyond Hope and Memory: A Conclusion

This book commenced with a familiar story about the putative death of irony after September 11, 2001, and I want to conclude with another familiar story. An army general, seeking to reassure the people of Baghdad about his nation's honorable intentions, invited the city to cooperate with the occupying force and to rejoice in newfound freedom after generations of tyranny: "our armies do not come into your cities and lands as conquerors or enemies, but as liberators." A few months later and thousands of miles away, a New York cultural critic grimly assessed the state of American democracy, where public support for the war was marshaled both by soaring appeals to obedient patriotism and by demonstrably false claims reproduced in papers such as the *New York Times*. "Only in a world where irony was dead," he wrote, "could an intellectual class enter war at the head of such illiberal cohorts in the avowed cause of world-liberalism and world democracy." The "Proclamation of Baghdad" was delivered by British lieutenant general Sir Frederick Stanley Maude, and the American critic was Randolph Bourne. The year was 1917.[1]

If you didn't know before reading the preceding chapters, you know now that Randolph Bourne was talking about John Dewey and Woodrow Wilson rather than about Thomas Friedman and George W. Bush. Whether or not you could enumerate the differences between General Maude and Dick Cheney, the anecdote both provides and withholds information to produce a series of recognizable ironies: an irony of history imperially repeating itself in the Middle East; a verbal irony, where

I knowingly told one story while referring to something else; a cosmic irony of unintended consequences, where a war marketed by the need to destroy terrorists actually produced more terror and more terrorists, and so forth. To the degree that one depicts or recognizes these differences as irony—as a series of represented disjunctions between historical facts and the values that attend them in order to guide the limited interpretation of those facts—it is at least plausible that this narrative successfully invites critique. This might be a critique, say, of the ways in which information is repeatedly deployed in particular ways to arouse particular emotions (patriotic pride and fear chief among them) and a critique of how the emotional force of this information helps constitute public opinion, which then bolsters actions such as invasions and prolonged occupations by United States and allied military forces. Depending on how one decides to compare different presidential administrations, one might even begin thinking about the "threat" of "enemies" who are kept as faceless and nameless as the robotic drones used by Democratic and Republican administrations to kill them, or as grotesquely desperate as the one hundred hunger strikers—many exonerated, all imprisoned and tortured for a decade without charge—who, as I write these words, are being force-fed in Guantanamo Bay.

One can certainly draw these comparisons and invite these critiques without irony, and acknowledge that "irony" sometimes serves as a synonym for something like "skepticism." In the broad discursive figuration of irony within modernist culture, however, the rhetoric of irony manifestly subsumes and refuses this limited sense because writers insist that irony offers unique resources—whether as an "engine" or a "sin" or an "acid" or a "gyroscope"—for individuals to deploy in the face of intertwined facts and values that produce and sustain dramatically undemocratic forms of life. Indeed, to descry similarities between different instances of imperial militarism and the cultural discourses that rise in opposition to or support of that militarism is emphatically not to claim that the second verse is the same as the first: that is, neither an invitation to reduce different moments to mere repetition without difference nor the implication that irony or "war for oil in Iraq" meant precisely the same thing in 1918 as it does in 2013. Indeed, my argument has been precisely the opposite: when writers invoke "irony" as a distinguishing feature of—and hermeneutic lens for judging—their representation of events, it is invariably an assertion of heterogeneity that insists upon maintaining difference and that does so in full cognizance of the historical and rhetorical weight behind such invocations. Far from an invitation to withdraw into the private pleasures of resignation, these moments are also an invitation to become active investigators for the conditions—material, phenomenological, aesthetic, political—for which "irony" is an adequate descriptor. As I have also tried to show, the fact that irony is so notoriously slippery as a term and contentious in its implications serves to intensify rather than negate the form of active judgment required for democratic imagination and participation.

In the brief narrative case of General Maude and Randolph Bourne, the problem and solution of irony are perhaps epistemological and informational, insofar as irony "happens" once I know about World War I and Dick Cheney. The semantic work of the anecdote might even be described as well by "Enlightenment humanism" as by "literary modernism." The recurrent proximity of multifarious, multivalent "ironies" to terms like "aesthetics" and "democracy" within modernist discourse, however, simultaneously describes events, individuals, collectivities, *and* aesthetic values within a dynamic field of meaning. That it is a field of meaning to be constantly reconstituted and renegotiated under the aegis of "democracy"—defined not only against monarchism and fascism but against the perjured facsimile of democracy that Bourne, Glasgow, Dos Passos, and Ellison witnessed and decried—strongly suggests that the story of political irony has been frequently and reductively sanitized in a critical consensus about literary modernism. For all their obvious differences, writers from Bourne to Ellison evoke and invoke an aesthetics of irony to describe events and different forms of information (not simply "art") precisely to refuse easy oppositions between "commitment" and "withdrawal," as well as between instrumental reason and somatic reflex. Whether engaging a novel or a newspaper or a photograph or a film, the arousal of charm and emotion (*Reiz und Rührung*) that must be purged from Kantian judgments of pure taste is a fact not merely to be overcome by cultivating the impossible dream of disinterest (figured variously by Bourne as "not caring," or more famously by John Rawls as a "veil of ignorance") but rather a value to be incorporated into the disposition of percipients who must judge various forms of representation before and while and after acting. And it is the forms of representation and forms of disposition that become "ironic" and "political" insofar as the invocation of "irony" acknowledges pragmatic somatic realities as what prefigure action, not only what is produced after action. It is also an invocation that emphasizes the necessity of critical rationality for adjudicating the received values that too frequently masquerade as facts. In this regard, "politics" names the means by which dispositions are encouraged or discouraged in order to adjudicate hierarchies of value without deadly efficient recourse to faith, dogmatism, ideology, or convention.

192 / BEYOND HOPE AND MEMORY

There is nothing new in the claim that "democracy" is less about a particular system of governance or composition of specific legislation: the use of "democracy" to delineate the parameters of what is thinkable and sayable runs from early twentieth-century pragmatism through recent theorists of democracy. The modernist writers in this study figure irony as an aesthetic politics that actively democratizes the unsayable—in the sense that irony reassigns the onus of responsibility for thinking to the active percipient—as a means of encouraging the transvaluation of values that have become habitual and thus invisible. In re-theorizing conventional understandings of proceduralism, Amanda Anderson has written powerfully in "defense of the critical, dialogical, and even emancipatory potential of cultivated detachment—a potential that can be expressed in aesthetic modes like irony and parody as well as through the more serious mode of critical social theory."[2] The writers in this study might well agree with her reinvigoration of categories such as character as a means of disrupting norms and habits, they would include "modernism" as well as "postmodernism," and they would also insist that liberal values, democracy, and the possibility of critical rationality themselves must be submitted to the most rigorous forms of disruptive interrogation. Moreover, they would do so from within and in explicit opposition to modernist literary cultures that are frequently understood as a politically conservative step away (and sometimes not even that far) from sliding into the most grotesque forms of authoritarian atrocity.

It has long been far too easy to imagine that systems of political representation in the United States are a flawed but necessary alternative to other forms of representation; all the writers in this study express deep suspicion about the sufficiency of electoral politics and deny the category of the state as the unique location or goal of political activity. At the same time, none of these writers is blithely naive about the ways that words like "democracy" and "freedom" serve as sanitizing blinders for the perpetuation of base iniquity, and none retreats into easy abstraction as a means of avoiding real, pragmatic choices that have real, pragmatic effects on the mutilated bodies lying in trenches and hanging from lynching trees. Indeed, irony rises appropriately to the fore to emphasize the importance of decision in the face of such paradoxes; this is not in spite of but because of the fact that so much authoritarian terror against individuals and classes of people is perpetrated under the banner of representative democracy. And it is here that a consistent thread unites thinkers and writers who are so different in so many ways: in the claim that literary forms of unresolved irony, dispositions to those forms, and the use of "irony" to describe those forms are a means of forcibly expanding the field of political critique to include not only violations of representative democratic principles but the constitution of those principles in the first instance.

"If voting changed anything, they'd make it illegal," goes the anarchist motto against participation in electoral politics. The fact that "they" and "we" have in fact long made it illegal for large swaths of the population to vote—from the Constitutional Convention in 1787 to the "Voter ID" laws passed in 2012—is a ready riposte based in unimpeachable fact and must give pause. And yet in a U.S. presidential election year where one was offered a choice between two putatively opposed visions of the world— the explicit "hope" for a return to Clinton-era prosperity versus the conjured "memory" of a traditional America that only ever existed as an ideological fantasy—it is difficult to escape the conclusion that the very parameters of imagined possibility have become so delimited that one isn't so much offered a choice between "good" and "bad" political representatives so much as a demi-choice of a less terrible quasi-alternative. For all of the very real and important differences between candidates, neither acknowledges nor offers an alternative to what Sheldon Wolin calls the "inverted totalitarianism" of twenty-first-century American life, where gun- and pepper-spray-wielding police have "evolve[d] from the obvious but occasional agent of employers into an element within an evolving system of control, intimidation, and repression."[3] The great progressive victories of the past few years have been to expand the number of people who may participate in institutions long championed by conservatives as the cornerstone of state and civil society—marriage and the military—and slowly to withdraw from wars that were already unsustainable defeats. One surely can recognize how access to both institutions would materially improve some people's lives while admitting that the field of recognizable alternatives has considerably narrowed in the past century and searching for a vocabulary to describe potential activist responses. In this context, the genealogy of modernist irony instantiated by the writers under consideration here is worth returning to precisely because of their suspicion that machineries of representation in the United States could not dramatically change that which most needed changing: the machineries of representation themselves and the imaginations of people who participate in them. The pragmatic alternative they propose is a dialogic form of literary irony that would enable people to recognize and perhaps alter the ways in which they had become active participants in their own alienation from democratic forms of life.

F. R. Ankersmit, not only connecting but equating representation with democracy, has claimed that "Romantic irony is . . . both the genesis of democracy and its nemesis: it defined the nature and purpose of political representation, but, in the end, it undermines representation in a way similar to how representation gradually became an irrelevancy in contemporary art."[4] The modernist "irony" in this study demands that we move further, to recognize that democracy is only viable when the pragmatic facts and values of "political" and "aesthetic" representation are constantly negated and renegotiated, which cannot be limited either to a feature of texts or a feature of people or a feature of events. In 1955, R.W.B. Lewis drew upon Ralph Waldo Emerson's identification of an intellectual two-party system of reformist "Hope" and conservative "Memory." The writers in this study ask us to join neither the political Party of Hope nor the political Party of Memory but a literary-political third party: a party for which, Lewis insists, "there is no proper name: unless we call it the party of Irony."[5] The modernist party of irony properly names all three, insisting that "choice" and "decision" are intertwined practices of feeling and thinking, seeking and refusing conventional and unconventional forms of affiliation, and drawing connections among them in order to imagine nonrepresentative forms of life that are nonetheless worthy of the name "democracy."

NOTES

Irony and How It Got That Way: An Introduction

1. J.A.K. Thomson, *Irony: An Historical Introduction* (Cambridge, MA: Harvard University Press, 1927), 139.

2. *Vanity Fair* editor Graydon Carter, qtd. in David Kirkpatrick, "Pronouncements on Irony Draw a Line in the Sand," *New York Times*, September 24, 2001, sec. C9; Roger Rosenblatt, "The Age of Irony Comes to an End," *Time*, September 24, 2001; Gerry Howard, editorial director for Broadway Books, qtd. in Michiko Kakutani, "The Age of Irony Isn't Over After All," *New York Times*, October 9, 2001, sec. E1; David Beers, "Irony Is Dead! Long Live Irony!" n.d., www.salon.com/mwt/feature/2001/09/25/irony_lives/?sid=1048586.

3. Joan Didion, *Fixed Ideas: America Since 9.11* (New York: New York Review of Books, 2003), 10; Joan Didion, qtd. in Andy Newman, "Irony Is Dead. Again. Yeah, Right," *New York Times*, November 23, 2008, http://www.nytimes.com/2008/11/23/fashion/23irony.html.

4. R. Jay Magill Jr., *Chic Ironic Bitterness* (Ann Arbor: University of Michigan Press, 2007), ix; Russell Leslie Peterson, *Strange Bedfellows: How Late-Night Comedy Turns Democracy into a Joke* (New Brunswick, NJ: Rutgers University Press, 2008), 18.

5. Jay McInerney, "Getting It Together," *New York Times*, August 28, 2005, http://www.nytimes.com/2005/08/28/books/review/28MCINER.html.

6. Paul Krugman, "Republicans and Medicare," *New York Times*, February 11, 2010, http://www.nytimes.com/2010/02/12/opinion/12krugman.html.

7. R.W.B. Lewis, *The American Adam: Innocence, Tragedy and Tradition in the Nineteenth Century* (Chicago: University of Chicago Press, 1955), 196.

8. Theodor W. Adorno, *Minima Moralia: Reflections from Damaged Life*, trans. E.F.N. Jephcott (London: Verso, 1974), 211; Theodor W. Adorno, *Minima Moralia: Reflexionen Aus Dem Beschädigten Leben*, Gesammelte Schriften 4 (Frankfurt am Main: Suhrkamp, 1980), 239; Bosley Crowther, "The Irony of It: A Gentle Reminder

That Satire Is Very Scarce These Days—And Some Fun!" *New York Times*, August 22, 1943, X3.

9. Randolph Bourne, "The War and the Intellectuals," in *The Radical Will: Selected Writings, 1911–1918*, ed. Olaf Hansen (New York: Urizen Books, 1977), 308.

10. It's difficult to know when and where to stop providing examples of this language—perhaps in 1792, when Peter Pindar's "Ode to Irony" lamented, "Thou, who formest pills to purge the spleen, / No more in Britain must thou dare be seen!" (9)—partially because serious people have been considering irony in a serious way ever since Aristotle's instructions to Alexander about virtue and political rhetoric, and partially because the word itself is so overdetermined and subject to constant revision. Peter Pindar, "Ode to Irony," in *Odes of Importance, &c*, new ed. (Dublin, 1792), 9.

11. James Huneker, *Unicorns* (New York: Charles Scribner's Sons, 1917), 7; F. McD. C. Turner, *The Element of Irony in English Literature* (Cambridge: Cambridge University Press, 1926).

12. "Irony," *The Living Age* 7, no. 4 (September 1899): 58; Claire Colebrook, *Irony*, The New Critical Idiom (New York: Routledge, 2004), 1; Paul de Man, "The Concept of Irony," in *Aesthetic Ideology*, trans. Andrzej Warminski, vol. 65, Theory and History of Literature (Minneapolis: University of Minnesota Press, 1996), 165. Colebrook is a rare exception when she warns against drawing a "distinction between irony as a figure of speech and irony as a theory of meaning" because "such a distinction is neither possible nor valuable" (17). I believe I am the first to take her at her word as a methodology for sustained literary analysis.

13. Edgar Johnson, *A Treasury of Satire* (New York: Simon and Schuster, 1945), 24.

14. Frances Theresa Russell, *Satire in the Victorian Novel* (New York: Macmillan, 1920), 121; H. Gomperz, "Interpretation," *Erkenntnis: Journal of Unified Science* 7 (1938): 229. By 2007, the editors of *Irony in Language and Thought: A Cognitive Science Reader*—Raymond W. Gibbs Jr. and Herbert L. Colston—compiled six hundred pages of attempts to say otherwise. Raymond W. Gibbs Jr. and Herbert L. Colston, eds., *Irony in Language and Thought* (New York: Lawrence Erlbaum Associates, 2007).

15. Edward Said, *The World, the Text, and the Critic* (Cambridge, MA: Harvard University Press, 1983), 159.

16. Richard Rorty, *Contingency, Irony, and Solidarity* (Cambridge: Cambridge University Press, 1989), 83.

17. Hayden White, *Metahistory: The Historical Imagination in Nineteenth-Century Europe* (Baltimore: Johns Hopkins University Press, 1973), 38.

18. Richard Rorty, *Achieving Our Country: Leftist Thought in Twentieth-Century America* (Cambridge, MA: Harvard University Press, 1998), 8.

19. Ibid., 39.

20. Herbert Marcuse, *An Essay on Liberation* (Boston: Beacon Press, 1969), 63.

21. Denise Riley, *The Words of Selves: Identification, Solidarity, Irony* (Stanford, CA: Stanford University Press, 2000), 162; Cynthia Willett, *Irony in the Age of Empire: Comic Perspectives on Democracy & Freedom* (Bloomington: University of Indiana Press, 2008), 13; Donna J. Haraway, "A Manifesto for Cyborgs: Science, Technology, and Socialist Feminism in the 1980s," in *The Gendered Cyborg: A Reader*, ed. Gill Kirkup et al. (New York: Routledge, 2000), 51. That irony would inspire the most contested claims to be stated as simple fact is not only limited to politics: within the space of a few years, equally insightful critics can state that "Irony, of all literary figures, is

the slipperiest, the most difficult to detect" and characterize "that most transparent of styles, irony." Paula Bennett, *Poets in the Public Sphere: The Emancipatory Project of American Women's Poetry, 1800–1900* (Princeton, NJ: Princeton University Press, 2003), 129; Nina Miller, *Making Love Modern: The Intimate Public Worlds of New York's Literary Women* (New York: Oxford University Press, 1999), 245. My point here is that there is no external criterion of value that would allow us to decide which of these two positions is correct but that as a dialectical opposition they illuminate a much broader discourse.

22. Viveca Greene, "Critique, Counternarratives, and Ironic Intervention in *South Park* and Stephen Colbert," in *A Decade of Dark Humour: How Comedy, Irony, and Satire Shaped Post-9/11 America*, ed. Ted Gournelos and Viveca Greene (Jackson: University Press of Mississippi, 2011), 128; Mark W. Van Wienen, *Partisans and Poets: The Political Work of American Poetry in the Great War* (Cambridge: Cambridge University Press, 1997), 244; Alain Badiou, *Metapolitics*, trans. Jason Barker (London: Verso, 2005), xi.

23. Agnes Repplier, "The Mission of Humour," in *Americans and Others* (Boston: Houghton Mifflin, 1912), 31; Dale M. Bauer, *Sex Expression and American Women Writers, 1860–1940* (Chapel Hill: University of North Carolina Press, 2009), 107.

24. Eugene E. Rovillain, "The Latest Mexican Revolution," *Atlantic Monthly*, October 1920, 567; George Saintsbury, "Irony," *The Dial* 82, no. 3 (March 1927): 181–87.

25. Theodor W. Adorno, *Notes to Literature*, trans. Shierry Weber Nicholsen, vol. 1 (New York: Columbia University Press, 1991), 306; Johnson, *A Treasury of Satire*, 4.

26. J. R. Pole, "An Anatomy of American Irony," *Raritan* 24, no. 1 (Summer 2004): 113; Jonathan Franzen, "The Liberal Form: An Interview with Jonathan Franzen," *boundary 2* 36, no. 2 (2009): 31–54.

27. H. L. Mencken, *The American Language: An Inquiry into the Development of English in the United States*, 2nd ed. (New York: Alfred A. Knopf, 1921), 191; Gilbert Seldes, *The Seven Lively Arts* (New York: Harper and Brothers, 1924), 60, 119.

28. Terry Eagleton, *The Illusions of Postmodernism* (Oxford: Blackwell, 1996), 47. Not all British writers have claimed a particular prerogative; in the 1920s, comedic dramatist Frank Stayton bucked the trend by claiming that "Irony has never been very popular in England, and never will be." Frank Stayton, *Threads* (New York: Century Co., 1921), 44. He was outnumbered by writers like Rebecca West, who claimed national characteristics derived from the "irony with which our military past has infused our spirit; for irony is the form of humor that can most easily be practiced by men who are keeping a stiff upper lip on land or sea, and we have done a lot of that." Rebecca West, "These American Women," *Harper's Monthly Magazine*, November 1925, 725. George Saintsbury viewed irony as an actual genetic trait, "not only in literary expression but in living character English blood . . . seems to have secreted in its complex composition more of the ironic virtue or virus than any other" ("Irony," 184). In these cases as in others, social and political conditions are thought to infuse individual character with the power of irony, which can then be translated into identifiable literary form. Thus Ibrahim Muhawi sees irony as a salient feature of recent Palestinian writing because "an exile by definition lives in a state of existential irony, where the lived present is characterised by a longing for an absent meaning," which "point[s] to a heightened sense of irony in Palestinian literature." Ibrahim Muhawi, "Irony and the Poetics of Palestinian Exile," in *Literature and Nation in the Middle East*, ed. Yasir Suleiman and Ibrahim Muhawi (Edinburgh: Edinburgh University Press, 2006), 31–47.

29. Alan Wilde, *Horizons of Assent: Modernism, Post-Modernism, and the Ironic Imagination* (Philadelphia: University of Pennsylvania Press, 1987), 10.

30. Miranda Fricker, "Feminism in Epistemology: Pluralism Without Postmodernism," in *The Cambridge Companion to Feminism in Philosophy*, ed. Miranda Fricker and Jennifer Hornsby (Cambridge: Cambridge University Press, 2000), 163n19.

31. Robert Genter, *Late Modernism: Art, Culture, and Politics in Cold War America* (Philadelphia: University of Pennsylvania Press, 2010), 317; Fredric Jameson, *The Seeds of Time* (New York: Columbia University Press, 1996), 113.

32. Jameson, *The Seeds of Time*, 92, 118; Walter Jost, "Philosophy and Literature—and Rhetoric," in *A Companion to the Philosophy of Literature*, ed. Gary Hagberg and Walter Jost (Oxford: Blackwell, 2010), 47.

33. Pericles Lewis, *The Cambridge Introduction to Modernism* (Cambridge: Cambridge University Press, 2007), 250; Philip Tew, "Glossary," in *The Modernism Handbook*, ed. Philip Tew and Alex Murray (New York: Continuum, 2009), 207; Leonard Diepeveen, "Learning from Philistines: Suspicion, Refusing to Read, and the Rise of Dubious Modernism," in *New Directions in American Reception Study*, ed. Philip Goldstein and James L. Machor (New York: Oxford University Press, 2008), 174.

34. Lewis, *Cambridge Introduction to Modernism*, 229.

35. Gunter Martens, "Literary Modernism, Critical Theory and the Politics of Irony," in *Modernism*, ed. Astradur Eysteinsson and Vivian Liska (Philadelphia: John Benjamins, 2007), 1:93. Glenn Willmott makes a particularly interesting version of these claims: "The general point to be made about modernist irony, then, is this: a binary structure built, as we see it here, on the quicksands of abjection . . . is synthetic and open-ended. In this sense, it is dialectical: it launches us toward an alterity yet to be realized, built on the ruins of irony itself" in which the life of irony requires the very death of irony. Glenn Willmott, *Modernist Goods: Primitivism, the Market and the Gift* (Toronto: University of Toronto Press, 2008), 129. In the 1990s, of course, "postmodern" irony was taken to be responsible for a wave of apathy toward pressing problems of politics; this is the sense in which legendary ironist David Foster Wallace described irony as a "new junta" behind television's "power to jettison connection and castrate protest," which was "fueled by the very ironic postmodern self-consciousness it had first helped fashion." David Foster Wallace, "E Unibus Pluram: Television and U.S. Fiction," in *A Supposedly Fun Thing I'll Never Do Again* (Boston: Little, Brown, 1997), 35.

36. Michael North, *Reading 1922: A Return to the Scene of the Modern* (Oxford: Oxford University Press, 1999), 208.

37. Paul Allen Miller, "Ethics and Irony," *SubStance* 38, no. 3 (2009): 66.

38. Jonathan Lear, *A Case for Irony* (Cambridge, MA: Harvard University Press, 2011), 38, ix.

39. Jameson, *The Seeds of Time*, 113.

40. Martens, "Literary Modernism, Critical Theory and the Politics of Irony," 89.

41. Morton White, *Social Thought in America: The Revolt Against Formalism* (New York: Viking, 1949), 9.

42. Claire Colebrook, *Irony in the Work of Philosophy* (Lincoln: University of Nebraska Press, 2002), 17.

43. Ludwig Wittgenstein, *Philosophical Investigations/Philosophische Untersuchungen*, trans. G.E.M. Anscombe, 2nd ed. (Oxford: Blackwell, 1953), 20; Gary Handwerk,

"Romantic Irony," in *The Cambridge History of Literary Criticism*, ed. Marshall Brown (Cambridge: Cambridge University Press, 2000), 5:203. While I don't ignore New Critical statements about irony—far from it—I do focus on the oppositional language of irony to the New Criticism. For the one writer whose career coincides directly with the institutional dominance of the New Criticism—Ralph Ellison—I attempt to show how a formalist reading itself, when framed by the language of irony, might still have more activist political intentions than conventional understandings of New Criticism admit.

44. Amanda Anderson, for example, has argued that it is "not the form of irony itself that is good or bad: detachment, whatever form it takes or predominantly allies itself with, is always situated—it is always a detachment from a particular mode of experience, a social situation, or a form of identity." Amanda Anderson, *The Powers of Distance: Cosmopolitanism & the Cultivation of Detachment* (Princeton, NJ: Princeton University Press, 2001), 175. In this situation, her equation of irony with detachment is not only perfectly coherent but squarely within well-established convention. It is not the only conventional understanding, however; one word bears literary and aesthetic connotations in ways that the other does not, and the very portability of the term frequently occludes equally conventional equations of irony with political engagement, especially when the words "politics" and "modernism" are at stake. The equation of personal "detachment" itself with withdrawal from politics—as opposed to a non-electoral form of aesthetic political action—is just as situated in a particular historical situation that is occluded by unreflective elision.

45. Thomas Aquinas, *Summa Theologiæ*, ed. T. C. O'Brien, vol. 41 (Cambridge: Cambridge University Press, 2006), 192; Ezra Pound, "Things to Be Done," *Poetry* 9, no. 6 (March 1917): 314.

46. One sees a salient example of this in the recurrent impulse to declare an "age of irony." To praise or blame a particular "age of irony" is to make tacit political claims about desirable dispositions on the world. It is one task of this project to trace a genealogy for these claims, even as the content of such claims for pundits in September 2001 was seemingly different from a liberal theologian's observation in 1952 that "Our age is involved in irony because so many dreams of our nation have been so cruelly refuted by history" (Reinhold Niebuhr, *The Irony of American History* [New York: Charles Scribner's Sons, 1952], 2), or from a decision in 1926 that "The bewildering days of Charles II and his portentous successor were neither natural nor healthy; no Age of Irony could be" (Turner, *The Element of Irony in English Literature*, 15), or from the question in 1994: "Will there ever be another—safe—'age of irony'? Did one ever really exist?" (Linda Hutcheon, *Irony's Edge: The Theory and Politics of Irony* [New York: Routledge, 1994], 204), or from the diagnosis of "an all too ironic age" (Ayon Roy, "Hegel Contra Schlegel; Kierkegaard Contra De Man," *PMLA* 124, no. 1 [January 2009]: 121).

47. Adorno, *Minima Moralia: Reflections from Damaged Life*, 98; Adorno, *Minima Moralia: Reflexionen Aus Dem Beschädigten Leben*, 108.

48. Walter Rideout, *The Radical Novel in the United States, 1900–1954: Some Interrelations of Literature and Society* (New York: Columbia University Press, 1992), 220.

49. Max Eastman, *Enjoyment of Living* (New York: Harper & Brothers, 1948), 210.

50. Dick Howard, *Political Judgments* (Lanham, MD: Rowman and Littlefield, 1996), 5.

51. W. D. Hudson, ed., *The Is-Ought Question: A Collection of Papers on the Central Problem in Moral Philosophy* (New York: Macmillan/St. Martin's Press, 1969), 11.

52. Hutcheon, *Irony's Edge*, 50.

53. William E. Connolly, "Foreword: The Left and Ontopolitics," in *A Leftist Ontology: Beyond Relativism and Identity Politics* (Minneapolis: University of Minnesota Press, 2009), xi.

54. Ibid., xiii.

55. Jacques Rancière, *The Politics of Aesthetics: The Distribution of the Sensible*, trans. Gabriel Rockhill (New York: Continuum, 2004), 18, 39.

56. Jacques Rancière, "Does Democracy Mean Something?" in *Dissensus: On Politics and Aesthetics*, trans. Steven Corcoran (New York: Continuum, 2010), 52, 58.

57. John Dewey, *Ethics*, in *John Dewey: The Later Works, 1925–1953*, ed. Jo Ann Boydstun, vol. 7 (Carbondale: Southern Illinois University Press, 1985), 350.

58. F. R. Ankersmit, *Aesthetic Politics: Political Philosophy Beyond Fact and Value* (Stanford, CA: Stanford University Press, 1996), 181.

59. Ibid., 358.

60. Donald A. Schön, "Generative Metaphor: A Perspective on Problem-Setting in Social Policy," in *Metaphor and Thought*, ed. Andrew Ortony, 2nd ed. (New York: Cambridge University Press, 1993), 137.

61. Benjamin De Casseres, "Caricature and New York," *Camera Work* 26 (April 1909): 17.

62. Mary McCarthy, "Class Angles and a Wilder Classic," 1938, in *A Bolt from the Blue and Other Essays* (New York: New York Review of Books, 2002), 22.

63. Ralph Ellison, "Beating That Boy," in *Shadow and Act* (New York: Vintage International, 1995), 95.

1 / The Eye in Irony: New York, Nietzsche, and the 1910s.

1. Hilaire Belloc, "On Irony," in *On Anything* (London: Methuen & Co., 1910), 18–22; Friedrich Nietzsche, *Ecce Homo*, ed. Oscar Levy, trans. Anthony M. Ludovici, vol. 17, Complete Works of Friedrich Nietzsche (New York: Russell & Russell, 1964).

2. Paul Fussell, *The Great War and Modern Memory* (New York: Oxford University Press, 1975), 35.

3. Harold Stearns, *Liberalism in America: Its Origin, Its Temporary Collapse, Its Future* (New York: Boni and Liveright, 1919), 173.

4. Randolph Bourne, "John Dewey's Philosophy," in *The Radical Will: Selected Writings, 1911–1918*, ed. Olaf Hansen (New York: Urizen Books, 1977), 332.

5. See Randolph Bourne, "Trans-National America," in *The Radical Will: Selected Writings, 1911–1918*, ed. Olaf Hansen (New York: Urizen Books, 1977), 248–64.

6. Lewis Mumford, "The Image of Randolph Bourne," *New Republic*, September 24, 1930, 151.

7. John Dos Passos, *U.S.A.: The 42nd Parallel; 1919; The Big Money* (New York: Library of America, 1996), 448–49; Noam Chomsky, *American Power and the New Mandarins* (New York: Pantheon Books, 1967), 7; Paul Rosenfeld, "Randolph Bourne," *The Dial* 75, no. 6 (December 1923): 545.

8. Daniel Aaron, "American Prophet," *New York Review of Books*, November 23, 1978, 37.

9. Casey Nelson Blake, *Beloved Community: The Cultural Criticism of Randolph Bourne, Van Wyck Brooks, Waldo Frank & Lewis Mumford* (Chapel Hill: University of North Carolina Press, 1990), 68.

10. Leslie J. Vaughan, *Randolph Bourne and the Politics of Cultural Radicalism* (Lawrence: University Press of Kansas, 1997), 48; Ross Posnock, "The Politics of Non-identity: A Genealogy," *boundary* 2 19, no. 1 (Spring 1992): 50. Posnock states this position most eloquently; Vaughan's book in many ways amplifies and extends Posnock's basic argument, while focusing primarily on Bourne's work and his historical context rather than his position in a larger genealogy of critical theory.

11. Bourne himself encouraged such readings of "The Life of Irony" in a letter to a friend: "This last essay, 'The Life of Irony,' I hurried off to the publisher without reading over and slunk around for a day or two, feeling what a fool and incapable I was, and sure that it would be summarily rejected, and with such scorn that I should never get even another hearing. And now as I read it over it quite charms me: I wonder how I could ever have expressed so completely the apotheosis of a whole side of me which makes my talk and comment on friends and events and books with my friends, such a sparkling joy to me." Letter to Prudence Winterrowd, March 2, 1913, in *Letters of Randolph Bourne: A Comprehensive Edition*, ed. Eric J. Sandeen (Troy, NY: Whitson Publishing, 1981), 75.

12. Randolph Bourne, "The Life of Irony," in *Youth and Life* (Freeport, NY: Books for Libraries Press, 1967), 102.

13. Benjamin De Casseres, *Chameleon, Being a Book of My Selves* (New York: Lieber & Lewis, 1922), 179; Northrop Frye, "The Nature of Satire," in *The Educated Imagination and Other Writings on Critical Theory*, Collected Works of Northrop Frye 21 (Toronto: University of Toronto Press, 1996), 49.

14. Scholarly opinions and preferences vary on whether to translate Nietzsche's "*Umwertung*" as "revaluation" or "transvaluation." For a concise analysis, see Duncan Large, "A Note on the Term 'Umwerthung,'" *Journal of Nietzsche Studies* 39 (Spring 2010): 5–11.

15. Bourne, "Life of Irony," 108.

16. Colebrook, *Irony in the Work of Philosophy*, x.

17. Ibid., 221.

18. Bourne, "Life of Irony," 111.

19. William James, *The Meaning of Truth: A Sequel to "Pragmatism"* (New York: Longmans, Green, 1909), 205. Compare with Hume on the greater variability of "thought" in comparison to "sight," a view the manipulated photograph would seem to address; in the case of the manipulated photograph, it wouldn't matter whether the eyes were variable or not, as the object that the eyes were perceiving would be changed such that the "thought" would be concomitantly affected. In Book I, Section VI of the *Treatise*, Hume writes: "Our eyes cannot turn in their sockets without varying our perceptions. Our thought is still more variable than our sight; and all our other senses and faculties contribute to this change; nor is there any single power of the soul, which remains unalterably the same, perhaps for one moment. The mind is a kind of theatre, where several perceptions successively make their appearance." David Hume, *A Treatise of Human Nature*, ed. L. A. Selby-Bigge (Oxford: Oxford University Press, 1978), 253.

20. Bourne, "Life of Irony," 120.

21. Van Wyck Brooks, *America's Coming-of-Age* (Garden City, NY: Doubleday Anchor Books, 1958), 15.

202 / NOTES

22. Marius de Zayas, "Photography," *Camera Work* 41 (January 1913): 17, 20.

23. Lewis Hine, "Social Photography: How the Camera May Help in the Social Uplift," in *Classic Essays on Photography*, ed. Alan Trachtenberg (New Haven, CT: Leete's Island Books, 1980), 111.

24. John Dewey, *Psychology*, in *John Dewey: The Early Works, 1882–1898*, ed. Jo Ann Boydstun, vol. 2 (Carbondale: Southern Illinois University Press, 1991), 65.

25. Alfred Stieglitz, "Pictorial Photography," in *Classic Essays on Photography*, ed. Alan Trachtenberg (New Haven, CT: Leete's Island Books, 1980), 119.

26. Richard Rorty, *Consequences of Pragmatism* (Minneapolis: University of Minnesota Press, 1982), 163.

27. Bourne, "Life of Irony," 105.

28. Georg Lukács, *The Historical Novel*, trans. Hannah Mitchell and Stanley Mitchell (New York: Humanities Press, 1965), 198. Historian John Pettegrew remarks that "Irony involves radical relativism—a complex of thought best represented by Nietzsche, who is an important reference point for Bourne and Rorty and their shared assumptions of perspectivalism, antifoundationalism, and the ever present possibility of losing critical consciousness. Nietzsche, however, is where Bourne and Rorty part company." John Pettegrew, "Lives of Irony: Randolph Bourne, Richard Rorty, & a New Genealogy of Critical Pragmatism," in *A Pragmatist's Progress? Richard Rorty and American Intellectual History*, ed. John Pettegrew (Lanham, MD: Rowman and Littlefield, 2000), 104. I wholeheartedly agree with his assertion that "Bourne's 'Life of Irony' is a corrective to Rorty," though as my conclusion suggests I prefer to keep them in dialectical tension rather than conceiving of Bourne as supplanting or "correcting" Rorty's mistakes (105).

29. I burlesque this position only slightly. In a recent biography of Upton Sinclair, historian Kevin Mattson describes the events following the publication of *The Jungle* and a federal investigation that confirmed some of Sinclair's most distasteful findings: "Meat sales plummeted. People were talking about the book throughout the country. The public had awakened, and now it started demanding that something be done. . . . The result of all this was the Meat Inspection Act of 1906—a major piece of legislation that helped empower the federal government." Kevin Mattson, *Upton Sinclair and the Other American Century* (Hoboken, NJ: John Wiley and Sons, 2006), 66. In an analysis that reveals as much about Mattson's politics as about Sinclair's, the socialist novelist was profoundly disappointed in the very limited scope of the reform his novel produced, which to the historian "represented his desire to embrace utopia over the practical reforms that Roosevelt believed in" (66).

30. Vaughan, *Randolph Bourne and the Politics of Cultural Radicalism*, 53.

31. Thorstein Veblen, "Professor Clark's Economics," in *The Place of Science in Modern Civilization and Other Essays* (New York: B. W. Hubsch, 1939), 191.

32. Lloyd R. Morris, *The Young Idea: An Anthology of Opinion Concerning the Spirit and Aims of Contemporary American Literature* (New York: Duffield and Company, 1917), 206.

33. Adorno, *Minima Moralia: Reflections from Damaged Life*, 98; Adorno, *Minima Moralia: Reflexionen Aus Dem Beschädigten Leben*, 108.

34. Bourne, "The War and the Intellectuals," 315.

35. Ibid., 308.

36. Bourne, "Life of Irony," 106.

37. Randolph Bourne, "The Doctrine of the Rights of Man as Formulated by Thomas Paine," in *The Radical Will: Selected Writings, 1911–1918*, ed. Olaf Hansen (New York: Urizen Books, 1977), 246, emphasis added.

38. Robert Guay, "Genealogy and Irony," *Journal of Nietzsche Studies* 41 (Spring 2011): 26.

39. Friedrich Nietzsche, *Beyond Good and Evil: Prelude to a Philosophy of the Future*, ed. Oscar Levy, trans. Helen Zimmern, vol. 12, Complete Works of Friedrich Nietzsche (New York: Macmillan, 1914), 154; Friedrich Nietzsche, *Jenseits Von Gut Und Böse*, vol. Band 5, Sämtliche Werke (München: Deutscher Taschenbuch Verlag, 1980), 150.

40. Friedrich Nietzsche, *The Twilight of the Idols, or, How to Philosophise with the Hammer*, ed. Oscar Levy, trans. Anthony M. Ludovici, vol. 16, Complete Works of Friedrich Nietzsche (New York: Russell & Russell, 1964), 57; Friedrich Nietzsche, *Götzen-Dämmerung*, vol. Band 6, Sämtliche Werke (München: Deutscher Taschenbuch Verlag, 1980), 102; Randolph Bourne, "The Price of Radicalism," in *The Radical Will: Selected Writings, 1911–1918*, ed. Olaf Hansen (New York: Urizen Books, 1977), 298.

41. Steilberg calls Bourne "one of the first not strictly philosophical expounders of Nietzsche in America," who was therefore attentive to the ludic, figurative quality of Nietzsche's project. Hays Alan Steilberg, *Die Amerikanische Nietzsche-Rezeption Von 1896 Bis 1950. Monographien Und Texte Zur Nietzsche-Forschung 35* (Berlin: Walter de Gruyter, 1996), 137, my translation. Historian Robert Westbrook has written that "Insofar as James shaped the thinking of young radicals such as Randolph Bourne, Max Eastman, and Walter Lippmann, it was less as a pragmatic empiricist than as a romantic vitalist, a homegrown counterpart to Nietzsche or Bergson." Robert Westbrook, *Democratic Hope: Pragmatism and the Politics of Truth* (Ithaca, NY: Cornell University Press, 2005), 121. Until Jennifer Ratner-Rosenhagen's magisterial *American Nietzsche: A History of an Icon and His Ideas* (Chicago: University of Chicago Press, 2012), the influence of Nietzsche's thought on U.S. culture and history received relatively little attention, but see Patrick Bridgwater, *Nietzsche in Anglosaxony: A Study of Nietzsche's Impact on English and American Literature* (Leicester: Leicester University Press, 1972) and Manfred Pütz, ed., *Nietzsche in American Literature and Thought* (Columbia, SC: Camden House, 1995). For Nietzsche's figure in American anarchism, see Alan Antliff, *Anarchist Modernism: Art, Politics, and the First American Avant-Garde* (Chicago: University of Chicago Press, 2001).

42. Ratner-Rosenhagen, *American Nietzsche*, 151, 153.

43. All quotations come from the first complete works in English, published in 1909–11. This is not because of the superiority of the translations compared to more recent ones—far from it—but rather to present the language that was available to non-German speakers in the historical moment; page numbers in brackets are for the German, which I have included where significant translation issues occur. For all of the many virtues of Frances Nesbitt Oppel's work on gender and irony in Nietzsche, when she claims that "Although Nietzsche employs a narrow definition of irony—saying one thing and meaning the opposite—in fact he uses it expansively and dialectically, so that it becomes the means or instrument fashioning his perspectivism, or clash of viewpoints," she overlooks many other forms of irony that Nietzsche indicates. Frances Nesbitt Oppel, *Nietzsche on Gender: Beyond Man and Woman* (Charlottesville: University of Virginia Press, 2005), 90. The best, if not only, sustained account in

English of Nietzsche on irony—not the way that irony functions in Nietzsche's work but what Nietzsche *means* by "irony"—is Ernst Behler, "Nietzsche's Conception of Irony," in *Nietzsche, Philosophy and the Arts*, ed. David W. Conway, Salim Kemal, and Ivan Gaskell (New York: Cambridge University Press, 1998), 13–35.

44. Nietzsche, *Beyond Good and Evil*, 98; Nietzsche, *Jenseits Von Gut Und Böse*, 100.

45. H. L. Mencken, *The Philosophy of Friedrich Nietzsche*, 3rd ed. (Port Washington, NY: Kennikat Press, 1913), viii.

46. "Observations and Comments," *Mother Earth* 7, no. 9 (November 1912): 279.

47. Ibid.

48. Mencken, *The Philosophy of Friedrich Nietzsche*, x; B. M., "Friedrich Nietzsche," *Mother Earth* 7, no. 11 (1913): 383, emphasis added.

49. "Some American Criticisms of Nietzsche," *Current Literature* 44, no. 3 (March 1908): 295; "Will Nietzsche Come into Vogue in America?" *Current Literature* 49, no. 1 (July 1910): 65; Joseph Jacobs, "Works of Friedrich Nietzsche: A Critical Consideration of the German Philosopher, If Philosopher He Can Be Called, Based Upon the New English Translation of His Works—Many Recent Nietzsche Volumes," *New York Times*, May 7, 1910, sec. BR8; Huneker, *Unicorns*, 320.

50. Randolph Bourne, review of *Nietzsche* by Paul Elmer More (Boston: Houghton Mifflin, 1911); *Journal of Philosophy, Psychology and Scientific Methods* 9, no. 17 (August 15, 1912): 472.

51. Randolph Bourne, "A Modern Mind," *The Dial*, March 22, 1917, 239. Bourne's characterization of Parsons as a Nietzschean may surprise those who understand Nietzsche only as an exponent of the raving misogyny his rhetoric can seem to endorse. As always with Nietzsche, one must pay attention to the irony to understand positions that are criticized rather than endorsed. On this point, see Oppel, *Nietzsche on Gender*, especially the chapter titled "'Yes, Life Is a Woman': Irony, Metaphor, and 'Woman' in *The Gay Science*" (89–117).

52. Randolph Bourne, "Denatured Nietzsche," *The Dial*, October 25, 1917, 390.

53. Ibid.

54. Bourne, "Review of Nietzsche," 472.

55. Nietzsche, *Beyond Good and Evil*, 152; Nietzsche, *Jenseits Von Gut Und Böse*, 148.

56. Friedrich Nietzsche, *The Genealogy of Morals: A Polemic*, ed. Oscar Levy, trans. Horace B. Samuel, vol. 13, Complete Works of Friedrich Nietzsche (Edinburgh: T. N. Foulis, 1913), 153; Friedrich Nietzsche, *Zur Genealogie Der Moral*, vol. Band 5, Sämtliche Werke (München: Deutscher Taschenbuch Verlag, 1980), 383.

57. Nietzsche, *The Genealogy of Morals*.

58. Dewey, "Psychology," 65.

59. Nietzsche, *Twilight of the Idols*, 44; Nietzsche, *Götzen-Dämmerung*, 92.

60. Matthew Rampley, *Nietzsche, Aesthetics, and Modernity* (New York: Cambridge University Press, 2000), 172.

61. Nietzsche, *Twilight of the Idols*, 20; Nietzsche, *Götzen-Dämmerung*, 71.

62. Walter Lippmann, *A Preface to Politics* (New York and London: M. Kennerly, 1914), 200–201.

63. Ibid., 305. Six years and one world war later, Harold Stearns took up precisely this thread of thought from Lippmann, who by that time had moved on to arguing for a rational technocracy. Stearns wrote in 1919, "[i]n practically every modern democracy—but in America, as I shall try to show, most of all—it is largely the unconscious and impulsive motives which lead a man to mark his ballot in a particular way. The

whole development of the party system is a practical acknowledgment of the inadequacy of the private, individual judgment." Stearns, *Liberalism in America*, 149.

64. Lippmann, *Preface to Politics*, 208.

65. Edmund Wilson, "The Nietzschean Line," in *The Shores of Light: A Literary Chronicle of the Twenties and Thirties* (New York: Farrar, Straus, and Giroux, 1952), 490.

66. Jack London, *The Iron Heel* (New York: Review of Reviews, 1917), 6.

67. Emma Goldman, "Nietzsche on War," *Mother Earth* 9, no. 8 (October 1914): 60.

68. Tracy B. Strong, "Nietzsche's Political Misappropriation," in *The Cambridge Companion to Nietzsche*, ed. Bernd Magnus and Kathleen M. Higgins (New York: Cambridge University Press, 1996), 128.

69. Nietzsche, *Twilight of the Idols*, 54; Nietzsche, *Götzen-Dämmerung*, 100.

70. Lippmann, *Preface to Politics*, 87, 88.

71. Brooks, *America's Coming-of-Age*, 15; Lippmann, *A Preface to Politics*, 22.

72. Nietzsche, *Beyond Good and Evil*, 212; Nietzsche, *Jenseits Von Gut Und Böse*, 227.

73. H. L. Mencken, "Letter to Benjamin De Casseres" (MS, December 12, 1933), box 1: Folder H. L. Mencken—De Casseres 1927–1935, Benjamin De Casseres Papers, New York Public Library Rare Books and Manuscripts.

74. I. Graeber, "Benjamin De Casseres as I Know Him" (*The Jewish Tribune*, undated), box 28: Benjamin De Casseres Papers, New York Public Library Rare Books and Manuscripts.

75. Eugene O'Neill, forward to *Litanies of Negation*, by Benjamin De Casseres (New York: Gotham Book Mart, 1928), viii. Cf. Benjamin De Casseres, "'Denial Without End': Benjamin De Casseres' Parody of Eugene O'Neill's 'God Play' *Days Without End*," ed. Robert M. Dowling, *Eugene O'Neill Review* 30 (Fall 2008): 145–59.

76. O'Neill, forward, x.

77. Benjamin De Casseres, "Reply," in *The Young Idea: An Anthology of Opinion Concerning the Spirit and Aims of Contemporary American Literature*, ed. Lloyd R. Morris (New York: Duffield and Company, 1917), 146.

78. Benjamin De Casseres, "Insincerity: A New Vice," *Camera Work* 42–43 (July 1913): 16.

79. Randolph Bourne, "Theodore Dreiser," in *The Radical Will: Selected Writings, 1911–1918*, ed. Olaf Hansen (New York: Urizen Books, 1977), 461; Bourne, "The Life of Irony," 107.

80. Benjamin De Casseres, *Mencken and Shaw: The Anatomy of America's Voltaire and England's Other John Bull* (New York: Silas Newton, 1930), 51; De Casseres, "Insincerity: A New Vice," 17.

81. Benjamin De Casseres, "The Ironical in Art," *Camera Work* 38 (April 1912): 18; De Casseres, "Insincerity: A New Vice," 16.

82. Benjamin De Casseres, "James Branch Cabell," in *Works of Benjamin De Casseres* (New York: Blackstone Publishers, 1936), 1:46.

83. Bourne, "Life of Irony," 128.

84. De Casseres, "The Ironical in Art," 17.

85. De Casseres, "Caricature and New York," 17.

86. Benjamin De Casseres, "The Philosophers of Unrepentance," *Liberty (Not the Daughter but the Mother of Order)* 16, no. 4 (October 1907): 35, 21.

87. De Casseres, "Caricature and New York," 17.

88. Oscar Levy, "Letter to Benjamin De Casseres" (MS., November 16, 1936), box 1, Benjamin De Casseres Papers, New York Public Library Rare Books and Manuscripts.

89. Benjamin De Casseres, *Forty Immortals* (New York: J. Lawren, 1926), 37; Benjamin De Casseres, "The Psychology of Caricature," in *Mortals & Immortals: Caricatures by C. De Fornaro* (New York: n.p., 1911), n.p.; Benjamin De Casseres, *The Muse of Lies* (Newark, NJ: Rose Printers and Publishers, 1936), 36.

90. Benjamin De Casseres, *The Superman in America* (Seattle: University of Washington Press, 1929), 28.

91. Benjamin De Casseres, "Jules De Gaultier: Super-Nietzschean," *Forum*, January 1913, 28.

92. Benjamin De Casseres, *Platform of Benjamin De Casseres: Candidate for Mayor of New York*, poster, hand-dated 1907 and 1912, box 24, Benjamin De Casseres Papers, New York Public Library Rare Books and Manuscripts.

93. De Casseres, *Chameleon, Being a Book of My Selves*, 73.

94. De Casseres, "The Ironical in Art," 17; Benjamin De Casseres, "Heavens a Hippodrome and All the Actors Airplanes," *New York Times*, November 30, 1919, SM12.

95. Sämi Ludwig, *Pragmatist Realism: The Cognitive Paradigm in American Realist Texts* (Madison: University of Wisconsin Press, 2002), 102.

96. Amy Elias, *Sublime Desire: History and Post-1960s Fiction* (London: Johns Hopkins University Press, 2001), 146.

97. De Casseres, "Caricature and New York," 17; Lawrence Hatab, "Prospects for a Democratic Agon: Why We Can Still Be Nietzscheans," *Journal of Nietzsche Studies* 24 (Fall 2002): 145.

98. Mencken, *The Philosophy of Friedrich Nietzsche*, 200. Herman Siemens and Gary Shapiro have remarked that "Over the last twenty years or so Nietzsche's significance for political thought has become the single most hotly contested area of Nietzsche research, especially in the English-speaking world: Is Nietzsche a political thinker at all—or an antipolitical philosopher of values and culture?" Herman Siemens and Gary Shapiro, "Guest Editors' Introduction: What Does Nietzsche Mean for Contemporary Politics and Political Thought?" *Journal of Nietzsche Studies* 35–36, Special Issue: Nietzsche and Contemporary Politics (Spring/Autumn 2008): 3. My intention is not to enter this debate in a sustained way. Rather, I'm interested in the ways that the very framing of the question—whether particular kinds of writing are "political" or merely obtain to "values and culture"—is not the understanding of cultural and aesthetic politics among the thinkers I'm considering. For the kind of sustained close reading of Nietzsche as a philosopher of cultural politics with resonance for tyranny in the twenty-first century, see Tracy B. Strong, "Nietzsche and the Political: Tyranny, Tragedy, Cultural Revolution, and Democracy," *Journal of Nietzsche Studies* 35–36 (Spring/Autumn 2008): 48–66.

99. Frederic L. Paxson and Samuel B. Harding, eds., "Nietzsche," *War Cyclopedia: A Handbook for Ready Reference on the Great War* (Washington, DC: GPO, 1918).

100. Benjamin De Casseres, *Germans, Jews and France* (New York: Rose Printers and Publishers, 1935), 6.

101. Ibid.

102. Nietzsche, *Twilight of the Idols*, 94; Nietzsche, *Götzen-Dämmerung*, 133.

103. Benjamin De Casseres, "The Individual Against Moloch," in *Works of Benjamin De Casseres* (New York: Blackstone Publishers, 1936), 1:8.

104. Benjamin De Casseres, "Spinoza, the Father of Modernism," *Canadian Jewish Chronicle*, September 30, 1932, 33, clipping from *The Reflex*—a journal "Devoted to

the secular interests of the Jewish Race"—in De Casseres Papers of New York Public Library.

105. Benjamin De Casseres, "Letter," *Contempo* 1, no. 12 (November 15, 1931): 2; Upton Sinclair, "Letter to Benjamin De Casseres" (MS., September 23, 1939), box 1, Benjamin De Casseres Papers. New York Public Library Rare Books and Manuscripts. Sinclair's version of Socialism was simply not as hostile to basic notions of the individual as is commonly understood but took a more systemic and economic view of the situation than rhetorical bomb-throwers like De Casseres. Sinclair's letter to De Casseres continues, "But we have to have a new economic basis for the new individualism that we may be able to develop in America. Under our present industrial system we can develop only robots."

106. De Casseres, *Forty Immortals*, 12.

107. De Casseres, "The Individual Against Moloch," 9.

108. De Casseres, *Platform of Benjamin De Casseres: Candidate for Mayor of New York*.

109. Chantal Mouffe, *The Democratic Paradox* (London: Verso, 2000), 5, 9.

110. Rancière, "Does Democracy Mean Something?" 47.

111. Wendy Brown, *Politics Out of History* (Princeton, NJ: Princeton University Press, 2001), 137.

2 / Gendering Irony and Its History: Ellen Glasgow and the Lost 1920s

1. Benjamin De Casseres, "Review of Marian Cox, *The Dry Rot of Society*," *Current Opinion* 67, no. 5 (December 1919): 339; Djuna Barnes, *Ryder* (Normal, IL: Dalkey Archive Press, 1990), 209.

2. Some writers identify an epoch rather than a specific parentage: Ernst Behler, for example, attributes to Nietzsche the notion that "[h]istorically speaking, the origin of irony was 'the age of Socrates'" (94) and to Schlegel the idea that "the real origin of irony is to be found in philosophy." Ernst Behler, "Friedrich Schlegel and Novalis," in *A Companion to Continental Philosophy* (Oxford: Blackwell, 1999), 79. Two hundred fifty years before Behler and 150 years before Nietzsche, Giambattista Vico situated irony's emergence within speculative history: "irony certainly could not have begun," he wrote, "until the period of reflection [*L'ironia certamente non poté cominciare che da' tempi della riflessione*]. Giambattista Vico, *The New Science of Giambattista Vico: Unabridged Translation of the Third Edition (1744) with the Addition of "Practice of the New Science*," trans. Thomas Goddard Bergin and Max Harold Fisch (Ithaca, NY: Cornell University Press, 1984), 131; Giambattista Vico, *La Scienza Nuova Seconda*, ed. Fausto Nicolini (Bari, Gius, Laterza & Figli, 1953), 163. For those who identify an embodied parentage, the answer also varies: Søren Kierkegaard identified not the "age of Socrates" but Socrates himself as the "introducer" of irony, for "it is in Socrates that the concept of irony has its inception in the world." Søren Kierkegaard, *The Concept of Irony, with Constant Reference to Socrates*, trans. Lee M. Capel (Indianapolis: Indiana University Press, 1965), 47. G.W.F. Hegel was primarily concerned with attacking Romantic irony and thus limited his paternal origin story to that which "was invented [*erfunden*] by Friedrich von Schlegel," whom he deemed "the father of irony," even though there was a genetically "deeper root [*tieferen Grund*] . . . in Fichte's philosophy, in so far as the principles of this philosophy were applied to art." Georg Wilhelm Friedrich Hegel, *Aesthetics: Lectures on Fine Art*, trans. T. M. Knox, vol. 1 (Oxford: Oxford University Press, 1998), 66, 64; Georg Wilhelm Friedrich Hegel, *Ästhetik*,

ed. Friedrich Bassenge, vol. Band 1 (Berlin: Aufbau-Verlag, 1965), 93. Others have allegorized irony's alleged parentage: in the early nineteenth century, for example, when Karl Solger asserted a maternal lineage for irony by writing that "Mysticism is, when looking to the real world, the mother of irony [*Die Mystik ist . . . die Mutter der Ironie*]" or in 1945 when an American literary critic would claim that "Prudence is one of the parents of irony." Karl Solger, "Letter to Ludwig Tieck, 22 November, 1818," in *German Aesthetic and Literary Criticism: The Romantic Ironists and Goethe*, ed. Kathleen Wheeler (Cambridge: Cambridge University Press, 1984), 156; Johnson, *A Treasury of Satire*, 28. The language is Behler's rather than Nietzsche's; while Nietzsche speaks about the origin of tragedy, law, justice, evil, morality, opera, and language, he remains silent on the origin of irony. Kierkegaard states the case even more trenchantly in his prefatory theses with "Socrates introduced irony first [*Socrates primus ironiam introduxit*]." Kierkegaard, *The Concept of Irony, with Constant Reference to Socrates*, 348, my translation. For Vico, of course, irony's recurrent "beginning" is a part of a speculative rather than chronological historical moment in the development of human civilization. An offhanded, implicit claim underlies historian Jackson Lear's use of "The Birth of Irony" as a title for the origins of postmodern sensibilities in nineteenth-century advertising and consumerism in the months after September 11, 2001.

3. "THE BIRTH OF IRONY," *Judge's Library: A Monthly Magazine of Fun* 154 (January 1902): n.p.

4. Katherine Holland Brown, "The Birth of Irony," *Lippincott's Monthly Magazine*, June 1908, 750.

5. Rorty, *Contingency, Irony, and Solidarity*, xv, 28.

6. Ibid., 75.

7. See Craig B. Matarrese, "Satisfaction or Supersession? Expression, Rationality, and Irony in Hegel and Rorty," *Clio* 36, no. 1 (September 2006): 41–58.

8. Georg Wilhelm Friedrich Hegel, *Phenomenology of Spirit*, trans. A. V. Miller (Oxford: Oxford University Press, 1977), 288; Georg Wilhelm Friedrich Hegel, *Phänomenology Des Geistes*, ed. Allen B. Wessels and Heinrich Clairmont (Hamburg: Felix Meiner Verlag, 2006), 352.

9. Kimberly Hutchings, *Hegel and Feminist Philosophy* (Oxford: Wiley-Blackwell, 2003), 89.

10. Georg Wilhelm Friedrich Hegel, *Elements of the Philosophy of Right*, ed. Allen B. Wood, trans. H. B. Nisbet (Cambridge: Cambridge University Press, 1991), 207.

11. Hegel, *Aesthetics: Lectures on Fine Art*, 1:67. There is clearly some overlap: his attack on the immorality of Friedrich von Schlegel's novel *Lucinde* appears not in the *Aesthetics* but in §164 of his *Elements of the Philosophy of Right*; his attack on Fichte's egoism and its danger to "morals, law, things human and divine, sacred and profane" appears in the "Irony" section of the *Aesthetics*. Hegel, *Elements of the Philosophy of Right*, 65. But Hegel objects to the novel's suggestion that the "marriage ceremony is superfluous and a formality which could be dispensed with" (205) and further asserts that a "girl's vocation [*Bestimmung*] consists essentially only in the marital relationship; what is therefore required is that love should assume the shape of marriage, and that the different moments which are present in love should attain their truly rational relation to each other" (205 [317]). The *Phenomenology* also includes his influential analysis of *Antigone*, which he employs to characterize the role played by women within the community, the State, and history.

12. Michael Inwood, *A Hegel Dictionary* (Oxford: Blackwell, 1992), 146.

13. Hegel, *Phenomenology of Spirit*, 288; Hegel, *Phänomenology Des Geistes*, 352.

14. Jocelyn B. Hoy, "Hegel, Antigone, and Feminist Critique: The Spirit of Ancient Greece," in *The Blackwell Guide to Hegel's Phenomenology of Spirit*, ed. Kenneth R. Westphal (Oxford: Wiley-Blackwell, 2009), 177.

15. Seyla Benhabib, "On Hegel, Women and Irony," in *Situating the Self: Gender, Community and Postmodernism in Contemporary Ethics* (New York: Routledge, 1992), 247. Benhabib's analysis has become the standard of its class. She writes: "Hegel, on the one hand, views the development of subjectivity and individuality within the context of a human community; on the other hand, in assigning men and women to their traditional sex roles, he codifies gender-specific differences as aspects of a rational ontology that is said to reflect the deep structure of *Geist*. Women are viewed as representing the principles of particularity (*Besonderheit*), immediacy (*Unmittelbarkeit*), naturalness (*Natürlichkeit*), and substantiality (*Substanzialität*), while men stand for universality (*Allgemeinheit*), mediacy (*Vermittlung*), freedom (*Freiheit*), and subjectivity (*Subjektivität*)" (245–46).

16. Hutchings, *Hegel and Feminist Philosophy*, 108. By articulating what I consider the consensus view of Hegel here, I don't mean to suggest that there is not a good deal of continuing debate among feminist philosophers and theorists over how one should understand Hegel's dramatically gendered account of politics, for there is: whether his analysis should be understood as an internal critique of ancient Greek society, as an historical observation that undercuts his own account of progressive history, or as a transhistorical, essentializing gesture that endorses what it describes remain contentious issues.

17. Hoy, "Hegel, Antigone, and Feminist Critique," 184.

18. Benhabib, "On Hegel, Women and Irony," 256.

19. Hegel, *Phenomenology of Spirit*, 288; Hegel, *Phänomenology Des Geistes*, 353.

20. In fact, for all the emphasis placed on Judith Butler as a theorist of irony, since the early *Gender Trouble* she rarely has recourse to the term itself, preferring "parody" as the figure most aptly suited to performative models of gender. This stands in contrast with Irigaray, who as early as 1974 famously quoted and analyzed Hegel for the title of an influential section of *Speculum of the Other Woman*: "The Eternal Irony of the Community" (214–26).

21. Lydia Rainford, *She Changes by Intrigue: Irony, Femininity and Feminism* (Amsterdam: Rodopi, 2005), 3.

22. Ibid., 54.

23. Hutcheon, *Irony's Edge*, 31.

24. Rainford, *She Changes by Intrigue*, 4.

25. Hutcheon, *Irony's Edge*, 32.

26. Haraway, "A Manifesto for Cyborgs," 50.

27. Ibid.

28. Naomi Schor, *Bad Objects: Essays Popular and Unpopular* (Durham, NC: Duke University Press, 1995), 183n19. Schor invokes Wayne Booth's "stable irony" here while recognizing that her political goals are incongruent with Booth's: "This resemblance is, however, at best only partial: Booth's agenda in promoting stable irony is fundamentally conservative (see Susan Suleiman, "Interpreting Ironies," *Diacritics* 6 [Summer 1976]: 15–21), and mine is not" (ibid.). For a less identifiably poststructuralist, more lyrically oriented account of political irony with feminist goals, see Riley, *The Words of Selves*, particularly "Echo, Irony, and the Political" (146–86).

29. Miller, *Making Love Modern*, 245. "A further problem with the term 'irony' is that it is troped, if not gendered, as masculine," Eileen Gillooly writes. "In its comic incarnation, irony presumes not only an *alazon* but an *eiron* or figure of disguised authority: an awkward posture for the feminine to maintain in almost any existent culture." Eileen Gillooly, *Smile of Discontent: Humor, Gender, and Nineteenth-Century British Fiction* (Chicago: University of Chicago Press, 1999), xxii. Or, as Naomi Schor states the case succinctly, "it is generally acknowledged that with the spectacular exception of Jane Austen, irony does not feature prominently in the history of women's fiction. The ironist in Western discourse has until recently almost always been male." Schor, "Fetishism and Its Ironies," in *Bad Objects*, 106.

30. Russell, *Satire in the Victorian Novel*, 121.

31. Ibid., 295.

32. Katha Pollitt, "Talk the Talk, Walk the Slutwalk," *The Nation*, July 18, 2011, 9.

33. As an anonymous and sympathetic critic described in 1914, "misogynists . . . in every age have insisted in Schopenhauer's manner that woman lacks the sense of humor." "Is the Greatest Humorist in English Literature a Woman?" *Current Opinion*, February 1914. Barbara Ellen Levy remarks that only two collections of "women's humor" existed before 1976: Kate Sanborn's *The Wit of Women* (New York: Funk & Wagnalls, 1885) and Martha Bensley Bruere and Mary Ritter Beard's *Laughing Their Way: Women's Humor in America* (New York: Macmillan, 1934). See Levy, *Ladies Laughing: Wit as Control in Contemporary American Women Writers* (Amsterdam: Gordon and Breach, 1997).

34. Don Marquis, "If We Could Only See," in *The Revolt of the Oyster* (Garden City, NY: Doubleday, Page & Co., 1922), 28.

35. John Galsworthy, "The Patricians," *Atlantic Monthly*, December 1910, 799.

36. Elsewhere, the inability to produce or recognize irony is represented as a function of environment rather than as a natural, preexisting condition and provides a reminder that gender politics were never neatly discrete from class politics: in analyzing the Soviet Union a decade after the revolutions of 1917, for example, American journalist Anne O'Hare McCormick remarked that the women "*emigrés* of the old regime . . . manage to condescend to fate by meeting it carelessly, in its own mood of irony," but the "female of the proletarian species looks as incapable of irony as of fear." Here, the proletariat coincidentally lack irony in the same proportion that they lack a Y chromosome but as a result of environment and political economy rather than— or perhaps in conjunction with—genetic predisposition, for the proletarian woman "has never had a chance to rise to grace or stoop to folly." Anne O'Hare McCormick, "Daughters of the Revolution," in *The Hammer and the Scythe: Communist Russia Enters the Second Decade* (New York: Alfred A. Knopf, 1927), 155.

37. Florence Leftwich Ravenel, "The Eternal Feminine," in *Women and the French Tradition* (New York: Macmillan, 1918), 12.

38. Emma Goldman, "The Tragedy of Woman's Emancipation," in *Anarchism and Other Essays* (New York: Mother Earth Publishing Association, 1910), 229, 225.

39. John Barrow Allen, "Review of Frank Frankfort Moore's One Fair Daughter," *The Academy* (November 17, 1894): 396.

40. "Books and Bookmen," *Harper's Weekly*, June 27, 1903, 1096.

41. Considering sarcasm as a species of irony dates at least to the early modern period: in *The Art of Rhetoric*, where Vico actually includes *litotes/extenuatio* as part of synecdoche rather than irony, he remarks that "Included among the species of irony is

sarcasm (*sarcasmus*) or a hostile mockery directed to one who is already dead or to one at the point of death." Giambattista Vico, *The Art of Rhetoric (Institutiones Oratoriae, 1711–1741)*, ed. Giorgio A. Pinton and Arthur W. Shippee (Amsterdam: Rodopi, 1996), 149.

42. Emily Thornwell, *The Lady's Guide to Perfect Gentility* (New York: Derby & Jackson, 1856), 149.

43. Kate Tannatt Woods, "Sarcasm Among Women," *Ladies' Home Journal* 8, no. 2 (January 1891): 8.

44. For Nietzsche on *Spottlust*, see Chapter 1. The idea that women needed to resist their natural proclivity for wounding verbal irony changed over the course of the next few decades, such that by 1920 a column in the popular *Youth's Companion* magazine would advise readers that "Sympathy is not incompatible with irony, whereas it is incompatible with sarcasm. The motive in resorting to irony is usually interest in the contradictory and unexpected turn taken by the course of events or by the human being on whom attention is fixed." Furthermore, "There may be humor in irony, but there is no humor in sarcasm. There is often a quality of wistfulness in irony, but in sarcasm there is no such feminine or appealing trait." "Irony and Sarcasm," *The Youth's Companion*, August 12, 1920, 470.

45. Margaret E. Sangster, *Good Manners for All Occasions: Including Etiquette of Cards, Wedding Announcements and Invitations* (New York: Cupples & Leon, 1910), 239.

46. Helen Thomas Follett and Wilson Follett, *Some Modern Novelists: Appreciations and Estimates* (New York: Henry Holt, 1919), 293.

47. Ibid.

48. Edith Wharton, "The Descent of Man," in *The Descent of Man and Other Stories* (New York: Charles Scribner's Sons, 1904), 9.

49. John Peale Bishop, "Mr. Fitzgerald Sees the Flapper Through," in *F. Scott Fitzgerald: The Critical Reception*, American Critical Tradition 5 (New York: B. Franklin, 1978), 72; F. Scott Fitzgerald, *The Beautiful and Damned* (New York: Penguin Classics, 1998), 5.

50. Georg Lukács, *The Theory of the Novel: A Historico-Philosophical Essay on the Forms of Great Epic Literature*, trans. Anna Bostock (Cambridge, MA: MIT Press, 1971), 93.

51. Fitzgerald, *The Beautiful and Damned*, 49, 337.

52. Handwerk, "Romantic Irony," 5:203.

53. Ezra Pound, "Irony, Laforgue, and Some Satire," *Poetry* 11, no. 2 (November 1917): 95, my emphasis.

54. Joseph Wood Krutch, "A Note on Irony," *The Nation*, November 1, 1922, 473.

55. It is not surprising, then, that Krutch's explicit connection of science, evolution, and irony wasn't the only suggestion that a species of post-Darwinian irony was itself evolving and that its natural habitat would be larger than a technical vocabulary of literary criticism. A cluster of poems appearing in various prominent places from 1914 to 1925, for example, suggests an oddly morbid admixture of naturalism, imagism, reason, and emotion under the titular concept of irony. In 1914, Amy Lowell's "Irony" described a fossilized coastal scene where "bleach / The skeletons of fishes, every bone / Polished and stark, like traceries of stone," where reader and narrator are resigned to a world in which "living things, who suffer pain, / May not endure till time can bring them ease." Amy Lowell, "Irony," in *Sword Blades and Poppy Seed* (New York:

Macmillan, 1914), 63. Louis Untermeyer's poem "Irony," collected in Harriet Monroe's 1917 *The New Poetry*, sounded a more explicitly naturalistic note about a world where "Eternity is thrust upon / A bit of earth, a senseless stone," and where "There is no kind of death to kill / The sands that lie so meek and still. . . . / But Man is great and strong and wise—And so he dies." Louis Untermeyer, "Irony," in *The New Poetry: An Anthology*, ed. Harriet Monroe and Alice Corbin Henderson (New York: Macmillan, 1917), 352. By 1925, Wyman Sidney Smith's "Ironies" first describes the opposition between romantic aspirations and the disappointing realities that punctuate daily life—"That we shall love and not be loved / And see love killed by the mere turning of a rose petal"—before returning to the familiar note of death that juxtaposes still-useful primitive industrial technology with primitive prehistory, both of which lead but to the grave: "Some lose their lives because a pulley slips; In other days the dew made climbing dangerous, / Or wind dropped cocoanuts on heads from high palm trees. / Accidents? / How so?" Wyman Sidney Smith, "Ironies," *The Nation*, October 7, 1925. Published in the year of the Scopes "Monkey" Trial, Smith provides an explicitly Darwinian answer to his own question, as the poem's concluding line provides an epitaph for a permanently deflated sense of human importance: "Ironies are monkeys in us still."

56. Jennifer Bajorek, *Counterfeit Capital: Poetic Labor and Revolutionary Irony* (Stanford, CA: Stanford University Press, 2009), 9.

57. Thus in 1922, Louis Untermeyer—not only a poet but an editor and writer for Left journals such as *Masses, Liberator,* and *New Masses*—expanded the subtext of his earlier poem into an explicit critical vocabulary. Recalling how a mere "generation ago, the ladies of our land were singing faintly and in sweetly splashing platitudes," he strongly advised his readers to "witness the edged concision of such women's work as H.D.'s, Edna Millay's and others" because their "temper is almost opposed; a fresh vigor finds its expression in more and more intellectual condensations. It luxuriates in lyrics that are frequently as ironic as they are introspective." Louis Untermeyer, "A Shelf of Recent Books: The Impulse of Irony," *The Bookman: A Review of Books and Life* 55, no. 6 (August 1922): 635. Throughout the first decades of the twentieth century, irony manifestly signifies much more than harmonized tensions held in a New Critical equipoise that had yet to be theorized and is figured as a perceptible aesthetic quality produced from an internal state or disposition: an "impulse of irony [that] assumes a strange variety of almost opposed forms; it colors the works of modernists of every school." As usual, this "impulse" is figured variously as an ontological predisposition, an expression of will, a feature of consciousness in its historical development, a function of external conditions, and a formal quality of texts, simultaneous products of both individual technique and historicized literary value. This was, according to Untermeyer, due to the fact that when "the literature of a nation progresses from naïveté to sophistication, its increasing intellectuality begins to sound the overtones of irony." Again, it has long been a critical convention to acknowledge, if not despair, at the difficulty of employing only one definition of irony at a time; when reading immanently from within the critiques themselves, it becomes apparent that writers like Untermeyer specifically employ irony *because* of its legibly polysemous ambiguity, and in a way that is more frequently and explicitly associated with democratic pluralism than with political quietism.

58. Lewis Campbell, "Note. On the So-Called Irony of Sophocles," in *Sophocles*, ed. Lewis Campbell, vol. 1, 2nd ed. (Oxford: Clarendon Press, 1879), 126.

59. Thomson, *Irony*, 139, my emphasis.

60. Campbell, "Note. On the So-Called Irony of Sophocles," 127.

61. Ibid.

62. George Meredith, "An Essay on Comedy," in *Comedy*, ed. Wylie Sypher (Baltimore: Johns Hopkins University Press, 1980), 37.

63. Recently, for example, Susan Edmunds characterized Flannery O'Connor as "Schooled in the precepts of New Criticism," which meant precisely that "she absorbed a set of literary and critical values dominated by the refusal of sentimentality and a corresponding privileging of modernist irony, objectivity, and detachment." Susan Edmunds, *Grotesque Relations: Modernist Domestic Fiction and the U.S. Welfare State* (Oxford: Oxford University Press, 2008), 182.

64. Alain Locke, "Negro Youth Speaks," in *The New Negro* (New York: Macmillan, 1992), 52. For an excellent synopsis of the way that sentimental tears were imagined by the Left (and modernist poetics) to have moved from eighteenth-century masculinity to twentieth-century (degenerate) femininity, see Paula Rabinowitz, "Melodrama/Male Drama: The Sentimental Contract of American Labor Films," in *Black & White & Noir: America's Pulp Modernism* (New York: Columbia University Press, 2002), especially pp. 121–26. For a critique that understands Locke as an antiradical force, see especially Barbara Foley, *Specters of 1919: Class and Nation in the Making of the New Negro* (Urbana. University of Illinois Press, 2003), 1 70.

65. Seth Moglen, *Mourning Modernity: Literary Modernism and the Injuries of American Capitalism* (Stanford, CA: Stanford University Press, 2007), 7.

66. For the relationship between sentimentality and masculinity in this period, see Christopher Breu, *Hard-Boiled Masculinities* (Minneapolis: University of Minnesota Press, 2005), esp. "The Hard-Boiled Male Travels Abroad," 83–114. See also Leonard Cassuto, *Hard-Boiled Sentimentality: The Secret History of American Crime Stories* (New York: Columbia University Press, 2009), esp. "Crime and Sympathy: Theodore Dreiser, Ernest Hemingway," 23–46.

67. Susan Rosenbaum argues that "irony does not remove modernist writers from the sentimental tradition but rather constitutes a position within the historical discourse of poetic affect. The antisentimental bias has resulted in a rigidified understanding of irony's aims and effects: positioning modernism (early and late) as part of a longer culture of sensibility can help us to see that conventions of irony work toward varied ends in sentimental culture." Susan Rosenbaum, "Elizabeth Bishop's Theater of War," in *Reading the Middle Generation Anew: Culture, Community, and Form in Twentieth-Century American Poetry*, ed. Eric L. Haralson (Iowa City: University of Iowa Press, 2006), 55.

68. Ernest Hemingway, *The Sun Also Rises* (New York: Charles Scribner's Sons, 1926), 113, 114.

69. As one scholar recently put it, "There appears to be, for most Hemingway scholars, no subject more banal than 'irony in Hemingway,' because there is unanimity about the fact that Hemingway is a great practitioner of modernist irony, which serves as a synonym for 'distance' and 'internal freedom' of the protagonists." William Dow, "The Perils of Irony in Hemingway's *The Sun Also Rises*," *Etudes Anglaises* 58 (February 2005): 178.

70. Michael G. Kammen writes that the exchange in *The Sun Also Rises* is essentially a resentful personal attack on Gilbert Seldes, who had publicly praised the "irony and pity" of *The Great Gatsby*: "All the insiders on the scene knew perfectly well that

Hemingway had aimed a sharp arrow at Seldes." Michael J. Kammen, *The Lively Arts: Gilbert Seldes and the Transformation of Cultural Criticism in the United States* (Oxford: Oxford University Press, 1996), 54.

71. Hemingway, *The Sun Also Rises*, 116.

72. John Pettegrew, *Brutes in Suits: Male Sensibility in America, 1890–1920* (Baltimore: Johns Hopkins University Press, 2007), 320, 321.

73. Jessica Burstein, "A Few Words About Dubuque: Modernism, Sentimentalism, and the Blasé," *American Literary History* 14, no. 2 (Summer 2002): 248.

74. Elizabeth Francis, *The Secret Treachery of Words: Feminism and Modernism in America* (Minneapolis: University of Minnesota Press, 2002), 112; Rosenbaum, "Elizabeth Bishop's Theater of War," 55.

75. Gillooly, *Smile of Discontent*, xxii.

76. Susan Goodman, *Civil Wars: American Novelists and Manners, 1880–1940* (Baltimore: Johns Hopkins University Press, 2003), 112.

77. Julius Rowan Raper, "Ellen Glasgow," in *A Companion to the Literature and Culture of the American South* (Malden, MA: Blackwell, 2004), 403.

78. Wilson Follett, "Sentimentalist, Satirist, and Realist: Notes on Some Recent Fiction," *Atlantic Monthly* (October 1916): 491.

79. Ellen Glasgow, *A Certain Measure: An Interpretation of Prose Fiction* (New York: Harcourt, Brace and Co., 1938), 224.

80. Ellen Glasgow, *Virginia* (New York: Doubleday, Page & Co., 1913), 430.

81. Ellen Glasgow, "The Novel in the South," in *Ellen Glasgow's Reasonable Doubts: A Collection of Her Writings*, ed. Julius Rowan Raper (Baton Rouge: Louisiana State University Press, 1988), 72.

82. Ellen Glasgow and James Branch Cabell, *Of Ellen Glasgow: An Inscribed Portrait* (New York: Maverick Press, 1938).

83. Glasgow, *A Certain Measure*, 54.

84. Ellen Glasgow, "I Believe," in *Ellen Glasgow's Reasonable Doubts: A Collection of Her Writings*, ed. Julius Rowan Raper (Baton Rouge: Louisiana State University Press, 1988), 243. "I have tried to interpret the vanished [Southern] lady with sympathy, though not entirely without that cutting edge of truth which we call irony," she wrote about her early (1913) novel *Virginia* (Glasgow, *A Certain Measure*, 78); she further opposes "sympathy" and "irony" when writing that "Although, in the beginning, I had intended to deal ironically with both the Southern lady and Victorian tradition, I discovered, as I went on, that my irony grew fainter, while it yielded at last to sympathetic compassion" (Glasgow, *Virginia*, 79). In a biography written in 1942 and published posthumously, she wrote of seeking after Maupassant, "a style that was touched with beauty and yet tinctured with irony." Ellen Glasgow, *The Woman Within* (New York: Harcourt Brace, 1954), 126.

85. Ellen Glasgow, "What I Believe," in *Ellen Glasgow's Reasonable Doubts: A Collection of Her Writings*, ed. Julius Rowan Raper (Baton Rouge: Louisiana State University Press, 1988), 222.

86. Glasgow, *A Certain Measure*, 28.

87. Lauren Berlant has shown how "the critique of patriarchal familialism that sentimental texts constantly put forth can be used to argue against the normativity of the family; at the same time, the sacred discourse of family values also sustained within this domain works to preserve the fantasy of the family

as a space of sociability in which flow, intimacy, and identification across difference can bridge life across generations and model intimate sociability for the social generally." Lauren Berlant, *The Female Complaint: The Unfinished Business of Sentimentality in American Culture* (Durham, NC: Duke University Press, 2008), 21.

88. Recent work has shown how "Women writers and artists catalyzed this synthesis, and their work in the magazines that promoted a popular version of modernism forged connections between elements of modern culture—irony and intimacy, wit and sentiment, private love and public space, sophisticated artifice and political critique—that are often seen as separate or contradictory." Elizabeth Majerus, "'Determined and Bigoted Feminists': Women, Magazines, and Popular Modernism," in *Modernism*, ed. Astradur Eysteinsson and Vivian Liska (Amsterdam: John Benjamins, 2007), 2:621.

89. Glasgow, *The Woman Within*, 104.

90. Glasgow further creates a kind of economy of irony, wherein less or more is available to be drawn upon in compensation: "Sophisticated wit and sparkling irony must be drained away from this bare and steady chronicle of simple lives [in a return to the realism of *Vein of Iron*]. Years earlier, I had said that Southern literature needed blood and irony; and in writing of a social tradition that had become lifeless from immobility, I found that through an infusion of satire alone could the dry bones be made to appear animate" (*A Certain Measure*, 178–79).

91. Edwin Mims, "The Social Philosophy of Ellen Glasgow," *Social Forces* 4, no. 3 (March 1926): 495–503.

92. James Southall Wilson, "Ellen Glasgow: Ironic Idealist," *Virginia Quarterly Review* 15, no. 1 (Winter 1939): 121–26; Henry Seidel Canby, "SRL Award to Ellen Glasgow," *Saturday Review of Literature* 23, no. 24 (April 5, 1941): 10.

93. Alfred Kazin, *On Native Grounds: An Interpretation of Modern American Prose* (New York: Reynal & Hitchcock, 1942), 260, 257. Despite the time and milieu in which her career peaked, and despite the more damning relegation of her work in recent years to the margins of "Southern Literature" or "Women's Literature," Glasgow forthrightly asserted that she thought of herself as a critic "not of Southern nature, but of human nature . . . not of Southern characteristics (whatever that may mean!), but of the springs of human conduct and the common heritage of mankind." Ellen Glasgow, *Letters of Ellen Glasgow*, ed. Blair Rouse (New York: Harcourt, Brace, 1958), 116. This was a note she sounded repeatedly: "I have always written, or tried to write, not of Southern characteristics, but of human beings." Glasgow 135 to Martha Saxton, September 17, 1932, in Ellen Glasgow, *Perfect Companionship: Ellen Glasgow's Selected Correspondence with Women*, ed. Pamela Matthews (Charlottesville: University of Virginia Press, 2005).

94. Walter Kalaidjian, *The Edge of Modernism: American Poetry and the Traumatic Past* (Baltimore: Johns Hopkins University Press, 2006), 131.

95. Ibid., 135. "In standard versions of American literary and critical history, the social politics of Southern Agrarianism is either simply elided or contained in a *cordon sanitaire* from, on the one hand, the modernist poetics of the Fugitives and, on the other, the disciplinary formalism of New Criticism" (ibid.).

96. Glasgow, "The Novel in the South," 75. "I feel that I write better when my pen is barbed with satire, and I cannot be satirical about Virginia Woolf. Now, if only it were Mr Ernest Hemingway and his school of sophisticated barbarians."

Ellen Glasgow to Irita Van Doren, early September [1933], in Glasgow, *Perfect Companionship*, 139.

97. Ellen Glasgow, qtd. in Grace Stone, "Ellen Glasgow and Her Novels," *Sewanee Review* 50, no. 3 (September 1942): 297.

98. Ellen Glasgow, "No Valid Reason Against Giving Votes to Women: An Interview," in *Ellen Glasgow's Reasonable Doubts: A Collection of Her Writings*, ed. Julius Rowan Raper (Baton Rouge: Louisiana State University Press, 1988), 23.

99. Dorothy Scura, "A Knowledge in the Heart: Ellen Glasgow, the Women's Movement, and 'Virginia,'" *American Literary Realism, 1870–1910*, Special Issue: Women Writers of the Realistic Period (Winter 1990): 30.

100. Glasgow, "No Valid Reason," 25.

101. Ibid., 21.

102. Ellen Glasgow, "Feminism," in *Ellen Glasgow's Reasonable Doubts: A Collection of Her Writings*, ed. Julius Rowan Raper (Baton Rouge: Louisiana State University Press, 1988), 32.

103. Glasgow, *The Woman Within*, 163.

104. Lucy Delap, *The Feminist Avant-Garde: Transatlantic Encounters of the Early Twentieth Century* (Cambridge: Cambridge University Press, 2007), 110.

105. "By 1908, 'feminism' was already taking on some avant-garde connotations," Lucy Delap has shown; the National Association Opposed to Woman Suffrage in the United States declared, "Feminism is a movement born of a cubist and futurist age of extremes." Quoted in ibid., 2.

106. Glasgow, "What I Believe," 223.

107. Victoria McAlmon, "Free—for What?" in *These Modern Women: Autobiographical Essays from the Twenties*, ed. Elaine Showalter (Old Westbury, NY: Feminist Press, 1978), 115.

108. Lorine Livingston Pruette, "The Evolution of Disenchantment," in *These Modern Women: Autobiographical Essays from the Twenties*, ed. Elaine Showalter (Old Westbury, NY: Feminist Press, 1978), 73.

109. Ann E. Towns, *Women and States: Norms and Hierarchies in International Society* (Cambridge: Cambridge University Press, 2010), 71, 72.

110. As one historian of the U.S. suffrage movement wrote the year before the ratification of the Nineteenth Amendment, the "Declaration of Independence was called naught but mocking irony unless women had the ballot," which emerges as an entirely reasonable phrase to describe the glaring discrepancy between the facts of political exclusion and the putatively exceptional values of American democracy (especially given that the ratification of the Fourteenth Amendment in 1868 introduced specific and positive rather than implicit sex discrimination into the Constitution). Indeed, "irony" seems almost uniquely capable of critically describing the moment where participation in the public sphere was itself framed as an uncivilizing degradation from which women should be protected: allowing women to enter the public sphere, the argument went, would necessarily degrade them to the level of men and deprive children and society of the soothing, civilizing, pacifying force that women supposedly "naturally" provided. Kirk Harold Porter, *A History of Suffrage in the United States* (Chicago: University of Chicago Press, 1918), 234.

111. Recent scholarship has expanded and complicated, but perhaps not fundamentally shifted, the historical consensus that "the enfranchisement made little

difference in the lives of women or to the American political system" or that the "Nineteenth Amendment did not mark a 'Great Divide.'" Lorraine Gates Schuyler, *The Weight of Their Votes: Southern Women and Political Leverage in the 1920s* (Chapel Hill: University of North Carolina Press, 2006), 3. Put plainly, "Far from the legislative 'reign of terror' that antisuffragists had feared," Schuyler continues, by the late 1920s "enfranchised women 'became neither an independent force in American politics nor an interest group within the parties whose loyalty had to be preserved'" (190). Schuyler argues against this consensus.

For the first five years or so after women gained the vote, there was indeed the desired surge in legislation that women's groups had long lobbied for, ranging from food purity laws to pre- and postnatal funding to states in 1921 (Sheppard-Towner Maternity and Infancy Protection Act) to establishing in 1922 that a woman's citizenship was not a malleable function of her marital status (Cable Act, or "Married Women's Independent Nationality Act"). Yet, as Anna Harvey notes, after 1924 "the success rates for women's organizations in both Congress and the party organizations diminished dramatically" and "in the period between the New Deal years and 1970 only two congressional acts that appeared to be designed to provide benefits to women as a group were passed." Anna Lil Harvey, *Votes Without Leverage: Women in American Electoral Politics, 1920–1970* (Cambridge: Cambridge University Press, 1998), 6, 9.

While perhaps seemingly obvious to anyone who has voted or had political hopes for the U.S. electoral system, there is a broader theoretical divide that describes competing emphases on the seemingly different political goals of fundamentally and primarily affecting the material bases of political economy and fundamentally and primarily affecting the conditions under which political actors and citizens experience the dignity and respect within a social and political order: call this divide, as a representative exchange between political theorists Nancy Fraser and Axel Honneth does, the question of whether to pursue *Redistribution or Recognition*? The feminist politics of the postsuffrage era saw just such deep disagreements about the goals and desirability of electoral politics in the first instance. When the Equal Rights Amendment was first sent to Congress in 1923, for example, support among women's groups was hardly unanimous; much opposition stemmed from the belief that women's practical experiences—as well as real sexual differences between men and women—required protective labor legislation aimed specifically at women. As Vanessa May recently describes the conflict, Progressive women's groups "championed the positive effect that protective labor legislation had on women's working conditions and vehemently opposed the ERA. They met opposition, however, from early feminists, who called for absolute gender equality under the law, and conservative women's groups, who generally resisted state intervention in the marketplace." Vanessa May, *Unprotected Labor: Household Workers, Politics, and Middle-Class Reform in New York, 1870–1940* (Chapel Hill: University of North Carolina Press, 2011), 110.

112. Glasgow to Mary Johnston, August 15, 1906, in Glasgow, *Perfect Companionship*, 29.

113. Glasgow, *The Woman Within*, 91. Giving the opening address at the Southern Writers Conference in 1931, Glasgow sounded a distinctly Nietzschean/Jamesian note: "there is not one truth alone but many truths," she said, because

"modern psychology or the Theory of Relativity or both together have demolished our conception of truth as an established principle superior to and apart from the thinking subject. We no longer think of truth as a fixed pattern outside of ourselves at which we may nibble for crumbs as mice at a loaf." Ellen Glasgow, "Opening Speech of the Southern Writers Conference," in *Ellen Glasgow's Reasonable Doubts: A Collection of Her Writings*, ed. Julius Rowan Raper (Baton Rouge: Louisiana State University Press, 1988), 92.

114. Glasgow, *The Woman Within*, 172, 173.

115. John Dewey, "The New Psychology," in *John Dewey: The Early Works, 1882–1898* (Carbondale: Southern Illinois University Press, 1985), 1:51; William James, "Pragmatism's Conception of Truth," in *Pragmatism and Four Essays from The Meaning of Truth* (New York: Meridian Books, 1967), 150.

116. William James, *A Pluralistic Universe* (New York: Longmans, Green, 1920), 304.

117. William James, *Habit* (New York: Henry Holt, 1914), 3.

118. Glasgow, "I Believe," 229; Ellen Glasgow, "Evasive Idealism in Literature," in *Literature in the Making by Some of Its Makers* (New York: Harper & Brothers, 1917), 234.

119. Glasgow, "I Believe," 234–35.

120. William James, "The Will," in *Talks to Teachers on Psychology: And to Students on Some of Life's Ideals* (New York: Henry Holt, 1914), 184. This was quite different from the debunked notion of early psychologists, insofar as it is thoroughly embodied in "motor effect," "an alteration of heart-beats or breathing, or a modification in the distribution of blood, such as blushing or turning pale; or else a secretion of tears" (170). Yet the "will" isn't merely a disembodied idea, on the one hand, or a pure physical action, on the other, but a sort of intermediary compounding of inhibitions and impulses. It is, moreover, a term for a collective faculty with explicitly political valences: "An Oriental despot requires little ability" to inhibit his ideas, since there are no institutional checks; "Your parliamentary rulers," on the other hand, "your Lincoln, your Gladstone, are the strongest type of man, because they accomplish results under the most intricate possible conditions" (180). Thus "from the point of view of the psychological machinery, it would be hard to say whether [Napoleon] or Gladstone was the larger volitional quantity; for Napoleon disregarded all the usual inhibitions, and Gladstone, passionate as he was, scrupulously considered them in his statesmanship" (181).

121. James, "Pragmatism's Conception of Truth," 149.

122. Ibid.

123. George Santayana, "The Comic Mask," in *Soliloquies in England and Later Soliloquies* (New York: Charles Scribner's Sons, 1922), 137.

124. Dorothy Scura remarks that *The Romantic Comedians* holds a "singular . . . place among Glasgow's nineteen novels. Although wit and satire are present in all her work, *The Romantic Comedians* is almost pure comedy." Dorothy Scura, afterword to *The Romantic Comedians*, by Ellen Glasgow (Charlottesville: University Press of Virginia, 1995), 243. Susan Goodman, the best critic of Glasgow's comedies, remarks that "Novels of manners work by appearing to endorse what they ultimately reject," which serves as a more than passable definition of irony but not the same sense of irony that Glasgow seemed to have in mind. Goodman, *Civil Wars*, 5.

125. Benjamin De Casseres, "The March of Events," in *Ellen Glasgow: The Contemporary Reviews*, ed. Dorothy M. Scura (Cambridge: Cambridge University Press, 1992), 473; Dorothea Lawrance Mann, "Ellen Glasgow: Citizen of the World," in *Ellen Glasgow: The Contemporary Reviews*, ed. Dorothy M. Scura (Cambridge: Cambridge University Press, 1992), 284; Carl Van Vechten, "A Virginia Lady Dissects a Virginia Gentleman," in *Ellen Glasgow: The Contemporary Reviews*, ed. Dorothy M. Scura (Cambridge: Cambridge University Press, 1992), 277, 278. For perhaps the best reading of *The Romantic Comedians* as a comedy of manners, see Goodman, *Civil Wars*, esp. 119–29.

126. Ellen Glasgow, *The Romantic Comedians* (Charlottesville: University Press of Virginia, 1995), 229, 54.

127. While Shakespeare's Cordelia enacts her own advice to "Love, and be silent," Glasgow's protagonist is haunted by the memory of a differently silent Cordelia: his dead wife, whose abnegation of her own desires has elevated her from woman to "hostel" and "angel." It is her presence that suggests the ridiculousness of Cordelia's principle of silent devotion to the Law embodied in her father (as the Judge embodied the Law for Glasgow's Cordelia). That is, the injunction to "love, and be silent" is the apotheosis of the Hegelian version of a woman's proper relationship to public affairs, filtered as that disposition is through the private sphere of the family.

128. Glasgow, "Feminism," 27.

129. Ellen Glasgow, "Some Literary Woman Myths," in *Ellen Glasgow's Reasonable Doubts: A Collection of Her Writings*, ed. Julius Rowan Raper (Baton Rouge: Louisiana State University Press, 1988), 36.

130. Glasgow, "Feminism," 27. Glasgow employs irony to attack the "immemorial woman myths in a modern comedy of manners," finding that "The sting of its irony, I saw, must lie in the point of its truth." Glasgow, *A Certain Measure*, 225.

131. James, *Habit*, 65.

132. Ibid., 52.

133. Glasgow, "Some Literary Woman Myths," 37, 36.

134. Ibid., 38.

135. Ellen Glasgow, "Impressions of the Novel," in *Ellen Glasgow's Reasonable Doubts: A Collection of Her Writings*, ed. Julius Rowan Raper (Baton Rouge: Louisiana State University Press, 1988), 150.

136. Immanuel Kant, *Groundwork of the Metaphysics of Morals*, ed. Mary Gregor (Cambridge: Cambridge University Press, 1997), 13.

137. Ibid., 53, 12. Consider William James's assertion that "Freedom's first deed should be to affirm itself"; or that "genuine determinism" is flawed because "not the *impotence* but the *unthinkability* of free-will is what it affirms." William James, *The Principles of Psychology*, vol. 2 (New York: Henry Holt, 1905), 573, 574.

138. Goldman, "The Tragedy of Woman's Emancipation," 228.

139. Drucilla Cornell, *Moral Images of Freedom: A Future for Critical Theory* (New York: Rowman and Littlefield, 2008), 34.

140. Glasgow, "Some Literary Woman Myths," 37. Cf. Lisa Hollibaugh's argument that "Glasgow's own variable use of Darwin's theory reflects her growing sense of optimism concerning the position of women within the workings of Darwinian ideas of inheritance." Lisa Hollibaugh, "'The Civilized Uses of Irony': Darwinism, Calvinism, and Motherhood in Ellen Glasgow's Barren," *Mississippi Quarterly* 59, no. 1/2 (Winter–Spring 2006): 52.

141. Cleanth Brooks and Robert Penn Warren, "Letter to the Teacher," in *Understanding Fiction* (New York: F. S. Crofts, 1943), xviii.

142. Rorty, *Contingency, Irony, and Solidarity*, 87.

143. In 1938, Glasgow introduced a new edition of *The Romantic Comedians* by calling attention to her desire for "a touch that was light, penetrating, satirical. The comic sprit may be wistful, but it is never solemn; a heavy-footed comedy, or tragicomedy, is doomed to disaster. [. . .] My one regret, if it may be called a regret, is that, to the hasty reader, the ironic overtones may seem occasionally to deny the tragic mood of the book. For there is tragedy in the theme, though it is tragedy running, like the 'divine things' of Nietzsche, 'on light feet.'" Glasgow, *The Romantic Comedians*, xiv. Cf. Nietzsche's remark that "'all good things are light, everything divine runs along on delicate feet': first principle of my aesthetics." Friedrich Nietzsche, "The Case of Wagner: A Musician's Problem," in *The Anti-Christ, Ecce Homo, Twilight of Idols, and Other Writings* (Cambridge: Cambridge University Press, 2005), 231–62.

144. Glasgow, *A Certain Measure*, 207.

145. Glasgow, *The Romantic Comedians*, xiii.

146. Benhabib, "On Hegel, Women and Irony," 257.

147. As political theorist Cynthia Willett has recently argued: "Against the rational, self-engaged life with all its proclivities to disconnect from historical memory and participation in social and political life, comedy sets the stage for freedom as subversion and re-engagement—the key elements for a democratic political ethics. In this vision of democratic ethics, freedom does not contrast with equality and solidarity as analytically distinct and conflicting values. The pragmatic spirit of comedy defines freedom in terms of them." Willett, *Irony in the Age of Empire*, 9.

148. Fitzgerald, *The Beautiful and Damned*, 21–22.

149. Charles Altieri, *The Art of Twentieth Century American Poetry: Modernism and After* (Oxford: Blackwell, 2006), 177; Bennett, *Poets in the Public Sphere*, 152.

150. Barnes, *Ryder*, 150.

3 / The Focus of Satire: Public Opinions of Propaganda in the U.S.A. of John Dos Passos

1. T. V. Smith, "The Democratic Process," *Public Opinion Quarterly* 2, no. 1, Special Supplement: Public Opinion in a Democracy (January 1938): 19; McCarthy, "Class Angles and a Wilder Classic," 18.

2. As Fredric V. Bogel rightly points out, the relationship of irony to satire is itself vexed in ways that have rarely been accounted for: "The traditional way of linking them has been to regard irony as one of the literary techniques that lend indirectness and artifice to the element of attack and thus redeem satire from charges of mere aggression. But they are linked in other, perhaps profounder, ways as well, for satiric doubleness—one aspect of which is a problematic rather than merely oppositional relation of satirist to satiric object—is as essential to satire as ambiguity is to irony, and the two forms are consequently linked by the fact that each has a double structure and each, therefore, poses challenges of a particular kind for the reader." Fredric V. Bogel, *The Difference Satire Makes: Rhetoric and Reading from Jonson to Byron* (Ithaca, NY: Cornell University Press, 2001), 66. As satire evolved into its recognizably twentieth-century forms, the doubleness of both irony and satire expands dramatically into a multiplicity that exceeds numeration and instead is better viewed in the specific (perhaps almost infinite) ways that its meanings are contingently stabilized.

3. Alfred W. Jones, "Satire and Sentiment," in *Essays Upon Authors and Books* (New York: Stanford and Swords, 1849), 113; Richard Garnett, "Satire," *Encyclopedia Britannica*, 1911.

4. Jonathan Greenberg, *Modernism, Satire, and the Novel* (Cambridge: Cambridge University Press, 2011), 64.

5. Glasgow, *A Certain Measure*, 28; Thomson, *Irony*, 139.

6. In Weisenburger's analysis, Frye's diagnosis exemplifies a kind of modernist terrorizing of "Others," wherein "satire could not address the central anxieties of modernity and even seemed complicitous with the worst forms of modern, propagandistic consensus-building." Steven Weisenburger, *Fables of Subversion: Satire and the American Novel, 1930–1980* (Athens: University of Georgia Press, 1995), 2. Weisenburger does not include *U.S.A.* as an example. See Frye, "The Nature of Satire," 43.

7. Northrop Frye, *Anatomy of Criticism: Four Essays* (Princeton, NJ: Princeton University Press, 1957), 223.

8. Juvenal, "Satire I," in *Juvenal and Persius*, trans. G. G. Ramsay, vol. 91, Loeb Classical Library (Cambridge, MA: Harvard University Press, 1996), 5.

9. Adorno, *Minima Moralia: Reflections from Damaged Life*, 209; Adorno, *Minima Moralia: Reflexionen Aus Dem Beschädigten Leben*, 237.

10. James Hannay, *Satire and Satirists* (London: David Bogue, 1854), 269.

11. "Why Have We No Satire?" *Atlantic Monthly*, July 1899, 143; "No Satire," *Life*, September 18, 1919, 498.

12. Ambrose Bierce, *The Unabridged Devil's Dictionary*, ed. David E. Schultz and S. J. Joshi (Athens: University of Georgia Press, 2002), 208.

13. Adorno, *Minima Moralia: Reflections from Damaged Life*, 209.

14. Herman Scheffauer, "The Death of Satire," *The Living Age* (July 12, 1913): 86, 89, 86.

15. Thomas Seltzer, "Satire," *The Masses* 4, no. 3 (December 1912): 9.

16. Brooks, *America's Coming-of-Age*, 19.

17. "Why Have We No Satire?" 143.

18. Ambrose Bierce, "The Passing of Satire," *Life*, July 8, 1909, 65.

19. "No Satire," *Life*, September 18, 1919, 498.

20. James Livingston, "On Richard Hofstadter and the Politics of 'Consensus History,'" *boundary 2* 34, no. 3 (Fall 2007): 42.

21. Adorno, *Minima Moralia: Reflections from Damaged Life*, 211.

22. One might expand this duality to anticipate a split within the Frankfurt School itself, as theorists of the public sphere such as Jürgen Habermas diverged from Adorno and Horkheimer.

23. Frederick Elmore Lumley, *Means of Social Control* (New York: Century Co., 1925), 257.

24. Ibid., 257, 253, 259.

25. Ruth McKenney, *Industrial Valley* (New York: Harcourt, Brace, 1939), 65.

26. Although Dos Passos always conceived of the trilogy as a single novel—and he edited the individual volumes before issuing *U.S.A.*—the novels were published as he finished them: *The 42nd Parallel* in 1930, *1919* in 1932, and *The Big Money* in 1936. John Rohrkemper counts thirty-one essays about and reviews of Dos Passos published in 1938; he does not, however, include Sartre's 1938 essay, which was not published in English until 1957. John Rohrkemper, *John Dos Passos: A Reference Guide* (Boston: G. K. Hall, 1980), 44–49.

27. Lionel Trilling, "The America of John Dos Passos," *Partisan Review* 4 (April 1938): 26; Mike Gold, "The Keynote to Dos Passos' Works," *Daily Worker*, February 26, 1938, 7; Jean-Paul Sartre, "John Dos Passos and '1919,'" in *Literary Essays*, trans. Annette Michelson (New York: Wisdom Library, 1957), 93; Delmore Schwartz, "John Dos Passos and the Whole Truth," in *Selected Essays of Delmore Schwartz*, ed. Donald A. Dike and David H. Zucker (Chicago: University of Chicago Press, 1970), 229.

28. Michael Denning seems to view this fact as a defect of the novel, claiming that Dos Passos's epigrammatic announcement that "mostly *U.S.A.* is the speech of the people" is at odds with a literary style of "anti-populist, Taylorized colloquialism" and consistent distancing of characters' voices from mimetic accuracy; I claim this distance as a necessary precondition for both irony and satire rather than as a rhetorical blind spot. Michael Denning, *The Cultural Front* (London: Verso, 1998), 177.

29. This is as true today as it was in 1938. Juan Antonio Suárez, for example, concludes that for all its promising engagement with Left political cinema, finally "*USA* deflates the progressive potential attached to the ideologies and practice of newsreel and camera-eye aesthetics in 1930s Left media culture. Rather than instruments of knowledge and agitation, the Newsreels and Camera Eye fragments embody confusion, deceit, and noise. The utopianism of the Left newsreel/camera-eye film tradition remains a road not taken, a possibility of the cultural system alluded to but not actualized in Dos Passos's trilogy." Juan Antonio Suárez, *Pop Modernism: Noise and the Reinvention of the Everyday* (Cambridge: Cambridge University Press, 2007), 109.

30. Schwartz, "John Dos Passos and the Whole Truth," 245; Sartre, "John Dos Passos and '1919,'" 96.

31. It may well be because the politics of the novel have been largely evaluated by such politically committed critics that its political significance remains controversial. The fact that Dos Passos himself later underwent a well-publicized transformation from committed Wobbly-sympathizing radical to committed Cold Warrior certainly hasn't helped. His rightward political migration—along with Max Eastman, Walter Lippmann, E. E. Cummings, and many others—from identifiably radical writer of the 1910s to Goldwater Republican of the 1960s is well-known. As Michael Denning writes, "his move to the radical right lost him his left-wing admirers, while the undisputed sense that his early works are his finest has made him a difficult icon for the right." Denning, *The Cultural Front*, 177. In what must have been sarcasm, Dos Passos declared in 1930 to Edmund Wilson that he had become a "middle-class liberal"; the state of Kentucky indicted him a year later for criminal syndicalism (for speaking publicly in favor of the Harlan County miners' strike) and in 1932 he publicly endorsed the Communist ticket for president, suggesting a stripe of middle-class liberalism that would shock the average middle-class liberal. Dos Passos, *U.S.A.*, 1251. In 1934, Dos Passos quite illiberally wrote in a letter to John Howard Lawson that "I've been reading the Industrial Worker weekly with considerable pleasure—I still feel more in common with the wobbly line of talk than any other—and their clever absorption of technocracy data and their cheerful kidding of the comrats is a great relief after the humorless monotone of the Daily Worker." John Dos Passos, *The Fourteenth Chronicle: The Letters and Diaries of John Dos Passos*, ed. Townsend Ludington (Boston: Gambit, 1973), 447.

32. Rancière, *The Politics of Aesthetics*, 61.

33. In the words of novelist E. L. Doctorow, "the *circumstances themselves* are occasionally flashed to us by means of the so-called 'Newsreels' that *interrupt* the text."

E. L. Doctorow, forward to *The Big Money* (Boston: Houghton Mifflin, 2000), ix, my emphasis. The Library of America edition of the novels reproduces a portion of a preface to the 1937 Modern Library edition of *The 42nd Parallel*, in which Dos Passos suggests that the Newsreels were to serve this purpose, at least partially. As he described the interwoven modes of the novel, "*The Camera Eye* aims to indicate the position of the observer and *Newsreel* to give an inkling of the common mind of the epoch. Portraits of a number of real people are interlarded in the pauses in the narrative because their lives seem to embody so well the quality of the soil in which Americans of these generations grew" (Dos Passos, *U.S.A.*, 1268). My reading, however, takes the phrase "common mind" as significantly different than the historical "circumstances" that subsequent critics have understood him to mean; for the increasingly individualist Dos Passos, I'm not sure that "common mind" was totally free of sinister overtones.

34. In this reading, the stream-of-consciousness, autobiographical narration in the "Camera Eye" primarily calls attention to the ostensibly transparent reportage of the conventional narrative sections and the novel's Newsreels. As Donald Pizer persuasively argues, "The Camera Eye mode is the consciousness of the author; the remainder of the work is the American world at large that the author has sought to depict as accurately as possible." Donald Pizer, *Dos Passos' U.S.A.: A Critical Study* (Charlottesville: University Press of Virginia, 1988), 56. By "accurate," of course, we are meant to understand "objective," a stance repeatedly assumed by even the novel's most perceptive critics: in the words of Justin Edwards, "by 'editing' the Camera Eyes with the narratives, Dos Passos is able to call attention to the objectivity of the narrative sections and the extremely personal content of the Camera Eye fragments through Eisenstein's theory of juxtapositional imaging" (Justin Edwards, "The Man with the Camera Eye: Cinematic Form and Hollywood Malediction in John Dos Passos' *The Big Money*," *Literature/Film Quarterly* 27, no. 4 [1999]: 250), which consequently produces what Alfred Kazin calls "the truth of the camera eye" (*On Native Grounds*, 359). We are thus finally left with three different kinds of information in the novel: the "fictionally" true, the "subjectively" true, and the "objectively" true; we are to understand that Dos Passos has attempted to the best of his abilities to render even his subjective judgments as objectively as possible, in the service of producing something approximating "historical" truth. By "objectively" true I do not exclude the wholly "subjective" function of the "Camera Eye," though by "realism" I have a primarily taxonomic definition in mind. That is, in broader terms, the stream of consciousness of the "Camera Eye" is as much an attempt accurately to portray a state of affairs (in this case, the state of a mind) as the more conventionally naturalist prose sections attempt to portray the objective unfolding of a variety of events.

35. Johnson, *A Treasury of Satire*, 12; Pizer, *Dos Passos' U.S.A.: A Critical Study*, 185.

36. Finally, I'm not particularly interested in the generic divisions between "satire" *strictu sensu* and "the novel" that has satiric aspects. As Charles Knight has written, "There are satiric novels . . . and there are novels that are satires . . . but the distinctions between the two are approximate and subjective, depending in large part on how the generic energies of the text strike a particular reader in a particular reading. The question is not usually whether the identification is correct but whether it generates interesting ideas about the work identified or fruitfully extends an idea of satire and its functions." Charles A. Knight, *The Literature of Satire* (Cambridge: Cambridge University Press, 2004), 14.

37. Denning, *The Cultural Front*, 167.

38. Kazin, *On Native Grounds*, 497. Kazin's reference is itself ironic, as he is apparently referring to the famous photograph by Margaret Bourke-White, "Flood Victims, Louisville, Kentucky, 1937." Rather than itinerant African American farmers forced by poverty to seek charity, however, the photograph is actually of refugees waiting for assistance after being displaced by the Louisville flood of that same year, and the NAM billboard actually reads "World's Highest Standard of Living." The valences of the photograph's irony change dramatically when one has the additional information provided in the original context, though such a reversed-meaning model is still conceivable. See Sean Callahan, ed., *The Photographs of Margaret Bourke-White* (Greenwich, CT: New York Graphic Society, 1972), 136–37.

39. Amber Day, *Satire and Dissent: Interventions in Contemporary Political Debate* (Bloomington: Indiana University Press, 2011), 4.

40. Bliss Perry, *The American Mind* (New York: Houghton Mifflin, 1912), 205.

41. Rancière, *The Politics of Aesthetics*, 13.

42. Among critics of Dos Passos, Thomas Strychacz is a notable exception in this regard: framing the novel in terms of the profession of public relations and noting the "radical instability in the trilogy's ironic meanings"; this is what William Solomon means when he describes how "the irony of the Newsreels often achieves its effect through a turning of 'language inside out,' through the manipulation and twisting of words, redirecting or perverting their original, ostensibly referential meanings toward something else." Thomas Strychacz, *Modernism, Mass Culture, and Professionalism* (Cambridge: Cambridge University Press, 1993), 141; William Solomon, *Literature, Amusement, and Technology in the Great Depression* (Cambridge: Cambridge University Press, 2002), 200. In this regard, irony serves to amplify rather than deflate the necessity of actively engaging disparate parts of the novel: as Barbara Foley has written, "The onions may be miscommandeered military rations or hijacked goods. It does not matter whether any of these interpretive speculations is 'true.' What matters is that Dos Passos's method invites—indeed, requires—the reader to incorporate apparently random fragments into a dialectical paradigm. To read this Newsreel and relate it to surrounding narrative elements is to engage in conscious totalization," a function that irony requires to be a constant process that looks more like a "negative dialectical paradigm." Barbara Foley, *Radical Representations: Politics and Form in U.S. Proletarian Fiction, 1929–1941* (Durham, NC: Duke University Press, 1993), 431.

43. Mark Wollaeger, *Modernism, Media, and Propaganda: British Narrative from 1900 to 1945* (Princeton, NJ: Princeton University Press, 2006), xiv.

44. Kenneth Burke, *A Grammar of Motives* (Berkeley: University of California Press, 1969), 400.

45. John Dos Passos, *One Man's Initiation—1917* (New York: George H. Doran Co., 1922), 25, 36.

46. Ibid., 115.

47. John Dos Passos, *Manhattan Transfer* (Boston: Houghton Mifflin, 2000), 195.

48. Dos Passos, *U.S.A.*, 25.

49. Ibid., 91. Lennard Davis has traced the intimately related history of novels and the news and demonstrated how a hierarchy of informational value was established several centuries before Dos Passos: "The ideologizing of language . . . created the conditions for legal intervention into the realm of the discourse to diffuse the politicizing of news/novels, which then created the conditions for a definition of fact and fiction in which the former could be repressed and the latter more or less ignored." Lennard

Davis, *Factual Fictions: The Origins of the English Novel* (Philadelphia: University of Pennsylvania Press, 1997), 83.

50. Dos Passos, *U.S.A.*, 374. In a series of trials, *The Masses* was finally suppressed by the U.S. government. In his ruling, Judge Learned Hand articulated an interestingly pragmatist perspective on the relationship among language, the press, and public opinion when he wrote: "Words are not only the keys of persuasion, but the triggers of action, and those which have no purport but to counsel the violation of law cannot by any latitude of interpretation be a part of that public opinion which is the final source of government in a democratic state." Learned Hand, *Masses Publishing Co. v. Patten* (S.D.N.Y. 1917), 244 F. 535, 540.

51. Walter Lippmann, *Liberty and the News* (New York: Harcourt, Brace and Howe, 1920), 3.

52. Thomas Jefferson, "Letter to John Norvell. (14 June 1807)," in *Jefferson: Political Writings*, ed. Joyce Appleby and Terence Ball, Cambridge Texts in the History of Political Thought (Cambridge: Cambridge University Press, 1999), 274.

53. Michael Sproule, *Propaganda and Democracy: The American Experience of Media and Mass Persuasion* (New York: Cambridge University Press, 1997), 26.

54. Alexander Hamilton, "Number 84," in *The Federalist: A Commentary on the Constitution of the United States* (New York: Random House, 2000), 550.

55. In 1929, journalist Seldes tried to "realize the hope of every one of my colleagues who says: 'Some day I am going to take a holiday and write THE TRUTH BEHIND THE NEWS' by documenting corruption of the press." George Seldes, *You Can't Print That! The Truth Behind the News, 1918–1928* (New York: Garden City Publishing, 1929), 18. Almost a decade later, Seldes would still observe that "There is a growing suspicion that the press is no longer what it claims to be, the 'Tribune of the People,' the 'Voice of the Public,' the 'Upholder of Truth,' the 'Defender of Public Liberty,' as thousands of newspaper mastheads daily proclaim it. In the 1920s millions undergoing disillusion vaguely realized that they had been deceived by newspaper war propaganda. In the 1930s the myths of cyclical depressions and prosperity-around-the-corner again shook the confidence of the public." George Seldes, *Freedom of the Press* (New York: Garden City Publishing, 1937), ix.

56. Dos Passos, *U.S.A.*, 879.

57. Ibid., 544. Dos Passos published these lines in 1932, the same year he prevailed over the attempted censorship of *1919*, when Harper and Brothers wanted to remove the satirical portrait of J. P. Morgan from the novel. Dos Passos refused and arranged for Harcourt, Brace to publish the book.

58. George Creel, *The Creel Report: Complete Report of the Chairman of the Committee on Public Information, 1917:1918:1919* (New York: Da Capo Press, 1972), 43.

59. Ibid., 40. American literature was a key component of the government's efforts: Creel reported that the United States distributed 94,848 copies of *The Battle Line of Democracy: Prose and Poetry of the World War*, Committee on Public Information (Washington, DC: GPO, 1917) throughout the nation in 1917 alone (Creel, *Creel Report*, 455). This tactic must have depressed radical champions of Walt Whitman, whose "Long, Too Long, America" and "Beat! Beat! Drums!" were included in the volume.

60. George Creel, *How We Advertised America: The First Telling of the Amazing Story of the Committee on Public Information That Carried the Gospel of Americanism to Every Corner of the Globe* (New York: Harper & Brothers, 1920), 3.

61. Dos Passos, *U.S.A.*, 449.

62. Fussell, *The Great War and Modern Memory*, 8.

63. Dos Passos, *U.S.A.*, 449.

64. Creel, *How We Advertised America*, 4.

65. Ibid., 5.

66. United States, Cong. Senate, *The National Association of Manufacturers*, Violations of Free Speech and Rights of Labor (Washington, DC: GPO, n.d.), 228.

67. The notion of "educating" the public didn't occur only in the figurative classrooms of the nation. As the *Creel Report* noted, public- and private-school classrooms provided a neatly efficient way to reach students and teachers directly: thus, "the division commenced the publication of the National School Service, a 16-page paper issued twice a month to every one of the 520,000 teachers in the United States. In many respects this publication was one of the most remarkable features of the war, for it gave to the schools the needs and messages of Government in concise and usable form and to the Government a direct medium for reaching the 20,000,000 homes represented in the schools" (Creel, *Creel Report*, 19).

68. Dos Passos, *U.S.A.*, 223.

69. Ibid., 239. In 1939, the La Follette Committee of the U.S. Senate, which investigated corporate use of propaganda to influence legislation via public opinion, concluded: "The leaders of the [NAM] resorted to 'education.' ... They asked not what the weaknesses and abuse of the economic structure had been and how they could be corrected, but instead paid millions to tell the public that nothing was wrong and that grave dangers lurked in the proposed remedies.... The association also considered its propaganda material an effective weapon in the fight against labour unions." Cited in Alex Carey, *Taking the Risk Out of Democracy: Corporate Propaganda Versus Freedom and Liberty*, ed. Andrew Lohrey (Urbana: University of Illinois Press, 1997), 26.

70. Dos Passos, *U.S.A.*, 86; Thorstein Veblen, *Theory of Business Enterprise* (New York: Charles Scribner's Sons, 1920), 385. The influence of Veblen on Dos Passos has long been recognized. Alfred Kazin noted the extent to which Dos Passos himself resembled "Thorstein Veblen—whose mordant insights even more than Marx's revolutionary critique give a base in social philosophy to *U.S.A.*" Kazin, *On Native Grounds*, 345.

71. See Melvin Landsberg, *Dos Passos' Path to U.S.A.: A Political Biography, 1912–1936* (Boulder, CO: Colorado Associated University Press, 1972), 161–63, 210–11.

72. Dos Passos, *U.S.A.*, 1199.

73. Ibid., 253. As Jonathan Greenberg argues, it is precisely the role of satire to combat sentimentalism: "If the sentimental, then, represents what is seen as most coercive about emotion—its mobilization of feeling for the purpose of assimilating affective life to 'dominant cultural attitudes'—then satire is a major, perhaps an essential, component of the modernist resistance to such coercion. Satire—with its sibling concept, the grotesque—often seeks to undermine precisely those dominant, conventional, or clichéd forms of representation that are based on stirring a reader's compassion." Greenberg, *Modernism, Satire, and the Novel*, 53.

74. Dos Passos, *U.S.A.*, 219, 233.

75. Ibid., 1195. As Noam Chomsky points out in his introduction to Alex Carey's *Taking the Risk Out of Democracy*, the concept of "public opinion" had been understood to precede and legitimate overt force long before Dos Passos, Dewey, and the Creel Committee. Thus Chomsky quotes David Hume's *First Principles of Government*, wherein Hume asserts: "When we enquire by what means this wonder is brought

about, we shall find, that as Force is always on the side of the governed, the governors have nothing to support them but opinion. 'Tis therefore, on opinion only that government is founded; and this maxim extends to the most despotic and most military governments, as well as to the most free and most popular." Hume, quoted in Noam Chomsky, introduction to Carey, *Taking the Risk Out of Democracy*, xii.

76. For a discussion of rhetorical politics in the 1930s, see Solomon, *Literature, Amusement, and Technology in the Great Depression*, esp. 806–14.

77. Dos Passos, *U.S.A.*, 616. The lines rather depressingly foreshadow the U.S. media's prominent use of misinformation to garner popular support for the ongoing war in Iraq, as well as the government's production and distribution of propaganda disguised as "news" segments to promote that war. Parallels between the 1910s and the first years of the twenty-first century are especially salient when Dos Passos depicts the colonial struggle over the region that would become Iraq; or when a Newsreel suggests that the horrors of World War I were partially produced because "oil was trumps" (570); or when Dos Passos decries new fighting over what was "oriental Baghdad long ago" (240).

78. Ibid., 617. As Dos Passos—anticipating Michel Foucault—suggests in this characterization of "distance," genuine power increasingly resides in quasi- or extra-institutional—albeit increasingly pervasive—structures that are not only defiantly and self-consciously *beyond* the control of individual political agents but outside the control even of the most organized collectivity. As such, power seems to exist quite outside the mandate of anything resembling *either* popular sovereignty *or* the wise, rational modulation of a synecdochal representative. As the genuine power traditionally expressed in and by "the State" has grown increasingly distant from and invisible to the individual, the State has—in a seeming paradox—grown more and more intrusive into the personal lives of citizens who have no choice but to rely on tottering edifices of "rights" and "natural law" to defend their personal choices.

79. United States, Cong. Senate, *The National Association of Manufacturers*, 228.

80. John Dewey, *The Public and Its Problems* (New York: Henry Holt, 1927), 116.

81. My analysis here draws directly from Ankersmit, *Aesthetic Politics*.

82. Dos Passos, *U.S.A.*, 617.

83. Ibid., 1199.

84. "If any mood predominates in American writing it is that of gentle satire. This tendency to satire, usually vague and kindly, sometimes bitter with the unconvinced bitterness of a middle-aged lady who thinks herself worldly wise, is the one feature pervading all that can be called American among the mass of foreign-inspired writing in this country." John Dos Passos, "Against American Literature," in *Travel Books and Other Writings, 1916–1940* (New York: Library of America, 2003), 587.

85. John Dos Passos, "Wanted: An Ivy Lee for Liberals," *New Republic*, August 13, 1930, 371.

86. Ibid.

87. Ibid., 372.

88. Ibid.

89. Ibid., my emphasis.

90. Dos Passos, *U.S.A.*, 547.

91. Dos Passos, "Wanted: An Ivy Lee for Liberals," 372.

92. Ibid.

93. Ibid.

94. Ibid.

95. See Michael Warner, *Publics and Counter-Publics* (New York: Zone Books, 2002), particularly the introduction and first chapter.

96. Creel, *Creel Report*, 53.

97. In the posthumously published *Century's Ebb*, Dos Passos included a biography of John Dewey, who had only appeared fleetingly and sneeringly in the Randolph Bourne section of *U.S.A.* Dewey's biography in *Century's Ebb* is titled "American Philosophy, 1859–1952" and indicates the ambivalence with which the American Left viewed Dewey during and after he supported U.S. entry into World War I. As Dos Passos wrote, Dewey "embodied the American virtues, tolerance, altruism, sympathy with the poor and oppressed, impatience with dogmatism, but as the philosopher of democracy, he failed us in the hour of need." John Dos Passos, *Century's Ebb: The Thirteenth Chronicle* (Boston: Gambit, 1975), 113.

98. Lippmann's experience helping Wilson sell the war had convinced him beyond doubt of the extent to which the manipulation of language enabled the manipulation of the public. The continuing relevance of this insight has been made recently by such media critics as Michael Massing (see Michael Massing, "Iraq, the Press and the Election," *New York Review of Books*, December 16, 2004). As recalled by Michael Sproule, Walter Lippmann and a colleague analyzed "1000 articles on Russia appearing in the *New York Times* between March, 1917 and March, 1920, which they compared to the actual turn of events. They concluded that 'the news as a whole is dominated by the hopes of the men who composed the news organization.'" Sproule, *Propaganda and Democracy*, 20.

99. Lippmann, *Liberty and the News*, 55.

100. Ibid.

101. Dos Passos, *U.S.A.*, 1160.

102. Dewey gave generally favorable (albeit mixed) reviews to both of Lippmann's books; in *The Public and Its Problems*, Dewey also directly acknowledged his debt to Lippmann for the idea that "the Public seems to be lost; it is certainly bewildered" in a footnote: "See Walter Lippmann's 'The Phantom Public.' To this as well as to his 'Public Opinion,' I wish to acknowledge my indebtedness, not only as to this particular point, but for ideas involved in my entire discussion even when it reaches conclusions diverging from his." Dewey, *The Public and Its Problems*, 116.

103. John Dewey, "Education as Politics," in *John Dewey: The Middle Works, 1899–1924*, ed. Jo Ann Boydstun (Carbondale: Southern Illinois University Press, 1985), 13:331.

104. Dewey, *The Public and Its Problems*, 3.

105. Ibid., 184.

106. Ibid., 210.

107. Walter Lippmann, *The Phantom Public: A Sequel to "Public Opinion"* (New York: Macmillan, 1930), 48.1930

108. As early as his *Preface to Politics*, which doesn't address the issue of the media as thoroughly as his subsequent books, Lippmann averred a connection between a form of "literacy" and the possibility of expressing an individual preference: "No amount of charters, direct primaries, or short ballots will make a democracy out of an illiterate people. Those portions of America where there are voting booths but no schools cannot possibly be described as democracies. Nor can the person who reads one corrupt newspaper and then goes out to vote make any claim to having registered his will. He may have a will, but he has not used it." Lippmann, *Preface to Politics*, 305.

109. Dewey would agree with Lippmann that agreeing upon a common sign-system is roughly equivalent to forming a metaphorical "general will." As Mark Garrett Cooper suggests in his book on early cinema and politics, Lippmann and Dewey also agreed that previous theorists of liberal democracy had failed to note just how central the construction of signs was to the definition of social and public spheres and that this was a failure of mistaking figurative signs for literal ones. Cooper writes that "Unlike Lippmann . . . Dewey strongly distinguished between symbols that enable a community to think itself (true, public communication) and those that merely create social cohesion (and by implication serve private interests)." He further notes that "Lippmann and Dewey banished the possibility that a non-ideological publicity might emerge within existing forms. Along with it, they dismissed any notion that a group could govern itself absent self-conscious manipulation of the signs that define it." Mark Garrett Cooper, *Love Rules: Silent Hollywood and the Rise of the Managerial Class* (Minneapolis: University of Minnesota Press, 2003), 99, 104.

110. Warner, *Publics and Counter-Publics*, 115.

111. Dos Passos, *U.S.A.*, 354. It is worth noting that the always credulous Janey—who quits her first job only because she's convinced that her Jewish employers are German sympathizers—is also an avid reader of Victorian novels and identifies with the characters in a way that Dos Passos prevents: "When she read she used to imagine she was the heroine, that the weak brother who went to the bad but was a gentleman at core and capable of every sacrifice, like Sidney Carton in *A Tale of Two Cities* was Joe and that the hero was Alec" (126).

112. W. C. Blum, "A Moralist in the Army," *The Dial*, December 1921, 607; Horace Gregory, "Review of *The Big Money*," *New York Herald Tribune Books*, August 9, 1936, 5.

113. John Chamberlain, "John Dos Passos Satirizes an America 'On the Make,'" *New York Times Book Review*, March 2, 1930, 5.

114. Michael North's *Camera Works: Photography and the Twentieth Century Word* (Oxford: Oxford University Press, 2005) is an excellent and notable exception and is still the best treatment of the role that historical discourses about visuality play in the novel. North writes that "If the social problem that *U.S.A.* is supposed to confront is not just class division but also the fragmentation of the public into a mass of individualized spectators, then how could the form of the trilogy itself be read except as another symptom or a collection of symptoms? If modernism itself is so thoroughly implicated in the bemusement of the public, then how would it have been any different if the partially autobiographical Savage had gone on to write *U.S.A.* instead of enlisting in Moorehouse's advertising army? Is the form of *U.S.A.* perhaps a form of despair, of acquiescence in the face of social facts, as leftwing critics have long claimed in the case of other modernist masterworks?" (155). I read the visual aspects of the novel as actively engaging the aesthetic sensibilities of "consumers" with a sophisticated eye toward critically refunctioning those sensibilities.

115. John Dos Passos, "Satire as a Way of Seeing," in *Occasions and Protests* (Chicago: Henry Regnery, 1964), 21.

116. Ibid. Lippmann's discussion of visual instruction in his *Public Opinion* echoes strongly here: "There is a connection between our vision and the facts, but it is often a strange connection. A man has rarely looked at a landscape, let us say, except to examine its possibilities for division into building lots, but he has seen a number of landscapes hanging in the parlor. And from them he has learned to think of a landscape

as a rosy sunset, or as a country road with a church steeple and a silver moon. One day he goes to the country, and for hours he doesn't see a single landscape. Then the sun goes down looking rosy. At once he recognizes a landscape and exclaims that it is beautiful. But two days later, when he tries to recall what he saw, the odds are that he will remember chiefly some landscape in a parlor." Walter Lippmann, *Public Opinion* (New York: The Free Press, 1965), 58.

117. Dos Passos, "Satire as a Way of Seeing," 31–32.

118. Frye, "The Nature of Satire," 49.

119. Dos Passos, "Satire as a Way of Seeing," 30.

120. Mabel Dwight, "Satire in Art," in *Art for the Millions: Essays from the 1930s by Artists and Administrators of the WPA Federal Art Project*, ed. Francis V. O'Connor (Greenwich, CT: New York Graphic Society, 1973), 151.

121. Dos Passos, "Satire as a Way of Seeing," 31.

122. "Forward," *Public Opinion Quarterly* 1, no. 1 (January 1937): 3.

123. Ibid., 4.

124. United States, Cong. Senate, *The National Association of Manufacturers*, 226.

125. Dos Passos, *U.S.A.*, 625, 177.

126. The 1938 edition also featured a new two-page prologue, titled "U.S.A.," which Dos Passos wrote for the occasion. Thus the first word that the reader actually sees is "U.S.A.," followed by a table of contents. The word "Newsreel" signals the start of the first installment.

127. For filmic readings of Dos Passos, see Edwards, "The Man with the Camera Eye"; Stephen Hock, "'Stories Told Sideways Out of the Big Mouth': John Dos Passos's Bazinian Camera Eye," *Literature/Film Quarterly* 33, no. 1 (2005): 20–27; and especially Suárez, *Pop Modernism*.

128. Creel, *Creel Report*, 47. In an exemplary scene, J. Ward Moorehouse is colluding with a private client and a U.S. congressman—Senator Planet—to their mutual financial advantage. As the deal draws to a close, the client invites Moorehouse to a party: "how about coming down for a little dip tomorrow? Pathé Newsreel is going to be there. . . . It would be worth your while in your business" (Dos Passos, *U.S.A.*, 1193). Via such personal and corporate arrangements, the War Department distributed five hundred feet of film per week to newsreel services, including Pathé, in 1918. They also successfully employed Hollywood studios to produce feature films. As a free "public service" the films were a flop; when features like "Pershing's Crusaders" were given impressive premieres and viewers were charged the same price as they were to see other films, however, the public flocked to pay for its own indoctrination. Within a year, ticket receipts not only paid for the free distribution of the films to neutral countries and to domestic "patriotic" organizations but showed a profit of almost 100 percent. See Creel, *Creel Report*, 53 and passim.

129. Gertrude Stein, *Narration: Four Lectures* (Chicago: University of Chicago Press, 1935), 35.

130. Dos Passos, *U.S.A.*, 373, 375.

131. One way of reading the language of visuality in Dos Passos would be as a revision of Dewey's sensual hierarchy. For Dewey, the visuality of print and film were impossible substitutes for the *viva voce* intercourse of a genuine community:

> *The connections of the ear with vital and out-going thought and emotion are immensely closer and more varied than those of the eye. Vision is a spectator; hearing is a participator.* Publication is partial and the public which results is

partially informed and formed until the meanings it purveys pass from mouth to mouth. There is no limit to the liberal expansion and confirmation of limited personal intellectual endowment which may proceed from the flow of social intelligence when that circulates by word of mouth from one to another in the communications of the local community. That and that only gives reality to public opinion. Dewey, *The Public and Its Problems*, 218–19, my emphasis.

132. Howard, *Political Judgments*, 5.

133. Charles Altieri has articulated the interplay of emotional affect and literary evaluation and concluded that the proper approach to texts is that of "generous irony," an account that approximates the disposition—without the political resonance—that I am attempting to theorize. In his words, the idea of generous irony "goes a long way toward summarizing how engaging aesthetic aspects of our affective lives can bring us a potentially richer account of the values governing these lives than we find in more epistemically oriented analyses." Charles Altieri, *The Particulars of Rapture: An Aesthetics of the Affects* (Ithaca, NY: Cornell University Press, 2003), 230.

134. Dewey, *The Public and Its Problems*, 123.

135. John Dos Passos, "Washington and Chicago, IL: Spotlights and Microphones," *New Republic*, July 27, 1932, 179.

136. United States, Cong. Senate, *The National Association of Manufacturers*, 240, my emphasis.

137. John Dos Passos, *Rosinante to the Road Again* (New York: George H. Doran Co., 1922), 93.

138. McCarthy, "Class Angles and a Wilder Classic," 18.

139. Dos Passos, *U.S.A.*, 895.

4 / Visible Decisions: Irony, Law, and the Political Constitution of Ralph Ellison

1. See Frederick Douglass, "What to the Slave Is the Fourth of July?: An Address Delivered in Rochester, New York, on 5 July 1852," in *The Life and Writings of Frederick Douglass*, ed. Philip S. Foner, vol. 2: *Pre–Civil War Decade, 1850–1860* (New York: International Publishers Co., 1950), 371. The entire speech was delivered on July 5, 1852. Van Vechten is discussing the controversial title to his novel *Nigger Heaven* and is quoted by Kathleen Pfeiffer in her introduction to Carl Van Vechten, *Nigger Heaven* (Urbana: University of Illinois Press, 2000), xv.

2. Ralph Ellison, *Invisible Man* (New York: Vintage Books, 1981), 13, 573.

3. Lawrence B. Holland, "Ellison in Black and White: Confession, Violence and Rhetoric in *Invisible Man*," in *Black Fiction: New Studies in the Afro-American Novel Since 1945*, ed. Robert A. Lee (New York: Barnes and Noble, 1980), 72.

4. Houston A. Baker Jr., "Failed Prophet and Falling Stock: Why Ralph Ellison Was Never Avant-Garde," *Stanford Humanities Review* 7, no. 1 (1999): 5. Baker is hardly the first to make this charge. As the civil rights movement saw the emergence of increasingly militant forms of Black Nationalism, eliding Ellison's life with that of his narrator became increasingly common. As Harold Cruse reported in *The Crisis of the Negro Intellectual*, communist theoretician Herbert Aptheker had publicly remarked that "I would say that [Ellison's] work, since the *Invisible Man*, even though he is not here and I prefer not to talk that way in his absence, but in terms of what he has published and also his published assertions, he has made himself rather not particularly visible in the struggles of the Negro people." Cruse went on to predict (correctly) that "The truth is

that the radical leftwing will never forgive Ellison for writing *Invisible Man*, no matter what Ellison does or does not do about the 'struggle.'" Harold Cruse, *The Crisis of the Negro Intellectual* (New York: William Morrow, 1967), 508, 509.

5. Irving Howe, "Black Boys and Native Sons," *Dissent* 10, no. 4 (Autumn 1963), 362.

6. As Lawrence Jackson notes, the essay "became nearly a creed for future black writers and intellectuals and many liberal whites who advanced the cause of racial integration." Lawrence Jackson, "Ralph Ellison's Politics of Integration," in *A Historical Guide to Ralph Ellison*, ed. Steven C. Tracy (Oxford: Oxford University Press, 2004), 194.

7. Ralph Ellison, "The World and the Jug," in *Shadow and Act* (New York: Vintage International, 1995), 109. Ellison wasn't the only prominent literary intellectual to indict Howe's retarded sense of irony in the mid-1960s: Wayne Booth dismissed Howe's 1965 review of Flannery O'Connor's "Everything That Rises Must Converge" on the grounds that the review "showed a failure to perceive the depths of irony the story offers." Wayne Booth, *A Rhetoric of Irony* (Chicago: University of Chicago Press, 1974), 168n8.

8. Barbara Foley, *Wrestling with the Left: The Making of Ralph Ellison's Invisible Man* (Durham, NC: Duke University Press, 2010), 2.

9. United States, Cong. Senate, *Testimony of Langston Hughes (accompanied by His Counsel, Frank Dr. Reeves)*, Executive Sessions of the Senate Permanent Subcommittee on Investigations of the Committee on Government Operations (Washington, DC: GPO, 2003), 980. The use of "irony" and "satire" as specific terms was not offhanded; in his prepared statement accepted by the Senate Committee, Hughes wrote: "Perhaps the most misunderstood of my poems was 'Goodbye Christ.' Since it is an ironic poem (and irony is apparently a quality not readily understood in poetry by unliterary minds) it has been widely misinterpreted as an anti-religious poem." Quoted in Arnold Rampersad, *The Life of Langston Hughes*, vol. 2: 1941–1967, 2nd ed. (Oxford: Oxford University Press, 2002), 214.

10. Howe, "Black Boys and Native Sons," 363. Of course, this was the decade when the part of the literary Left that included Irving Howe was almost wholly absent in person and in writing from the public struggle for civil rights. By the time Howe charged Ellison with misrepresenting the experience of African Americans, however, the pages of his journal *Dissent* were directly addressing the injustices suffered by African Americans; see Carol Polsgrove's excellent *Divided Minds: Intellectuals and the Civil Rights Movement* (New York: W. W. Norton, 2001), where she convincingly indicts the mainstream white and Jewish literary establishment for overlooking matters of racial justice. As Alan Wald has argued, in this respect "the behavior of the bulk of the New York intellectuals in the 1950s undermined the validity of the whole anti-Stalinist current of thought and even somewhat redeemed the Communist, fellow-traveling, and progressive liberals who acted heroically by comparison." Wald also includes an excellent description of the "deradicalization" of Howe in particular, who "vehemently turned against the New Left of the 1960s and early 1970s, caricaturing its aims and activities, and even flirted briefly with the incipient neoconservatives." Alan Wald, *The New York Intellectuals: The Rise and Decline of the Anti-Stalinist Left from the 1930s to the 1980s* (Chapel Hill: University of North Carolina Press, 1987), 311–12.

11. Foley, *Wrestling with the Left*, 344.

12. Jackson, "Ralph Ellison's Politics of Integration," 174. Jackson continues: "Black writers resisted the New Criticism (beyond merely the crude examples of color prejudice written early by Allen Tate, Donald Davidson, and [Robert Penn] Warren)

principally because of their discomfort with the intrinsic value of the text or literary artifact. They remained suspicious of the ideas that meaning could be certified objectively inside of a text and that the external circumstances producing literature and the determinations of communities reading literature had limited influence on the creation of fine art" (189).

13. A full evaluation of the rightfully controversial politics of New Criticism is obviously far beyond the scope of my argument. A bibliography of attacks on New Criticism would look very much like a tendentious literary history of the academy after 1930; for an alternative genealogy and defense of New Criticism, see Mark Jancovich, *The Cultural Politics of the New Criticism* (Cambridge: Cambridge University Press, 1993).

14. Barbara Foley, "Renarrating the Thirties in the Forties and Fifties," *Prospects: An Annual of American Cultural Studies* 20 (2000): 462.

15. Ibid., 463.

16. Daniel Bell, *The End of Ideology: On the Exhaustion of Political Ideas in the Fifties* (New York: Free Press, 1965), 300. I certainly don't mean to diminish the invaluable critical work of Barbara Foley or to collapse manifold differences between her work and Bell's *The End of Ideology*. Indeed, there is a way in which establishing "irony" as the primary heuristic for understanding *Invisible Man* would be perfectly consonant with Ellison's evolving personal conservatism, especially as he would later deploy the term to describe political negation, describing Tod Clifton's political devolution as learning "that more was involved in his experience than the simple black & white matter of selling out or being sold out. He had, in other words, learned irony, a bitter, masochistic irony." Ralph Ellison, "Letter to John Lucas," in *Ralph Ellison's Invisible Man: A Casebook*, ed. John F. Callahan (Oxford: Oxford University Press, 2004), 51.

17. Eugene Clay, "The Negro in Recent American Literature," in *American Writers' Congress*, ed. Henry Hart (New York: International Publishers, 1935), 149.

18. Langston Hughes, "To Negro Writers," in *American Writers' Congress*, ed. Henry Hart (New York: International Publishers, 1935), 140. For the role of African American literary and political theorists on the Left, see especially Foley, *Specters of 1919* and Anthony Dawahare, *Nationalism, Marxism, and African-American Marxism Between the Wars: A New Pandora's Box* (Jackson: University Press of Mississippi, 2003).

19. Lawrence Jackson, *Ralph Ellison: Emergence of Genius* (New York: John Wiley, 2002), 426. As I indicate earlier—especially Chapter 2—"New Criticism" refers to a diverse set of practices and assumptions, among which irony is a central, but hardly stable or unified, concept. The diversity of those who came to be called the American New Critics ranged from the early, reactionary and racist Southern agrarian nostalgia of Allen Tate, Donald Davidson, and John Crowe Ransom to the later work of Cleanth Brooks and Robert Penn Warren, who developed what might be understood as a democratic emphasis on how to read literature without benefit of an elite classical education. The fact is that New Criticism was not monolithic, nor did New Critics use "irony" as an iconic synonym for detachment and withdrawal, though their baseline assumption is that the primary touchstone of literary value should not be strictly ideological in nature. In this they were hardly unique in the history of literary criticism.

20. Ellison, *Invisible Man*, 581.

21. As one 1954 *Phylon* reviewer concluded about the novel, "The only avenue open to the Negro who wants to keep his self-respect is complete withdrawal. This seems to

be the meaning of the final episode." Nick Aaron Ford, "Four Popular Negro Novelists," *Phylon: The Atlanta University Review of Race & Culture* 15, no. 1 (Qtr 1954): 35.

22. Cleanth Brooks and Robert Penn Warren, *Understanding Fiction* (New York: F. S. Crofts, 1943), 13. Brooks and Warren's subjunctive objections to irony sound curiously similar to the line of historians whom literary critics are most fond of quoting (as I do in the introduction), such as Hayden White's proclamation in *Metahistory*: "As the basis of a world view, irony tends to dissolve all belief in the possibility of positive political actions. In its apprehension of the essential folly or absurdity of the human condition, it tends to engender belief in the 'madness' of civilization itself and to inspire a Mandarin-like disdain for those seeking to grasp the nature of social reality" (38).

23. Of all the New Critics, Robert Penn Warren probably used the term "irony" most explicitly in a manner that engaged the twin issues of morality and representation, a fact that is rarely noted by those who invoke irony as metonymic for New Criticism and New Critics as metonymic for disengaged readings of literature. In 1942, for instance, Penn Warren wrote an essay detailing the accomplishments of Katherine Anne Porter, in which he explicitly raises the possibility of different kinds of ironies, and certainly different kinds of literature, that might engage with the practical world that is often considered to be the realm of more politically engaged criticism:

> The skeptical and ironical bias is, I think, important in Miss Porter's work, and it is true that her work wears an air of detachment and contemplation. But, I should say, her irony is an irony with a center, never an irony for irony's sake. It simply implies, I think, a refusal to accept the code, the formula, the ready-made solution, the hand-me-down morality, the word for the spirit. It affirms, rather, the constant need for exercising discrimination, the arduous obligation of the intellect in the face of conflicting dogmas, the need for a dialectical approach to matters of definition, the need for exercising as much of the human faculty as possible." Robert Penn Warren, "Katherine Anne Porter (Irony with a Center)," *Kenyon Review* 4, no. 3 (Winter 1942): 42.

24. Cleanth Brooks, *The Well-Wrought Urn* (New York: Harcourt, Brace & World, 1947), 3, 18.

25. Ibid., 210.

26. Kazin, *On Native Grounds*, 491. As early as 1941, literary critic Oscar Cargill opined: "The only possibility of Fascism in this country lies, not in the popularity of the doctrines of Fascism, but rather in the debility of the public will through wide acceptance of the philosophy of Naturalism." Oscar Cargill, *Intellectual America: Ideas on the March* (New York: Macmillan, 1941), 175.

27. Ralph Ellison, *Shadow and Act* (New York: Vintage International, 1995), 26.

28. Ibid., 103.

29. James Baldwin, "Many Thousands Gone," in *Notes of a Native Son* (Boston: Beacon Press, 1984), 31.

30. Ralph Ellison, "Society, Morality, and the Novel," in *The Collected Essays of Ralph Ellison*, ed. John F. Callahan (New York: Modern Library, 1995), 706.

31. As Lawrence Jackson claims, not only did Ellison's writing feature "trademark razor-sharp irony," but "his career and his life hinged upon irony." Jackson, *Ralph Ellison: Emergence of Genius*, xiii, ix. The best critics of Ellison's irony theorize him specifically as a Romantic ironist and thereby help complete a version of the

Hegelian and Schlegelian aesthetic-political debate I describe in Chapter 2. Ronald A. T. Judy, for example, argues that "Schlegel's understanding of irony derives much of its force from Fichte's system, and it is Fichte's thinking about the self that most parallels Ellison's thinking about irony." Ronald A. T. Judy, "Irony and the Asymptotes of the Hyperbola," *boundary 2* 25, no. 1 (1998): 162. More recently, Kevin Bell has also understood Ellison as a Romantic ironist, following Paul de Man's reading of Friedrich Schlegel's "On Incomprehensibility" to argue that "De Man himself, also proceeding from Schlegel's investigations, underscores Ellison's denial of simplistic social concords, political justifications, and claims of final truth. For de Man, the tendency to read irony in such tightly piloted fashion is to miss its function." Kevin Bell, *Ashes Taken for Fire: Aesthetic Modernism and the Critique of Identity* (Minneapolis: University of Minnesota Press, 2007), 179. Champions of both Ellison and Romantic irony serve up philosophical defenses, focusing on irony to refight the political and aesthetic opposition of "Paul de Man v. Wayne Booth" (aka "Schlegel v. Hegel Redux"). When Arnold Rampersad describes Ellison as "aware of this irony, [but] he did not yet possess the vision and the courage to resolve it," one should recognize the enormous philosophical and political history behind seemingly innocuous phrasing. Arnold Rampersad, *Ralph Ellison: A Biography* (New York: Vintage Books, 2008), 107.

32. Douglass, "What to the Slave Is the Fourth of July?" 371. Douglass was aware of irony's multiple definitions and prescribed rhetorical irony as a tonic for situational irony: in the same speech, he remarks that "To drag a man in fetters into the grand illuminated temple of liberty, and call upon him to join you in joyous anthems, were inhuman mockery and sacrilegious irony" (368).

33. Ellison, "Beating That Boy," 99.

34. Lucas Morel remarks that "Given Ellison's appreciation of the 'sacred principles' of the American founding, as well as his consistent observations of its failed practice, it is surprising to find so little written in the 50 years since the novel's publication that makes 'visible' the politics of *Invisible Man*—especially the contradiction between ideal and practice that Ellison explores in the novel." Lucas E. Morel, ed., *Ralph Ellison and the Raft of Hope: A Political Companion to Invisible Man* (Lexington: University Press of Kentucky, 2004), 2.

35. Brooks, *The Well-Wrought Urn*, 207.

36. Richard Kostelanetz, "An Interview with Ralph Ellison," in *Conversations with Ralph Ellison*, ed. Amritjit Singh and Maryemma Graham (Jackson: University Press of Mississippi, 1995), 94.

37. Ralph Ellison, "Letter to Kenneth Burke," November 23, 1945, located in and used with permission of the Kenneth Burke Archives of Pennsylvania State University Library. Many characterizations and invocations of "The New Criticism" rely upon the exclusion of Burke from their ambiguously defined ranks.

38. Christian Lander, "#50: Irony," *Stuff White People Like*, February 3, 2008, http://stuffwhitepeoplelike.com/2008/02/03/50-irony/.

39. Jerry Gafio Watts, *Heroism & the Black Intellectual: Ralph Ellison, Politics, and Afro-American Intellectual Life* (Chapel Hill: University of North Carolina Press, 1994), 29; Clive Bell, *Since Cezanne* (New York: Harcourt, Brace, 1922), 216. Cf. J. A. Rogers's "Jazz at Home" in *The New Negro*, which claims that "The negroes who invented [jazz] called their songs the 'Blues,' and they weren't capable of satire or deception. Jazz was their explosive attempt to cast off the blues and be happy, carefree happy. . . . It is the

revolt of the emotions against repression." J. A. Rogers, "Jazz at Home," in *The New Negro*, ed. Alain Locke (New York: Macmillan, 1992), 217.

40. Alain Locke, "From Native Son to Invisible Man: A Review of the Literature of the Negro for 1952," *Phylon: The Atlanta University Review of Race & Culture* 14, no. 1 (1953): 35.

41. Ralph Ellison, *Conversations with Ralph Ellison*, ed. Ed. Maryemma Graham and Amritjit Sing (Jackson: University Press of Mississippi, 1995), 204.

42. Russell Ames, "Protest and Irony in Negro Folksong," *Science & Society* 3 (1950): 196.

43. Baldwin, "Many Thousands Gone," 43.

44. Brooks, *The Well-Wrought Urn*, 210; Ralph Ellison, "On Being the Target of Discrimination," in *The Collected Essays of Ralph Ellison*, ed. John F. Callahan (New York: Modern Library, 1995), 825.

45. Barbara Foley claims that Ellison's "irony" in "World and the Jug" is merely of the verbal variety, wherein one "means" the opposite of what the words literally say: "While critics of the novel are divided over whether the invisible man will actually emerge," she writes, "only once—in his exchange with Irving Howe—did Ellison suggest that the invisible man's claim to be a world of 'infinite possibilities' should be taken ironically." Foley, *Wrestling with the Left*, 422n1.

46. Kenneth Warren, *So Black and So Blue: Ralph Ellison and the Occasion of Criticism* (Chicago: University of Chicago Press, 2002), 21.

47. Lippmann, *Preface to Politics*, 298–99.

48. Interestingly, Paul de Man rightly excepted Kenneth Burke, writing on his lecture notes to "The Concept of Irony" "alazon is Am. criticism (not Burke)." Paul de Man, "The Concept of Irony," in *Aesthetic Ideology*, trans. Andrzej Warminski, Theory and History of Literature, vol. 65 (Minneapolis: University of Minnesota Press, 1996), 165.

49. The extent to which some critics imagine a seamless convertibility between Ellison's criticism and his novel occasionally reaches absurd proportions. Such is the case when Beth Eddy objects to a troubling development wherein Ellison is even "being claimed, I believe, by critics who do not interpret him as he asks in his essays to be interpreted." Beth Eddy, *The Rites of Identity: The Religious Naturalism and Cultural Criticism of Kenneth Burke and Ralph Ellison* (Princeton, NJ: Princeton University Press, 2003), 6.

50. In the past fifteen years, critics have begun to take Burke seriously as an influence on Ellison's work. Starting with Timothy Parrish's excellent "Ralph Ellison, Kenneth Burke, and the Form of Democracy," *Arizona Quarterly: A Journal of American Literature, Culture, and Theory* 51, no. 3 (Autumn 1995): 117–48, the body of work includes essays and portions of books by Albrecht, Arac, Genter, Pease, and Eddy. See James Albrecht, "Saying Yes and Saying No: Individualist Ethics in Ellison, Burke, and Emerson," *PMLA* 114, no. 1 (January 1999): 46–63; Jonathan Arac, "Toward a Critical Genealogy of the U.S. Discourse of Identity: Invisible Man After Fifty Years," *boundary 2* 30, no. 2 (Summer 2003): 195–216; Robert Genter, "Toward a Theory of Rhetoric: Ralph Ellison, Kenneth Burke, and the Problem of Modernism," *Twentieth Century Literature: A Scholarly and Critical Journal* 48, no. 2 (Summer 2002): 191–214; Donald E. Pease, "Ralph Ellison and Kenneth Burke: The Nonsymbolizable (Trans)Action," *boundary 2* 30, no. 2 (2003): 65–96; and Eddy, *The Rites of Identity*. The best and most recent work is Foley, *Wrestling with the Left*, 92–103, and especially Genter, *Late Modernism*, 273–308.

51. Kenneth Burke, *Language as Symbolic Action: Essays on Life, Literature, and Method* (Berkeley: University of California Press, 1966), 46.

52. Bryan Crable, *Ralph Ellison and Kenneth Burke: At the Roots of the Racial Divide* (Charlottesville: University of Virginia Press, 2012), 60.

53. Ellison, *Shadow and Act*, xxiii.

54. Ibid., 177.

55. Ellison, *Conversations with Ralph Ellison*, 364. Pease sees Ellison's fictional project not so much as a perfection or revision of Burkean theories as an extension of them into terrain that Burke himself could neither envision nor adequately understand. As Pease writes, "Whereas Burke's symbolic actions took place in the realm of the symbolizable, the shadows Ellison understood to be the primary integers of the American racist order populated a nonsymbolizable terrain that lay outside the realm of symbolic action about which Burke theorized" and that "Ellison's shadows nevertheless haunted Burke's theory of symbolic actions with representations of beliefs and enactments Burke could neither fully analyze nor adequately describe." Pease, "Ralph Ellison and Kenneth Burke," 73.

56. Ellison, "Letter to Kenneth Burke." These lines are dated November 29, 1945; his letter to Burke the previous week had expressed many of the same sentiments.

57. Ellison, "Letter to Kenneth Burke," November 23, 1945. The words "for politics" are a handwritten addendum in the version Ellison sent to Burke. Ellison's copy is held in Part I: box I:38, Ralph Ellison Papers, Manuscript Division, Library of Congress, Washington, DC.

58. Ralph Ellison, *Going to the Territory* (New York: Random House, 1986), 19.

59. Kenneth Burke, "Key Words for Critics," *Kenyon Review* 4, no. 3 (Winter 1942): 129.

60. Ellison, *Shadow and Act*, 140.

61. Ibid., 137.

62. Ellison, *Going to the Territory*, 338.

63. Charles Humboldt, "The Novel of Action," *Mainstream: A Literary Quarterly* 1, no. 4 (Fall 1947): 392.

64. Louis Menand, "Richard Wright: The Hammer and the Nail," in *American Studies* (New York: Farrar, Straus, and Giroux, 2002), 83.

65. Such an opposition makes perfect sense in the context of *Native Son*: the soliloquy with which Bigger's attorney concludes the novel is nothing if not unironically earnest (and ineffective, at least in terms of Bigger's trial).

66. As E. L. Doctorow writes of the Constitution, "It uses none of the tropes of literature to create empathic states in the mind of the reader. It does not mean to persuade. It abhors metaphor as nature abhors a vacuum." E. L. Doctorow, *Jack London, Hemingway, and the Constitution: Selected Essays, 1977–1992* (New York: Random House, 1993), 120. One finds similar statements by judges and other experts in American jurisprudence. As eminent jurist Benjamin Cardozo opined in 1926, "Metaphors in law are to be narrowly watched, for starting as devices to liberate thought, they end often by enslaving it." Benjamin N. Cardozo, *Berkey v. Third Avenue Railway* (1926), 244 N.Y. 84, 94, 155 N.E. 58.

67. Burke, *A Grammar of Motives*, 506.

68. Burke, "Key Words for Critics," 130.

69. Ibid., 130–31.

70. Burke, *A Grammar of Motives*, 399; Ellison, *Going to the Territory*, 19.

71. Burke, *A Grammar of Motives*, 503. Burke's magisterial statement about the relationship among metaphor, metonymy, synecdoche, and irony appeared in the *Kenyon Review* six years before its publication as an appendix to *A Grammar of Motives*. See Kenneth Burke, "Four Master Tropes," *Kenyon Review* 3, no. 4 (Autumn 1941): 421–38.

72. Burke, *A Grammar of Motives*, 503.

73. Ibid., 505.

74. Ibid., 510.

75. As Macdonald wrote in his seminal 1946 essay *The Root Is Man*, the "Radical approach" does not "deny the importance and validity of science in its own proper sphere, or of historical, sociological and economic studies," but "rather defines a sphere which is outside the reach of scientific investigation, and whose value judgments cannot be proved." Dwight Macdonald, *The Root Is Man: Two Essays in Politics* (Alhambra, CA: Cunningham Press, 1953), 18. Most critics and biographers focus on Ellison's refusal to sign and criticism of MacDonald's petition in support of Robert Lowell (and against the war in Vietnam) at the White House in 1965. Macdonald was perhaps the only one of the New York Intellectuals who focused much of his intellectual and political activity on the issue of race in the 1940s; he had agitated and organized to help desegregate the armed forces and war industries, and at a time when organs like *Partisan Review* chose to ignore the "race problem" almost entirely, Macdonald was militant and unrelenting in his polemical investigations of both causes and effects of American racism. Lawrence Jackson's speculation that Ellison may have had a chance to publish an essay in *politics* is best ignored; the explanation that Ellison may have been politically irked because "McDonald [*sic*] was zealously anti-communist by 1947, seeing no difference between Nazi fascism and the USSR's protectionist strategies" is unfortunate. Jackson, *Ralph Ellison: Emergence of Genius*, 360.

76. Ellison, *Shadow and Act*, 17.

77. Burke, *A Grammar of Motives*, 340.

78. Ibid., 511.

79. An interesting exception to this appears in Burke's discussion of Romantic irony, which he opposes with "true irony": "There is, to be sure, a brand of irony, called 'romantic irony' . . . that did, as a matter of fact, arise as an aesthetic opposition to cultural philistinism, and in which the artist considered himself *outside of* and *superior* to the rôle he was rejecting. And though not 'essentially *the* poetic attitude,' it is essentially *a* poetic attitude, an attitude exemplified by much romantic art." Ibid., 514.

80. Ellison, *Invisible Man*, xv.

81. Ibid., xviii.

82. Ellison, *Shadow and Act*, 143.

83. Burke, *A Grammar of Motives*, 514.

84. Ellison, *Invisible Man*, 7, 5.

85. See the work of Mark Naison, primarily "From Eviction Resistance to Rent Control: Tenant Activism in the Great Depression," in *The Tenant Movement in New York City, 1904–1984*, ed. Ronald Lawson (New Brunswick, NJ: Rutgers University Press, 1986). For more comprehensive background on the role of the CPUSA in the eviction resistance and rent strikes, see Mark Naison, *Communists in Harlem During the Depression* (Urbana: University of Illinois Press, 2005).

86. Ellison, *Going to the Territory*, 321.

87. Ibid., 323.

88. Ibid., 321.

89. Ellison, *Invisible Man*, 281. The scene strongly echoes the description of the madmen turning on their supervisor, Supercargo, earlier in the novel: "'So you like to kick, huh?' a tall man said, aiming a shoe at the attendant's head. The flesh above his right eye jumped out as though it had been inflated. [...] I watched the spot as though compelled, just beneath the lower rib and above the hip-bone, as Sylvester measured carefully with his toe and kicked as though he were punting a football. Supercargo let out a crown like an injured horse" (84).

90. Ellison, *Going to the Territory*, 17; Ellison, *Shadow and Act*, 35.

91. Ellison, *Going to the Territory*, 17. Michael Magee has written interestingly about the Emersonian legacy of both Burke and Ellison, situating Ellison in a genealogy of American pragmatism: "Emerson and Ellison take the Declaration of Independence, the Constitution, the Bill of Rights, as exhibits A, B, and C in their historicized description of how language operates and what it can do. The ramifications of their insistence need to be made clear. These 'exhibits' were *active documents* against which the *acted* document of culture could be compared." Michael Magee, "Ralph Ellison: Pragmatism, Jazz and the American Vernacular," *Transactions of the Charles S. Peirce Society* 39, no. 2 (Spring 2003): 231.

92. Ellison, *Going to the Territory*, 328.

93. Ibid., 331.

94. Burke, *A Grammar of Motives*, 349.

95. Ibid., 376.

96. As Burke writes of legal positivism, which he associates directly with the rise of logical positivism and American pragmatism:

> "positive" law has tried to uphold the fiction that the Constitutional enactment itself is the criterion for judicial interpretations of motive. It would abandon "natural law" or "divine law" as criteria, looking only to the Constitution itself and not to any scientific, metaphysical, or theological doctrines specifying the nature of the "Constitution behind the Constitution" as the ultimate test of a judgment's judiciousness. And since it is simply impossible to so confine the circumference of the scene in which occurs the given act that is to be judged, i.e., since an act in the United States has not merely the United States Constitution as its background, but all sorts of factors originating outside it, the fiction of positive law has generally served to set up the values, traditions, and trends of business as the Constitution-behind-the-Constitution that is to be consulted as criterion. In effect, therefore, the theory of "positive law" has given us courts which are the representatives of business in a mood of mild self-criticism. Ibid., 363.

97. Ibid., 377.

98. Ellison, *Going to the Territory*, 248.

99. Ibid., 249.

100. For a useful synopsis of the past and uncertain future of "law as literature" movement in both literary and legal studies, see Julie Stone Peters, "Law, Literature, and the Vanishing Real: On the Future of an Interdisciplinary Illusion," *PMLA* 10, no. 2 (March 2005): 442–53.

101. Burke, *A Grammar of Motives*, 387.

102. Gilles Deleuze, *Difference and Repetition*, trans. Paul Patton (New York: Continuum, 2004), 6.

103. See Gary Orfield, *Reviving the Goal of an Integrated Society: A 21st Century Challenge* (Los Angeles: Civil Rights Project/Proyecto Derechos Civiles at UCLA, 2009).

104. Michael J. Klarman, *From Jim Crow to Civil Rights: The Supreme Court and the Struggle for Racial Equality* (New York: Oxford University Press, 2004), 6. Novelist John Barth phrased the issue rather more poetically in 1956, observing that "men . . . are ever attracted to the *bon mot* rather than the *mot juste*, and judges, no less than other men, are often moved by considerations more aesthetic than judicial." John Barth, *The Floating Opera* (New York: Doubleday, 1967), 92. Klarman is careful to stipulate that, while "changes in the social and political context of race relations preceded and accounted for changes in judicial decision making," "this is not to say that the Court decisions did not matter, only that they reflected social attitudes and practices more than they created them" (443). This is not simply a quirk that obtains in particular cases such as civil rights legislation but is, as Burke and Ellison pointed out, a function of how the Constitution itself articulates its principles. As Klarman continues, "the text of the Constitution fails to supply dispositive answers to most questions. 'Equal protection' does not plainly forbid separate but equal, and 'state action' under the Fourteenth and Fifteenth amendments is hardly self-defining. [. . .] *Grovey* (1935), which sustained the constitutionality of white primaries, proved unpalatable to the justices in 1944, not because its legal reasoning was faulty, but because during World War II they found black disfranchisement offensive" (448).

105. Ellison, *Shadow and Act*, 105.

106. Burke, *A Grammar of Motives*, 516.

107. Ellison, *Invisible Man*, 490.

108. Ellison, *Shadow and Act*, 25; Ellison, *Invisible Man*, 10.

109. Ellison, *Invisible Man*, 14. The novel is filled with such references to both Jack and the Bear (and the manuscript version even more so). One of the most provocative appears in the Golden Day episode, wherein the narrator reports that "The one who called himself a composer was banging away the one wild piece he seemed to know on the out-of-tune piano, striking the keyboard with fists and elbows and filling in other effects in a bass voice that moaned like a bear in agony" (85).

110. Linda Hutcheon, *A Theory of Parody: The Teachings of Twentieth-Century Art Forms* (Urbana: University of Illinois Press, 1985), 7. "Parody," Hutcheon writes, "is a form of imitation, but imitation characterized by ironic inversion, not always at the expense of the parodied text. [. . .] This ironic playing with multiple conventions, this extended repetition with a critical difference, is what I mean by modern parody" (6–7).

111. Ellison was surely aware of the gesture toward Upton Sinclair's novel, and the manuscript alternates between referring to the "tenement jungle" and properly naming the doomed building "The Jungle." Part I: box I:143, folder 10, page A, Ralph Ellison Papers, Manuscript Division, Library of Congress, Washington, DC.

112. As historian Richard Wightman Fox shows, leading figures of mid-century liberalism such as Lewis Mumford, Reinhold Niebuhr, and Lionel Trilling emphasized personal responsibility in the 1940s but in a version not to be understood as the sort of low-grade abdication of collective responsibility familiar to readers of Horatio Alger. Rather, "the term 'responsibility' came in the 1940s to connote a refusal to be swept into social enthusiasms. . . . The responsible self was the self in balance . . . devoted in principle to justice, reticent and discriminating in concrete commitment. The posture of responsibility provided a dominant model for intellectual life in the postwar world." Richard Wightman Fox, "Tragedy, Responsibility,

and the American Intellectual, 1925–1950," in *Lewis Mumford: Public Intellectual*, ed. Thomas P. Hughes and Agatha C. Hughes (New York: Oxford University Press, 1990), 335. This also describes Ellison's own public emphasis on personal responsibility, such as when Ellison asserted that naturalist fiction "performs a function similar to that of the stereotype: it conditions the reader to accept the less worthy values of society, and it serves to justify and absolve our sins of social irresponsibility. With unconscious irony it advises stoic acceptance of those conditions of life which it so accurately describes and which it pretends to reject" (Ellison, *Shadow and Act*, 40); such fiction encouraged "one-sided interpretation" that "relieves the individual of personal responsibility for the health of democracy. Not only does it forget that a democracy is a collectivity of *individuals*, but it never suspects that the tenacity of the stereotype springs exactly from the fact that its function is no less personal than political" (ibid., 28).

113. Ellison, *Shadow and Act*, 102.

114. Ellison, *Invisible Man*, 14.

115. As Fraser and Honneth describe their debate, "One of us, Axel Honneth, conceives recognition as the fundamental, overarching moral category, while treating distribution as a derivative. Thus, he reinterprets the socialist ideal of redistribution as a subvariety of the struggle for recognition. The other one, Nancy Fraser, denies that distribution can be subsumed under recognition. Thus, she proposes a 'perspectival dualist' analysis that casts the two categories as co-fundamental and mutually irreducible dimensions of justice." Nancy Fraser and Axel Honneth, *Redistribution or Recognition: A Political-Philosophical Exchange*, trans. Joel Golb, James Ingram, and Christiane Wilke (London: Verso, 2003), 3.

116. Ellison, "Beating That Boy," 95.

117. See Ralph Ellison, "Eyewitness Story of Riot: False Rumors Spurred Mob," *New York Post*, August 2, 1943, 4.

118. Ellison, *Invisible Man*, 267.

119. Burke, *A Grammar of Motives*, 512.

120. Ibid., 516. Burke rightly and usefully stipulates that a "similar synecdochic form is present in all theories of political representation, where some part of the social body (either traditionally established, or elected, or coming into authority by revolution) is held to be 'representative' of the society as a whole. The pattern is essential to Rousseau's theory of the *volonte general*, for instance. And though there are many disagreements within a society as to what part should represent the whole and how this representation should be accomplished, in a complex civilization any act of representation automatically implies a synecdochic relationship (insofar as the act is, or is held to be, 'truly representative')." Ibid., 508.

121. Burke, *A Grammar of Motives*, 579.

122. Ibid., 517. I obviously take "casuistries" here in the sense of ethical principles applied to particular cases rather than the secondary sense of disingenuous invocation of such principles.

123. Ellison, *Invisible Man*, 567.

124. Burke, *A Grammar of Motives*, 335. It is possible that Ellison got the metaphor from Burke, who had written in *Attitudes Toward History* that changes of identity give the changed agent new empirical abilities wherein he "sees around corners" and "is 'prophetic,' endowed with 'perspective'" (qtd. in Genter, "Toward a Theory of Rhetoric," 209). After Ellison, the critic R.W.B. Lewis employed the metaphor as well when he wrote:

the best of our fiction has from the outset been neither exclusively hopeful nor exclusively nostalgic, because it has been both. There were many dreary examples of fiction of both extremes. But the quality of anything like a genuine and enduring fiction could not help being "ironic": in the sense that all genuine fiction is, by nature, ironic. For fiction, whether comic or tragic, dramatizes the interplay of compelling opposites: the real peeping around the corner of the illusory, or the real exploding in the midst of the apparent, in whatever terms of manners, psychology, or sheer picaresque adventure the novelist has seized upon. R.W.B. Lewis, *The American Adam: Innocence Tragedy and Tradition in the Nineteenth Century* (Chicago: University of Chicago Press, 1955), 91.

125. Ellison, *Invisible Man*, 13.

126. Burke, *A Grammar of Motives*, 517.

127. Ellison, *Invisible Man*, 514, my emphasis.

128. Mouffe, *The Democratic Paradox*, 34. There have been some notable attempts to read *Invisible Man* as proposing new forms of democratic practice; the most convincing are Meili Steele, "Metatheory and the Subject of Democracy in the Work of Ralph Ellison," *New Literary History* 27, no. 3 (1996): 473–502 and Parrish, "Ralph Ellison, Kenneth Burke, and the Form of Democracy."

129. Ellison, *Invisible Man*, 580, 581.

130. I am suggesting here an alternative to the conception of choice, decision, and action that, for example, James Forman proposes in *The Making of Black Revolutionaries*: "To decide to do nothing is to make a decision, I felt. Since we have only one life and there is only one certainty in life, death, then a person must choose what he is going to do with his life. He makes that decision whether he recognizes it or not. We choose by our inaction." James Forman, *The Making of Black Revolutionaries* (New York: Macmillan, 1972), 107.

131. Burke, *A Grammar of Motives*, 400.

132. Ibid., 399.

133. Ellison, *Going to the Territory*, 112.

134. Cf. James Baldwin's 1951 essay "Many Thousands Gone," which (among other things) insightfully discusses relationships between novelistic and political representation, between *Darstellung* and *Vertretung*: "Leaving aside the considerable question of what relationship precisely the artist bears to the revolutionary, the reality of man as a social being is not his only reality and that artist is strangled who is forced to deal with human beings solely in social terms; and who has, moreover, as Wright had, the necessity thrust on him of being the representative of some thirteen million people. It is a false responsibility (since writers are not congressmen) and impossible, by its nature, of fulfillment." Baldwin, "Many Thousands Gone," 33.

135. Mouffe, *The Democratic Paradox*, 11.

136. Burke, *A Grammar of Motives*, 351.

137. Pragmatically, this is leading to the "pure choice" described by Andrew Norris: "Pure choice takes the form of irony," Norris writes, "as only irony displays the simultaneous emptiness and quasi-divine power of the decision. A just decision, say, would reveal me as just, but as such as bound by the tenets of justice. Only an empty, ironic choice allows for the assertion of the ultimate mastery of the self, unbound by any commitment or any defining characteristic." Andrew Norris, "Willing and Deciding: Hegel on Irony, Evil, and the Sovereign Exception," *Diacritics* 37, no. 2–3

(Summer–Fall 2007): 142. Rather, the novel represents the negative condition of the "pure choice," which is a subjective precondition for just, pragmatic decisions.

138. Ellison, *Invisible Man*, 573.

Beyond Hope and Memory: A Conclusion

1. Sir Frederick Stanley Maude, "The Proclamation of Baghdad," 2003, http://harpers.org/archive/2003/05/0079593; Bourne, "The War and the Intellectuals."

2. Amanda Anderson, *The Way We Argue Now: A Study in the Cultures of Theory* (Princeton, NJ: Princeton University Press, 2006), 66.

3. Sheldon S. Wolin, *Democracy Incorporated: Managed Democracy and the Specter of Inverted Totalitarianism* (Princeton, NJ: Princeton University Press, 2008), 214.

4. Ankersmit, *Aesthetic Politics*, 245.

5. Lewis, *The American Adam*, 7. Lewis's critical study culminates in reflections on what kind of fiction would instantiate the Party of Irony and might thus serve as a potential corrective to the mordant skepticism that Lewis felt was a characteristic feature of so much mid-century writing. He concludes: "in most of what I take to be the truest and most fully engaged American fiction after the second war, the newborn or self-breeding or orphaned hero is plunged again and again, for his own good and for ours, into the spurious, disruptive rituals of the actual world. We may mention especially *Invisible Man*, by Ralph Ellison . . . in which the hero is willing, with marvelously inadequate equipment, to take on as much of the world as is available to him, without ever fully submitting to any of the world's determining categories" (198).

Bibliography

Aaron, Daniel. "American Prophet." *New York Review of Books*, November 23, 1978.

Adorno, Theodor W. *Minima Moralia: Reflections from Damaged Life.* Trans. E.F.N. Jephcott. London: Verso, 1974.

———. *Minima Moralia: Reflexionen Aus Dem Beschädigten Leben.* Gesammelte Schriften 4. Frankfurt am Main: Suhrkamp, 1980.

———. *Notes to Literature.* Trans. Shierry Weber Nicholsen. Vol. 1. New York: Columbia University Press, 1991.

Albrecht, James. "Saying Yes and Saying No: Individualist Ethics in Ellison, Burke, and Emerson." *PMLA* 114, no. 1 (January 1999): 46–63.

Allen, John Barrow. "Review of Frank Frankfort Moore's One Fair Daughter." *The Academy* (November 17, 1894): 396–97.

Altieri, Charles. *The Art of Twentieth Century American Poetry: Modernism and After.* Oxford: Blackwell, 2006.

———. *The Particulars of Rapture: An Aesthetics of the Affects.* Ithaca, NY: Cornell University Press, 2003.

Ames, Russell. "Protest and Irony in Negro Folksong." *Science & Society* 3 (1950): 193–213.

Anderson, Amanda. *The Powers of Distance: Cosmopolitanism & the Cultivation of Detachment.* Princeton, NJ: Princeton University Press, 2001.

———. *The Way We Argue Now: A Study in the Cultures of Theory.* Princeton, NJ: Princeton University Press, 2006.

Ankersmit, F. R. *Aesthetic Politics: Political Philosophy Beyond Fact and Value.* Stanford, CA: Stanford University Press, 1996.

Antliff, Alan. *Anarchist Modernism: Art, Politics, and the First American Avant-Garde.* Chicago: University of Chicago Press, 2001.

Aquinas, Thomas. *Summa Theologiæ*. Ed. T. C. O'Brien. Vol. 41. Cambridge: Cambridge University Press, 2006.

Arac, Jonathan. "Toward a Critical Genealogy of the U.S. Discourse of Identity: Invisible Man After Fifty Years." *boundary 2* 30, no. 2 (Summer 2003): 195–216.

Badiou, Alain. *Metapolitics*. Trans. Jason Barker. London: Verso, 2005.

Bajorek, Jennifer. *Counterfeit Capital: Poetic Labor and Revolutionary Irony*. Stanford, CA: Stanford University Press, 2009.

Baker, Houston A. Jr. "Failed Prophet and Falling Stock: Why Ralph Ellison Was Never Avant-Garde." *Stanford Humanities Review* 7, no. 1 (1999): 4–11.

Baldwin, James. "Many Thousands Gone." In *Notes of a Native Son*, 24–45. Boston: Beacon Press, 1984.

Barnes, Djuna. *Ryder*. Normal, IL: Dalkey Archive Press, 1990.

Barth, John. *The Floating Opera*. New York: Doubleday, 1967.

Bauer, Dale M. *Sex Expression and American Women Writers, 1860–1940*. Chapel Hill: University of North Carolina Press, 2009.

Beers, David. "Irony Is Dead! Long Live Irony!" N.d. www.salon.com/mwt/feature/2001/09/25/irony_lives/?sid=1048586.

Behler, Ernst. "Friedrich Schlegel and Novalis." In *A Companion to Continental Philosophy*, 68–82. Oxford: Blackwell, 1999.

———. "Nietzsche's Conception of Irony." ed. David W. Conway, Salim Kemal, and Ivan Gaskell, 13–35. New York: Cambridge University Press, 1998.

Bell, Clive. *Since Cezanne*. New York: Harcourt, Brace, 1922.

Bell, Daniel. *The End of Ideology: On the Exhaustion of Political Ideas in the Fifties*. New York: Free Press, 1965.

Bell, Kevin. *Ashes Taken for Fire: Aesthetic Modernism and the Critique of Identity*. Minneapolis: University of Minnesota Press, 2007.

Belloc, Hilaire. "On Irony." In *On Anything*, 18–22. London: Methuen & Co., 1910.

Benhabib, Seyla. "On Hegel, Women and Irony." In *Situating the Self: Gender, Community and Postmodernism in Contemporary Ethics*, 242–59. New York: Routledge, 1992.

Bennett, Paula. *Poets in the Public Sphere: The Emancipatory Project of American Women's Poetry, 1800–1900*. Princeton, NJ: Princeton University Press, 2003.

Berlant, Lauren. *The Female Complaint: The Unfinished Business of Sentimentality in American Culture*. Durham, NC: Duke University Press, 2008.

Bierce, Ambrose. "The Passing of Satire." *Life*, July 8, 1909.

———. *The Unabridged Devil's Dictionary*. Ed. David E. Schultz and S. J. Joshi. Athens: University of Georgia Press, 2002.

"THE BIRTH OF IRONY." *Judge's Library: A Monthly Magazine of Fun* 154 (January 1902).

Bishop, John Peale. "Mr. Fitzgerald Sees the Flapper Through." In *F. Scott Fitzgerald: The Critical Reception*. American Critical Tradition 5. New York: B. Franklin, 1978.

Blake, Casey Nelson. *Beloved Community: The Cultural Criticism of Randolph Bourne, Van Wyck Brooks, Waldo Frank & Lewis Mumford.* Chapel Hill: University of North Carolina Press, 1990.

Blum, W. C. "A Moralist in the Army." *The Dial*, December 1921.

Bogel, Fredric V. *The Difference Satire Makes: Rhetoric and Reading from Jonson to Byron.* Ithaca, NY: Cornell University Press, 2001.

"Books and Bookmen." *Harper's Weekly*, June 27, 1903, 1096.

Booth, Wayne. *A Rhetoric of Irony.* Chicago: University of Chicago Press, 1974.

Bourne, Randolph. "Denatured Nietzsche." *The Dial*, October 25, 1917.

———. "The Doctrine of the Rights of Man as Formulated by Thomas Paine." In *The Radical Will: Selected Writings, 1911–1918*, ed. Olaf Hansen, 233–47. New York: Urizen Books, 1977.

———. "John Dewey's Philosophy." In *The Radical Will: Selected Writings, 1911–1918*, ed. Olaf Hansen, 331–35. New York: Urizen Books, 1977.

———, *The Letters of Randolph Bourne: A Comprehensive Edition.* Ed. Eric J. Sandeen. Troy, NY: Whitson Publishing, 1981.

———. "The Life of Irony." In *Youth and Life*, 99–132. Freeport, NY: Books for Libraries Press, 1967.

———. "A Modern Mind." *The Dial*, March 22, 1917.

———. "The Price of Radicalism." In *The Radical Will: Selected Writings, 1911–1918*, ed. Olaf Hansen, 298–300. New York: Urizen Books, 1977.

———. Review of *Nietzsche* by Paul Elmer More. Boston: Houghton, Mifflin. 1911. *Journal of Philosophy, Psychology and Scientific Methods* 9, no. 17 (August 15, 1912): 471–73.

———. "Theodore Dreiser." In *The Radical Will: Selected Writings, 1911–1918*, ed. Olaf Hansen, 457–61. New York: Urizen Books, 1977.

———. "Trans-National America." In *The Radical Will: Selected Writings, 1911–1918*, ed. Olaf Hansen, 248–64. New York: Urizen Books, 1977.

———. "Twilight of Idols." In *The Radical Will: Selected Writings, 1911–1918*, ed. Olaf Hansen, 336–47. New York: Urizen Books, 1977.

———. "The War and the Intellectuals." In *The Radical Will: Selected Writings, 1911–1918*, ed. Olaf Hansen, 307–18. New York: Urizen Books, 1977.

Breu, Christopher. *Hard-Boiled Masculinities.* Minneapolis: University of Minnesota Press, 2005.

Bridgwater, Patrick. *Nietzsche in Anglosaxony: A Study of Nietzsche's Impact on English and American Literature.* Leicester: Leicester University Press, 1972.

Brooks, Cleanth. *The Well-Wrought Urn.* New York: Harcourt, Brace & World, 1947.

Brooks, Cleanth, and Robert Penn Warren. "Letter to the Teacher." In *Understanding Fiction*, vii–xix. New York: F. S. Crofts, 1943.

———. *Understanding Fiction.* New York: F. S. Crofts, 1943.

Brooks, Van Wyck. *America's Coming-of-Age.* Garden City, NY: Doubleday Anchor Books, 1958.

Brown, Katherine Holland. "The Birth of Irony." *Lippincott's Monthly Magazine*, June 1908.

Brown, Wendy. *Politics Out of History*. Princeton, NJ: Princeton University Press, 2001.

Burke, Kenneth. "Four Master Tropes." *Kenyon Review* 3, no. 4 (Autumn 1941): 421–38.

———. *A Grammar of Motives*. Berkeley: University of California Press, 1969.

———. "Key Words for Critics." *Kenyon Review* 4, no. 3 (Winter 1942): 126–32.

———. *Language as Symbolic Action: Essays on Life, Literature, and Method*. Berkeley: University of California Press, 1966.

Burstein, Jessica. "A Few Words About Dubuque: Modernism, Sentimentalism, and the Blasé." *American Literary History* 14, no. 2 (Summer 2002): 227–54.

Callahan, John, ed. *Ralph Ellison's Invisible Man: A Casebook*. Oxford: Oxford University Press, 2004.

Callahan, Sean, ed. *The Photographs of Margaret Bourke-White*. Greenwich, CT: New York Graphic Society, 1972.

Campbell, Lewis. "Note. On the So-Called Irony of Sophocles." In *Sophocles*, ed. Lewis Campbell. Vol. 1. 2nd ed. Oxford: Clarendon Press, 1879.

Canby, Henry Seidel. "SRL Award to Ellen Glasgow." *Saturday Review of Literature* 23, no. 24 (April 5, 1941): 10.

Cardozo, Benjamin N. *Berkey v. Third Avenue Railway* 244 N.Y. 84, 94, 155 N.E. 58 (1926).

Carey, Alex. *Taking the Risk Out of Democracy: Corporate Propaganda Versus Freedom and Liberty*. Ed. Andrew Lohrey. Urbana: University of Illinois Press, 1997.

Cargill, Oscar. *Intellectual America: Ideas on the March*. New York: Macmillan, 1941.

Cassuto, Leonard. *Hard-Boiled Sentimentality: The Secret History of American Crime Stories*. New York: Columbia University Press, 2009.

Chamberlain, John. "John Dos Passos Satirizes an America 'On the Make.'" *New York Times Book Review*, March 2, 1930.

Chomsky, Noam. *American Power and the New Mandarins*. New York: Pantheon Books, 1967.

Clay, Eugene. "The Negro in Recent American Literature." In *American Writers' Congress*, ed. Henry Hart, 145–53. New York: International Publishers, 1935.

Colebrook, Claire. *Irony*. The New Critical Idiom. New York: Routledge, 2004.

———. *Irony in the Work of Philosophy*. Lincoln: University of Nebraska Press, 2002.

Connolly, William E. "Foreword: The Left and Ontopolitics." In *A Leftist Ontology: Beyond Relativism and Identity Politics*, ix–xx. Minneapolis: University of Minnesota Press, 2009.

Cooper, Mark Garrett. *Love Rules: Silent Hollywood and the Rise of the Managerial Class*. Minneapolis: University of Minnesota Press, 2003.

Cornell, Drucilla. *Moral Images of Freedom: A Future for Critical Theory*. New York: Rowman and Littlefield, 2008.

Crable, Bryan. *Ralph Ellison and Kenneth Burke: At the Roots of the Racial Divide*. Charlottesville: University of Virginia Press, 2012.

Creel, George. *The Creel Report: Complete Report of the Chairman of the Committee on Public Information, 1917:1918:1919*. New York: Da Capo Press, 1972.

———. *How We Advertised America: The First Telling of the Amazing Story of the Committee on Public Information That Carried the Gospel of Americanism to Every Corner of the Globe*. New York: Harper & Brothers, 1920.

Crowther, Bosley. "The Irony of It: A Gentle Reminder That Satire Is Very Scarce These Days—And Some Fun!" *New York Times*, August 22, 1943.

Cruse, Harold. *The Crisis of the Negro Intellectual*. New York: William Morrow, 1967.

Dane, Joseph A. *The Critical Mythology of Irony*. 1990. Athens: University of Georgia Press, 2011.

Davis, Lennard. *Factual Fictions: The Origins of the English Novel*. Philadelphia: University of Pennsylvania Press, 1997.

Dawahare, Anthony. *Nationalism, Marxism, and African-American Marxism Between the Wars: A New Pandora's Box*. Jackson: University Press of Mississippi, 2003.

Day, Amber. *Satire and Dissent: Interventions in Contemporary Political Debate*. Bloomington: Indiana University Press, 2011.

De Casseres, Benjamin. "Advertisement for Marian Cox, The Dry Rot of Society." *Current Opinion* 67, no. 5 (December 1919): 339.

———. "Caricature and New York." *Camera Work* 26 (April 1909): 17–18.

———. *Chameleon, Being a Book of My Selves*. New York: Lieber & Lewis, 1922.

———. "'Denial Without End': Benjamin De Casseres' Parody of Eugene O'Neill's 'God Play' *Days Without End*." Ed. Robert M. Dowling. *Eugene O'Neill Review* 30 (Fall 2008): 145–59.

———. *Forty Immortals*. New York: J. Lawren, 1926.

———. *Germans, Jews and France*. New York: Rose Printers and Publishers, 1935.

———. "Heavens a Hippodrome and All the Actors Airplanes." *New York Times*, November 30, 1919.

———. "The Individual Against Moloch." In *Works of Benjamin De Casseres*, 1:7–16. New York: Blackstone Publishers, 1936.

———. "Insincerity: A New Vice." *Camera Work* 42–43 (July 1913): 15–17.

———. "The Ironical in Art." *Camera Work* 38 (April 1912): 17–19.

———. "James Branch Cabell." In *Works of Benjamin De Casseres*, 1:45–47. New York: Blackstone Publishers, 1936.

———. "Jules De Gaultier: Super-Nietzschean." *Forum*, January 1913.

———. "Letter." *Contempo* 1, no. 12 (November 15, 1931): 2.

———. "The March of Events." In *Ellen Glasgow: The Contemporary Reviews*, ed. Dorothy M. Scura, 473. Cambridge: Cambridge University Press, 1992.

———. *Mencken and Shaw: The Anatomy of America's Voltaire and England's Other John Bull.* New York: Silas Newton, 1930.

———. *The Muse of Lies.* Newark, NJ: Rose Printers and Publishers, 1936.

———. "The Philosophers of Unrepentance." *Liberty (Not the Daughter but the Mother of Order)* 16, no. 4 (October 1907): 35.

———. *Platform of Benjamin De Casseres: Candidate for Mayor of New York.* Poster, hand-dated in pencil with "1907" and "1912?" Box 24. New York Public Library Rare Books and Manuscripts.

———. "The Psychology of Caricature." In *Mortals & Immortals: Caricatures by C. De Fornaro.* New York: n.p., 1911.

———. "Reply." In *The Young Idea: An Anthology of Opinion Concerning the Spirit and Aims of Contemporary American Literature,* ed. Lloyd R. Morris, 146–47. New York: Duffield and Company, 1917.

———. "Spinoza, the Father of Modernism." *Canadian Jewish Chronicle,* September 30, 1932.

———. *The Superman in America.* Seattle: University of Washington Press, 1929.

De Man, Paul. "The Concept of Irony." In *Aesthetic Ideology,* ed. Andrzej Warminski, 163–84. Theory and History of Literature, vol. 65. Minneapolis: University of Minnesota Press, 1996.

De Zayas, Marius. "Photography." *Camera Work* 41 (January 1913): 17–20.

Delap, Lucy. *The Feminist Avant-Garde: Transatlantic Encounters of the Early Twentieth Century.* Cambridge: Cambridge University Press, 2007.

Deleuze, Gilles. *Difference and Repetition.* Trans. Paul Patton. New York: Continuum, 2004.

Denning, Michael. *The Cultural Front.* London: Verso, 1998.

Dewey, John. "Education as Politics." In *John Dewey: The Middle Works, 1899–1924,* ed. Jo Ann Boydstun, 13:329–34. Carbondale: Southern Illinois University Press, 1985.

———. *Ethics.* In *John Dewey: The Later Works, 1925–1953,* ed. Jo Ann Boydstun. Vol. 7. Carbondale: Southern Illinois University Press, 1985.

———. "The New Psychology." In *John Dewey: The Early Works, 1882–1898,* 1:48–60. Carbondale: Southern Illinois University Press, 1985.

———. "Practical Democracy." Review of *The Phantom Public,* by Walter Lippmann. 1925. *John Dewey: The Later Works, 1925–1953.* Ed. Jo Ann Boydstun, 2:213–20. Carbondale: Southern Illinois University Press, 1985.

———. "Psychology." In *John Dewey: The Early Works, 1882–1898.* Ed. Jo Ann Boydstun. Vol. 2. Carbondale: Southern Illinois University Press, 1991.

———. *The Public and Its Problems.* New York: Henry Holt, 1927.

———. Review of *Public Opinion,* by Walter Lippmann. 1922. *John Dewey: The Middle Works 1899–1924.* Ed. Jo Ann Boydstun. 13:337–44. Carbondale: Southern Illinois University Press, 1985.

Didion, Joan. *Fixed Ideas: America Since 9.11.* New York: New York Review of Books, 2003.

Diepeveen, Leonard. "Learning from Philistines: Suspicion, Refusing to Read, and the Rise of Dubious Modernism." In *New Directions in American Reception Study*, ed. Philip Goldstein and James L. Machor, 159–78. New York: Oxford University Press, 2008.

Doctorow, E. L. Forward to *The Big Money*, vii–xi. Boston: Houghton Mifflin, 2000.

———. *Jack London, Hemingway, and the Constitution: Selected Essays, 1977–1992*. New York: Random House, 1993.

Dos Passos, John. "Against American Literature." In *Travel Books and Other Writings, 1916–1940*, 587–90. New York: Library of America, 2003.

———. *Century's Ebb: The Thirteenth Chronicle*. Boston: Gambit, 1975.

———. *The Fourteenth Chronicle: The Letters and Diaries of John Dos Passos*. Ed. Townsend Ludington. Boston: Gambit, 1973.

———. *Manhattan Transfer*. Boston: Houghton Mifflin, 2000.

———. *One Man's Initiation—1917*. New York. George H. Doran Co., 1922.

———. *Rosinante to the Road Again*. New York: George H. Doran Co., 1922.

———. "Satire as a Way of Seeing." In *Occasions and Protests*, 20–33. Chicago. Henry Regnery, 1964.

———. *U.S.A.: The 42nd Parallel; 1919; The Big Money*. New York: Library of America, 1996.

———. "Wanted: An Ivy Lee for Liberals." *New Republic*, August 13, 1930.

———. "Washington and Chicago, IL: Spotlights and Microphones." *New Republic*, July 27, 1932.

Douglass, Frederick. "What to the Slave Is the Fourth of July?: An Address Delivered in Rochester, New York, on 5 July 1852." In *The Life and Writings of Frederick Douglass*, ed. Philip S. Foner, vol. 2, *Pre–Civil War Decade, 1850–1860*, 359–88. New York: International Publishers Co., 1950.

Dow, William. "The Perils of Irony in Hemingway's *The Sun Also Rises*." *Etudes Anglaises* 58 (February 2005): 178–92.

Dwight, Mabel. "Satire in Art." In *Art for the Millions: Essays from the 1930s by Artists and Administrators of the WPA Federal Art Project*, ed. Francis V. O'Connor, 151–54. Greenwich, CT: New York Graphic Society, 1973.

Eagleton, Terry. *The Illusions of Postmodernism*. Oxford: Blackwell, 1996.

Eastman, Max. *Enjoyment of Living*. New York: Harper & Brothers, 1948.

Eddy, Beth. *The Rites of Identity: The Religious Naturalism and Cultural Criticism of Kenneth Burke and Ralph Ellison*. Princeton, NJ: Princeton University Press, 2003.

Edmunds, Susan. *Grotesque Relations: Modernist Domestic Fiction and the U.S. Welfare State*. Oxford: Oxford University Press, 2008.

Edwards, Justin. "The Man with the Camera Eye: Cinematic Form and Hollywood Malediction in John Dos Passos' *The Big Money*." *Literature/Film Quarterly* 27, no. 4 (1999): 245–54.

Elias, Amy. *Sublime Desire: History and Post-1960s Fiction*. London: Johns Hopkins University Press, 2001.

Ellison, Ralph. "Beating That Boy." In *Shadow and Act*, 95–101. New York: Vintage International, 1995.

———. *Conversations with Ralph Ellison*. Ed. Maryemma Graham and Amritjit Singh. Jackson: University Press of Mississippi, 1995.

———. "Eyewitness Story of Riot: False Rumors Spurred Mob." *New York Post*, August 2, 1943.

———. *Going to the Territory*. New York: Random House, 1986.

———. *Invisible Man*. New York: Vintage Books, 1981.

———. "Letter to John Lucas." In *Ralph Ellison's Invisible Man: A Casebook*, ed. John F. Callahan, 50–52. Oxford: Oxford University Press, 2004.

———. "Letter to Kenneth Burke." November 23, 1945. Located in and used with permission of the Kenneth Burke Archives of Pennsylvania State University Library.

———. "On Being the Target of Discrimination." In *The Collected Essays of Ralph Ellison*, ed. John F. Callahan, 825–32. New York: Modern Library, 1995.

———. Ralph Ellison Papers. Manuscript Division, Library of Congress. Washington, DC.

———. *Shadow and Act*. New York: Vintage International, 1995.

———. "Society, Morality, and the Novel." In *The Collected Essays of Ralph Ellison*, ed. John F. Callahan, 699–729. New York: Modern Library, 1995.

———. "The World and the Jug." In *Shadow and Act*. New York: Vintage International, 1995.

Fitzgerald, F. Scott. *The Beautiful and Damned*. New York: Penguin Classics, 1998.

Foley, Barbara. *Radical Representations: Politics and Form in U.S. Proletarian Fiction, 1929–1941*. Durham, NC: Duke University Press, 1993.

———. "Renarrating the Thirties in the Forties and Fifties." *Prospects: An Annual of American Cultural Studies* 20 (2000): 455–66.

———. *Specters of 1919: Class and Nation in the Making of the New Negro*. Urbana: University of Illinois Press, 2003.

———. *Wrestling with the Left: The Making of Ralph Ellison's Invisible Man*. Durham, NC: Duke University Press, 2010.

Follett, Helen Thomas, and Wilson Follett. *Some Modern Novelists: Appreciations and Estimates*. New York: Henry Holt, 1919.

Follett, Wilson. "Sentimentalist, Satirist, and Realist: Notes on Some Recent Fiction." *Atlantic Monthly*, October 1916.

Ford, Nick Aaron. "Four Popular Negro Novelists." *Phylon: The Atlanta University Review of Race & Culture* 15, no. 1 (Qtr 1954): 29–39.

Forman, James. *The Making of Black Revolutionaries*. New York: Macmillan, 1972.

"Forward." *Public Opinion Quarterly* 1, no. 1 (January 1937): 3–5.

Fox, Richard Wightman. "Tragedy, Responsibility, and the American Intellectual, 1925–1950." In *Lewis Mumford: Public Intellectual*, ed. Thomas P. Hughes and Agatha C. Hughes, 323–38. New York: Oxford University Press, 1990.

Francis, Elizabeth. *The Secret Treachery of Words: Feminism and Modernism in America*. Minneapolis: University of Minnesota Press, 2002.

Franzen, Jonathan. "The Liberal Form: An Interview with Jonathan Franzen." *boundary 2* 36, no. 2 (2009): 31–54.

Fraser, Nancy, and Axel Honneth. *Redistribution or Recognition: A Political-Philosophical Exchange*. Trans. Joel Golb, James Ingram, and Christiane Wilke. London: Verso, 2003.

Fricker, Miranda. "Feminism in Epistemology: Pluralism Without Postmodernism." In *The Cambridge Companion to Feminism in Philosophy*, ed. Miranda Fricker and Jennifer Hornsby, 146–65. Cambridge: Cambridge University Press, 2000.

Frye, Northrop. *Anatomy of Criticism: Four Essays*. Princeton, NJ: Princeton University Press, 1957.

———. "The Nature of Satire." In *The Educated Imagination and Other Writings on Critical Theory*, 39–57. Collected Works of Northrop Frye 21. Toronto: University of Toronto Press, 1996.

Fussell, Paul. *The Great War and Modern Memory*. New York: Oxford University Press, 1975.

Galsworthy, John. "The Patricians." *Atlantic Monthly*, December 1910.

Garnett, Richard. "Satire." *Encyclopedia Britannica*, 1911.

Genter, Robert. *Late Modernism: Art, Culture, and Politics in Cold War America*. Philadelphia: University of Pennsylvania Press, 2010.

———. "Toward a Theory of Rhetoric: Ralph Ellison, Kenneth Burke, and the Problem of Modernism." *Twentieth Century Literature: A Scholarly and Critical Journal* 48, no. 2 (Summer 2002): 191–214.

Gibbs, Raymond W. Jr., and Herbert L. Colston, eds. *Irony in Language and Thought*. New York: Lawrence Erlbaum Associates, 2007.

Gillooly, Eileen. *Smile of Discontent: Humor, Gender, and Nineteenth-Century British Fiction*. Chicago: University of Chicago Press, 1999.

Glasgow, Ellen. *A Certain Measure: An Interpretation of Prose Fiction*. New York: Harcourt, Brace and Co., 1938.

———. "Evasive Idealism in Literature." In *Literature in the Making by Some of Its Makers*. New York: Harper & Brothers, 1917.

———. "Feminism." In *Ellen Glasgow's Reasonable Doubts: A Collection of Her Writings*, ed. Julius Rowan Raper, 26–36. Baton Rouge: Louisiana State University Press, 1988.

———. "I Believe." In *Ellen Glasgow's Reasonable Doubts: A Collection of Her Writings*, ed. Julius Rowan Raper, 228–45. Baton Rouge: Louisiana State University Press, 1988.

———. "Impressions of the Novel." In *Ellen Glasgow's Reasonable Doubts: A Collection of Her Writings*, ed. Julius Rowan Raper, 140–49. Baton Rouge: Louisiana State University Press, 1988.

———. *Letters of Ellen Glasgow*. Ed. Blair Rouse. New York: Harcourt, Brace, 1958.

———. "No Valid Reason Against Giving Votes to Women: An Interview." In *Ellen Glasgow's Reasonable Doubts: A Collection of Her Writings*, ed. Julius Rowan Raper, 19–26. Baton Rouge: Louisiana State University Press, 1988.

———. "The Novel in the South." In *Ellen Glasgow's Reasonable Doubts: A Collection of Her Writings*, ed. Julius Rowan Raper, 68–82. Baton Rouge: Louisiana State University Press, 1988.

———. "Opening Speech of the Southern Writers Conference." In *Ellen Glasgow's Reasonable Doubts: A Collection of Her Writings*, ed. Julius Rowan Raper, 90–97. Baton Rouge: Louisiana State University Press, 1988.

———. *Perfect Companionship: Ellen Glasgow's Selected Correspondence with Women.* Ed. Pamela Matthews. Charlottesville: University of Virginia Press, 2005.

———. *The Romantic Comedians.* Charlottesville: University Press of Virginia, 1995.

———. "Some Literary Woman Myths." In *Ellen Glasgow's Reasonable Doubts: A Collection of Her Writings*, ed. Julius Rowan Raper, 36–45. Baton Rouge: Louisiana State University Press, 1988.

———. *Virginia.* New York: Doubleday, Page & Co., 1913.

———. "What I Believe." In *Ellen Glasgow's Reasonable Doubts: A Collection of Her Writings*, ed. Julius Rowan Raper, 219–27. Baton Rouge: Louisiana State University Press, 1988.

———. *The Woman Within.* New York: Harcourt Brace, 1954.

Glasgow, Ellen, and James Branch Cabell. *Of Ellen Glasgow: An Inscribed Portrait.* New York: Maverick Press, 1938.

Gold, Mike. "The Keynote to Dos Passos' Works." *Daily Worker*, February 26, 1938.

Goldman, Emma. "Nietzsche on War." *Mother Earth* 9, no. 8 (October 1914): 60–64.

———. "The Tragedy of Woman's Emancipation." In *Anarchism and Other Essays*, 219–32. New York: Mother Earth Publishing Association, 1910.

Gomperz, H. "Interpretation." *Erkenntnis: Journal of Unified Science* 7 (1938): 225–32.

Goodman, Susan. *Civil Wars: American Novelists and Manners, 1880–1940.* Baltimore: Johns Hopkins University Press, 2003.

Graeber, I. "Benjamin De Casseres as I Know Him" (*The Jewish Tribune*, undated). Box 28, Benjamin De Casseres Papers. New York Public Library Rare Books and Manuscripts.

Greenberg, Jonathan. *Modernism, Satire, and the Novel.* Cambridge: Cambridge University Press, 2011.

Greene, Viveca. "Critique, Counternarratives, and Ironic Intervention in South Park and Stephen Colbert." In *A Decade of Dark Humour: How Comedy, Irony, and Satire Shaped Post-9/11 America*, ed. Ted Gournelos and Viveca Greene, 119–36. Jackson: University Press of Mississippi, 2011.

Gregory, Horace. "Review of *The Big Money*." *New York Herald Tribune Books*, August 9, 1936.

Guay, Robert. "Genealogy and Irony." *Journal of Nietzsche Studies* 41 (Spring 2011): 26–49.

Hamilton, Alexander. "Number 84." In *The Federalist: A Commentary on the Constitution of the United States*, 550–51. New York: Random House, 2000.

Hand, Learned. *Masses Publishing Co. v. Patten* (S.D.N.Y. 1917).

Handwerk, Gary. "Romantic Irony." In *The Cambridge History of Literary Criticism*, ed. Marshall Brown, 5:203–25. Cambridge: Cambridge University Press, 2000.

Hannay, James. *Satire and Satirists*. London: David Bogue, 1854.

Haraway, Donna J. "A Manifesto for Cyborgs: Science, Technology, and Socialist Feminism in the 1980s." In *The Gendered Cyborg: A Reader*, ed. Gill Kirkup, Linda Uanes, Kath Woodwar, and Fiona Hovenden, 50–57. New York: Routledge, 2000.

Harvey, Anna Lil. *Votes Without Leverage: Women in American Electoral Politics, 1920–1970*. Cambridge: Cambridge University Press, 1998.

Hatab, Lawrence. "Prospects for a Democratic Agon: Why We Can Still Be Nietzscheans." *Journal of Nietzsche Studies* 24 (Fall 2002): 132–47.

Hegel, Georg Wilhelm Friedrich. *Aesthetics: Lectures on Fine Art*. Trans. T. M. Knox. Vol. 1. Oxford: Oxford, 1998.

———. *Ästhetik*. Ed. Friedrich Bassenge. Vol. Band 1. Berlin: Aufbau-Verlag, 1965.

———. *Elements of the Philosophy of Right*. Ed. Allen B. Wood. Trans. H. B. Nisbet. Cambridge: Cambridge University Press, 1991.

———. *Phänomenology Des Geistes*. Ed. Allen B. Wessels and Heinrich Clairmont. Hamburg: Felix Meiner Verlag, 2006.

———. *Phenomenology of Spirit*. Trans. A. V. Miller. Oxford: Oxford University Press, 1977.

Hemingway, Ernest. *The Sun Also Rises*. New York: Charles Scribner's Sons, 1926.

Hine, Lewis. "Social Photography: How the Camera May Help in the Social Uplift." In *Classic Essays on Photography*, ed. Alan Trachtenberg, 110–13. New Haven, CT: Leete's Island Books, 1980.

Hock, Stephen. "'Stories Told Sideways Out of the Big Mouth': John Dos Passos's Bazinian Camera Eye." *Literature/Film Quarterly* 33, no. 1 (2005): 20–27.

Holland, Lawrence B. "Ellison in Black and White: Confession, Violence and Rhetoric in *Invisible Man*." In *Black Fiction: New Studies in the Afro-American Novel Since 1945*, ed. Robert A. Lee, 54–73. New York: Barnes and Noble, 1980.

Hollibaugh, Lisa. "'The Civilized Uses of Irony': Darwinism, Calvinism, and Motherhood in Ellen Glasgow's Barren." *Mississippi Quarterly* 59, no. 1/2 (Winter–Spring 2006): 31–63.

Howard, Dick. *Political Judgments*. Lanham, MD: Rowman and Littlefield, 1996.

Howe, Irving. "Black Boys and Native Sons." *Dissent* 10, no. 4 (Autumn 1963): 353–68.

Hoy, Jocelyn B. "Hegel, Antigone, and Feminist Critique: The Spirit of Ancient Greece." In *The Blackwell Guide to Hegel's Phenomenology of Spirit*, ed. Kenneth R. Westphal, 172–89. Oxford: Wiley-Blackwell, 2009.

Hudson, W. D., ed. *The Is-Ought Question: A Collection of Papers on the Central Problem in Moral Philosophy.* New York: Macmillan/St. Martin's Press, 1969.

Hughes, Langston. "To Negro Writers." In *American Writers' Congress*, ed. Henry Hart, 139–41. New York: International Publishers, 1935.

Humboldt, Charles. "The Novel of Action." *Mainstream: A Literary Quarterly* 1, no. 4 (Fall 1947): 389–407.

Hume, David. *A Treatise of Human Nature.* Ed. L. A. Selby-Bigge. Oxford: Oxford University Press, 1978.

Huneker, James. *Unicorns.* New York: Charles Scribner's Sons, 1917.

Hutcheon, Linda. *Irony's Edge: The Theory and Politics of Irony.* New York: Routledge, 1994.

———. *A Theory of Parody: The Teachings of Twentieth-Century Art Forms.* Urbana: University of Illinois Press, 1985.

Hutchings, Kimberly. *Hegel and Feminist Philosophy.* Oxford: Wiley-Blackwell, 2003.

Inwood, Michael. *A Hegel Dictionary.* Oxford: Blackwell, 1992.

"Irony." *The Living Age* 7, no. 4 (July, August, September 1899). Orig. *Spectator.* Boston: The Living Age Company, 58–60.

"Irony and Sarcasm." *The Youth's Companion*, August 12, 1920.

"Is the Greatest Humorist in English Literature a Woman?" *Current Opinion*, February 1914, 139.

Jackson, Lawrence. *Ralph Ellison: Emergence of Genius.* New York: John Wiley, 2002.

———. "Ralph Ellison's Politics of Integration." In *A Historical Guide to Ralph Ellison*, ed. Steven C. Tracy, 171–205. Oxford: Oxford University Press, 2004.

Jacobs, Joseph. "Works of Friedrich Nietzsche: A Critical Consideration of the German Philosopher, If Philosopher He Can Be Called, Based Upon the New English Translation of His Works—Many Recent Nietzsche Volumes." *New York Times*, May 7, 1910, sec. BR8.

James, William. *Habit.* New York: Henry Holt, 1914.

———. *The Meaning of Truth: A Sequel to "Pragmatism."* New York: Longmans, Green, 1909.

———. *A Pluralistic Universe.* New York: Longmans, Green, 1920.

———. "Pragmatism's Conception of Truth." In *Pragmatism and Four Essays from The Meaning of Truth.* New York: Meridian Books, 1967.

———. *The Principles of Psychology.* Vol. 2. New York: Henry Holt, 1905.

———. "The Will." In *Talks to Teachers on Psychology: And to Students on Some of Life's Ideals*, 169–96. New York: Henry Holt, 1914.

Jameson, Fredric. *The Seeds of Time*. New York: Columbia University Press, 1996.

Jancovich, Mark. *The Cultural Politics of the New Criticism*. Cambridge: Cambridge University Press, 1993.

Jefferson, Thomas. "Letter to John Norvell. (14 June 1807)." In *Jefferson: Political Writings*, ed. Joyce Appleby and Terence Ball, 273–76. Cambridge Texts in the History of Political Thought. Cambridge: Cambridge University Press, 1999.

Johnson, Edgar. *A Treasury of Satire*. New York: Simon and Schuster, 1945.

Jones, Alfred W. "Satire and Sentiment." In *Essays Upon Authors and Books*, 113–19. New York: Stanford and Swords, 1849.

Jost, Walter. "Philosophy and Literature—and Rhetoric." In *A Companion to the Philosophy of Literature*, ed. Gary Hagberg and Walter Jost, 38–51. Oxford: Blackwell, 2010.

Judy, Ronald A. T. "Irony and the Asymptotes of the Hyperbola." *boundary 2* 25, no. 1 (1998): 161–90.

Juvenal. "Satire I." In *Juvenal and Persius*, trans. G. G. Ramsay, 91:2–15. Loeb Classical Library. Cambridge, MA: Harvard University Press, 1996.

Kakutani, Michiko. "The Age of Irony Isn't Over After All," *New York Times*, October 9, 2001, sec. E1.

Kalaidjian, Walter. *The Edge of Modernism: American Poetry and the Traumatic Past*. Baltimore: Johns Hopkins University Press, 2006.

Kammen, Michael J. *The Lively Arts: Gilbert Seldes and the Transformation of Cultural Criticism in the United States*. Oxford: Oxford University Press, 1996.

Kant, Immanuel. *Groundwork of the Metaphysics of Morals*. Ed. Mary Gregor. Cambridge: Cambridge University Press, 1997.

Kazin, Alfred. *On Native Grounds: An Interpretation of Modern American Prose*. New York: Reynal & Hitchcock, 1942.

Kierkegaard, Søren. *The Concept of Irony, with Constant Reference to Socrates*. Trans. Lee M. Capel. Indianapolis: Indiana University Press, 1965.

Kirkpatrick, David. "Pronouncements on Irony Draw a Line in the Sand." *New York Times*, September 24, 2001, sec. C9.

Klarman, Michael J. *From Jim Crow to Civil Rights: The Supreme Court and the Struggle for Racial Equality*. New York: Oxford University Press, 2004.

Knight, Charles A. *The Literature of Satire*. Cambridge: Cambridge University Press, 2004.

Kostelanetz, Richard. "An Interview with Ralph Ellison." In *Conversations with Ralph Ellison*, ed. Amritjit Singh and Maryemma Graham, 87–97. Jackson: University Press of Mississippi, 1995.

Krugman, Paul. "Republicans and Medicare." *New York Times*, February 11, 2010. http://www.nytimes.com/2010/02/12/opinion/12krugman.html.

Krutch, Joseph Wood. "A Note on Irony." *The Nation*, November 1, 1922.

Lander, Christian. "#50: Irony." *Stuff White People Like*. February 3, 2008. http://stuffwhitepeoplelike.com/2008/02/03/50-irony/.

Landsberg, Melvin. *Dos Passos' Path to U.S.A.: A Political Biography, 1912–1936*. Boulder, CO: Colorado Associated University Press, 1972.

Large, Duncan. "A Note on the Term 'Umwerthung.'" *Journal of Nietzsche Studies* 39 (Spring 2010): 5–11.

Lear, Jonathan. *A Case for Irony*. Cambridge, MA: Harvard University Press, 2011.

Levy, Barbara Ellen. *Ladies Laughing: Wit as Control in Contemporary American Women Writers*. Amsterdam: Gordon and Breach, 1997.

Levy, Oscar. "Letter to Benjamin De Casseres." MS., November 16, 1936. Box 1. Benjamin De Casseres Papers. New York Public Library Rare Books and Manuscripts.

Lewis, Pericles. *The Cambridge Introduction to Modernism*. Cambridge: Cambridge University Press, 2007.

Lewis, R.W.B. *The American Adam: Innocence, Tragedy and Tradition in the Nineteenth Century*. Chicago: University of Chicago Press, 1955.

Lippmann, Walter. *Liberty and the News*. New York: Harcourt, Brace and Howe, 1920.

———. *The Phantom Public: A Sequel to "Public Opinion."* New York: Macmillan, 1930.

———. *A Preface to Politics*. New York and London: M. Kennerly, 1914.

———. *Public Opinion*. New York: The Free Press, 1965.

Livingston, James. "On Richard Hofstadter and the Politics of 'Consensus History.'" *boundary 2* 34, no. 3 (Fall 2007): 33–46.

Locke, Alain. "From Native Son to Invisible Man: A Review of the Literature of the Negro for 1952." *Phylon: The Atlanta University Review of Race & Culture* 14, no. 1 (1953): 34–44.

———. "Negro Youth Speaks." In *The New Negro*. New York: Macmillan, 1992.

London, Jack. *The Iron Heel*. New York: Review of Reviews, 1917.

Lowell, Amy. "Irony." In *Sword Blades and Poppy Seed*, 63. New York: Macmillan, 1914.

Ludwig, Sämi. *Pragmatist Realism: The Cognitive Paradigm in American Realist Texts*. Madison: University of Wisconsin Press, 2002.

Lukács, Georg. *The Historical Novel*. Trans. Hannah and Stanley Mitchell. New York: Humanities Press, 1965.

———. *The Theory of the Novel: A Historico-Philosophical Essay on the Forms of Great Epic Literature*. Trans. Anna Bostock. Cambridge, MA: MIT Press, 1971.

Lumley, Frederick Elmore. *Means of Social Control*. New York: Century Co., 1925.

M., B. "Friedrich Nietzsche." *Mother Earth* 7, no. 11 (1913): 383–89.

Macdonald, Dwight. *The Root Is Man: Two Essays in Politics*. Alhambra, CA: Cunningham Press, 1953.

Magee, Michael. "Ralph Ellison: Pragmatism, Jazz and the American Vernacular." *Transactions of the Charles S. Peirce Society* 39, no. 2 (Spring 2003): 227–58.

Magill, R. Jay Jr.. *Chic Ironic Bitterness.* Ann Arbor: University of Michigan Press, 2007.

Majerus, Elizabeth. "'Determined and Bigoted Feminists': Women, Magazines, and Popular Modernism." In *Modernism*, ed. Astradur Eysteinsson and Vivian Liska, 2:619–36. Amsterdam: John Benjamins, 2007.

Mann, Dorothea Lawrance. "Ellen Glasgow: Citizen of the World." In *Ellen Glasgow: The Contemporary Reviews*, ed. Dorothy M. Scura, 284–85. Cambridge: Cambridge University Press, 1992.

Marcuse, Herbert. *An Essay on Liberation.* Boston: Beacon Press, 1969.

Markovits, Elizabeth. *The Politics of Sincerity: Plato, Frank Speech, and Democratic Judgment.* University Park: Pennsylvania State University Press, 2008.

Marquis, Don. "If We Could Only See." In *The Revolt of the Oyster*, 18–37. Garden City, NY: Doubleday, Page & Co., 1922.

Martens, Gunter. "Literary Modernism, Critical Theory and the Politics of Irony." In *Modernism*, ed. Astradur Eysteinsson and Vivian Liska, 1:89–105. Philadelphia: John Benjamins, 2007.

Massing, Michael. "Iraq, the Press and the Election." *New York Review of Books*, December 16, 2004, 26–32.

Matarrese, Craig B. "Satisfaction or Supersession? Expression, Rationality, and Irony in Hegel and Rorty." *Clio* 36, no. 1 (September 2006): 41–58.

Mattson, Kevin. *Upton Sinclair and the Other American Century.* Hoboken, NJ: John Wiley and Sons, 2006.

Maude, Sir Frederick Stanley. "The Proclamation of Baghdad." N.d. http://harpers.org/archive/2003/05/0079593.

May, Vanessa. *Unprotected Labor: Household Workers, Politics, and Middle-Class Reform in New York, 1870–1940.* Chapel Hill: University of North Carolina Press, 2011.

McAlmon, Victoria. "Free—for What?" In *These Modern Women: Autobiographical Essays from the Twenties*, ed. Elaine Showalter, 110–15. Old Westbury, NY: Feminist Press, 1978.

McCarthy, Mary. "Class Angles and a Wilder Classic." In *A Bolt from the Blue and Other Essays*, 17–24. New York: New York Review of Books, 2002.

McCormick, Anne O'Hare. "Daughters of the Revolution." In *The Hammer and the Scythe: Communist Russia Enters the Second Decade*, 154–77. New York: Alfred A. Knopf, 1927.

McInerney, Jay. "Getting It Together." *New York Times*, August 28, 2005. Rev. of *Indecision*, by Benjamin Kunkel. http://www.nytimes.com/2005/08/28/books/review/28MCINER.html.

McKenney, Ruth. *Industrial Valley.* New York: Harcourt, Brace, 1939.

Menand, Louis. "Richard Wright: The Hammer and the Nail." In *American Studies*, 76–90. New York: Farrar, Straus, and Giroux, 2002.

Mencken, H. L. *The American Language: An Inquiry into the Development of English in the United States.* 2nd ed. New York: Alfred A. Knopf, 1921.

———. "Letter to Benjamin De Casseres." MS, December 12, 1933. Box 1, folder H. L. Mencken—De Casseres 1927–1935. Benjamin De Casseres Papers. New York Public Library Rare Books and Manuscripts.

———. *The Philosophy of Friedrich Nietzsche.* 3rd ed. Port Washington, NY: Kennikat Press, 1913.

Meredith, George. "An Essay on Comedy." In *Comedy,* ed. Wylie Sypher, 3–60. Baltimore: Johns Hopkins University Press, 1980.

Miller, Nina. *Making Love Modern: The Intimate Public Worlds of New York's Literary Women.* New York: Oxford University Press, 1999.

Miller, Paul Allen. "Ethics and Irony." *SubStance* 38, no. 3 (2009): 51–71.

Mims, Edwin. "The Social Philosophy of Ellen Glasgow." *Social Forces* 4, no. 3 (March 1926): 495–503.

Moglen, Seth. *Mourning Modernity: Literary Modernism and the Injuries of American Capitalism.* Stanford, CA: Stanford University Press, 2007.

Morel, Lucas E., ed. *Ralph Ellison and the Raft of Hope: A Political Companion to Invisible Man.* Lexington: University Press of Kentucky, 2004.

Morris, Lloyd R. *The Young Idea: An Anthology of Opinion Concerning the Spirit and Aims of Contemporary American Literature.* New York: Duffield and Company, 1917.

Mouffe, Chantal. *The Democratic Paradox.* London: Verso, 2000.

Muhawi, Ibrahim. "Irony and the Poetics of Palestinian Exile." In *Literature and Nation in the Middle East,* ed. Yasir Suleiman and Ibrahim Muhawi, 31–47. Edinburgh: Edinburgh University Press, 2006.

Mumford, Lewis. "The Image of Randolph Bourne." *The New Republic,* September 24, 1930.

Naison, Mark. *Communists in Harlem During the Depression.* Urbana: University of Illinois Press, 2005.

———. "From Eviction Resistance to Rent Control: Tenant Activism in the Great Depression." In *The Tenant Movement in New York City, 1904–1984,* ed. Ronald Lawson. New Brunswick, NJ: Rutgers University Press, 1986.

Newman, Andy. "Irony Is Dead. Again. Yeah, Right." *New York Times,* November 23, 2008. http://www.nytimes.com/2008/11/23/fashion/23irony.html.

Niebuhr, Reinhold. *The Irony of American History.* New York: Charles Scribner's Sons, 1952.

Nietzsche, Friedrich. *Beyond Good and Evil: Prelude to a Philosophy of the Future.* Ed. Oscar Levy. Trans. Helen Zimmern. Vol. 12. Complete Works of Friedrich Nietzsche. New York: Macmillan, 1914.

———. "The Case of Wagner: A Musician's Problem." In *The Anti-Christ, Ecce Homo, Twilight of Idols, and Other Writings,* 231–62. Cambridge: Cambridge University Press, 2005.

———. *Ecce Homo.* Ed. Oscar Levy. Translated by Anthony M. Ludovici. Vol. 17. The Complete Works of Friedrich Nietzsche. New York: Russell & Russell, 1964.

——. *The Genealogy of Morals: A Polemic.* Ed. Oscar Levy. Trans. Horace B. Samuel. Vol. 13. Complete Works of Friedrich Nietzsche. Edinburgh: T. N. Foulis, 1913.

——. *Götzen-Dämmerung.* Vol. Band 6. Sämtliche Werke. München: Deutscher Taschenbuch Verlag, 1980.

——. *Jenseits Von Gut Und Böse.* Vol. Band 5. Sämtliche Werke. München: Deutscher Taschenbuch Verlag, 1980.

——. *The Twilight of the Idols, or, How to Philosophise with the Hammer.* Ed. Oscar Levy. Trans. Anth Ludovici. Vol. 16. Complete Works of Friedrich Nietzsche. New York: Russell & Russell, 1964.

——. *Zur Genealogie Der Moral.* Vol. Band 5. Sämtliche Werke. München: Deutscher Taschenbuch Verlag, 1980.

"No Satire." *Life,* September 18, 1919, 498.

Norris, Andrew. "Willing and Deciding: Hegel on Irony, Evil, and the Sovereign Exception." *Diacritics* 37, no. 2–3 (Summer–Fall 2007): 135–56.

North, Michael. *Camera Works: Photography and the Twentieth Century Word.* Oxford: Oxford University Press, 2005.

——. *Reading 1922: A Return to the Scene of the Modern.* Oxford: Oxford University Press, 1999.

"Observations and Comments." *Mother Earth* 7, no. 9 (November 1912): 279.

O'Neill, Eugene. "Forward." In *Litanies of Negation,* by Benjamin De Casseres, vii–xi. New York: Gotham Book Mart, 1928.

Oppel, Frances Nesbitt. *Nietzsche on Gender: Beyond Man and Woman.* Charlottesville: University of Virginia Press, 2005.

Orfield, Gary. *Reviving the Goal of an Integrated Society: A 21st Century Challenge.* Los Angeles: Civil Rights Project/Proyecto Derechos Civiles at UCLA, 2009.

Parrish, Timothy. "Ralph Ellison, Kenneth Burke, and the Form of Democracy." *Arizona Quarterly: A Journal of American Literature, Culture, and Theory* 51, no. 3 (Autumn 1995): 117–48.

Paxson, Frederic L., and Samuel B. Harding, eds. "Nietzsche." *War Cyclopedia: A Handbook for Ready Reference on the Great War.* Washington, DC: GPO, 1918.

Pease, Donald E. "Ralph Ellison and Kenneth Burke: The Nonsymbolizable (Trans)Action." *boundary 2* 30, no. 2 (2003): 65–96.

Perry, Bliss. *The American Mind.* New York: Houghton Mifflin, 1912.

Peters, Julie Stone. "Law, Literature, and the Vanishing Real: On the Future of an Interdisciplinary Illusion." *PMLA* 10, no. 2 (March 2005): 442–53.

Peterson, Russell Leslie. *Strange Bedfellows: How Late-Night Comedy Turns Democracy into a Joke.* New Brunswick, NJ: Rutgers University Press, 2008.

Pettegrew, John. *Brutes in Suits: Male Sensibility in America, 1890–1920.* Baltimore: Johns Hopkins University Press, 2007.

——. "Lives of Irony: Randolph Bourne, Richard Rorty, & a New Genealogy of Critical Pragmatism," in *A Pragmatist's Progress? Richard Rorty and*

American Intellectual History, ed. John Pettegrew, 103–34 (Lanham, MD: Rowman and Littlefield, 2000.

Pindar, Peter. "Ode to Irony." In *Odes of Importance, &c*, 9. New ed. Dublin, 1792.

Pizer, Donald. *Dos Passos' U.S.A.: A Critical Study*. Charlottesville: University Press of Virginia, 1988.

Pole, J. R. "An Anatomy of American Irony." *Raritan* 24, no. 1 (Summer 2004): 113–32.

Pollitt, Katha. "Talk the Talk, Walk the Slutwalk." *The Nation*, July 18, 2011.

Polsgrove, Carol. *Divided Minds: Intellectuals and the Civil Rights Movement*. New York: W. W. Norton, 2001.

Porter, Kirk Harold. *A History of Suffrage in the United States*. Chicago: University of Chicago Press, 1918.

Posnock, Ross. "The Politics of Nonidentity: A Genealogy." *boundary 2* 19, no. 1 (Spring 1992): 34–68.

Pound, Ezra. "Irony, Laforgue, and Some Satire." *Poetry* 11, no. 2 (November 1917): 93–98.

———. "Things to Be Done." *Poetry* 9, no. 6 (March 1917): 312–14.

Pruette, Lorine Livingston. "The Evolution of Disenchantment." In *These Modern Women: Autobiographical Essays from the Twenties*, ed. Elaine Showalter, 69–73. Old Westbury, NY: Feminist Press, 1978.

Pütz, Manfred, ed. *Nietzsche in American Literature and Thought*. Columbia, SC: Camden House, 1995.

Rabinowitz, Paula. "Melodrama/Male Drama: The Sentimental Contract of American Labor Films." In *Black & White & Noir: America's Pulp Modernism*, 121–42. New York: Columbia University Press, 2002.

Rainford, Lydia. *She Changes by Intrigue: Irony, Femininity and Feminism*. Amsterdam: Rodopi, 2005.

Rampersad, Arnold. *The Life of Langston Hughes*. Vol. 2: 1941–1967. 2nd ed. Oxford: Oxford University Press, 2002.

———. *Ralph Ellison: A Biography*. New York: Vintage Books, 2008.

Rampley, Matthew. *Nietzsche, Aesthetics, and Modernity*. New York: Cambridge University Press 2000.

Rancière, Jacques. "Does Democracy Mean Something?" In *Dissensus: On Politics and Aesthetics*, trans. Steven Corcoran, 45–61. New York: Continuum, 2010.

———. *The Politics of Aesthetics: The Distribution of the Sensible*. Trans. Gabriel Rockhill. New York: Continuum, 2004.

Raper, Julius Rowan. "Ellen Glasgow." In *A Companion to the Literature and Culture of the American South*, 403–19. Malden, MA: Blackwell, 2004.

Ratner-Rosenhagen, Jennifer. *American Nietzsche: A History of an Icon and His Ideas*. Chicago: University of Chicago Press, 2012.

Ravenel, Florence Leftwich. "The Eternal Feminine." In *Women and the French Tradition*, 3–38. New York: Macmillan, 1918.

Repplier, Agnes. *Americans and Others*. Boston: Houghton Mifflin, 1912.

Rideout, Walter. *The Radical Novel in the United States, 1900–1954: Some Inter-relations of Literature and Society*. New York: Columbia University Press, 1992.

Riley, Denise. *The Words of Selves: Identification, Solidarity, Irony*. Stanford, CA: Stanford University Press, 2000.

Rogers, J. A. "Jazz at Home." In *The New Negro*, ed. Alain Locke, 216–24. New York: Macmillan, 1992.

Rohrkemper, John. *John Dos Passos: A Reference Guide*. Boston: G. K. Hall, 1980.

Rorty, Richard. *Achieving Our Country: Leftist Thought in Twentieth-Century America*. Cambridge, MA: Harvard University Press, 1998.

———. *Consequences of Pragmatism*. Minneapolis: University of Minnesota Press, 1982.

———. *Contingency, Irony, and Solidarity*. Cambridge: Cambridge University Press, 1989.

Rosenbaum, Susan. "Elizabeth Bishop's Theater of War." In *Reading the Middle Generation Anew: Culture, Community, and Form in Twentieth-Century American Poetry*, ed. Eric L. Haralson. Iowa City: University of Iowa Press, 2006.

Rosenblatt, Roger. "The Age of Irony Comes to an End." *Time*, September 24, 2001.

Rosenfeld, Paul. "Randolph Bourne." *The Dial* 75, no. 6 (December 1923): 545–60.

Rovillain, Eugene E. "The Latest Mexican Revolution." *Atlantic Monthly*, October 1920.

Roy, Ayon. "Hegel Contra Schlegel; Kierkegaard Contra De Man." *PMLA* 124, no. 1 (January 2009): 107–26.

Russell, Frances Theresa. *Satire in the Victorian Novel*. New York: Macmillan, 1920.

Said, Edward. *The World, the Text, and the Critic*. Cambridge, MA: Harvard University Press, 1983.

Saintsbury, George. "Irony." *The Dial* 82, no. 3 (March 1927): 181–87.

Sangster, Margaret E. *Good Manners for All Occasions: Including Etiquette of Cards, Wedding Announcements and Invitations*. New York: Cupples & Leon, 1910.

Santayana, George. "The Comic Mask." In *Soliloquies in England and Later Soliloquies*. New York: Charles Scribner's Sons, 1922.

Sartre, Jean-Paul. "John Dos Passos and '1919.'" In *Literary Essays*, trans. Annette Michelson, 88–96. New York: Wisdom Library, 1957.

Scheffauer, Herman. "The Death of Satire." *The Living Age* (July 12, 1913): 82–90.

Schön, Donald A. "Generative Metaphor: A Perspective on Problem-Setting in Social Policy." In *Metaphor and Thought*, ed. Andrew Ortony. 2nd ed. New York: Cambridge University Press, 1993.

Schor, Naomi. "Fetishism and Its Ironies." In *Bad Objects: Essays Popular and Unpopular*, 105–12. Durham, NC: Duke University Press, 1995.

Schuyler, Lorraine Gates. *The Weight of Their Votes: Southern Women and Political Leverage in the 1920s*. Chapel Hill: University of North Carolina Press, 2006.

Schwartz, Delmore. "John Dos Passos and the Whole Truth." In *Selected Essays of Delmore Schwartz*, ed. Donald A. Dike and David H. Zucker, 229–45. Chicago: University of Chicago Press, 1970.

Scura, Dorothy. Afterword to *The Romantic Comedians*, by Ellen Glasgow, 241–65. Charlottesville: University Press of Virginia, 1995.

———. "A Knowledge in the Heart: Ellen Glasgow, the Women's Movement, and 'Virginia.'" *American Literary Realism, 1870–1910*, Special Issue: Women Writers of the Realistic Period (Winter 1990): 30–43.

Seldes, George. *Freedom of the Press*. New York: Garden City Publishing, 1937.

———. *You Can't Print That! The Truth Behind the News, 1918–1928*. New York: Garden City Publishing, 1929.

Seldes, Gilbert. *The Seven Lively Arts*. New York: Harper and Brothers, 1924.

Seltzer, Thomas. "Satire." *The Masses* 4, no. 3 (December 1912): 9.

Siemens, Herman, and Gary Shapiro. "Guest Editors' Introduction: What Does Nietzsche Mean for Contemporary Politics and Political Thought?" *Journal of Nietzsche Studies* 35–36, Special Issue: Nietzsche and Contemporary Politics (Spring/Autumn 2008): 3–8.

Sinclair, Upton. "Letter to Benjamin De Casseres." MS., September 23, 1939. Box 1. Benjamin De Casseres Papers. New York Public Library Rare Books and Manuscripts.

Smith, T. V. "The Democratic Process." *Public Opinion Quarterly* 2, no. 1. Special Supplement: Public Opinion in a Democracy (January 1938): 15–20.

Smith, Wyman Sidney. "Ironies." *The Nation*, October 7, 1925.

Solger, Karl. "Letter to Ludwig Tieck, 22 November, 1818." In *German Aesthetic and Literary Criticism: The Romantic Ironists and Goethe*, ed. Kathleen Wheeler, 155–56. Cambridge: Cambridge University Press, 1984.

Solomon, William. *Literature, Amusement, and Technology in the Great Depression*. Cambridge: Cambridge University Press, 2002.

"Some American Criticisms of Nietzsche." *Current Literature* 44, no. 3 (March 1908): 295.

Sproule, Michael. *Propaganda and Democracy: The American Experience of Media and Mass Persuasion*. New York: Cambridge University Press, 1997.

Stayton, Frank. *Threads*. New York: Century Co., 1921.

Stearns, Harold. *Liberalism in America: Its Origin, Its Temporary Collapse, Its Future*. New York: Boni and Liveright, 1919.

Steele, Meili. "Metatheory and the Subject of Democracy in the Work of Ralph Ellison." *New Literary History* 27, no. 3 (1996): 473–502.

Steilberg, Hays Alan. *Die Amerikanische Nietzsche-Rezeption Von 1896 Bis 1950*. Monographien Und Texte Zur Nietzsche-Forschung 35. Berlin: Walter de Gruyter, 1996.

Stein, Gertrude. *Narration: Four Lectures*. Chicago: University of Chicago Press, 1935.

Stieglitz, Alfred. "Pictorial Photography." In *Classic Essays on Photography*, ed. Alan Trachtenberg. New Haven, CT: Leete's Island Books, 1980.

Stone, Grace. "Ellen Glasgow and Her Novels." *Sewanee Review* 50, no. 3 (September 1942): 289–301.

Strong, Tracy B. "Nietzsche and the Political: Tyranny, Tragedy, Cultural Revolution, and Democracy." *Journal of Nietzsche Studies* 35–36 (Spring/Autumn 2008): 48–66.

———. "Nietzsche's Political Misappropriation." In *The Cambridge Companion to Nietzsche*, ed. Bernd Magnus and Kathleen M. Higgins, 119–47. New York: Cambridge University Press, 1996.

Strychacz, Thomas. *Modernism, Mass Culture, and Professionalism*. Cambridge: Cambridge University Press, 1993.

Suárez, Juan Antonio. *Pop Modernism: Noise and the Reinvention of the Everyday*. Cambridge: Cambridge University Press, 2007.

Tew, Philip. "Glossary." In *The Modernism Handbook*, ed. Philip Tew and Alex Murray, 199–214. New York: Continuum, 2009.

Thomson, J.A.K. *Irony: An Historical Introduction*. Cambridge, MA: Harvard University Press, 1927.

Thornwell, Emily. *The Lady's Guide to Perfect Gentility*. New York: Derby & Jackson, 1856.

Towns, Ann E. *Women and States: Norms and Hierarchies in International Society*. Cambridge: Cambridge University Press, 2010.

Trilling, Lionel. "The America of John Dos Passos." *Partisan Review* 4 (April 1938): 26–32.

Turner, F. McD. C. *The Element of Irony in English Literature*. Cambridge: Cambridge University Press, 1926.

United States. Cong. Senate. *The National Association of Manufacturers*. Violations of Free Speech and Rights of Labor. 76th Cong., 1st sess. Report no. 6, Part 6, Section 3. Washington, DC: GPO, n.d.

———. *Testimony of Langston Hughes (accompanied by His Counsel, Frank Dr. Reeves)*. Executive Sessions of the Senate Permanent Subcommittee on Investigations of the Committee on Government Operations. 83rd Cong., 1st Sess. Vol. 2. 1953. S. Prt. 107–84. Made public January 2003. Washington, DC: GPO, 2003.

United States Government. *The Battle Line of Democracy: Prose and Poetry of the World War*. Committee on Public Information. Washington, DC: GPO, 1917.

Untermeyer, Louis. "Irony." In *The New Poetry: An Anthology*, ed. Harriet Monroe and Alice Corbin Henderson, 352. New York: Macmillan, 1917.

———. "A Shelf of Recent Books: The Impulse of Irony." *The Bookman: A Review of Books and Life* 55, no. 6 (August 1922): 635.

Van Vechten, Carl. *Nigger Heaven*. Urbana: University of Illinois Press, 2000.

———. "A Virginia Lady Dissects a Virginia Gentleman." In *Ellen Glasgow: The Contemporary Reviews*, ed. Dorothy M. Scura, 277–78. Cambridge: Cambridge University Press, 1992.

Van Wienen, Mark W. *Partisans and Poets: The Political Work of American Poetry in the Great War.* Cambridge: Cambridge University Press, 1997.

Vaughan, Leslie J. *Randolph Bourne and the Politics of Cultural Radicalism.* Lawrence: University Press of Kansas, 1997.

Veblen, Thorstein. "Professor Clark's Economics." In *The Place of Science in Modern Civilization and Other Essays,* 180–230. New York: B. W. Hubsch, 1939.

———. *Theory of Business Enterprise.* New York: Charles Scribner's Sons, 1920.

Vico, Giambattista. *The Art of Rhetoric (Institutiones Oratoriae, 1711–1741).* Ed. Giorgio A. Pinton and Arthur W. Shippee. Amsterdam: Rodopi, 1996.

———. *The New Science of Giambattista Vico: Unabridged Translation of the Third Edition (1744) with the Addition of "Practice of the New Science."* Trans. Thomas Goddard Bergin and Max Harold Fisch. Ithaca, NY: Cornell University Press, 1984.

———. *La Scienza Nuova Seconda.* Ed. Fausto Nicolini. Bari, Gius, Laterza & Figli, 1953.

Wald, Alan. *The New York Intellectuals: The Rise and Decline of the Anti-Stalinist Left from the 1930s to the 1980s.* Chapel Hill: University of North Carolina Press, 1987.

Wallace, David Foster. "E Unibus Pluram: Television and U.S. Fiction." In *A Supposedly Fun Thing I'll Never Do Again,* 21–82. Boston: Little, Brown, 1997.

Warner, Michael. *Publics and Counter-Publics.* New York: Zone Books, 2002.

Warren, Kenneth. *So Black and So Blue: Ralph Ellison and the Occasion of Criticism.* Chicago: University of Chicago Press, 2002.

Warren, Robert Penn. "Katherine Anne Porter (Irony with a Center)." *Kenyon Review* 4, no. 3 (Winter 1942): 29–42.

Watts, Jerry Gafio. *Heroism & the Black Intellectual: Ralph Ellison, Politics, and Afro-American Intellectual Life.* Chapel Hill: University of North Carolina Press, 1994.

Weisenburger, Steven. *Fables of Subversion: Satire and the American Novel, 1930–1980.* Athens: University of Georgia Press, 1995.

West, Rebecca. "These American Women." *Harper's Monthly Magazine,* November 1925.

Westbrook, Robert. *Democratic Hope: Pragmatism and the Politics of Truth.* Ithaca, NY: Cornell University Press, 2005.

Wharton, Edith. "The Descent of Man." In *The Descent of Man and Other Stories,* 1–34. New York: Charles Scribner's Sons, 1904.

White, Hayden. *Metahistory: The Historical Imagination in Nineteenth-Century Europe.* Baltimore: Johns Hopkins University Press, 1973.

White, Morton. *Social Thought in America: The Revolt Against Formalism.* New York: Viking, 1949.

"Why Have We No Satire?" *Atlantic Monthly,* July 1899.

Wilde, Alan. *Horizons of Assent: Modernism, Post-Modernism, and the Ironic Imagination.* Philadelphia: University of Pennsylvania Press, 1987.

"Will Nietzsche Come into Vogue in America?" *Current Literature* 49, no. 1 (July 1910): 65.

Willett, Cynthia. *Irony in the Age of Empire: Comic Perspectives on Democracy & Freedom*. Bloomington: University of Indiana Press, 2008.

Willmott, Glenn. *Modernist Goods: Primitivism, the Market and the Gift*. Toronto: University of Toronto Press, 2008.

Wilson, Edmund. "The Nietzschean Line." In *The Shores of Light: A Literary Chronicle of the Twenties and Thirties*, 485–91. New York: Farrar, Straus, and Giroux, 1952.

Wilson, James Southall. "Ellen Glasgow: Ironic Idealist." *Virginia Quarterly Review* 15, no. 1 (Winter 1939): 121–26.

Wittgenstein, Ludwig. *Philosophical Investigations/Philosophische Untersuchungen*. Trans. G.E.M. Anscombe. 2nd ed. Oxford: Blackwell, 1953.

Wolin, Sheldon S. *Democracy Incorporated: Managed Democracy and the Specter of Inverted Totalitarianism*. Princeton, NJ: Princeton University Press, 2008.

Wollaeger, Mark. *Modernism, Media, and Propaganda: British Narrative from 1900 to 1945*. Princeton, NJ: Princeton University Press, 2006.

Woods, Kate Tannatt. "Sarcasm Among Women." *Ladies' Home Journal* 8, no. 2 (January 1891): 9.

Index